A 52-Week Bible Journey – Just For Kids!

ROUTE 52

Study
God's Plan

**52 Bible Lessons that Build
Bible Skills for Ages 8–12**

Standard
PUBLISHING
CINCINNATI, OHIO

All Scripture quotations, unless otherwise indicated, are taken from the HOLY BIBLE, NEW INTERNATIONAL VERSION®. NIV®· Copyright © 1973, 1978, 1984 by International Bible Society. Used by permission of Zondervan. All rights reserved.

Scripture quotations marked (*ICB*) are taken from the *International Children's Bible® New Century Version®*. Copyright © 1986, 1988, 1999 by Tommy Nelson™, a division of Thomas Nelson, Inc., Nashville, Tennessee 37214. Used by permission.

Lesson Writers: Alice Brown, Tara Fogelson, Kathy Johnson, Terri Lowe, Christine Spence, Bruce E. Stoker, Becky Thatcher, Kristi Walter
Syllabus Development: Linda Ford
Project Editor: Bruce E. Stoker
Cover Designer: Malwitz Design
Template Designer: Andrew Quach

Standard Publishing, Cincinnati, Ohio.
A division of Standex International Corporation.
© 2004 by Standard Publishing.
All rights reserved.
Printed in the United States of America.

10 09 08 07 06 05 04   9 8 7 6 5 4 3 2 1

ISBN 0-7847-1329-4

Introduction

The goal of this curriculum is to equip students to use their Bibles. Students should feel confident to pick up a Bible and locate a Bible verse. They should be able to use a Bible dictionary to uncover meaning and a concordance to find other verses on the same topic. They should be able to find Bible places on atlas maps. They will practice finding Bible answers to everyday questions that are soon to challenge them.

This 52-week curriculum is organized in biblical order except for Units 5, 11, and 12. Since the focus of the lessons is skill-building, basic memory verses are short. Memory work emphasizes the content of the unit. A memory challenge is listed to encourage older students or those with more Bible background.

Unit 1 (September) establishes the skills needed to unlock the Bible. Locating books, chapters, and verses,, reading and writing Bible references, naming the Bible books in order and using a Bible dictionary and concordance are all addressed.

Units 2–4 (October–December) and **6–10** (February–June) are taught in basic Bible order.

Unit 5 (January) is designed to trace God's loving message of salvation from the Old into the New Testament. Its placement allows the New Testament lessons to lead up to Easter in April.

Units 6–10 (February–June) introduce the life and teachings of Jesus and the growth of His church. (Note: Units 7 and 8 can be taught in reverse order when Easter occurs in March.)

Units 11, 12 (July, August) focus on teaching the chronology of Bible events and Bible people.

Bible Skills Handouts

There are many reproducible materials and other ideas throughout this book that can be applied to many lessons. For example, the Unit 2 introduction suggests the Bible Divisions Binder Activity Project (p. 37) that could be used throughout the course.

There are also many reproducible materials at the back of this book that can be used in every unit:

Bible Library (p. 296) lists the divisions, gives a brief description of each division, and lists the book(s) in each division.

Bible Cards (pp. 297, 298) includes the names of each Bible book and is designed to be copied and cut apart for use in games and activities.

Things We Know (p. 299) is a chart to help students track what they know about the Bible stages, eras, and time line segments.

For the Record (p. 300) is another chart that you and your students can use to track what and when they have mastered various Bible skills.

Sample Bible Dictionary (pp. 301, 302), *Sample Bible Concordance* (pp. 303, 304), *Bible Atlas Maps 1–3* (pp. 305-307), and *Index to Maps* (p. 308) will be used in lessons that help students learn how and when to use those Bible tools.

Time Line Segments (pp. 309-314) can be copied, cut apart, colored, and displayed on your classroom wall. Each page contains 2 segments, so you should have 12 segments in a completed time line. (If you don't prepare it at the beginning of the course, it is included in Unit 4.)

Time Line Pieces (pp. 315-318) can be copied and used for games in which students match, sort, explain, or describe people and events according to Bible chronology.

▼ Table of Contents ▲

Unit	Unit Title	Scripture	Unit Goals
Unit 1	The Bible Teaches Us How to Please God	**Psalm 119**—*God and His Word are trustworthy* **Joshua 1; John 20; Romans 15; 2 Timothy 3; 2 Peter 1**—*God's Word gives us hope and encouragement* **Genesis 1; Exodus 3; Leviticus 19; Numbers 14; Deuteronomy 7, 10, 32**—*The Bible tells about God* **Deuteronomy 6; Psalm 119**—*God's Word gives us directions for living*	**Students will** • Love and trust God's Word • Thank God for His Word • Praise God for who He is • Read God's Word and do what it says
Unit 2	Books of Law Tell Us How God's People Were Led	**Genesis 22, 28, 35**—*Patriarchs in Canaan* **Hebrews 11**—*People who lived by faith* **Genesis 37, 41, 45, 46**—*Joseph and family go to Egypt* **Exodus 20; Deuteronomy 5**—*Moses, the Exodus, and the Ten Commandments* **Matthew 22**—*Jesus teaches the Ten Commandments*	**Students will** • Believe God's promises • Accept God's plan • Restate the Ten Commandments • Explain how to follow God's commands
Unit 3	History and Poetry Tell About Choices God's People Made	**Joshua 24**—*Joshua and the conquest of Canaan* **Judges 2, 4–6, 8**—*Gideon and Deborah* **Genesis 13, 39; Exodus 19; Ruth 1, 2, 4; Joshua 1**—*Old Testament geography* **1 Samuel 7, 10, 15; 2 Samuel 5; 1 Kings 3**—*Israel wants a king* **Esther 2, 4, 7, 8**—*Esther saves the Jews* **Daniel 3**—*Daniel trusts God to protect him* **Psalm 23, 100**—*We are the sheep of God's pasture* **Proverbs 3**—*How to be wise* **Ecclesiastes 3**—*The wisdom of God's creation*	**Students will** • Choose to serve God • Know that following by faith means entering the unknown • Follow leaders who choose to obey God • Know that godly leaders choose to obey God even when it is difficult • Choose to follow God as a sheep follows its shepherd
Unit 4	Prophets Reveal That God Does What He Says	**Deuteronomy 13, 18; Mark 1; Luke 1; Hebrews 1; 2 Peter 1**—*Prophecies fulfilled in the New Testament* **Isaiah 7; Jeremiah 23; Matthew 1**—*Prophecies about Jesus' birth* **Isaiah 9; Hosea 3; Luke 1**—*Old Testament prophecies about the "Son of the Most High"* **Micah 5; Matthew 2; Luke 2**—*Prophecies point toward Bethlehem* **Luke 2**—*Simeon sees a prophecy fulfilled*	**Students will** • Tell the difference between true and false prophecy • Know Jesus' birth was part of God's plan • Celebrate God's promises and plan • Recognize that Jesus is God's promised Savior
Unit 5	God Planned, Promised, and Provided Salvation	**Genesis 3, 12; Matthew 1; John 3**—*God has a plan to save His people* **2 Chronicles 33**—*God has a plan to restore a relationship with His people* **John 20; Romans 3, 5, 6, 10**—*God's salvation is a plan for eternal life* **John 3; Acts 16, 26; 1 John 5**—*God's plan is for everyone*	**Students will** • Understand God's promise to save us from sin • Know that God restores us when we repent • Choose God's plan of salvation
Unit 6	Gospels Teach Us What Jesus Did	**Matthew 3, 4**—*Jesus is baptized and tempted* **Matthew 4, 9, 10**—*Jesus calls His disciples* **Matthew 9**—*Jesus heals a man* **Matthew 17**—*Jesus shows God's glory*	**Students will** • Know Scripture • Resist temptation • Do the work of disciples: Be workers for the harvest • Praise Jesus

	Unit Title	Scripture	Unit Goals
Unit 7	**Gospels Teach Us What Jesus Said**	**Matthew 5**—*The Beatitudes* **Matthew 6**—*The Lord's Prayer* **Matthew 13**—*The Parable of the Sower* **Luke 15**—*The "Lost" Parables* **Luke 10**—*The Good Samaritan*	**Students will** • Rejoice and be glad about Heaven • Pray • Hear and understand God's Word • Celebrate God's love • Show mercy
Unit 8	**Gospels Teach Us That Jesus Is Our Savior**	**John 11**—*Jesus raises Lazarus* **Exodus 12; Luke 22; 1 Corinthians 11**—*Jesus celebrates the Passover* **Matthew 26, 27; Mark 15, 16; 1 Corinthians 15**—*The crucifixion, burial, and resurrection of Jesus* **Luke 24; John 20**—*Jesus appears after the resurrection*	**Students will** • Praise God for His power • Remember Jesus for His sacrifice • Thank God for salvation • Praise Jesus that He is alive
Unit 9	**Acts Records How the Church Began and Grew**	**Matthew 28; Luke 24; Acts 1**—*The Great Commission* **Acts 2**—*The church begins on Pentecost* **Acts 11**—*Peter has a vision* **Acts 9**—*Saul's conversion* **Acts 13-28**—*Paul's missionary journeys*	**Students will** • Explain God's plan for His church • Identify the church as the body of believers in Christ • Recognize that the church is available to all who believe in Jesus the Christ • Recount that Saul repented, accepted Jesus as Lord, and preached in His name
Unit 10	**Letters Instruct the Church in Right Living**	**1 John 4; 1 Corinthians 13**—*Love one another* **Galatians 15**—*The Fruit of the Spirit* **Ephesians 6**—*The Armor of God* **James 1, 2**—*Be hearers and doers of the Word*	**Students will** • Love God and love one another • Make right choices • Equip themselves to stand for God • Show their faith by actions
Unit 11	**Old Testament People and Events Prepare for God's Plan**	**Genesis 1–10**—*The Creation, the Fall, and the Flood* **Genesis 11–50; Exodus; Deuteronomy**—*The Patriarchs and the 12 Tribes* **Joshua, Judges**—*Conquest of Canaan and the Judges* **1, 2 Samuel; 1, 2 Kings; 1, 2 Chronicles**—*Israel's Kings*	**Students will** • Recognize God's plan throughout history • Survey the Old Testament chronologically • Express thanks for God's gift of salvation planned from the beginning
Unit 12	**New Testament People and Events Spread God's Plan**	**Matthew; Mark; Luke; John**—*Building faith in Jesus* **Acts; Paul's letters; Peter's letters**—*Peter and Paul spread the gospel* **Acts**—*Christians working within the church* **1, 2, 3 John; Revelation**—*Hope for the future*	**Students will** • See the global impact of the gospel • Take responsibility as witnesses for Jesus • Identify areas in which students can serve

The Bible Teaches Us How to Please God

Lessons 1–4

Bible Skills
Read, write, and locate Bible
references
Recite Bible divisions

Memorize
2 Timothy 3:16

Memory Challenge
Psalm 119:9-11

Unit Overview

"Do your best to present yourself to God as one approved, a workman who does not need to be ashamed and who correctly handles the word of truth" (2 Timothy 2:15). In this first unit, students will begin to correctly handle the Word of truth. They will locate books, chapters, and verses, read and write Bible references, and name the divisions of Bible books.

Each lesson contains instructions and activities for each session. However, if you need some additional ideas for learning activities, several are included below. First is a short summary of the four sessions in this unit.

Summary

Lesson 1 teaches that God is trustworthy and that His Word is also trustworthy. It also shows that we obey God and His Word because we trust Him.

Lesson 2 focuses on the idea that the Bible is God's Word and that we should be thankful for it.

Lesson 3 teaches about what God's Word tells us that God himself is like and that we should praise God for who He is.

Lesson 4 shows that not only does the Bible tell us what God is like but what God wants us to be like and that we should read His Word and do what it says.

Hidden Books

Use masking tape to put the names of an Old Testament and a New Testament book on each student's back. Students must try to discover their books by asking questions that can be answered with yes or no. They may ask as many questions as they want, but they can guess at the book name only three times. Therefore, students should wait to guess a book until they are certain they know what it is. When a student guesses a book correctly, draw a star on the tape next to the book name. If the student guesses incorrectly, mark an *X* on the tape. When students have discovered their books, have them name the Bible books.

Next, students should arrange themselves in the order of the books of the Old Testament, then the New Testament.

Ball Toss

Sit together in a circle. If you have more than 12 students, sit in two circles. Toss a ball to one person. That person names the first division of the Old Testament and tells how many books are in it. He then tosses the ball to another person. Each person who catches the ball must say the next division and the number of books in it. You may want to make clue cards to post in your room for the first few times. Use the following list to help.

Law (5)	Gospels (4)
OT History (12)	NT History (1)
Poetry (5)	Letters (21)
OT Prophecy (17)	NT Prophecy (1)

Division Themes

The following themes have been selected to help your students learn that the books grouped in each division have something in common. Many themes are developed in the books of each division. The following, however, are dominant in each one.

Learn the Bible divisions and themes by repeating the following phrases with the indicated movements.

Law helps us know what God is like. *(point up)*

OT History teaches us to obey God. *(point backward)*

Poetry helps us worship God. *(conduct singing)*

OT Prophecy points to Jesus. *(point forward)*

The Gospels help us to know Jesus. *(draw a cross in the air)*

NT History helps us tell the good news. *(point to mouth)*

The Letters help us love one another. *(draw heart over heart; point to others)*

NT Prophecy points to Jesus' return *(extend arm; pull toward body)*

Chalkboard Game

On the chalkboard draw a rectangle. Label it "Menu." Assign each student one of the references listed below. Each student will find and read the verse to discover a kind of food. When he finds a food he will write the name of the food in the menu.

Hebrews 5:13	milk
1 Corinthians 8:13	meat
Psalm 119:103	honey
Matthew 4:4	bread
Numbers 15:20	cake
Daniel 1:12	vegetables
John 15:4	fruit

A variation on this game is to have students look in the following verses for things that can be found outdoors. Then they can draw the items on the chalkboard.

John 6:10	grass
Genesis 40:17	birds
Matthew 16:2	sky
1 Chronicles 16:33	trees
Hebrews 3:4	house
Matthew 13:30	barn
Ezekiel 47:6	river
Song of Solomon 2:12	flowers, doves

LESSON 1 — The Bible Is Wonderful and Dependable

Psalm 119

Lesson Aims

Students will
- Identify three parts of a Bible reference
- Describe God's Word as wonderful and dependable
- Declare that they love and trust God's Word

Materials
masking tape
paper in 9 different colors
envelopes
marker
container for the grab bag

▼ Building Study Skills ▲

Create a grab bag that will be used during this unit, Lessons 1 through 4. Each week students will receive a grab bag item by reciting the unit's memory verses to a sponsor. Items received in the grab bag will be used sometime during the lesson.

For today's lesson, print the memory verse, 2 Timothy 3:16, and the memory challenge, Psalm 119:9-11 on paper and post them so that students may read and study the verses as they arrive. If your group is large, make several copies of each.

Next, divide the following references into their book, chapter, and verse segments: Psalm 119:1; Psalm 119:18; Psalm 119:47; Psalm 119:89; Psalm 119:129; Psalm 119:137; Psalm 119:138; Psalm 119:160; Psalm 119:167. Include the colon punctuation with the number of the chapter. Write each segment on separate strips of the same color of paper. Use a different color of paper for each reference. Repeat references as needed in order to make one book, chapter, verse set for each student. Put each set in an envelope. Place the envelopes in the grab bag.

Use the masking tape to make three large squares side-by-side on the classroom floor. Label the first square "book." Label the middle square "chapter." Label the end square "verse."

As students arrive instruct them to study Psalm 119:9-11 which is posted near the grab bag. (Students will study and recite 2 Timothy 3:16 during the Reviewing Study Skills step.) After a few minutes, students may recite the passage or part of the passage. After a student recites the passage, give him permission to reach into the grab bag and retrieve an envelope. Then direct him to the three squares on the floor.

Say: **The envelopes that you hold contain the three parts of a Bible reference. What are those three parts? Look at the labels on these squares on the floor. Yes, a Bible reference contains the name of the book, the chapter of the book, and the verse in that chapter. Which of your papers names the book? Place it in the "book" square. Which of your papers names the chapter? Put it in the "chapter" square. Which of your papers names the verse? Put it in the "verse" square.** Help students as needed, but allow them to use their reasoning skills to determine the parts of the reference before offering help.

After all papers have been placed, stand by and point to the "book" square and ask: **How did you know which of your papers named the book?** (The paper contains a word or a name and not a number.) **Which Bible book are all of our references from?** (Psalms.) **Now look at the "chapter" square. How do we know that these papers tell us the chapter part of the Bible reference?** (They contain a number followed by a colon.) **The colon is an important part of a Bible reference. Why?** (It separates the chapter number from the verse number.) **Now look at the "verse" square. How did you know that these papers contained the verse number?** (It was a number without a colon following it.) **These references only have one verse. If the references had more than one verse, it would have some punctuation, but that punctuation is never the colon. We'll learn the other kinds of punctuation in a later lesson.**

At this time pick up all of the papers in random order and distribute three papers to each student. It does not matter if they each receive a book, a chapter, and a verse. Instruct students to look at the papers and place them in the correct squares. Check students' work and clear up any problems.

If students are advanced in this concept, have them form two teams. Each team member should write a Bible reference for the opposing team to separate into book, chapter, and verse. Have teams race.

After this, assign students a color and have them pick up the book, chapter, and verse papers in that color and bring the papers and their Bibles to the lesson area. Have Bibles available in the classroom for those students who don't have one of their own to use. These are hands-on assignments, and in order for students to get the full benefit of them, they must have a Bible to use. When situated, have students place their Bible reference in front of them in book, chapter, and verse order.

Say: **All of our Bible references are from the book of Psalms. Psalms tells us some important information about the Bible. Let's find out what that is. We'll begin by locating these Bible references in our Bibles. First, we will locate the book of Psalms. Let's do that together. Psalms is located approximately in the middle of the Bible. Open your Bible to the middle and you will probably open it somewhere in the book of Psalms. If not, you will open it to a book that is close to Psalms.** Have students do so and report the book and chapter where they opened their Bibles. Show them that the book and chapter—sometimes the verse—are located at the top of the page like guide words in a dictionary. Let them try again and again as time permits to open their Bibles to Psalms.

Introduce students to another way of finding a Bible book. Have them turn to the table of contents in the front of their Bibles. Point out that the books of the Bible are listed in order along with a page number. Some students will have Bibles that have a table of contents with the books listed in alphabetical order. Look at those pages together. Then have students find the page number for Psalms and turn to that page.

Once all students have their Bibles open to Psalms, ask: **Now that we have located the book, what must we find next?** (The chapter which is 119.) Have students to turn to chapter 119. **What do we locate after we have found the book and chapter?** (The verse which is different for each student.) Have students locate their particular verses within the chapter.

Ask: **How were you able to tell the difference between the chapter numbers and verse numbers in your Bibles?** (The chapter numbers are bigger and stand out. The verse numbers are small and similar in size to the words on the page.)

▼ Using Study Skills ▲

Before class cut into strips *Historical Facts About the Bible* and tape them to the bottom of chairs in the classroom. Also create a matching game on one wall of the classroom. Write the nine Bible references from Psalms on separate sheets of one color of paper. On the reverse side of the sheets, write one letter from the word *wonderful* so that when the sheets are turned over the word *wonderful* can be read. Place the Bible references horizontally on the wall just above eye level. Put them in numerical order according to verse.

Write summary sentences on separate sheets of the second color of paper. Do not include the verse number; it is given here for matching purposes. Summary

Materials
9 sheets each of 2 colors of
    paper
masking tape
Historical Facts About the Bible
    (p. 15)

sentences are: I am blessed when I obey God's laws (1). I want to see the wonderful things in God's laws (18). I want to obey God's laws because I love them (47). God's Word will last forever (89). I obey God's laws because they are wonderful (129). God always does what is right, and His laws are right (137). Because God's laws are right, I can trust them (138). God's everlasting Word is true (160). I will obey God's laws because I love them very much (167). Write the letters of the word *dependable* on the back of these papers, one letter per paper in the order given here. Make one extra sheet for the letter *e*. Scramble the order of these sheets and attach below the reference sheets. Attach the letter *e* sheet to the end of the summary row with the blank side showing.

In class have students take turns reading their verses. If more than one student has the same verse, allow those students to work as a team. After they have read their assigned verse, they are to determine which sentence summarizes it. When this is done, they are to post the matching summary under the matching verse.

When all nine Scriptures have been read and summarized, say: **We have learned some wonderful things about the Bible from the book of Psalms. What are some things we have learned?** (Have students answer.) **Did any of you already know some of these things about the Bible before we found them in the book of Psalms? What new things did you learn about the Bible?** (Discuss.)

Ask: **If you could use one or two words to describe all that we've read about the Bible today, what would they be?** Allow students to give their ideas. As students suggest words, write them on the blank paper that was posted at the end of the summary row. Write this heading on the paper: "God's Word Is . . ." then list the words the students give. Save room for the words *wonderful* and *dependable* which will be added later. Say: **These are some great words to use to describe the Bible. I thought of some words too. I spelled them out on the back of our matching game.** Have students take turns turning over the papers with the references to reveal the word *wonderful*. Do the same with the summary sentences to reveal the word *dependable*. Before turning over the last letter *e* in the word *dependable,* add the words *wonderful* and *dependable* to the list that the class made.

Say: **We know that the Bible is wonderful and dependable because of what the Bible says about itself. We also know from history that the Bible is wonderful and dependable. Look underneath your chair to find a piece of paper. It will tell one reason from history that the Bible is wonderful and dependable.** Allow students time to find a message underneath their chairs. Have students read the facts aloud and in numerical order. Say: **For many centuries, men have believed that the Bible is wonderful and dependable so they have preserved it for us to have today. History shows us that the Bible is wonderful and dependable. The entire chapter of Psalm 119 tells us over and over again how wonderful and dependable the Bible is. The Bible will last forever. We can count on it. We can trust the Bible to show us the right way to live. It is always right. When we follow it, we never have to wonder if there is a better way. There is no better way. All these are reasons why we can love and trust the Bible. Let's tell God how much we love and trust His wonderful and dependable Bible.**

Remove each of the summary sentences from the wall and distribute them among the students. If you have more than 10 students, some can double up on the same sentence. Ask students to take turns reading their sentences aloud as a prayer to God. Instruct them to say the word *you* in place of the word *God* and to say the word *your* in the place of the word *God's*. The list compiled by the class should be read to close the prayer.

▼ Responding to Study ▲

Materials
Bookmarks (p. 16), photocopied, or blank bookmarks for the students to decorate
markers, crayons, glitter, stickers
scissors
glue
pictures cut out of magazines, calendars, or church bulletins to decorate bookmarks

Ask: **What will you do now that you know how wonderful and dependable the Bible is? What will you do because you love and trust God's wonderful, dependable Word?** Discuss their answers. Say: **Today, we are learning and soon we will practice how to read Bible references and to find verses in the Bible. Learning to use the Bible is one way to show that we love and trust the Bible. Knowing how to find verses is an important step in studying the Bible for yourself. It is important that we learn how to study the Bible. Today, we are beginning a series of lessons that will teach us how to study the Bible. If you will commit yourself to this study—to learning how to navigate the Bible and to learning how to use Bible reference books— then gather in a circle. Put one hand in the middle of the circle and form a huddle. Repeat after me: I love and trust God's Word. I will learn to study it for myself. I promise to learn to use the Bible. I promise to read the Bible.** After students have made their promises, finalize them by having the group say "I promise" as a team would when it breaks from the huddle to play a game.

Say: **A second way that we are going to show our love for God's Word is by sponsoring a "Read the Bible Every Day" campaign. For the next four lessons, we are going to remind the people of our congregation to read their Bibles. We are going to help them remember that God's Word is wonderful and dependable. When we believe that God's Word is wonderful and dependable, we will read it.**

Choose one or both of the following options for students to do. Students will prepare this week for next week.

Option 1: Find out from the church office how many bulletins are printed each week. Divide that number by four and make that many copies of reproducible page 16 (the bookmarks). During this time have students decorate the bookmarks. You may also supply blank paper bookmarks so the students can create their own designs. If possible set up a time for students to insert the bookmarks into next week's bulletins. If your congregation is large and this would be a formidable project, choose one or several Bible school classes to focus upon for the campaign and make enough bookmarks for them.

Option 2: Have students practice and polish the reading of the summary sentences from the Using Study Skills step to present to the congregation. If you choose this option, make arrangements with the worship leader or minister ahead of time. Introduce the reading to the congregation in the following manner: **The members of (name of class) have declared this month 'Read the Bible Every Day' month. Our mission is to remind you and to encourage you to read your Bibles every day. It is our 'Read Your Bible Every Day' campaign. Today, we begin by presenting what the book of Psalms says about God's wonderful and dependable Word.**

▼ Reviewing Study Skills ▲

Materials
index cards
For the Record (p. 300)

Copy one *For the Record* chart for each student and write in the dates for your class sessions. You will need to extend the chart to accommodate more dates. Prepare index cards by writing one of the following references on separate cards: Psalm 104:21; Psalm 41:7; Psalm 47:1; Judges 5:16; John 20:13; Proverbs 29:2; Numbers 23:21; Matthew 9:24; Luke 15:25; Acts 12:17; Exodus 15:21; 2 Kings 4:35. Place the cards in the grab bag. If you have more than 12 students, copy some verses twice and students can reveal answers in pairs.

Gather students around the book, chapter, and verse squares. Use the following example to play a simple review game. Say: **Listen to this Bible reference: Genesis 10:1. What part of the reference is the numeral 1? Is it the book,** chapter, or verse? Stand in that square. What part of the reference is the word *Genesis*? Stand in that square. What part of the reference is the numeral 10? Stand in that square. Do this with several references: Exodus 3:7; Leviticus 19:1; Numbers 14:8; Deuteronomy 7:9; Matthew 1:7; Mark 2:4; Luke 15:15; John 3:16.

Say: **We've learned today that the Bible has a reference system made of three parts: the book, the chapter, and the verse. Long ago Bible scholars divided the books of the Bible into chapters and verses so that we could easily find an exact passage of Scripture. The book, chapter, and verse reference gives us a great tool for reading and studying the Bible. Now we are going to practice using Bible references to find information in our Bibles. Each one of you needs a Bible reference from our grab bag.** Have students study 2 Timothy 3:16 and then recite (with help, if needed) in order to obtain a Scripture reference from the grab bag.

Say: **When you receive your Scripture reference, locate it in the Bible and read it.** As students work, encourage those who struggle to locate a book to use the table of contents. As students read their verses, have them find a sound word such as clapping, whispering, or roaring. Tell them to keep their sound a secret. Later they will act out their sounds without making any noise. When all students are ready, gather them around the board.

Say: **I'm going to write a verse on the board. I will read it. Then you will read it back to me. After that, the person(s) who received that verse from the grab bag will act out the sound from the verse without making any noise, and we will guess the sound.**

It is important that you make the effort to write the verse on the board, to read it to the students, and then have the students read it to you. This will help students make a connection between the written and spoken versions of a reference.

Use these references: Psalm 104:21 (roar); Psalm 41:7 (whisper); Psalm 47:1 (clap); Judges 5:16 (whistling); John 20:13 (crying); Proverbs 29:2 (groan); Numbers 23:21 (shout); Matthew 9:24 (laughed); Luke 15:25 (music); Acts 12:17 (quiet); Exodus 15:21 (sing); 2 Kings 4:35 (sneezed).

After the game close with prayer: **Thank You, Lord for Your wonderful and dependable Word.** Then have students mark the grid for "I can find the book of Psalms" on their *For the Record* charts.

Historical Facts About the Bible

1. Forty men wrote the 66 books of the Bible over a period of 1500 years.

2. All 66 books and all 40 men wrote about the same message.

3. The one message they wrote was how God brought salvation to you and me.

4. Bible scholars call this unity. Only God's Word could be faithful to one message when 40 different men wrote it between 1400 B.C. and A.D. 96!

5. When the Bible was written, men used the Hebrew, Aramaic, and Greek languages.

6. In order to make more copies of the Bible, men had to copy it by hand.

7. Men would work for months to make one copy of the Bible.

8. They checked each line and counted each letter so they would not make any mistakes when copying.

9. The Bible books were copied on scrolls made of animal skins or papyrus and were kept in clay jars.

10. When the printing press was invented, copies of the Bible could be made faster, and more people could have their own Bibles.

11. This is when all 66 books of the Bible were put together in one volume.

12. The Bible has been translated into many languages. English was one of those languages.

13. Because many men were dependable in bringing the Bible to us, the Bible that we have today has the same message as it did when it was written long ago.

14. We know that the Bible is dependable because of how carefully Bible scholars preserved it, translated it, and copied it.

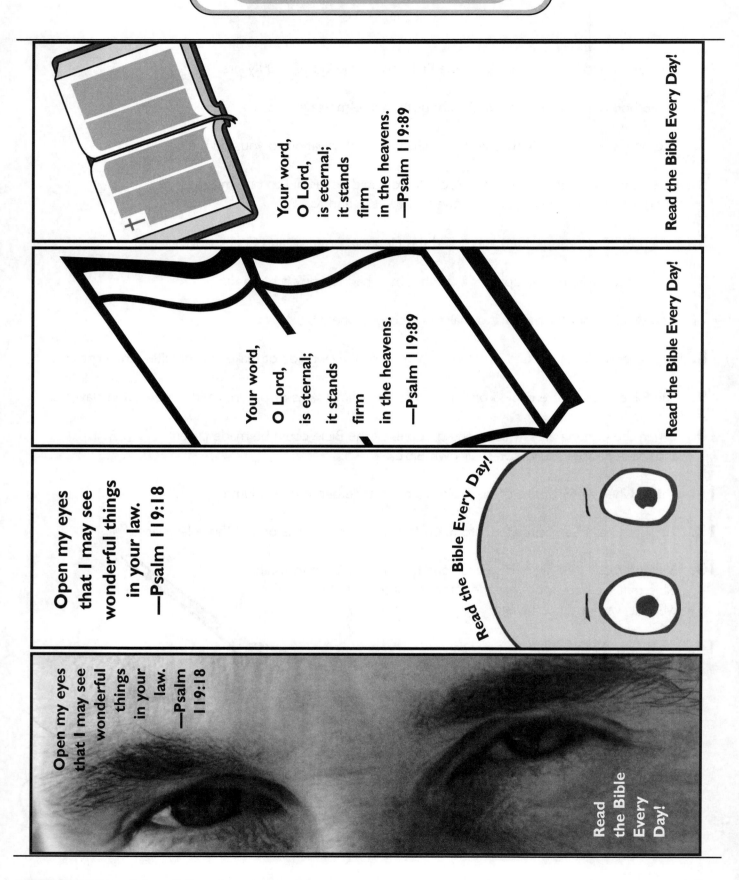

Your word,
O Lord,
is eternal;
it stands
firm
in the heavens.
—Psalm 119:89

Read the Bible Every Day!

Your word,
O Lord,
is eternal;
it stands
firm
in the heavens.
—Psalm 119:89

Read the Bible Every Day!

Open my eyes
that I may see
wonderful things
in your law.
—Psalm 119:18

Read the Bible Every Day!

Open my eyes
that I may see
wonderful
things
in your
law.
—Psalm
119:18

Read
the Bible
Every
Day!

The Bible Is God's Word to Us

Joshua 1; John 20; Romans 15; 2 Timothy 3; 2 Peter 1

Lesson Aims

Students will
- Locate the Old and New Testaments in their Bibles
- Produce a skit explaining the origin of the Bible
- Practice locating and reciting Bible references

▼ Building Study Skills ▲

Materials
large sheet of poster board
marker
scissors
index cards
tape
Bibles
bulletin board
darts or balls
staples and stapler
masking tape
Bible Bookshelf (p. 24)

Before class prepare the poster board by dividing it into two columns. Label the left column "Old Testament" and the right, "New Testament." Then evenly space the names of the four Old Testament divisions in the left column and the names of the four New Testament divisions in the right column. Refer to the *Bible Library* on page 296. When completed, cut the poster board into puzzle pieces. Make enough pieces for each student to have one. Write the names of the following Bible books, each on a separate index card: Psalms, Joshua, John, Romans, 2 Timothy, 2 Peter, Genesis, Malachi, Matthew, Revelation, Acts. Add books as necessary so that each student will have one. Pair a puzzle piece with an index card. Place this week's grab bag at a bulletin board. Staple each puzzle piece/index card pair to the bulletin board. Use the masking tape to mark a line several yards from the bulletin board.

As students arrive ask them to study Psalm 119:9-11 for a few minutes and then recite it to the grab bag manager. Since this is only the second week to work on memorizing these verses, help students as necessary. After a student has recited the passage, give him a dart. He is to stand behind the masking tape line and throw the dart (or a ball) at the bulletin board. Give that student the puzzle piece/index card pair that the dart or ball hits or hits closest to.

Gather students together in the lesson area. Instruct them to work together, using the puzzle pieces, to construct the puzzle and to tape it together. Using Bibles along with the poster board puzzle, explain the testaments and divisions of the Bible.

Say: **This chart shows us that the Bible has two major sections, which are called Testaments. The word *testament* means agreement or promise, so the Bible tells us about two agreements or promises that God made with mankind—an old agreement and a new agreement. Open your Bibles to the table of contents page. Find the two different testaments. Notice that each Testament has a number of separate books listed with it. The Old Testament books tell about events before the birth of Jesus. So the old agreement God made with people was the promise to send Jesus. The New Testament books tell about events after the birth of Jesus. So the New Testament books tell about the promise God made with people for salvation through Jesus.**

Let's find the Old Testament and the New Testament in our Bibles. The Old Testament takes about three-fourths of the Bible, and the New Testament takes about one-fourth. The first book of the Old Testament is Genesis. Find Genesis. Help students do so. **The last book of the Old Testament is Malachi, which is just before the first book of the New**

Testament, Matthew. **Keep your place in Genesis and find Matthew.** Help students do so. Then point out how the Old Testament is a larger portion of the Bible than the New Testament.

Next, we want to look at the four divisions of each Testament. Refer to the poster board puzzle that students assembled. **Bible scholars have divided the Old Testament into four sections or divisions. Let's name these together.** Point to each section while leading students in speaking the names: Law, History, Poetry, Prophecy.

Now let's name the New Testament divisions together: Gospels, History, Letters, Prophecy. Books in both the Old Testament and New Testament are grouped into one of these eight divisions. Books are grouped by content, and these eight divisions tell us what the content is.

You've each been given an index card with the name of a Bible book. Let's place those books in their divisions. One at a time have each student read the name of the book written on his index card. Tell what division the book belongs to and have the student place it in the space below that division on the poster board puzzle.

Psalms is a book of poetry; it belongs in Old Testament Poetry. Joshua is a book of history before Jesus, so it belongs in Old Testament History. John is a book about the life of Jesus, so it belongs in New Testament Gospels. Romans is a letter to the church in Rome, so it belongs in New Testament Letters. Second Timothy and 2 Peter are also letters that belong in New Testament Letters. Genesis is the first book of the Old Testament. It records the first laws that God gave to people, so it fits under Old Testament Law. Malachi was a prophet before Jesus, so this book is Old Testament Prophecy. Revelation is about events that haven't happened yet, so it is New Testament Prophecy. Acts is the only New Testament History book.

Our lesson today comes from an Old Testament book of History (point to the index card of Joshua), **a New Testament Gospel** (point to the index card of John), **and three New Testament Letters** (point to the index cards of Romans, 2 Timothy, and 2 Peter).

If you wish you may give each student a copy of the handout on page 24, *Bible Bookshelf.* Students can color the sets of books the same color, or they may cut apart and make an individual puzzle of the page instead of the group poster puzzle.

▼ Using Study Skills ▲

Distribute the handout pages and pencils. Check to see that each student has a Bible. Lead the class in completing blanks one through five. Write each reference (see below) on the board, read it, and instruct students to copy it into the correct blank, reading it as they write it. This may be a bit noisy, but allow students to speak aloud as they write. It will aid their skills in reading and writing Scripture references. Once each reference is written, have students locate each reference in their Bibles. Remind students how to locate references as needed.

Divide the students into five groups. Assign each group one of the five Scripture passages. Each group will find the answers for blanks that refer to its assigned Scripture passage.

Group 1: Joshua 1:8 answers blanks 21, 22, 23, 24, 25, 26.
Group 2: John 20:31 answers blanks 12, 13, 14, 27, 28.
Group 3: Romans 15:4 answers blanks 10, 11, 30, 31.
Group 4: 2 Timothy 3:14-17 answers blanks 9, 15, 16, 17, 18, 19, 20, 29. (This group could be divided into two groups: verses 15 and 17 answer blanks 15, 16, 29; verse 16 answers blanks 9, 17, 18, 19, 20.)
Group 5: 2 Peter 1:21 answers blanks 6, 7, 8.

When all the blanks have been filled, share answers as needed so that each student has a completed script. Assign students to the various parts. If fewer than nine students need parts, combine the reporters. If more than nine students need parts, assign two additional reporters to the second lines of Reporter #1 and #2. One student could do the videotaping. If needed present the skit more than one time, using a different cast each time. As time permits, practice the skit, tape it, and watch it.

After completing the news conference, ask students to name what they learned about the Bible from the skit. Write each item on the board. Then narrow the list to one overall summarizing statement. **All of these items on our list have something in common. What is that?** (The Bible.) **What one overall statement can we make about the Bible from this list?** (The Bible is God's Word.) **What are we to do with God's Word?** (Read it!) Say: **We've listened to proof that the Bible is God's Word. We can be confident that the Bible was given to us by God. Because of this we should read our Bibles every day.**

▼ Responding to Study ▲

Say: **Learning to use the Bible helps us when we read the Bible. Knowing how to find verses is an important step in reading and studying the Bible for yourself. Knowing how the Bible is put together will also help you study the Bible. Last week we committed ourselves to this study—to learn how to navigate our way through the Bible. Today, we will renew our pledge by saying the Pledge of Allegiance to the Bible.** Choose a student to hold the Bible and to lead students in the pledge: "I pledge allegiance to the Bible, God's holy Word—a lamp unto my feet, and a light unto my path. Its words will I hide in my heart that I may not sin against God." **We will also continue to help remind our church people to read the Bible every day. We are going to work on our "Read the Bible Every Day" campaign.**

Create surprise tubes with a message. Cut toilet paper tubes in half. Use a section of tissue paper that is about 4 inches longer than the tube (about 6 inches total). After wrapping, twist the paper at one end and tie with a curling ribbon. Through the open end insert a few pieces of wrapped candy and one copy of the "Read the Bible Every Day" message (p. 20). (Have the students color the messages if you have time.) Twist that end shut and tie with ribbon. Make as many as possible to distribute throughout the church. If your congregation is small, make enough for the average attendance. If your congregation is large, choose several Bible school classes and make the surprises for them. If appropriate, enlist your students to be greeters before worship where they can hand out the surprise tubes and instruct recipients to twist the tubes to open them.

Materials
toilet paper tubes
tissue paper
curling ribbon
clear tape
scissors
individually wrapped pieces of candy or gum
photocopy of messages (p. 20)

▼ Reviewing Study Skills ▲

Before class copy one set of the *Testaments and Divisions* from page 23 for each student. Place each set in an envelope and place in the grab bag.

Say: **Now we are going to practice our Bible skills. Each one of you needs an envelope from our grab bag.** Have students study 2 Timothy 3:16 and then recite it in order to select an envelope from the grab bag. When students receive their envelopes, direct them to work alone to place the divisions in order under the correct Testaments. Before they begin, make sure the poster puzzle from the Building Study Skills step is covered or removed. Then help students as needed until they are able to put the Testaments and divisions in order without help.

After students have successfully arranged the Testaments and divisions, play the following game where they will practice locating and reciting Bible references. Post the letters A through H, with the Scripture references indicated below, in random order around the room. Each student must have a Bible. Begin by

Materials
Testaments and Divisions (p. 23)
envelopes
For the Record (p. 300)
Bibles
individually wrapped pieces of candy
paper
marker

announcing the Bible division in which the reference will be located. Students are to choose a letter and reference, stand beside it, and then locate and read the reference from their Bibles. Announce the Scripture reference listed for that division. Students are to repeat the reference back to you (in unison if possible). Give students who are standing by the correct letter and reference a piece of candy. Instruct students to close their Bibles and repeat play.

Old Testament Law: E. Genesis 5:9
Old Testament History: B. Nehemiah 34:13
Old Testament Poetry: A. Proverbs 17:10
Old Testament Prophecy: F. Ezekiel 40:17
New Testament Gospels: C. Luke 10:42
New Testament History: G. Acts 2:14
New Testament Letters: D. Hebrews 11:30
New Testament Prophecy: H. Revelation 21:13

After the game, close with prayer: **Thank You, Lord for giving us Your Word. Thank You for the many men who listened to You as they wrote Your wonderful message to us.** Then have students mark the grids for "I can separate the Old Testament section from the New Testament" and "I can locate a specific chapter and verse for each" of the divisions on their *For the Record* charts.

Writers of the Bible News Conference

Scene: A news conference room with a table and four chairs facing the audience, a lectern, and an audience area for the reporters.

Mediator: Good evening, ladies and gentlemen. We are waiting the arrival of four of the 40 men who wrote the Bible. We understand that these writers are ready to tell us how they took part in writing the Bible and why it is important that we read our Bibles every day. If you will remember, the Bible has two Testaments— Old and New. It was written over a period of 1500 years by 40 different writers. Here come the four writers now: Joshua, John, Paul, and Peter. They will read a statement from the books they have written, and then they will answer questions.

(The four writers file in and take a seat at the table, facing the audience.)

Joshua: (steps up to the lectern) I am Joshua, conqueror of the promised land and writer of the Old

Testament History book Joshua. My statement comes from (1) _____.
<Write reference from Joshua.>
(Joshua reads the passage from the Bible then sits down.)

John: (steps up to lectern) I am John, the disciple whom Jesus loved and writer of the Gospel book John and

of 1, 2, and 3 John. My statement comes from (2) _____. (John reads the
<Write reference from John.>
passage from the Bible then sits down.)

Paul: (steps up to the lectern) I am Paul, missionary to the Gentiles and writer of several New Testament Letters including Romans and 1 and 2 Timothy. My first statement comes from (3)

_____. (Paul reads the passage from the Bible.) My second statement comes
<Write reference from Romans.>
from (4) _____. (Paul reads the passage from the Bible then sits down.)
<Write reference from 2 Timothy.>

Peter: (steps up to lectern) I am Simon Peter. I was once a fisherman until Jesus called me to be a fisher of

men. I am the writer of 1 and 2 Peter. My statement comes from (5) _____.
<Write reference from 2 Peter.>
(Peter reads the passage from the Bible and then sits down.)

Mediator: Now we will take questions.

Reporter #1: Will you explain how 40 men like yourselves were able to write the Bible over 1500 years without mistake and without contradiction?

Peter: I can explain how this happened. The Bible came from (6) _____ and not from
<2 Peter 1:21>

(7) _____. Men held the pens and wrote the words, but their thinking was carried along by the
<2 Peter 1:21>

(8) _____. We writers wrote what God was thinking.
<2 Peter 1:21>

Paul: God's Word certainly was written to (10) _____ us and to give us (11) _____.
<Romans 15:4>   <Romans 15:4>
Our hope is in Jesus.

Reporter #1: So are you telling us that the Bible is really the Word of God?

Paul: Yes, all of the words of the Bible are (9) _____-breathed, meaning that words came from God.
<2 Timothy 3:16>
It is His message. God whispered to every writer, so every writer wrote a portion of God's perfect message.

Reporter #2: This is very interesting. God must have had something very important to say to us since He had His message written down for people to read. What is God's message in the Bible?

John: God's message is the most remarkable and important message people ever received. It is the message

of salvation through God's Son, (12) _____. The Bible was written so that everyone
<John 20:31>

—people like you and me—would believe in Jesus Christ and have (13) _____ in His
<John 20:31>

(14) _____.
<John 20:31>

Reporter #2: I'm impressed. The Bible is useful to teach us about salvation through Jesus Christ. What else?

Paul: The Bible will make us (15) _____ about salvation. In addition, God's Word is so perfect
<2 Timothy 3:15>

that it will also equip the people of God for (16) _____ _____. God's Word does this by
<2 Timothy 3:17>

(17) _____, (18) _____, (19) _____, and
<2 Timothy 3:16>   <2 Timothy 3:16>   <2 Timothy 3:16>

(20) _____ in righteousness.
<2 Timothy 3:16>

Reporter #3: You've told us so far that the Bible is God's Word. It was written so that we would believe in
Jesus Christ and receive salvation and life through Him. You've also told us that the Bible—God's Word—
will equip us for good work. How will all this happen? What are we to do with the Bible?

Joshua: It's simple, really. We must begin by reading the Bible. We must read it every day. Next, we are to

(21) _____ on its words which means that we should think about it and memorize it.
<Joshua 1:8>

Second, we should see to it that the words never leave our (22) _____, that is we are to
<Joshua 1:8>

talk about it a lot. Third, we are to be (23) _____ to do everything (24) _____
<Joshua 1:8>   <Joshua 1:8>

in it. We are to follow and obey what God has written in His Word.

Reporter #4: Let me ask why. What is the point? Are there any rewards for doing all these things with
God's Word?

Joshua: For one thing, the person who reads, meditates on, talks about, and carefully obeys God's Word will

be (25) _____ and (26) _____.
<Joshua 1:8>   <Joshua 1:8>

John: Let's not forget that God's Word will lead a person to believe in (27) _____ _____,
<John 20:31>

which leads to (28) _____, a very important benefit of knowing God's Word.
<John 20:31>

Paul: I agree. Wisdom for (29) _____ is crucial. We also can't forget that God's Word
<2 Timothy 3:15>

equips us to do God's good work. A final reason that I would mention is that the encouragement in God's

Word gives us (30) _____ and (31) _____.
<Romans 15:4>   <Romans 15:4>

Peter: None of these wonderful and dependable words came from men. They are all the work of God, who
chose to send the message of salvation to people through 40 writers who wrote over a period of 1500 years.

Mediator: Thank you, gentlemen. This concludes our news conference with four of the 40 writers of the Bible.
We pray that this knowledge of the Bible and how it came to us has helped you to understand that the Bible
is the Word of God. We hope that it will inspire you to read your Bible every day. Thank you and goodbye.

 LESSON 2

Old Testament

New Testament

Letters

Prophecy

Gospels

History

Law

Poetry

Prophecy

History

Bible Bookshelf

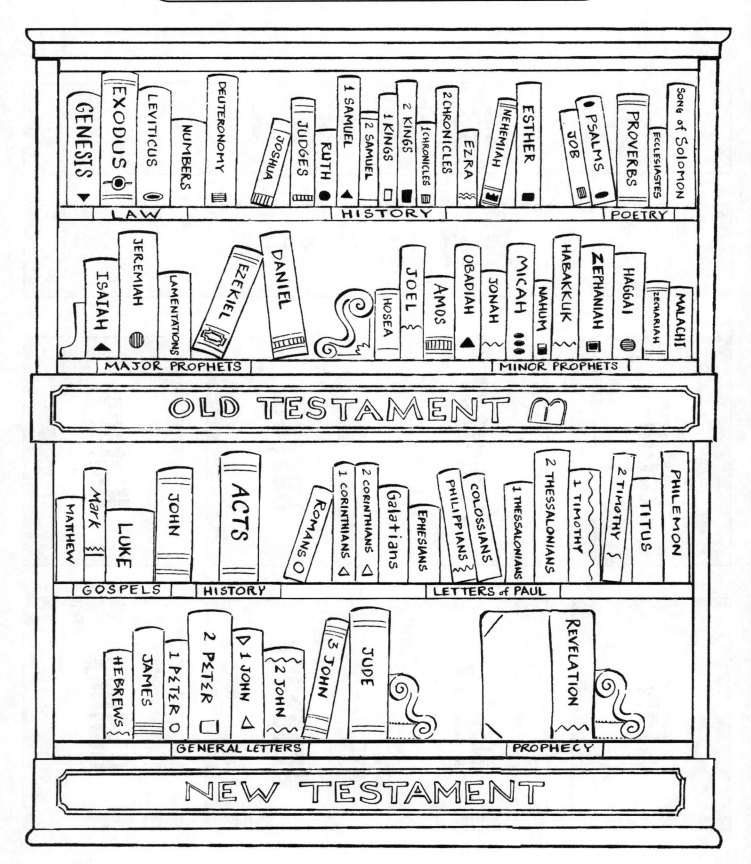

OLD TESTAMENT

LAW · HISTORY · POETRY

MAJOR PROPHETS · MINOR PROPHETS

NEW TESTAMENT

GOSPELS · HISTORY · LETTERS of PAUL

GENERAL LETTERS · PROPHECY

Genesis 1; Exodus 3; Leviticus 19; Numbers 14; Deuteronomy 7, 10, 32

Lesson Aims

Students will

- Read and write Scripture references correctly using five punctuation marks
- Research characteristics of God
- Create a visual and oral presentation encouraging others to read the Bible

▼ Building Study Skills ▲

Before class prepare the sticks of gum for the grab bag. If you have a small class, prepare gum for two teams. If you have a large class, prepare gum for the necessary number of teams to accommodate all students. Teams of five will be formed according to the gum flavor that each student draws from the grab bag. Prepare the sticks of gum by removing the paper wrapper from each piece of gum, leaving the foil wrapping intact. On the inside of the wrapper, write one of the following Scripture references: Genesis 1:1–2:3; Exodus 3:7-9; Leviticus 19:1, 2; Numbers 14:18; Deuteronomy 7:9; 10:17; 32:4. Rewrap the paper around the gum and tape closed. Make one set of references from each flavor of gum.

As students arrive ask them to study Psalm 119:9-11 and 2 Timothy 3:16 for a few minutes and then recite them to the grab bag manager. Students should be able to recite the passages without much help. After a student has recited both passages, instruct him to reach into the grab bag and take a piece of gum.

When everyone is finished, have students form teams according to the flavor of gum that they chose from the grab bag. Instruct students to hold their pieces of gum until you have given the following demonstration.

Say: **Punctuation is important when reading a Scripture reference. Each punctuation mark gives us instructions about what verses to read. We are going to look at five punctuation marks: the colon (:), the comma (,), the semicolon (;), the hyphen (-), and the dash (–).**

Make the following comments about each punctuation mark and write each example on the chalkboard as you read it to the class:

The colon separates chapter and verse: Joshua 1:1 (Joshua chapter one: verse one).

The comma separates two or more verses or chapters: (1) Psalm 119:129, 130 and (2) Psalm 19, 24, 36. Say the word *and* for a comma.

The semicolon separates references from different chapters of the same book and from different books: (1) Matthew 5:1; 6:2 and (2) Matthew 5:1; John 3:16.

The hyphen tells us to read without stopping from one verse through another verse: Mark 1:1-4. Say the word *through* for a hyphen.

The dash tells us to read without stopping from one chapter through another chapter: (1) Mark 3–7 and (2) Mark 3:5–7:3. Say the word *through* for a dash.

Follow this explanation by rereading each reference and reviewing each punctuation mark. Then have students practice with this activity. Give each team a pencil and a sheet of paper. Team members take turns reading the reference that is written on the inside of their paper gum wrappers. Another player on the team

Materials
grab bag
1 flavor of individually wrapped
    sticks of gum for every 5
    students
pencils
paper
Bibles
tape
chalkboard and chalk

must write the reference on the piece of paper. Each team uses one sheet of paper and no references are erased. Players take turns until each player has written a reference, and each has read a reference. After this, have the teams locate the references in their Bibles, one reference per team member.

▼ Using Study Skills ▲

Before class gather the ingredients for the trail mix. Make a set of 12 bags of separate trail mix ingredients for each team. For example, for four teams, put one-half cup of each ingredient in a separate bag. Attach to the bag a slip of paper containing a Scripture reference and scrambled word from the handout on page 29.

In class distribute the reproducible recipe card page and the 12 bags of ingredients to each team that was established in the Building Study Skills step. Instruct teams to work together to unscramble the words on each ingredient bag. Students should use the Scripture reference to determine the correct word. Then students should transfer the correct unscrambled words to the recipe card.

After checking the handout page, add the ingredients to a large bowl, one at a time after the following explanations. Copy the following descriptions and distribute them for students to read.

Say: **All of these different characteristics are a part of who God is. Knowing that God has these characteristics helps us know God. God wants us to know Him. The more we know about God, the more love we will have for Him, the more trust we will have in Him, and the deeper our relationship with Him will be. As we discuss each characteristic of God, we will add the snack mix ingredient with that quality written on it to the bowl.**

Creator: We learn in Genesis 1:1 that God is the creator of the world. God designed and made the Heavens and the earth and all living things. He made all of this out of nothing. We can count on God to know what is best for us because He created us. Reading the Bible teaches us that God is the creator. Knowing this helps us understand who God is.

Concerned: We learn in Exodus 3:7 that God was concerned about the suffering of the Israelites in Egypt. God cared about what was going on in the lives of the people He had created. God had a relationship with His people and because of that He wanted to help them in their sufferings. We can count on God to be concerned about what is happening in our lives. Reading the Bible teaches us that God is concerned for us. Knowing this helps us understand who God is.

Holy: We learn in Leviticus 19:2 that God is holy. The word *holy* helps us understand that God is perfect and righteous. Holy describes God's nature. If we wanted to use one word to describe all that God is, that word would be *holy*. Because God is holy, He deserves our worship, adoration, and praise. Reading the Bible teaches us that God is holy. Knowing this helps us understand who God is.

Loving: Numbers 14:18 tells us that God is loving. God showed us the greatest love of all when He sent Jesus to die on the cross for our sins. Because God loves us, He always does what is best for us. We can count on God to love us because He made us and gave His Son for us. Reading the Bible teaches us that God is loving. Knowing this helps us understand who God is.

Forgiving: We also learn in Numbers 14:18 that God is forgiving. Forgiving someone is canceling a debt. We are all in debt to God because of our sins. When God forgives us, He cancels our sin, and we are no longer in debt to Him. We can count on God's forgiveness when we ask for it through His Son Jesus Christ. Reading the Bible teaches us that God is forgiving. Knowing this helps us understand who God is.

Faithful: Deuteronomy 7:9 tells us that God is faithful. God is reliable, trustworthy, and loyal. Because God is faithful, we can find security in Him. He will never leave us or forsake us. Reading the Bible teaches us that God is faithful. Knowing this helps us understand who God is.

God of gods and Lord of lords: Deuteronomy 10:17 tells us that God is the

Materials

½ cup each of 12 different dry ingredients for a trail mix such as pretzels, dry cereal, candy-coated chocolates, crackers with various shapes, cinnamon candies, raisins, sunflower seeds, or nuts
resealable plastic bags
large bowl
Who Is God? (p. 29)
Recipe Cards (p. 30)
pencils

Note: Be sure that none of the children have food allergies before allowing them to eat!

God of gods and Lord of lords. God with a capital G refers to God in Heaven, the Father of our Savior Jesus Christ. God with a little g can be many other people or idols that people worship. Our God in Heaven is supreme over any god. Lord with a capital L is our Lord in Heaven, the Father of our Savior Jesus Christ. Lord with a little l refers to people who have power over other people. Our God in Heaven is Lord over any and all other lords. Reading the Bible teaches us that God is greater than rulers of people and anything that people might worship. Knowing this helps us understand who God is.

Is not partial: We learn in Deuteronomy 10:17 that God is not partial. Being partial means favoring or loving one person more than another person. God is not partial; He loves us all the same. We receive different gifts from God because we are each different people and need different things. The Bible teaches us that God loves us in just the way we need to be loved. Knowing this helps us understand who God is.

Mighty: Deuteronomy 10:17 tells us that God is mighty. Mighty is power and authority. God is mighty; He has power over all the earth. Whatever He speaks happens. When He created the world, He spoke and whatever He spoke happened. Reading the Bible teaches us that God is mighty. Knowing this helps us understand who God is.

Awesome: We know without reading in Deuteronomy 10:17 that God is awesome. Whenever we think about God, we are filled with awe and wonder at who He is and what He has done. Perhaps you are full of awe when you think about God's sending Jesus to the cross. Reading the Bible teaches us that God is awesome. Knowing this helps us understand who God is.

Perfect: We learn in Deuteronomy 32:4 that God is perfect. Nothing needs to be added to God or taken away from God or corrected in God. He is perfect. He has no flaws, faults, or defects. He is perfect. Reading the Bible teaches us that God is perfect. Knowing this helps us understand who God is.

Upright and Just: Deuteronomy 32:4 tells us that God is upright and just. God created the standards for uprightness and justness. A person who is upright is honest and does what is morally right. He knows what is right and sticks to what is right. Justness is God's standard of correctness. A person who is just conforms to what is morally upright or good. Reading the Bible teaches us that God is upright and just. Knowing this helps us understand who God is.

After the 12 ingredients are in the bowl and mixed together, ask: **What has happened now that we have added 12 different ingredients to the bowl and mixed them together?** (Discuss.) Say: **We have a fun snack to eat that is full of a lot of tasty ingredients. In the process we have looked at 12 different characteristics of God. What has happened now that we know 12 of God's characteristics?** (Discuss. We know God better. Our relationship with Him improved.) **God has many wonderful characteristics, and we can count on Him to be all of these things and more. Which one of these 12 characteristics of God's is your favorite; which quality about God do you like the best? Tell us why.** Discuss, giving each student a turn and share yourself.

▼ Responding to Study ▲

Say: **We've just used our Bible skills to learn about 12 of God's characteristics. Knowing how to use the Bible is an important skill to have. By using our skills, we can grow in our faith, and we can please God. We did that in our Bible study today.**

For the past two weeks, we have taken time during this part of the lesson to make a pledge to learn how to use the Bible. We will renew our pledge again today by using Psalm 119:9-11, which is our memory challenge this month. I will ask the question, "How can a young man keep his way pure?" You will answer, "By living according to your word." I will ask again, "How

Materials
colored pencils
markers
crayons
scissors
poster board

can a young man keep his way pure?" You will answer, "I seek you with all my heart; do not let me stray from your commands." Then I will ask a third time, "How can a young man keep his way pure?" You will answer, "I will hide your word in my heart that I might not sin against you." Do the activity as described. If students still struggle with this passage, use the printed poster of the passage for students to read.

Say: **Now that we have renewed our commitment to using the Bible, let's help others make a pledge—the pledge to read the Bible every day. We are going to work on our "Read the Bible Every Day" campaign.**

Have students create one poster board strip for each of God's characteristics learned in today's lesson. They should make these colorful and attractive. Next have students practice and prepare a presentation using the descriptions of each characteristic from the Using Study Skills step along with the poster strips they prepare here. Add the following final summary after the 12 characteristics have been read: "The Bible teaches us many more wonderful things about God beyond what we have presented today. The way to know God is to read about Him in the Bible. Who is God? God is creator, concerned, holy, loving, forgiving, faithful, God of gods and Lord of lords, not partial, mighty, awesome, perfect, upright, and just. Get to know Him. Read the Bible every day."

Make arrangements for students to present this information in worship service or for a Bible school class. Introduce the presentation in the following manner: **The members of (name of class) have declared this month "Read the Bible Every Day" month. Our mission is to remind you and to encourage you to read your Bibles every day. It is our "Read the Bible Every Day" campaign. Today, we will present some of the wonderful things the Bible tells us about God.**

▼ Reviewing Study Skills ▲

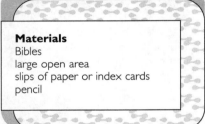

Materials
Bibles
large open area
slips of paper or index cards
pencil

Before class write the Scripture references given below on separate index cards. Do not reveal the color with the passage.

Direct students to play this version of tag. One person is it. He is the blue man. Blue man holding the index cards stands in the middle of the playing area. Players line up on one end of the area or along a wall with their Bibles. Blue man calls a Scripture reference from the following list of choices. Each reference contains a color. All players must find and read the reference to discover the color. Blue man must also find and read the passage. Players who are wearing any color mentioned in the passage must run from one end of the playing area to the other—wall to wall, if possible. Blue man may begin tagging players with the determined color as soon as he knows what it is, so the faster he is at locating verses the greater advantage he will have. Players wearing the specified color are only safe once they reach the opposite end or wall of the playing area. All those captured by blue man become his helpers. Students should read the entire verse because some contain more than one color.

White: Revelation 20:11; 2 Kings 5:27; Acts 1:10
Red: Exodus 15:22; Job 16:16; Matthew 16:3
Black: 1 Kings 18:45; Deuteronomy 4:11; Lamentations 4:8; Revelation 6:5
Green: Hosea 14:8; Proverbs 11:28; Luke 23:31; Genesis 1:30
Blue: Numbers 4:6
Yellow: Leviticus 13:30; Leviticus 13:36
Purple: Acts 16:14; Mark 15:17; Proverbs 31:22
Gray: Hosea 7:9; 1 Samuel 12:2; Job 15:10
Mixed: Daniel 5:29 (purple, gold); Exodus 38:18 (blue, purple); Isaiah 1:18 (white, red); Zechariah 1:8 (red, brown, white); Revelation 9:17 (red, blue, yellow); Jeremiah 10:9 (blue, purple); Esther 1:6 (white, blue, purple)

After the game close with prayer: **Thank You, Lord, for giving us Your Word. Thank You for teaching us about You and helping us to know who You are.**

Who Is God?

Who is God? Get to know Him. Read the Bible every day. Genesis 1:1	**God is** _____. REAROTC
Who is God? Get to know Him. Read the Bible every day. Exodus 3:7	**God is** _____. CERCONDEN
Who is God? Get to know Him. Read the Bible every day. Leviticus 19:2	**God is** _____. LOYH
Who is God? Get to know Him. Read the Bible every day. Numbers 14:18	**God is** _____. GNIVOL
Who is God? Get to know Him. Read the Bible every day. Numbers 14:18	**God is** _____. OGRVNGIFI
Who is God? Get to know Him. Read the Bible every day. Deuteronomy 7:9; 32:4	**God is** _____. LFHTAIFU
Who is God? Get to know Him. Read the Bible every day. Deuteronomy 10:17	**God is** _____. OGD & ORDL
Who is God? Get to know Him. Read the Bible every day. Deuteronomy 10:17	**God is not** _____. AARITPL
Who is God? Get to know Him. Read the Bible every day. Deuteronomy 10:17	**God is** _____. THGYMI
Who is God? Get to know Him. Read the Bible every day. Deuteronomy 10:17	**God is** _____. WEOMSAE
Who is God? Get to know Him. Read the Bible every day. Deuteronomy 32:4	**God is** _____. ERECTFP
Who is God? Get to know Him. Read the Bible every day. Deuteronomy 32:4	**God is** _____. TGPHURI & SUJT

Recipe: What Is God Like?

From the Pen of Moses
as written in the
Old Testament Books of Law

List of Characteristics
Genesis 1:1 _ _ _ _ _ _ _ _
Exodus 3:7 _ _ _ _ _ _ _ _ _ _
Leviticus 19:2 _ _ _ _ _
Numbers 14:18 _ _ _ _ _ _ _
Numbers 14:18 _ _ _ _ _ _ _ _ _ _ _
Deuteronomy 7:9; 32:4 _ _ _ _ _ _ _ _
Deuteronomy 10:17 _ _ _ of gods & _ _ _ _ of lords
Deuteronomy 10:17 Is not _ _ _ _ _ _ _ _
Deuteronomy 10:17 _ _ _ _ _ _ _
Deuteronomy 10:17 _ _ _ _ _ _ _
Deuteronomy 32:4 _ _ _ _ _ _ _
Deuteronomy 32:4 _ _ _ _ _ _ _ _ & _ _ _ _ _

Recipe: What Is God Like?

From the Pen of Moses
as written in the
Old Testament Books of Law

List of Characteristics
Genesis 1:1 _ _ _ _ _ _ _ _
Exodus 3:7 _ _ _ _ _ _ _ _ _ _
Leviticus 19:2 _ _ _ _ _
Numbers 14:18 _ _ _ _ _ _ _
Numbers 14:18 _ _ _ _ _ _ _ _ _ _ _
Deuteronomy 7:9; 32:4 _ _ _ _ _ _ _ _
Deuteronomy 10:17 _ _ _ of gods & _ _ _ _ of lords
Deuteronomy 10:17 Is not _ _ _ _ _ _ _ _
Deuteronomy 10:17 _ _ _ _ _ _ _
Deuteronomy 10:17 _ _ _ _ _ _ _
Deuteronomy 32:4 _ _ _ _ _ _ _
Deuteronomy 32:4 _ _ _ _ _ _ _ _ & _ _ _ _ _

The Bible Records God's Instructions

Deuteronomy 6; Psalm 119

Lesson Aims

Students will

- Find treasure using clues and a treasure map
- Pledge to learn how to use the Bible
- Participate in a Bible club game

▼ Building Study Skills ▲

Before class copy the handout from Lesson 2, cut apart, and place each set of labels in separate envelopes (one set per student). (Use sets prepared for Lesson 2 if they are still intact.) Place them along with the newspapers in the grab bag. As students arrive instruct them to review the memory passages for this unit: 2 Timothy 3:16 and Psalm 119:9-11. Students recite the passages to the grab bag manager in order to receive one envelope and two sheets of newspaper.

When all students have the materials needed, play this game. Students line up along one end of the room, standing on one sheet of newspaper. At the go signal, each player sorts through the slips of paper in his envelope to find the Old Testament title. He sets that on the floor next to the newspaper. Then he sets the newspaper sheet he is holding on the floor in front of him and steps onto it with both feet. He searches through his envelope to find the first Old Testament division slip. He places that on the floor next to the newspaper. He then picks up the first page, sets it in front of the one he's standing on, and steps onto it with both feet. Again, he reaches in his envelope to pull out the next Old Testament division and places it on the floor next to the newspaper. He repeats this process until he has left a trail behind him of the Old and New Testament divisions in their proper order. When the race is over, students may check each other's order.

After this, gather students in the lesson area. Instruct them to bring their newspaper sections with them. Have extra newspaper sections for those students whose newspapers didn't survive the race. Distribute markers. Dictate the lesson Scriptures and have students write them in large letters and numbers on their newspapers: Psalm 119:9-11, 33-35 and Deuteronomy 6:6-9. Check students' work, discuss the divisions where references are located (Old Testament Law and Poetry), and then instruct them to find the references in their Bibles. Once the references are found, have students tear a piece from the newspaper to mark each reference in their Bibles. They will be turning back and forth between the two references during the Using Study Skills step.

As time permits, dictate other passages for students to write.

Materials
2 sheets of newspaper per student
Testaments and Divisions (p. 23)
envelopes
wide-tip markers
grab bag

▼ Using Study Skills ▲

Before class make one copy of the *Clues* for each group of students. Separate the clues and sort them so that all the same clues are together. Then hide the clues as follows: Clue one will be handed to groups in the classroom. Clue two should be located on the wall in one of the building's hallways. Clue three should

Materials
copy paper
pencils
Clues (p. 35)
wrapped Bibles

be located on a mirror near the described chair. Clue four should be located beside one of the building's sinks. Then choose one of the entrances to the building and place the wrapped Bibles there, one for each group. If you have a large class, you will want to divide students into smaller groups for the treasure hunt. If this is the case, wrap one Bible for each group and then mark the packages so that each group will take only one package.

Say: **Today we are looking for a treasure. If we follow the instructions that are given to us, we will succeed. We will find a great treasure. In order to do this, we need help from our lesson Scriptures. We will also need a treasure map. Remember: Following instructions is a very important part of today's lesson.**

Give each student one piece of copy paper, and direct them to fold the paper in the following manner. Say: **We are going to make our treasure map. To do this, we will fold our papers into small squares so that when we open it, it will have 16 spaces. Then we will fill in the spaces with information from our Bibles.**

First, holding the paper horizontally, fold the paper in half, short end to short end. Make a good crease. Fold it in half again, short end to short end. Make a good crease. Fold it in half a third time, short end to short end. Finally, fold it in half a fourth time, short end to short end. Now open the paper and hold it horizontally. If you followed instructions, you now have a piece of paper with 16 spaces.

Direct students to number the squares from 1–16, starting in the upper left corner and continuing across the row. The second row should be numbers 5–8, the third should be 9–12, and the fourth should be 13–16. Make sure rows are numbered in this manner and not columns. If necessary explain that rows are horizontal and columns are vertical.

Say: **Now we will begin marking our map. Start by writing your name in space 10.** Have students write their name. **Our maps also need to be marked for direction, so we will write the letter *N* in space 8. Now we know which direction is north.**

Next I will dictate two Scripture reference. Write this reference in space 2: Psalm 119:9-11, 33-35. Students do so. **Next write Deuteronomy 6:6-9 in space 3.**

Now, let's answer some questions. In order to do this, we must use the two references we just wrote. We found these references earlier and marked them in our Bibles. What are the names used in these passages for the Bible, God's Word? We are going to list these in space 7. Help students locate this space. Then read both passages. Names for God's Word include the following: word (119:9), commands (119:10, 35), decrees (119:33), law (119:34), and commandments (6:6).

Ask: **What are we told to do with God's Word? We will list these in space 5.** Help students find this space. Then read both passages again. Actions for what to do with God's Word include the following: live (119:9), seek, (119:10), hide (119:11), follow (119:33), keep (119:33, 34), obey (119:34), talk about (6:7), and write (6:9).

Ask: **When are we to do these things with God's Word? In Deuteronomy 6:6-9, we will find four times when we are to talk about God's Word.** Students are to write the four times in the four corners of their maps. Space 1: sit at home. Space 4: walk along the road. Space 13: you lie down. Space 16: you get up.

Ask: **Where are we to keep God's Word? Read Psalm 119:11.** (heart) **Draw a heart in space 11. We are to keep God's Word in our hearts, but where are we to put God's Word so that we can see it every day? Read Deuteronomy 6:8, 9. Write the two places found in verse 8 in spaces 9 and 12.** (hands, foreheads) **Write the two places found in verse 9 in spaces 14 and 15.** (doorframes, gates)

Say: **Since these are God's commandments, we want to include God's name in one of our spaces. Write or draw a picture to represent God in space 6.**

Answers to clues (p. 35)
1. walk along the road; halls
2. sit at home; chair
3. you get up, you lie down, sink
4. doorframes

We have finished our maps, and we are ready to use them to find the treasure. We have four clues to follow. Some blanks in the clues will direct you to use your map. To fill in other blanks, you will have to use hints from the clue itself. When you've found the treasure, bring it back to our lesson area, and we will open it together. Divide students into groups if needed. Then stagger their starting times so that all may participate in the search for the treasure. Say: **Let's begin. Here is our first clue. We will need to fill in the missing parts.**

When all groups have located the treasure, have them unwrap the Bibles. Say: **Our greatest treasure is contained in God's Word. Why?** (It shows us the way to God through Jesus; it tells us how to live; it is our instruction book for life.) **We had to follow instructions today in order to find this treasure. What would have happened if we followed only a few of the instructions? What would happen if we just decided to search for the treasure on our own, without following any instructions? What if the person who created this treasure hunt didn't know were the treasure was? Could we rely on his instructions? No. Following instructions that were written by someone who knew where the treasure was made it easier for us to find the treasure. It also was a lot of fun to create our treasure map, solve the clues, and search.**

Today's treasure hunt can help us understand how important God's Word is to us. The Bible records God's instructions for us. It is like a treasure map. When we follow God's instructions, we will find God's best for us—God's treasure for us. Since God created us and knows us, we can rely on His instructions. Following God's instructions makes our lives full of blessings and full of fun.

What are we to do with the instructions in God's Word? Take your treasure maps. Fold them in half, short ends together. With the folded edge to the left and using the squares as a grid, tear off half of the upper left square (triangle shape). Do the same with the upper right corner. Next, starting at the lower left corner, tear the paper in a diagonal direction to the center of the right edge. This will remove half of the lower left square, all of the lower right corner, and half of the space above the lower right square.

Open the paper. Ask: **What shape is this?** (It is a heart.) **What is the message of the heart? Look in the center.** (Live, seek, hide, etc. God's words, commands, decrees, etc. in [name's] heart.)

▼ Responding to Study ▲

Say: **Knowing how to use the Bible is an important skill to have because the Bible records God's instructions to us. One of the instructions God gives to us is that we should hide His Word in our hearts. We transformed our treasure maps into a heart with the message that God instructs us to put His Word in our hearts.** Have students show their heart messages.

We will renew our pledge today to promise to learn how to use the Bible. We will add a new promise as well. We will promise to hide God's Word in our hearts. We are going to form a circle. Cross your right hand over your left and join hands. Make sure everyone has right over left or this won't work. **If you pledge to learn to study God's Word and to hide God's Word in your heart, take turns saying "I promise" then squeeze the hand of the person next to you. When everyone is finished, we will raise our arms with our hands still joined and turn to the outside of the circle.** Choose a student to begin.

Now it is time to work on our "Read the Bible Every Day" campaign. Let's help others make the same pledge we just made—to read God's Word and hide it in their hearts. To prepare mints, punch a hole in the paper surrounding the mint and a hole in the paper message. Tie the two together with the ribbon.

Materials
individually wrapped spearmint flavored candy rings
curling ribbon
hole punch
copies of *CommitMINT* (p. 36)

Make as many as possible to distribute to the entire congregation or to a Bible school class, depending on what you have chosen.

Recite Psalm 119:9-11 while folding and tearing a paper heart. Follow the directions given in the lesson to fold a piece of copy paper into 16 squares and then to tear it into a heart. Work out the timing so that when students say the word *heart* in verse 11, they open their papers to reveal the heart. Arrange for students to present this during the worship service. Introduce the students with the following: **The members of (name of class) have declared this month "Read the Bible Every Day" month. Our mission is to remind you and encourage you to read your Bible every day. It is our "Read the Bible Every Day" campaign. Today, the class will recite Psalm 119:9-11.**

▼ Reviewing Study Skills ▲

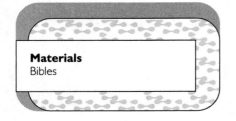

Materials
Bibles

Psalm 119:1, 18; Joshua 1:8;
John 20:30, 31; Romans 15:4;
2 Timothy 3:14-17; 2 Peter 1:21,
22; Deuteronomy 6:6-9;
Genesis 1:1-31; Exodus 3:7;
Leviticus 19:1, 2; Numbers
14:18; Psalm 119:9-11, 33-35

Play the following variation of Simon Says with the theme of a Bible club. The president of the club calls and acts out the commands. The club members must follow according to the directions given below. If a club member doesn't correctly follow the command, his membership dues expire, and he must leave the game. The last club member remaining in the game becomes the next president, and the game begins again. The president uses the phrase "new business" in place of Simon Says. Any club member who follows a command without the president saying "new business" must leave the game because his membership expired. All actions must continue or be held until the president says the next "new business." The president may give any command in any order. Encourage the president to use the "favorite verse" command often so that students will have ample practice locating verses and the president will have practice speaking references.

Command: Password. Club members cup their hands over their mouths and whisper John 3:16.

Command: Secret handshake. Club members find a partner and shake hands with right hands while holding their left hands behind their heads.

Command: Favorite verse: (Choose one of the references in the box at left.) The president chooses one reference to read after saying favorite verse. Club members take Bibles and locate the verse called by the president. Memberships expire for those who can't find the verse.

Command: Come to order. Members sit on the floor with legs and arms crossed.

Command: New Testament Gospels. Members form the sign language sign for Jesus by touching the center of the left palm with the middle right finger and then touching the center of the right palm with the middle left finger.

Command: New Testament Letters. Members drop to the floor on their stomachs and begin to write a letter.

Command: Old Testament Law. Members "draw" the outline of the Ten Commandment tablets, using both hands starting in the middle and moving up and out to form two tablets and meeting together at the bottom of the tablet.

Command: Old Testament History or New Testament History. Members pair up and form the letter *H* with their bodies.

Command: Old Testament Poetry. Members place one hand over their hearts and pretend to sing.

Command: Old Testament Prophecy or New Testament Prophecy. Members place their right hands above their eyes as if looking into the future.

Command: Meeting's adjourned. Members clear the playing area.

Command: All in favor say aye. Members raise hands and shout aye.

After the game, close with prayer: **Thank You, Lord, for giving us Your Word. Thank You for Your instructions to us. Help us to follow them. Thank You for teaching us about You and helping us to know who You are.**

Clues

1.

Are you ready to have a lot of fun?

Listen carefully to clue No. 1.

_____ that is enclosed between
<Space 4>

two long walls.

Look for clue No. 2 in one of this

building's _____.

2.

Many of you _____ in one of these.
<Space 1>

Now, listen closely to clue No. 2, please.

Every morning we all take time to fix our hair.

Look for clue No. 3 on a mirror near a

_____.

3.

In the morning _____ and at
<Space 16>

night _____.
<Space 13>

Rest assured that clue No. 3 will not

produce a frown.

It'll lead you to where you wash your

hands when they turn pink.

Look high and low for clue No. 4 near a

_____.

4.

Here it is—the last clue and the end of the

road.

Clue No. 4 will not leave you with a heavy

load.

And if you can't find this one, I won't take the

blame.

You'll have to look high above or below one of

this building's outdoor _____.
<Space 14>

CommitMINT

○ Make a **CommitMINT** to **READ THE BIBLE EVERY DAY.**	○ Make a **CommitMINT** to **READ THE BIBLE EVERY DAY.**
○ Make a **CommitMINT** to **READ THE BIBLE EVERY DAY.**	○ Make a **CommitMINT** to **READ THE BIBLE EVERY DAY.**
○ Make a **CommitMINT** to **READ THE BIBLE EVERY DAY.**	○ Make a **CommitMINT** to **READ THE BIBLE EVERY DAY.**
○ Make a **CommitMINT** to **READ THE BIBLE EVERY DAY.**	○ Make a **CommitMINT** to **READ THE BIBLE EVERY DAY.**
○ Make a **CommitMINT** to **READ THE BIBLE EVERY DAY.**	○ Make a **CommitMINT** to **READ THE BIBLE EVERY DAY.**
○ Make a **CommitMINT** to **READ THE BIBLE EVERY DAY.**	○ Make a **CommitMINT** to **READ THE BIBLE EVERY DAY.**
○ Make a **CommitMINT** to **READ THE BIBLE EVERY DAY.**	○ Make a **CommitMINT** to **READ THE BIBLE EVERY DAY.**
○ Make a **CommitMINT** to **READ THE BIBLE EVERY DAY.**	○ Make a **CommitMINT** to **READ THE BIBLE EVERY DAY.**
○ Make a **CommitMINT** to **READ THE BIBLE EVERY DAY.**	○ Make a **CommitMINT** to **READ THE BIBLE EVERY DAY.**

Books of Law Tell Us How God's People Were Led

Unit Overview

The stories, concepts, and information contained in the Books of the Law are the foundation on which much of the rest of Scripture is laid. If your students understand how God worked to develop the nation of Israel and establish His laws for them, they will be more ready to understand the world into which Jesus came and why He came. Likewise, the skills your students will be introduced to in this unit will lay the foundation for future Bible use and study.

The use of reference helps, like the Bible atlas and Bible dictionary will open doors of understanding for students that even many adults do not possess. Once again in this unit, the focus is on using the Bible with Bible content being the secondary aim. Make certain that your students handle their Bibles numerous times during each lesson. Allow them time to find Scripture references and discover Bible atlas and Bible dictionary answers on their own, even if you have to cut back on what you have time to accomplish. The practice and sense of accomplishment they receive from doing it on their own is more important than completing every activity in the lesson.

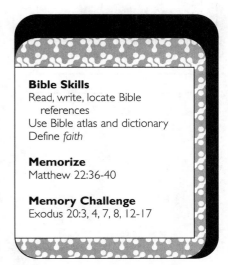

Bible Skills
Read, write, locate Bible references
Use Bible atlas and dictionary
Define *faith*

Memorize
Matthew 22:36-40

Memory Challenge
Exodus 20:3, 4, 7, 8, 12-17

Summary

Lesson 5 focuses on the patriarchs—Abraham, Isaac, and Jacob—and the promise God made to them, a promise for everyone. This is one of the primary threads that runs throughout the entire curriculum.

Lesson 6 encourages kids to accept God's plan, which was part of the promise to the patriarchs and focuses on the beginning of Israel as a nation, first in captivity.

Lesson 7 shows the power of God to keep His promise and emphasizes that there are responsibilities for us to follow in hoping in God's promise.

Lesson 8 shows that the Old Testament is not only relevant today but it was important to Jesus; it gives us examples of how we are to follow God's commands.

Use the following unit project throughout the rest of the year to help your students learn the divisions of the Bible.

Bible Division Binder Activity Project

Label the spine of each binder with a Bible division: *Law, History, Poetry, Prophecy, Gospels, History, Letters,* and *Prophecy.* Print the Bible books for each division on the front of the binders, or photocopy and cut out the Bible books from the *Bible Library* on page 296 and glue or tape them to the front of each binder. Make two signs that say *Old Testament* and *New Testament.* Put the Old Testament sign up on the left-hand side of an empty shelf; put the New Testament sign on the right side.

Photocopy and cut out one set of the *Bible Cards* to use throughout this book. If possible, laminate the cards to make them more durable. (Laminate after cutting apart the cards, or the laminate will peel.) Save the binders and cards to use throughout the unit.

Set up an area of your room to be the Bible Division activity area. Allow students to go to this area when they finish activities early or arrive before class begins. Provide activity sheets in the binder that correspond with the Bible division you are

Materials
Bible Cards (pp. 297, 298)
Bible Library (p. 296)
8 hardcover 3-ring binders
paper
3-hole notebook paper
markers
empty bookshelf
timer

studying. This month, the students will be learning from the books of Law and the assignments are found on page 43.

Following are suggested activities to include in the binder. Adapt these activities to be used with all Bible divisions.

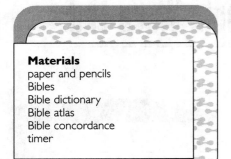

Materials
paper and pencils
Bibles
Bible dictionary
Bible atlas
Bible concordance
timer

Activity 1

Write the books of Law in order.

Find the first page of each book of Law in your Bible. Time yourself to see how quickly you can find all the pages. Print your time here.

Activity 2

Open your Bible to any page in the books of Law and point to a verse. Print the verse reference here.

Practice reading these references aloud: Genesis 22:3-7; Deuteronomy 34:1, 4, 8; Numbers 2:1-4; Leviticus 12; Exodus 11:8.

Now find the references above. Time yourself to see how quickly you can find each reference.

Activity 3

Find the following people from the books of Law in a Bible dictionary. Write one sentence about each person.

Miriam
Amram
Rebekah
Caleb
Seth

Open your Bible to any page in the books of Law. Find a name of a Bible person on your page. Look up the name in the Bible dictionary. If the name is in the Bible dictionary, write the name and what it says about the person. If the name is not in the dictionary, open your Bible again and choose another name.

Activity 4

Find the following places from the books of Law in a Bible atlas.

Mt. Ararat
Haran
Shechem
Nile River
Desert of Paran

Open your Bible to any page in the books of Law. Find the name of a Bible place. Look up the name in the index of the Bible atlas. Find the place in the atlas. If the name is not in the atlas, open your Bible again and choose another place.

Abraham, Isaac, and Jacob Believed God's Promise

LESSON 5

Genesis 22; 28; 35; Hebrews 11

Lesson Aims

Students will

- Recall persons and events from the first five books of the Bible
- Match Old Testament prophecies with their fulfillment
- Make a memory book string to review God's promises throughout the week

▼ Building Study Skills ▲

Prepare binders according to instructions for Unit 2 (p. 37).

Spread out the *Bible Cards* on the floor or a table. Ask the students to work together to find the five books of the Law and put them in order: Genesis, Exodus, Leviticus, Numbers, Deuteronomy. They may use the table of contents in their Bibles if they need help.

Say: **The first five books of the Bible are called the books of the Law. Say them together with me.** Point to each Bible book card as you say the name. **Why do you think these books are called the books of Law?** (Allow students to speculate.)

How many of you have heard of the Ten Commandments? Do you know what some of the Ten Commandments are? (Do not steal. Do not lie. Honor your father and mother.)

The Ten Commandments are a part of God's law that He gave to His people Israel. The books of the Law tell the story of how the people of Israel became God's people and how He gave the law to them. I'll give you some hints about the person who wrote the books of the Law, and you see if you can guess who it is. He grew up in the land of Egypt. He was a shepherd for 40 years before He led God's people. God spoke to him from a burning bush. When he was a baby, his mother put him in a basket in the river. He spoke to Pharaoh to tell him to let God's people go. Who is he? (Moses.)

The books of the Law are the first of eight sections in the Bible. There are four sections in the Old Testament and four sections in the New Testament. Let's work together to build a Bible library of the sections of the Bible.

Direct students to use the table of contents in their Bibles or the *Bible Library* to put the binders in order on the empty bookshelf. When they have placed the binders in order, point to and say the Bible division names together in order.

Pull out the books of the Law binder. Ask students to work in pairs. If you have more than 12 students, select groups of three. Give each group one of the pages from the binder and have the students work together to complete the instructions. Set a timer for 2–3 minutes or an appropriate amount of time depending on the skill of your students. When the timer sounds, have each group pass the activity instructions to the next group. Continue until all groups have had a chance to complete the activities or until time runs out.

Materials

Bible Cards (pp. 297, 298)
Bible Library (p. 296)
8 hardcover 3-ring binders
paper
3-hole notebook paper
markers
empty bookshelf
timer
Law Binder Page (p. 43), cut into strips with one activity per strip

---

▼ Using Study Skills ▲

Materials

Time Line Segments (pp. 309-314)
Bibles
sand in a container
5 cardboard boxes
soft ball that will fit into each box
paper to label the boxes
tape
large piece of poster board
markers

Option

In addition to having one class Bible time line, you may choose to photocopy enough time lines for all the students to have a copy of their own. Students can color or decorate their time lines and keep them in pocket folders.

Before the session, draw a line down the poster board lengthwise to create two columns. Label the left column "God made promises." Label the right column "God kept His promises." Place a paper label on the front and back side of each cardboard box. The first Scripture tells a promise God made to His people. The second Scripture tells a way God kept that promise. Set the boxes against one end of your room with the promise side facing out.

Genesis 22:17; Exodus 1:9, 20
Genesis 22:18; Galatians 3:8, 9
Genesis 28:10-13; Joshua 11:23
Genesis 28:14, 15; Acts 3:25, 26
Genesis 35:10-12; Matthew 1:2, 16

Ask: **From what section of the Bible were the verses we just found in our groups?** Point to the Bible library binders. **The verses were from the books of the Law. Our Bible story verses this month will talk about things that happened in the books of the Law. Does anyone remember any stories from those books?** If students need hints, give them familiar names and let them mention stories—Adam, Noah, Abraham, Joseph, Moses, and so on. Show them the time line pages and have them name the events from "Creation" through "Israel wanders 40 years."

Display the sand and/or dirt. Let the students handle and examine it. **Can anyone guess how many grains of sand/dirt there are in this container?** Accept student guesses. Set out a tiny amount on the table and let students count the grains. **How long do you think it would take us to count this whole jar of sand?** Too much time to finish in class. **This sand reminds us of a promise that God made to His people through Abraham, Isaac, and Jacob. God promised that they would have as many descendants as the number of grains of sand on the shore. God also promised that if they would obey Him and His laws, He would do some other things for them. We are going to play a game to help us learn some of God's promises and the way God kept His promises.**

Divide the students into two teams of no more than five. (If you have more than 10 students, make another set of cardboard boxes. This will ensure that every student has a chance to throw the ball and participate.)

Make sure students have their Bibles. Line students up against the opposite wall from the cardboard boxes. Let teams take turns trying to throw the ball into a box. When the ball lands in a box, the whole class reads the Scripture from the box. If needed, review how to read punctuation in references: for a comma, say the word *and*; for a hyphen, say the word *through*. For example, Genesis chapter 28, verses 10 through 13. Then guide the whole class to look up the Scripture on the box and ask the team to name promises found in the verses. A volunteer from the team may print the promises in the left-hand column on the poster board. Once a box has been used, remove it from the lineup. For the duplicate Scriptures, the second team should try to name different promises than the first team. Continue until all the boxes have been used. Following is a list of promises found in the Scripture.

Genesis 22:17—bless you; have as many descendants as the stars in the sky; have as many descendants as the sand on the seashore; descendants will possess cities of enemies.

Genesis 22:18—all nations on earth blessed because you obeyed me.

Genesis 28:10-13—give you the land on which you are lying.

Genesis 28:14, 15—descendants will be like the dust of the earth; all people on earth blessed by your offspring; I will not leave you.

Genesis 35:10-12—nation and kings will come from you; give this land to your descendants.

Display the promises listed on the poster board. **How do you think God kept some of these promises?** Accept student responses. Then set the cardboard boxes up again with the Scriptures about how God kept His promises facing out.

Play the game again, but students should look for the way God kept His promise in each Scripture. Then a student can print the way the promise was kept in the right-hand column on the poster board across from the original promise. Following is a list of the promises God kept.

Exodus 1:9, 20—the descendants of Abraham, Isaac, and Jacob were very numerous.

Galatians 3:8, 9—the gospel of Jesus blessed all nations of the earth.

Joshua 11:23—God gave Joshua and the nation of Israel the entire land.

Acts 3:25, 26—God sent Jesus to all nations to bless them.

Matthew 1:2, 16—Jesus, the greatest king of all, was a descendant of Abraham, Isaac, and Jacob.

▼ Responding to Study ▲

Ask: **Why do you think God kept His promise to Abraham, Isaac, and Jacob?** Allow for responses. Ask students to find Hebrews 11 in their Bibles. **This chapter is a very well-known chapter in the Bible. Do any of you know what it is called? I'll give you a hint. Look at the first two words of the chapter.** Allow students to guess. **This chapter is called the Faith Chapter.** Ask students to find verses 8 and 9 in the chapter. Read them aloud together. **Why do these verses say Abraham, Isaac, and Jacob received God's promises?** They obeyed God; they had faith. **What does it mean to have faith?** It means you believe what God says.

What are some promises God has made to us? He'll save us through Jesus, be with us, take care of us, and listen to our prayers. Read Deuteronomy 31:8 and Hebrews 13:5, 6 to the students to give them some specific promises God made. Print the students' answers on a white board or chalkboard.

We have to obey and have faith to receive God's promises too. Our unit memory verses tell us some ways we can obey. Help students find Matthew 22:36-40 in their Bibles. Allow plenty of time, depending on your students' activity level, for them to work on memorizing the verses. Do not rush them; they will gain a great sense of accomplishment from their memory work.

Say: **When we believe God's promises and obey Him, then He will keep His promises to us. We are going to use memory beads to help us remember some of God's promises.** Show the list of promises the students named. Ask them to choose several promises they will remember this week that will help them: for example, God's promise to answer prayer, His promise to protect, His promise to be with us all the time. Ask students to choose a different colored bead for each promise. Tie off knots at the end of lengths of string and allow students to string their beads. They may tie the string on their wrists or take them home to hang from their book bag or doorknob. Ask student volunteers to use their memory beads to tell the class which promises of God they will remember this week.

▼ Reviewing Study Skills ▲

Before the session, make different labels for the four boxes with the following information.

Name one of the books of the Law. (1 point)

Name which Testament the books of the Law are in. (1 point)

Name the books of the Law in order. (5 points)

Name any Scripture reference from the books of the Law. (2 points)

Put the labels on the boxes and set them up against the wall as in the Using Study Skills step.

Materials
Bibles
whiteboard or chalkboard
chalk/dry-erase marker
colored string
small colored beads (or small colored pasta that can be strung)

Bible Words
Bible Cards (pp. 297, 298)
4 of the cardboard boxes and ball used in the Using Study Skills step.
new labels for the boxes
For the Record (p. 300)

Divide the students into two teams. Place the *Bible Cards* in a jumbled heap on the table or floor. Let teams take turns seeing how quickly they can find the books of the Law cards and put them in order. Ask: **What do the books of the Law tell about?** They tell about how the people of Israel became God's people and how He gave the law to them.

Then have students work in pairs to test each other on looking up Scripture references. Give each pair a Bible and a blank piece of paper. One student in each pair should open the Bible to any page and print a Scripture reference, including book, chapter, and verse, on the paper. Then he should close the Bible and hand it and the paper to the other student. The second student in the pair should find the printed Scripture. Then the second student should open the Bible and find a verse to print on the paper. Time the groups and see how many Scriptures each group can find in the time limit.

If time permits, play a game with the ball and boxes similar to the game played in the Using Study Skills step. Allow students to work in two teams to throw the ball into the boxes. Allow the teams to continue throwing during each turn until the ball lands in a box. They should follow the instructions on the box the ball lands in. Do not remove the box when it is used. Boxes may be used multiple times. If they wish, students may use their Bibles for Box #4 (to find a Scripture reference).

In closing, read 2 Timothy 2:15 to the students. "Do your best to present yourself to God as one approved, a workman who does not need to be ashamed and who correctly handles the word of truth." Say: **You are learning to correctly handle God's Word of truth, the Bible. I know that God approves of your work.** Distribute the *For the Record* sheets and let students continue to check off skills they have learned and knowledge they have gained.

Law Binder Page

1. Choose one of the books of the Law printed below.

Genesis   **Exodus**   **Leviticus**   **Numbers**   **Deuteronomy**

Open your Bible to that book. Choose a chapter and verse in that book. Write your book, chapter, and verse reference below. Then pass the paper to the next group.

---

2. Find and read the reference below in your Bible. Write the promise God made in the verse. Then pass the paper to the next group.
Genesis 28:15

---

3. Find and read the reference below in your Bible. Write the promise God made in the verse. Then pass the paper to the next group.
Exodus 20:12

---

4. Find and read the reference below in your Bible. Write the promise God made in the verse. Then pass the paper to the next group.
Leviticus 26:3, 4

---

5. Find and read the reference below in your Bible. Write the promise God made in the verse. Then pass the paper to the next group.
Numbers 33:53

---

6. Find and read the reference below in your Bible. Write the promise God made in the verse.
Deuteronomy 31:8

Lesson Aims

Students will
- Locate and use five features of a Bible atlas—map number, grid, column, row, index
- Interpret events in the life of Joseph as positive or negative
- Recall events in their own lives that were sad or bad and acknowledge that God can use them for good

Materials

Bible Cards (pp. 297, 298)
Bible Library (p. 296)
Bible division binders and shelf labeled Old and New Testament used last week
Using a Bible Atlas (p. 48)
Bible Atlas Maps 1–3 (pp. 305-307)
Index to Maps (p. 308)
large sheet of paper
marker
Bibles
full-size Bible Atlas

▼ Building Study Skills ▲

If you do not have a full-size Bible atlas, check your church's library or ask one of the church staff to help you. Spread out the *Bible Cards* and ask students to work together to see how quickly they can identify and put in order the cards for the books of the Law. Ask: **What do the books of the Law tell us about?** (They tell how the people of Israel became God's people, and how God gave the law to them.) **Who wrote the books of the law?** (Moses)

Ask students to work together to place the Bible division binders in order on the shelf. Have them place as many as they can without consulting another reference. When they need help, they may look at the *Bible Library* chart or the table of contents in their Bibles. When they have placed the binders in order, say the divisions together.

Ask: **What do you know about a Bible atlas? How is it like a regular atlas? How is it different?** Allow students to share ideas and guesses. Write their ideas on a large sheet of paper. **A Bible atlas has maps like a regular atlas. The maps show places mentioned in the Bible.**

Ask the students to look in the backs of their Bibles to find maps. (Some Bibles will not have maps.) Then allow them to look at the Bible atlas you brought. Point out the titles to some of the maps. Ask them to find a map that might show places from the books of the Law.

Distribute full-size Bible atlases to the students and allow them to spend a few minutes looking at the maps and notations. Then distribute reproducible page 48 and read and discuss the information together. Allow students to work in pairs to find each of the features listed on the page—map number, grid, column, row, index. Use *Bible Atlas Map 1* as the sample.

If students need further instruction, find the same features on *Bible Atlas Maps 2, 3.* When you are confident your students understand the atlas, have them work in pairs to complete the practice activity at the bottom of page 48. If you wish, have the students race to see which pair can complete the activity correctly first.

▼ Using Study Skills ▲

Label the black poster board **Bad**. Label the white poster board **Good**. Display the posters together on a wall of your classroom. On one side of each construction paper strip, print one of the following Scripture references. The events in each Scripture are provided for your reference.

1. **Genesis 37:3, 4**—Joseph's brothers hate him.
2. **Genesis 37:17, 18**—Joseph's brothers plot to kill him.
3. **Genesis 37:26-28**—Joseph's brothers sell him to the Midianites.
4. **Genesis 39:1, 2**—Joseph is a slave to Potiphar and prospers in his house.
5. **Genesis 39:20**—Joseph's master puts him in prison.
6. **Genesis 39:21**—Joseph is put in charge of those in prison.
7. **Genesis 41:15, 16, 28**—Joseph interprets Pharaoh's dreams.
8. **Genesis 41:39-41**—Pharaoh puts Joseph in charge of all Egypt.
9. **Genesis 45:7**—God put Joseph in Egypt to help save his family.
10. **Genesis 46:2-4**—God promises Jacob He will make him into a great nation.

Show students the Good and Bad posters. Say: **Today we are going to talk about a man named Joseph. What do you know about Joseph?** Allow students to share information they remember about Joseph. **We are going to read Bible verses that show us God's plan for Joseph's life.** Show students the Scriptures on the construction paper strips, and practice reading the Scripture references aloud together. For example: 1. Genesis, chapter 37, verses 3 and 4; 3. Genesis, chapter 37, verses 26 through 28.

Ask students to work in pairs. Give each pair one or two of the construction paper strips 1–8. Save strips 9 and 10 to read later. Each pair should find the Scripture printed on the strip, decide if the Scripture tells about a good or bad event in Joseph's life, and print a sentence on the strip telling about what happens in the Scripture. When the pairs have completed their strips, ask them to take turns coming forward in order (1–8), reading the sentence on the strip, and attaching it to the Good or Bad poster.

Was God's plan for Joseph's life good or bad? How do you think Joseph felt about God's plan when his brothers hated him and sold him as a slave? How do you think he felt about God's plan when he was put into prison? When he was made ruler of Egypt? Ask students to find Genesis 45:7 and Genesis 46:2-4 in their Bibles. Read the Scripture aloud together and decide what sentence to print on strips 9 and 10. **What do these verses tell us about God's plan for Joseph's life?** (God used everything that happened to Joseph to save his family and make them a great nation. Even the very bad things that happened, God used for good.) Ask the students to move all the events to the **Good** poster board. **Even though these things were very painful and sad for Joseph, God used them for good. They were part of His plan.**

If you have time or if your students need some movement, allow them to act out Joseph's story. Characters include: Jacob, Joseph, Joseph's brothers, Midianite merchants, Potiphar, prison warden, Pharaoh. If needed, students can play more than one character. They can use the poster board strips as references for each event. If you wish, provide props, such as towels for head coverings, a brightly-colored robe or shirt for Joseph, rope to tie Joseph's hands, a ring or chain for Joseph as ruler of Egypt, a crown for Pharaoh.

Give students the opportunity to use the Bible atlas skills they practiced in the Building Study Skills step. Print the following Scripture references on poster board or white board. The Scriptures are similar to the ones the students found in the previous activity. Ask the groups to look at the Scriptures and name the places found in the Scriptures. The names are provided below for your reference. As the groups find the names, print them beside each Scripture.

Genesis 37:14-18—Hebron, Shechem, Dothan
Genesis 37:26-28—Midian, Egypt
Genesis 45:7, 10, 25—Goshen, Canaan

Materials
Bibles
Bible Atlas Maps 1–3 (pp. 305-307), one for each student
full-size Bible atlas
light-colored construction paper strips
tape or reusable adhesive
poster board, 1 black and 1 white sheet
poster board or white board
markers or colored pencils
highlighters

Genesis 46:1-4—Beersheba

Distribute *Bible Atlas Maps 1–3* to the students. Divide the class into groups of 3–4 students. Instruct the groups to work together to find some of the places listed on the poster board on Map 1 of their Bible atlases. **You will not find every place listed on the map. Highlight on your maps the names of as many places as you can find. Be ready to tell me which places you could not find on the map.** If you wish, have groups race to see who can complete the activity first. Places found on the map are Midian, Egypt, Goshen, and Canaan. Places not found on the map are Hebron, Shechem, Dothan, and Beersheba.

Guide the group to use a full-size Bible atlas to find the places not found on the sample Bible atlas map—Hebron, Shechem, Dothan, and Beersheba. Students can take turns looking up the names in the index, finding the correct map, and locating each place on the map.

▼ Responding to Study ▲

Ask: **Do any of you remember what Hebrews chapter 11 is called?** If students don't remember, have them find Hebrews 11 and read the title: Faith. Say: **Last week in this chapter, we read about the faith of Abraham, Isaac, and Jacob. Today, we're going to read about the faith of Joseph.** Ask students to find verses 21 and 22 and read them aloud together. **Think about the Scriptures about Joseph that we read earlier. How did Joseph show he had faith in God's plan?** (Wherever Joseph was, whether in slavery or in prison or in charge of Egypt, he obeyed God and did his best.) **Joseph had faith in God's plan for him, even when things were going very badly for him. He showed his faith by obeying God, by doing what our memory verses say.** Ask students to find Matthew 22:36-40 in their Bibles. Practice reading and saying the verses aloud together.

Ask: **What are some sad or bad things that have happened to you? What are some good things that have happened?** Allow students to share. Do not rush them, but allow everyone who wishes to have a chance to speak. Insist that students show respect by listening carefully as each person speaks. Listening is a good way they can do what the memory verse says—show love to their neighbors. **God can use the bad and the good things in your life as part of His plan, just like He did with Joseph. When you have faith in God, you obey Him and follow Him no matter what happens. You believe that God's plan for you is good.**

Take out a small slice of lemon for each student. Let everyone who wishes taste one of the lemon pieces. Say: **These lemons by themselves are too sour. But when we mix them with sugar, water, and ice, we can make delicious lemonade.**

If you have time, allow the students to help make lemonade. If not, simply provide lemonade for them to drink. **That's what God does for us. He mixes together all the things in our life—bad and good—and brings about the best for us.**

▼ Reviewing Study Skills ▲

Play a review game using candy-coated chocolates. Print the following instructions on a poster board.

Purple—Find one of the following features on your Bible atlas: map number, grid, column, row, index.

Yellow—Find one of the books of the Law in your Bible: Genesis, Exodus, Leviticus, Numbers, Deuteronomy.

Materials
Bibles
small slices of lemon for the students to taste
supplies for making lemonade —juicer, pitcher, spoon, measuring cup, lemons, sugar, water, ice—or cups of prepared lemonade
Optional: popcorn or another snack to go with the lemonade

Materials
Bibles
Bible Atlas Maps 1–3 used in previous lesson steps
For the Record (p. 300)
poster board and marker
candy-coated chocolates
bowl

Red—Find one of the following places on your Bible atlas: Nile River, Damascus, Nazareth, Bethlehem, Judea.

Orange—Name a book of the Law.

Blue—Tell which Testament the books of the Law are in.

Green—Open your Bible to a New Testament book.

Brown—Name any Scripture reference from the books of the Law.

Divide the class into two or three teams (5–6 students per team). Take two each of purple, yellow, and red candy-coated chocolates and one each of orange, blue, green, and brown candies out of the bowl and place them on the table. Ask teams to take turns choosing a different color of candy and doing the review instruction that corresponds with that color. As teams find the features, books, and places for the purple, yellow, and red candies, cross out the ones they complete. If teams complete their review instruction correctly, every member of each team gets candy to eat. Once all the candies on the table are used, take more candies from the bowl and begin again. Continue until time is up or candies are gone.

Distribute the *For the Record* sheets and have students check off skills they have gained. Most students should be able to check off that they have located a specific chapter and verse for each book of Law and that they can recite the books of Law. If students think they know the Bible divisions, they can recite them to you and check that box on their charts as well.

In closing, ask students to find Deuteronomy 31:8 in their Bibles. Read the verse with the students. "The Lord himself goes before you and will be with you; he will never leave you nor forsake you. Do not be afraid; do not be discouraged." Say: **God kept this promise to Joseph when He was with him through both the bad and the good things that happened. God will be with you as well, whatever His plan is for you.** Close with prayer, thanking God for being with the students and for your students' commitment to learning His Word.

Using a Bible Atlas

A Bible atlas is a book with maps of Bible lands.

1. Use a Bible atlas when you want to find the location of a Bible place.

2. Use a Bible atlas to find the physical features of Bible lands, such as mountains, deserts, and forests.

3. Some Bible atlases give a brief history about Bible events.

Find these things on your *Bible Atlas Maps.*

1. Each map in an atlas has a map number. Find Map 1 in your sample atlas.

2. Each map has a grid. A grid is made of lines running from top to bottom and side to side. These lines are the longitude and latitude markings of the map. Find the grid lines on Map 1 in your sample atlas.

3. Each column of squares in the grid is given a number, and each row of squares is given a letter, or vice versa. Find the column numbers and row letters for Map 1.

4. Each square of the grid has its own number and letter combination, such as B2. Square B2 is where row B overlaps with column 2. Find B2 on Map 1. What body of water do you find in that square?

5. An atlas uses map numbers and grid numbers to create an index. The index tells us where to look on a certain map to find the place we want to locate. The map number is first, and the grid letter/number combination is second. In a map index, place names are listed in alphabetical order. Find the index in your sample atlas. On which map would you find Haran? In what grid would you find Haran?

Follow the instructions below to fill in the blanks and find a reference from today's story.

_____ What sea would you find on Map 2, Grid B2? Write the first letter of the sea in the blank.

_____ What river do you find on Map 1, Grid B4? Write the first letter in the blank.

_____ Find Assyria by looking in your index and finding it on the map. What city is in the same grid as Assyria? Write the first letter of the city in the blank.

_____ Find Cyrene in the index and find it on the map. What sea is in the same grid square as Cyrene? Write the second letter of the sea in the blank.

_____ What desert would you find on Map 1, Grid C2? Write the first letter of the desert in the blank.

_____ What country would you find on Map 3, Grid A1? Write the first letter of the country in the blank.

_____ What Dead thing would you find on Map 2, Grid C2? Write the first letter of the Dead thing in the blank.

_____ In which row would you find the city of Babylon? Write the number in the blank.

_____ On which map would you find the Red Sea? Write the number in the blank.

_____ In which row would you find the Tigris River? Write the number in the blank.

_____ On which map would you find the Persian Gulf? Write the number in the blank.

Now write the letters and numbers in order to spell out a reference from today's story.

									:		

LESSON 6

Lesson Aims

Students will

- Research Bible terms using a Bible dictionary
- Compare parallel passages of the Ten Commandments
- Paraphrase one or more of the Ten Commandments

▼ Building Study Skills ▲

Begin by playing a Bible book relay. Divide students into two teams. Place two sets of jumbled *Bible Cards*, Genesis—Ecclesiastes, facedown at one end of the room. Teams line up at the other end of the room. At your signal, players take turns running down to their pile of cards, choosing a card from the pile, and deciding if it is a book of the Law. If the card is not a book of the Law, it is placed in a discard pile. If the card is a book of the Law, the student should tape it to the wall or floor. The first team to have the books of the Law taped in order wins the game.

Have the students work together to place the Bible division binders in order on the shelf. Have them place as many as they can without consulting another reference. They may look at the *Bible Library* or the table of contents in their Bibles if they need help. When they have placed the binders in order, say the divisions together. Practice saying the divisions from memory. Remind students that when they master this skill, they can mark it off on their *For the Record* charts.

Ask: **Have any of you ever used a Bible dictionary? What do you think a Bible dictionary is used for?** Allow students to share ideas. Write their ideas on a large sheet of paper. **A Bible dictionary tells about the meaning of Bible words and people.** Allow students to look through the full-size Bible dictionary you brought. Then distribute the copies of the *Sample Bible Dictionary* and page 52. Read over the information on page 52 together and help students look in the *Sample Bible Dictionary* to find the features listed.

Then help students work together to find the same features in the full-size Bible dictionary. When the students understand the features of the Bible dictionary, ask them to work in pairs to complete the activity at the bottom of page 52, using their *Sample Bible Dictionary.*

▼ Using Study Skills ▲

Ask: **Who remembers what Bible person we read about last week?** (Joseph) **How did Joseph show His faith in God?** (He obeyed and followed God and believed in God's plan even when things in his life were going badly.) **Do you remember the land where Joseph was ruler, the land where the people of Israel moved during the famine?** (the land of Egypt) **The people of Israel stayed in Egypt for 430 years! Today we are going to talk about what happened when they left the land of Egypt.** Point out the segments on the time line—Joseph through the Exodus. Ask students to find Hebrews 11:23, 27-29. Guide the students to make a mural of the information in the verses. They can use the

Materials
2 sets of *Bible Cards*, Genesis–
    Ecclesiastes (p. 297)
tape or reusable adhesive
Bible division binders
Using a Bible Dictionary (p. 52)
Sample Bible Dictionary (pp. 301,
    302)
Bible dictionary
large sheet of paper

Materials
"Nation" and "Land" *Time Line
    Segments* (pp. 309, 310)
large sheet of paper or white
    board and marker
Sample Bible Dictionary (pp. 301,
    302)
full-size Bible dictionary
regular dictionary
roll paper or other large sheet
    of paper for a mural
markers or colored pencils
paper
camcorder or tape recorder

segments on the time line as a guide for the sections of their mural, beginning with "Slavery in Egypt 400 years" and ending with "Exodus." Assign pairs or groups of students to each section. Students may consult a Bible dictionary for further information about the people and events. Suggested words to look up: Moses, Egypt, Passover, firstborn, Red Sea. When the students are finished, hang the mural on the wall.

Sometime after Moses and the Israelites crossed the Red Sea, God gave Moses the Ten Commandments. What do you know about the Ten Commandments? Allow students to answer and print their ideas on paper or white board. **Let's read in our Bibles to see whether or not our ideas about the Ten Commandments were right.** Divide the students into two groups. Ask group 1 to find Exodus 20:1-17 in their Bibles. Ask group 2 to find Deuteronomy 5:6-21 in their Bibles. **The two Scriptures you have found are called "parallel" passages. That means that they are two different parts of Scriptures that tell about exactly the same thing. Listen to how these verses are the same.** Ask the groups to take turns reading aloud together the verses you call out.

Exodus 20:2, 3; Deuteronomy 5:6, 7
Exodus 20:4-6; Deuteronomy 5:8-10
Exodus 20:7; Deuteronomy 5:11
Exodus 20:8-10; Deuteronomy 5:12-15
Exodus 20:12; Deuteronomy 5:16
Exodus 20:13; Deuteronomy 5:17
Exodus 20:14; Deuteronomy 5:18
Exodus 20:15; Deuteronomy 5:19
Exodus 20:16; Deuteronomy 5:20
Exodus 20:17; Deuteronomy 5:21

Ask: **Why do you think these Scriptures are so much alike?** Allow students to respond. **Do you remember who wrote the books of Exodus and Deuteronomy?** (Moses wrote both books. Moses was the one to whom God gave the Ten Commandments.)

Say: **We are going to use our Bible dictionaries to help us understand more about the Ten Commandments. You are going to be investigative reporters, and we are going to tape you telling what the Commandments mean. You are going to *paraphrase* each Commandment. Does anyone know what it means to *paraphrase*?** Allow students to guess. ***Paraphrasing* may sound like a hard word, but it just means to put something in your own words. For example, I could paraphrase the first part of the pledge of allegiance. *I pledge allegiance to the flag* means that "I promise I will be faithful to my country."**

Divide students into pairs. Assign each pair one or more Commandments. Commandments 2, 4, and 10 should be assigned singly since they have more information to research. Students may use their *Sample Bible Dictionaries*, a full-size Bible dictionary, and a regular dictionary. When the students are ready, videotape or tape record their Commandments and paraphrases in order. Have someone prepare the completed recording to play back during the Responding to Study step.

▼ Responding to Study ▲

Before class, print each Commandment and its Scripture reference on a piece of paper.

You shall have no other gods before me. Exodus 20:3
You shall not make for yourself an idol. Exodus 20:4
You shall not misuse the name of the Lord your God. Exodus 20:7
Remember the Sabbath day by keeping it holy. Exodus 20:8
Honor your father and your mother. Exodus 20:12
You shall not murder. Exodus 20:13
You shall not commit adultery. Exodus 20:14

NOTE: Save the Ten Commandments papers to use next week in the Using Study Skills step.

Materials
Bibles
paper
markers
tape or reusable adhesive
video or cassette made during the Using Study Skills step
TV and VCR or cassette player

You shall not steal. Exodus 20:15

You shall not give false testimony against your neighbor. Exodus 20:16

You shall not covet. Exodus 20:17

Tape the Commandments to 10 different student volunteers' backs. If you have fewer than 10 students, you may tape more than one Commandments to some students.

Have students take turns standing in front of the class. Each should turn his back to show the class the Commandment. Then the class should take turns saying the Commandment in their own words until the student guesses which Commandment is on his back. Then help the student tape the Commandment in the correct order on the wall.

When the students have guessed all the Commandments, allow them to view or listen to the recording they made in the Using Study Skills step.

Ask: **Who remembers our memory verse for this unit?** Ask student volunteers to read or recite Matthew 22:36-40. **Who does our memory verse tell us to love?** (God and our neighbor)

▼ Reviewing Study Skills ▲

Before the session, print the numbers 1–20 on 20 index cards. Make a set of cards for every 4–5 students in your class.

Review the Commandments. Give each student a flashlight. Read paraphrases or parts of paraphrases of the Commandments and have students point their flashlights at the correct Commandment on the wall from the Responding to Study step. (Option: If you do not have enough flashlights for each student, provide two flashlights. Let students take turns racing each other by twos to see who can shine their flashlight on the correct Commandment first as you give clues.)

Play a Books of the Bible game. Divide students into groups of 4 or 5. Give each group two shuffled sets of the books of the Law *Bible Cards* and a set of shuffled index cards numbered 1–20. Each student will also need a Bible. Students should take turns drawing a book of the Law card and two number cards. The first number card will be the chapter, the second number card will be the verse. When all students in the group have found the reference in their Bibles, continue with the next player. If you wish, groups may compete to see who can use all its cards and find its references first.

Give each student a *Sample Bible Dictionary*. Say: **Tell me the occupation, or jobs, of the following people.** Pause after each one for students to stand and share their answers. Answers are provided for your reference.

Amos—shepherd

Micah—prophet

James—fisherman

Rhoda—servant girl

Philip—apostle, deacon, or evangelist

Cornelius—Roman centurion

What is another name for Holy City? (Jerusalem)

What is the first entry word? (Almighty)

What is the definition of *doctrine*? (teachings; something that is taught)

When did Claudius Caesar reign? (A.D. 41-54)

What Scripture reference is provided for the word *Zion*? (Revelation 14:1)

Praise the students for their work and their knowledge. Read 2 Timothy 2:15 to the students. Ask: **What is the word of truth?** (the Bible) **You are doing your best to learn how to use God's Word. That pleases God. You are good workers for God.** Distribute the *For the Record* sheets and help students to continue to fill in the skills they have gained.

Materials
Bibles
books of the Law *Bible Cards* (p. 297), 2 sets for every 4–5 students
index cards
Sample Bible Dictionary (p. 301, 302)
flashlights, one for each student
For the Record (p. 300)

A Bible dictionary is a reference book for Bible words.

1. Use a Bible dictionary to find biblical information about Bible words.
2. Use a Bible dictionary to identify Bible people and places.

Find these things in the *Sample Bible Dictionary.*

1. Guide words are listed at the top of each page. The word on the left is the first word on that page. The word on the right is the last word on that page. Guide words help you locate entry words. All words in a dictionary are listed in alphabetical order. Since the guide words show the first and last words on a page, only words that fit between them alphabetically are on that page.
2. Entry words are all the words listed in the dictionary.
3. Along with the listing of the word is its pronunciation. The pronunciation tells how to say the word.
4. Following the pronunciation is the word's definition. The definition tells what the word means. Sometimes a word has more than one meaning.
5. Many words in Bible dictionaries include a Scripture reference that indicates where that word is used in the Bible.
6. Some words are illustrated.

Use the *Sample Bible Dictionary* to answer the following questions.

1. Under what entry would you look to find out about foreign altars?

2. Patmos is a
    river   desert   island

3. What was Amos's occupation?

4. What does it mean to repent?

5. What does the name *Genesis* mean?

6. Zion is another name for what city?

 LESSON 7

Jesus Taught Us How to Obey

Exodus 20; Matthew 22

Lesson Aims

Students will

- Recite a memory verse using hand motions
- Act out one or more of the Ten Commandments
- Choose one way to show love to someone else

▼ Building Study Skills ▲

Before class, label two containers "Old Testament." Label two containers "New Testament." Divide the students into two teams. Give each team a shuffled set of *Bible Cards* and an Old and New Testament container. Make sure students have their Bibles. Ask teams to sit in a circle. Students should take turns choosing a book card and putting it in the Old or New Testament container. If students need help, they can look in the table of contents of their Bibles.

Ask students to place the Bible division binders in order on the shelf. Say the Bible division names together. This is the last week you will be focusing on the books of Law, so make sure all students can recite the books of Law in order. Ask: **Who wrote the books of Law?** (Moses) **What do the books of Law tell us about?** (They tell us how God's people became His people and how God gave the law to Moses.) **What are some of the people and places you've learned about in the books of Law?** Encourage students to share what they remember from the past lessons about Abraham, Isaac, Jacob, Joseph, and Moses.

Point to the New Testament division binders. **The New Testament tells us about Jesus' life and teachings and about His apostles' teachings. Today we are going to learn some things Jesus taught about the law God gave Moses. Let's practice using our New Testament so we will be ready to learn about Jesus.**

Have the students find the beginning of the New Testament in their Bibles. Have them close their Bibles several times and practice finding the New Testament until they are fairly comfortable opening their Bibles to the New Testament.

Distribute paper and pencils to the students. Ask them to work in pairs. Let one pair at a time take turns being the teacher and dictating one of the following references to the class. The other students should decide how to write the reference on their papers. They can look in the table of contents of their Bibles if they need help with spelling. References follow: John 14:6; Ephesians 6:1-4; Matthew 26:1, 5, 6; 1 Corinthians 13:4-7; Revelation 22:20, 21; 2 Timothy 2:15.

After each reference is read, print it correctly on a markerboard and have the students check their work. When all six references have been dictated, have the students find each reference in their Bibles. Remind them that all the references are in the New Testament, so if they begin by opening their Bibles to the New Testament, they will be closer to the page number they need.

Materials
Bibles
2 sets of *Bible Cards*
4 small containers
Bible division binders
paper
pencils

▼ Using Study Skills ▲

Materials

Bibles
Ten Commandments papers
   used last week
tape or reusable adhesive
cassette recorder and cassette
2 signs that say "Love God" and
   "Love your neighbor"
Bible dictionary
Ten Commandments Match-Up
   (p. 56)

Suggestions for Motions

love—place hands over heart
Lord your God—raise hands
   toward Heaven
heart—trace a heart shape
   over your heart
mind—point to your head
first—hold up one finger
second—hold up two fingers
neighbor—point to those next
   to you
all the law and prophets—hold
   out hands as though encom-
   passing everything
two—hold up two fingers

Before the session, record Matthew 22:36-40 on the cassette recorder. Display the Ten Commandments papers on the wall.

Ask: **Which of these Commandments do you think is the most important?** Ask the students to point to or stand by the command they think is the most important.

In our memory verses, Jesus tells us which commands are the most important. What do our memory verses say? Ask the students to find Matthew 22:36-40 in their Bibles. Play the verses you recorded and ask the students to follow along in their Bibles. Then play them again, having the students say the verses aloud with the recording.

Ask the students to work together to come up with simple motions for Jesus' words in verses 37-40. Some suggestions are found in the box in the margin.

Play the recording and have the students practice doing the motions. When they are comfortable with the motions, ask them to speak along with the recording. When the verses are memorized, the students should be able to speak and perform the motions without the recording.

Ask: **What did Jesus mean when He said the "Law" and the "Prophets"?** Ask students to look up these words in a Bible dictionary. Point out the Law and Prophecy divisions of the Old Testament and the books contained in each. **The commands that Jesus told the teacher of the law actually are taken from the books of the Law.** Ask half of your students to find Deuteronomy 6:5 (love God) in their Bibles. Ask the other half to find Leviticus 19:18 (love neighbors). Have student volunteers read the verses aloud. **Which of these verses tell us to love God? To love our neighbors?**

Say: **The Ten Commandments that we studied last week tell us ways that we can love God and love our neighbors. Let's decide which Commandments tell us how to love God and which tell us how to love our neighbors.** Remove the Commandments from the wall. Place the two signs, "Love God" and "Love your neighbor," on the wall. Ask students to decide which commands should be attached under each heading. Commandments 1-4 talk about loving God. Commandments 5–10 talk about loving our neighbors.

Say: **Jesus and His followers talked a lot about God's laws. Let's see if we can match these New Testament verses with the Ten Commandments they talk about.** Divide the students into small groups or pairs (6 or fewer groups). Give each group one or more copies of *Ten Commandments Match-Up*. The group should locate and read each verse in their Bibles, decide which Commandment it matches, and decide how to act out the verse. Matching New Testament references and Commandments follow:

Mark 12:29, 30—1. You shall have no other gods.
1 Corinthians 8:4—2. You shall not make idols or worship them.
Matthew 5:33—3. You shall not misuse the name of the Lord your God.
Luke 13:14—4. Remember the Sabbath day by keeping it holy.
Colossians 3:20—5. Honor your father and your mother.
Matthew 5:21, 22a—6. You shall not murder.
Matthew 5:27, 28—7. You shall not commit adultery.
Ephesians 4:28—8. You shall not steal.
Colossians 3:9—9. You shall not give false testimony.
Luke 12:15—10. You shall not covet.

When the groups are prepared, ask them to act out the verses. The rest of the class will guess which Commandment the verse matches.

Say: **In Matthew chapter 5, verse 17, Jesus said that He did not come to destroy the Law, but to do what it said. Jesus taught us more about obeying the Law and about what was really important in the Law.**

▼ Responding to Study ▲

Say: **We are going to talk about ways you can show love for God and for your neighbors.** Ask students to find 2 Timothy 2:15 in their Bibles. Read the verse to the group. **How does this verse say you can be approved by God?** (Study and handle His Word.) **What is the Word of truth?** (God's Word, the Bible) **You are showing your love for God by learning to study His Word. When you work hard in our class and when you study your Bible at home, you are showing love for God.**

Ask: **What is something special a friend or family member has done for you? What is something you would really like a friend or family member to do for you?** Some ideas: my brother to play a game with me; my mom to make cookies; my friend to play what I choose; my friend to draw me a picture.

Look at our list. We have just made a great list of ways we can show love to our neighbors. When we do some of these things, we are truly loving our neighbors as we love ourselves. Distribute the craft foam and other supplies. Help students make magnets to remind them of the way they will show love. They can draw and cut shapes out of the foam. Then they can decorate and write on their shapes the way they will show love. They could print Scriptures on the foam, draw pictures, or write sentences. If you wish, provide beads or small foam shapes for the students to decorate their foam. When the students have completed their foam reminders, help them add adhesive-backed magnets on the backs. You may wish to use a small dab of craft glue to attach the magnet more securely.

Put the completed magnets in resealable bags and set them in a safe place to dry until class is over.

Materials
Bibles
large sheet of paper or poster
   board
craft foam
scissors
markers
adhesive-backed magnets
craft glue (optional)
resealable plastic bags

▼ Reviewing Study Skills ▲

Before class, gather the following items to be used as clues to correspond with the Scriptures.

Matthew 5:13—salt
Acts 2:46—slice of bread
Revelation 18:13—cinnamon or olive oil
Luke 21:2—two pennies
Mark 4:21—bowl

John 6:10—small bunch of grass
James 1:23—small mirror
Colossians 2:14—nails
1 Corinthians 10:4—rock
Romans 12:20—a piece of charcoal

Display the items on a table or surface where the entire group can see them. Be sure each student has a Bible. Call out Scripture references (or write them on the board). Ask students to find the reference in their Bibles and discover which item on the table they find in the verse. As soon as they find the item, they should stand. Choose a student to tell you the correct item.

Place the Bible dictionary at one end of the room. Place the Bible atlas at the other. Tell students that you will call out Bible questions. They should decide whether they should look in a Bible dictionary or a Bible atlas to find the answer to the question. If needed, quickly review the use of these references.

What was Cain's occupation? (dictionary)
In what country would you find the Nile River? (atlas)
What was Bible-times bread like? (dictionary)
What river flows between the Sea of Galilee and the Dead Sea? (atlas)
How do you pronounce the name G-A-D-A-R-A? (dictionary)
What mountain is close to the city of Jerusalem? (atlas)
How do you spell the name Ephraim? (dictionary)

Distribute the *For the Record* sheets. Be sure all students have been able to check off the tasks learned in this unit—quoting the books of Law, locating a specific chapter and verse for each book of the Law.

Materials
Bibles
Bible dictionary
Bible atlas
salt
slice of bread
cinnamon or olive oil
2 pennies
bowl
small bunch of grass
small mirror
nails
rock
piece of charcoal

Ten Commandments Match-Up

Read each of the Scriptures. Decide which of the Ten Commandments the New Testament passage refers to, and write the number of the Commandment on the blank.

Matthew 5:21, 22 _____

Matthew 5:27, 28 _____

Matthew 5:33 _____

Mark 12:29, 30 _____

Luke 12:15 _____

Luke 13:14 _____

1 Corinthians 8:4 _____

Ephesians 4:28 _____

Colossians 3:9 _____

Colossians 3:20 _____

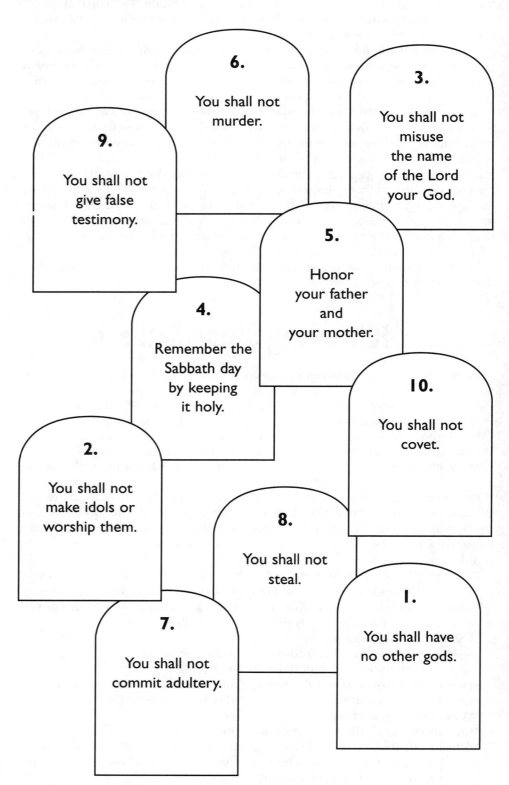

6. You shall not murder.

3. You shall not misuse the name of the Lord your God.

9. You shall not give false testimony.

5. Honor your father and your mother.

4. Remember the Sabbath day by keeping it holy.

10. You shall not covet.

2. You shall not make idols or worship them.

8. You shall not steal.

7. You shall not commit adultery.

1. You shall have no other gods.

LESSON 8

History and Poetry Tell About Choices God's People Made

Unit Overview

The books of Old Testament History contain an overview of the period of Israel's history leading up to the time before the New Testament. The students' knowledge of this time will give them a frame of reference for understanding the messages of the Prophets. The books of Poetry give us insight into the Hebrew mind and into the character of God. In the books of History, your students will see examples of people who chose to follow or not to follow God and the consequences of their choices. In the books of Poetry, your students will find specific instructions for those who choose to follow God. The knowledge from both of these Old Testament divisions will prepare them to make right choices.

Continue to focus on their Bible handling and study skills. In this unit, students will be introduced to the Bible concordance and will gain further experience in using a Bible atlas and dictionary. They will work on memorizing the books of the Old Testament and will become proficient in finding verses throughout the Old Testament. Be ready to take the time your students need to gain these Bible skills. It is better for the students to finish only one task or skill on their own, than for them to complete several activities without doing all the research and Bible handling themselves.

If your students need further work on basic Bible skills, use the Reviewing Study Skills steps from Unit 2.

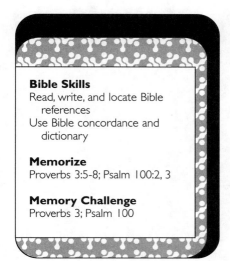

Bible Skills
Read, write, and locate Bible references
Use Bible concordance and dictionary

Memorize
Proverbs 3:5-8; Psalm 100:2, 3

Memory Challenge
Proverbs 3; Psalm 100

Bible Division Binder Activity Project

If you chose to do the Bible Division Binder Activity Project in Unit 2, make activity sheets relevant to the books of History and Poetry, adapting activities developed for the books of Law. See Unit 2, pages 37 and 38, for a complete explanation of this project.

Summary

Lesson 9 is a broad survey of the history of Israel and the judges. The major point of the lesson is choosing obedience to God.

Lesson 10 uses Bible geography as the framework for introducing the story of Ruth and the concept of walking by faith.

Lesson 11 focuses on the choices that the leaders of God's people made. Students will use their Bible skills to research the Divided Kingdom and evaluate the kings of Israel and Judah.

Lesson 12 requires students to use their Bible skills to research the books of Esther and Daniel, and shows that even godly leaders have difficult choices to make.

Lesson 13 is an overview of Bible Poetry and gives the students experience in interpreting figurative language.

Bible Era Rhyme

Use the following rhyme to help students learn the eras of Bible history shown in the time line. When students have the rhyme memorized, have them add the motions described on the next page.

After CREATION came man's sinful FALL.
Through the PATRIARCHS God blessed us all.
The EXODUS and CONQUEST led to the promised land.
JUDGES delivered the nation from the enemy's hand.
Many KINGS ruled while God's PROPHETS spoke His word.
The unfaithful nation fell; God's message wasn't heard.
After the march into EXILE came the captives' RETURN.
Faithfulness to God had to be learned.
JESUS' LIFE brought us salvation and ended our search.
Believers saved through Jesus became the EARLY CHURCH.

Motions

Creation

Stretch arms high over head. Start with hands together, then move hands apart and down to make a large circle. This motion represents the world.

Fall

Bend down at the knees and touch the floor. The motion represents the fall from God's favor due to sin.

Patriarchs

Stand tall with feet apart and hands on hips. The motion represents the authority of fathers.

Exodus

Use both arms to make a sweeping motion across from left to right. This motion represents the movement of Israel from Egypt to the promised land.

Conquest

Stand with feet apart, both arms stretched over head with fists clenched. This motion represents the victories the Israelites had when taking the promised land.

Judges

Hit the open left palm with a clenched right fist as if hitting a gavel on a table. This motion represents the fall of the gavel used by modern judges.

Kings

Put thumbs and index fingers together to form an oval shape. Set on top of head with thumbs and index fingers on head. This represents the crown associated with kings.

Prophets

Reach both arms up with palms open as a child would reach up to a parent. Then bring hands to chest level and open as if holding a book. This represents the idea that prophets received messages from God.

Exile

Hang head low and cross hands at the wrists behind the back as if in handcuffs. The motion represents capture.

Return

March in place with head held high. This represents the confidence of the children of Israel as they returned home.

Jesus' Life

Form a cross with body (feet together and arms extended). This symbol represents our salvation and forgiveness through Jesus.

Early Church

Bring hands together over head to form a church steeple. This motion represents a church building which represents the people of the church.

Joshua and Judges Challenged People to Turn to God — LESSON 9

Lesson Aims

Students will

- Research the lives of Joshua, Deborah, and Gideon and illustrate posters about them
- Use a Bible dictionary to identify other judges
- Make a pledge to serve God this week

▼ Building Study Skills ▲

Have students work together to put the Bible division binders on the shelf in order. They may use the *Bible Library* or the table of contents in their Bibles if they need help. Ask: **What does the first division, the books of Law, tell about?** (Students should remember from the last unit. The books of Law tell about the law God gave to Moses and how the Hebrew people became God's people.) **Who wrote the books of Law?** (Moses) **During this unit, we are going to be learning about the next two sections in the Old Testament. What are their names?** (History and Poetry) **What books of the Bible are in each section?** Students may look on their *Bible Library* charts. Tell them how to pronounce any names they are unsure about. Be sure to point out that the *1* and *2* in Samuel, Kings, and Chronicles are said as *first* and *second.*

Ask students to sort through the *Bible Cards* and put the first 19 books of the Bible in order. They can use the *Bible Library* chart for reference. Say the names aloud together in order. Then shuffle the cards and repeat the process, having students put them in order and say the books again. Do not expect students to memorize the book order today. Simply familiarize them with the names of the divisions and books.

Show the full-size concordance to the students. Say: **This book is called a Bible concordance. Does anyone have any idea what a Bible concordance is?** Have students share their ideas. **A Bible concordance is a reference book like a Bible dictionary and a Bible atlas.** Distribute copies of the handout page 62 to the students and review the information together. Ask the students to follow the instructions on the page to find the features in the *Sample Bible Concordance* and in a full-size Bible concordance. Then ask them to follow the steps at the bottom of the page to find the verse reference in the sample concordances.

If students need more practice with the basic steps of using the concordance, choose other verses from the *Sample Bible Concordance* for them to practice finding. Suggestions follow. The key word in each verse is italicized and the verse location is provided for your reference. "Man does not live on *bread* alone" (Matthew 4:4). "We have found the *Messiah* (that is, the Christ)" (John 1:41).

When your students are comfortable looking up verses in their sample concordances, ask them to work in pairs to find any verse in their Bibles. Let each pair take turns reading their verse aloud to the rest the group. The group can work together to identify a key word or words and look up the words in the full-size concordance to identify the Scripture reference for the verse.

Materials
Bibles
Bible division binders
Bible Cards, Genesis–Song of Solomon (p. 297)
Bible Library (p. 296)
Sample Bible Concordance (pp. 303, 304)
Using a Concordance (p. 62)
poster board
markers
full-size Bible concordance

▼ Using Study Skills ▲

Materials
Bibles
full-size Bible concordance
Bible dictionary
Bible Library (p. 296)
3 poster board
drawing or construction paper
markers
tape
chalkboard or white board
chalk or dry-erase markers

Before the session, title three posters: Joshua, Deborah, Gideon. Print the following Scriptures across the bottom of pieces of drawing or construction paper. A short description of the Scripture is provided for your reference.

Numbers 13:23-25; 14:5-8—Joshua gives good report about land.

Joshua 6:1-5, 20, 21—Jericho's walls fall.

Joshua 24:1, 2, 14, 15—Joshua challenges people to obey God.

Judges 2:6-8—Joshua dies.

Judges 4:1-4, 14-16; 5:1, 31—Deborah judges and defeats Sisera.

Judges 6:1, 7, 8, 12; 7:19-22; 8:28—call of Gideon; Midian defeated.

Today we are going to talk about three leaders of Israel who chose to serve God. We are going to make posters to show how these leaders served God. Give pairs of students one of the pieces of paper on which you have written a Scripture reference. Ask the pairs to find and read the Scripture in their Bibles and decide how they will illustrate the verses on the paper. They can illustrate the story in the verses, or they can draw a symbol that reminds them of the verses. Provide a Bible dictionary and encourage students to look up any terms or places they do not understand. Encourage the students to keep their drawings simple if time is limited.

When the students have completed their illustrations, ask pairs to come forward and share what their Scripture told and what the illustration shows. Then help them tape the illustration to the correct poster.

Ask: **How did Joshua choose to serve God?** Students may look at the poster to remind them. (He gave a good report about the land to which God sent them even when other men did not. He led the people of Israel to defeat Jericho. He promised to serve God even if the rest of Israel did not. He served God all his days.)

How did Deborah serve God? (She led God's people. She trusted God and went into battle against Sisera.)

How did Gideon serve God? (He led God's people to defeat the Midianites.)

In what division of the Bible are the stories about Joshua, Deborah, and Gideon? (History)

The books of History tell us about three parts of the nation of Israel's history—when they were ruled by God, when they were ruled by kings, and when they were freed from captivity and returned to their homeland. The books of Joshua and Judges are in the first part of the History division. They tell about a time when the people of Israel were ruled by God. The way God ruled His people at that time was by judges. Do any of you know what a judge is? Allow students to respond. They may know that a modern-day judge makes decisions in a courtroom. Help students to look up the term "judge" in a Bible dictionary and read about what judges did. **We can read about most of the judges that God sent in the book of Judges.**

Print the following list of names on a chalkboard and have students take turns looking up the names in the Bible dictionary to determine if they were judges or not: **Ehud,** Jabez, **Othniel, Jephthah,** Eleazar, Melchizedek, **Samson, Jair, Shamgar.** (Names in bold are judges.)

Draw a large circle on the chalkboard. At four evenly-spaced intervals within the circle, print the following four Scripture references: Judges 2:11; Judges 2:14; Judges 2:16, 18; Judges 2:19. Draw arrows connecting all the references. Judges 2:19 should be connected to Judges 2:11 to make one continuous cycle. Say: **The reason God's people needed judges was because they were caught in a big circle. Let's read some verses to see if we can figure out what that circle was.** Beginning with Judges 2:11, ask the students to find the references in their Bibles. Read the verse or verses together and decide what to print by that reference in the circle. A short description is provided below for your reference.

2:11—People did evil in sight of the Lord.

2:14—God handed them over to their enemies.

2:16, 18—God sent judges who saved them from their enemies.

2:19—The judge died.

Ask: **Who were the three judges we just read and made posters about?** (Deborah, Joshua, and Gideon) **Who were the Israelites' enemies when Deborah was judge?** (Sisera and his army) **Who were the Israelites' enemies when Gideon was judge?** (the Midianites) **God sent judges over and over and over again, and the Israelites disobeyed God over and over and over again. How many judges did we find in our list of names?** (Refer to the list on the board. They found six judges, plus they learned that Deborah and Gideon were judges.) **We've named eight judges in class today. The book of Judges mentions 12 judges God sent to help His people. That means that God's people turned away from God 12 times. Each time God sent a leader to help them come back to Him.**

▼ Responding to Study ▲

Before the session, print the memory verses, Psalm 100:2, 3 and Proverbs 3:5-8 on chalkboard or white board. Print the proclamation in large letters on a sheet of paper and make copies of the proclamation for your students.

Joshua, Deborah, and Gideon chose to serve God, even when others didn't. We have the same choice that Joshua, Deborah, and Gideon had. Our memory verses tell us some ways we can choose to serve God. Ask students to find Psalm 100:2, 3 and Proverbs 3:5-8 in their Bibles. Read the verses aloud or ask student volunteers to read them.

What ways do these verses tell us to serve God? Students can refer to the verses you have written on the board. Print their suggestions on the board: worship God, sing songs to Him, trust Him even when we don't understand, talk about Him in everything we do, don't be a know-it-all, show respect for God.

Distribute the proclamations to the students. Ask them to fill in the blanks and name a way or ways they will choose to serve God this week. Encourage them to think about how they can serve at their homes, schools, or with their friends. When they have finished, ask students who are willing to share with the class how they will serve. Then roll the proclamations and tie each with a ribbon.

▼ Reviewing Study Skills ▲

Before the session, print the following Scriptures on a piece of paper. Key words are italicized and references are provided for your information only. Make a copy of the Scriptures for each student in your class.

Jesus declared, "I am the ***bread*** of life." (John 6:35)

All your ***words*** are true. (Psalm 119:160)

For all have ***sinned*** and fall short of the glory of God. (Romans 3:23)

Do not let this Book of the ***Law*** depart from your mouth. (Joshua 1:8)

Therefore, go and make ***disciples*** of all nations. (Matthew 28:19)

Jesus Christ is the same ***yesterday*** and today and forever. (Hebrews 13:8)

Play a review game with the *Sample Bible Concordance*. Distribute the papers to your students and ask them to work in pairs to find the Scripture references for the verses by looking in their concordances. If students need help, give them a clue by telling the key word in the verse. You may wish to have students race to see who can find all the verses first.

Divide students into two teams. Give each team a set of shuffled *Bible Cards* Genesis–Song of Solomon. At your signal, teams should work to lay out the cards in order. They may use the *Bible Library* chart or table of contents in their Bibles. The first team to put the cards in order wins. If you have time, play again.

Distribute the *For the Record* charts and allow students to continue filling them in.

Materials
Bibles
chalkboard or white board
chalk or dry-erase marker
copies of the proclamation
    below
6" lengths of ribbon

I, _____, do promise to serve God. During this week, I will serve Him by
_____
_____
_____.

Signed this _____ day of the month of _____ in the year _____.

Materials
2 copies of *Bible Cards*,
    Genesis–Song of Solomon
    (p. 297)
Sample Bible Concordance
    (p. 303, 304)
paper
marker

A concordance is a reference book for finding Bible verses.

　1. Use a concordance when you can remember some of the words of a Bible verse, but you want to know where to find it in the Bible.

　2. Use a concordance to find out what the Bible says about a certain topic or person.

Find these things in the *Sample Bible Concordance.*

　1. Guide words are listed at the top of each page. They help us locate the words we want. Words are listed in alphabetical order. Only words that fit between the guide words are listed on that page.

　2. Key words are all the words listed in the concordance. Key words are the important words from the verse we wish to locate.

　3. Entries include the Scripture reference and a partial quotation of that verse.

　4. Bible book names in each entry are usually abbreviated by using only a couple of letters from the name (Ge for Genesis, Ex for Exodus, and so on.)

　5. Key words in each entry are also abbreviated by using the first letter of the word.

　6. Each entry is on a separate line in Bible order—Old Testament quotes before New Testament quotes.

Practice finding a verse in the *Sample Bible Concordance.* Follow these steps to find the verse below.

　"The Lord is my shepherd, I shall lack nothing."
　1. Choose an important word—a key word—from the verse. Did you choose the word *shepherd?*

　2. Find the word *shepherd* in the concordance. Under the key word you will find Scripture references containing the key word. Notice how the word *shepherd* is abbreviated with its first letter.

　3. Read the references to locate the entry that reads like the verse you want to find. Did you find Psalm 23:1?

　4. Find the reference in your Bible to be sure it is the verse you want.

Follow Where God Leads

Genesis 13, 39; Exodus 19; Ruth 1, 2, 4; Joshua 1

Lesson Aims

Students will
- Make and/or use maps to locate the sites of Bible events
- Recount times in their lives when it was hard to follow God
- State one way they will have faith and follow God this week

▼ Building Study Skills ▲

Have the students place the Bible division binders in order on the shelf. Talk about the two divisions of the Old Testament after the books of Law. Ask: **What is the name of the division after the books of Law?** (History) **How many books are in the History section?** (12) **These books tell about the history of the nation of Israel while God was preparing them for the coming of His Son, Jesus. Look at your *Bible Library* chart. Notice how the History books can be divided into three sections. What are the names of the three sections?** (Theocracy, Monarchy, and Post Exile) **Can you read on the *Bible Library* chart and tell me what each of these means?** Allow students to share what they find. **A *theocracy* is a nation that is ruled by God. During this period, the nation of Israel was ruled by God. What are the names of the people we studied last week who helped lead the nation of Israel under God's rule?** (Joshua, Deborah, Gideon) **What are the names of the three Bible books of the *Theocracy* period?** (Joshua, Judges, Ruth) **A *monarchy* is a nation ruled by a king. The country of England used to be a monarchy that was ruled by the King of England. During the *monarchy* period, the nation of Israel was ruled by different kings. What are the six books of the *Monarchy* period?** (1 and 2 Samuel; 1 and 2 Kings; 1 and 2 Chronicles) Be sure to point out to the students that the names of the books are said as *first* and *second,* not *one* and *two.* **To *exile* someone means to send them away or throw them out. The people of Israel were thrown out of their country when another nation captured it. During the *Post Exile* period, the people of Israel were allowed to return home to their country. What are the three books of the *Post Exile* period?** (Ezra, Nehemiah, Esther)

What is the name of the division after History? (Poetry) **How many books are in the Poetry division?** (Five) **Read about this division on your *Bible Library* chart. What does it say about the books of Poetry?** (They contain songs, stories, and wise sayings from the Hebrew people.)

Divide the students into groups of 4–5. Distribute the *Bible Cards* to the groups. Ask them to work together to lay out the cards in order from Genesis to Song of Solomon. Say: **Name the five books of Law. Name the 12 History books. Name the five Poetry books.** Ask the students to turn over the five books of Law cards and practice saying the first 19 books of the Bible in order. Then ask the groups to choose one card at a time to turn over each time before they say the books. Don't expect them to memorize all the book names today, but encourage them to memorize as many as they can in the time allotted.

Distribute the *Bible Atlas Maps 1–3*, copies of page 67, and brown and blue candy-coated chocolates to the students. Ask the students to work in pairs to follow

Materials
Bibles
set of *Bible Cards,* Genesis–Song of Solomon (p. 297) for every 4–5 students
Bible Library (p. 296)
Bible division binders
Bible Atlas Map 3 (p. 307)
Brown and blue candy-coated chocolates, or other candies or markers
By Land or By Sea (p. 67)

Option
If you wish, give the students another kind of candy in two colors, or simply use paper circles for the activity.

the instructions on page 67. The blue candies should make an X on the completed page. Answers follow: Ephesus to Crete—by sea; Ephesus to Lystra—by land; Ephesus to Alexandria—by sea; Ephesus to Derbe—by land; Ephesus to Athens—by sea; Ephesus to Iconium—by land; Ephesus to Paphos—by sea; Ephesus to Phrygia—by land; Ephesus to Salamis—by sea.

Materials
masking tape
poster board
markers
Bibles
Bible atlas
construction paper

▼ Using Study Skills ▲

Before class, make a large masking tape map outline on your classroom floor. See the illustration below. The map should be as large as possible to allow the students to move around on it.

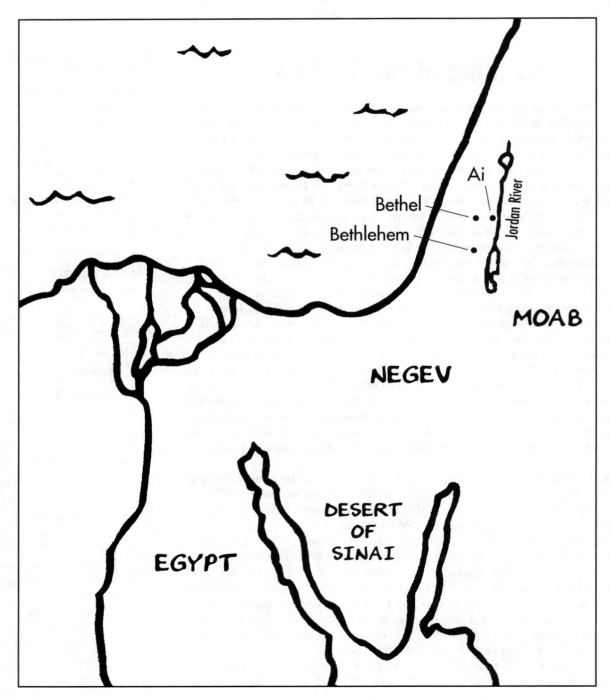

If your students are capable (and if you have time), help the students to create the map in masking tape on the floor. Give them the simple outline map for reference, and provide these labels for them to position on the floor:

Negev	Moab	Egypt
Bethel	Ai	Bethlehem
Desert of Sinai	Jordan River	

Option

If it is not practical for you to have a map on the floor, draw a mural-size map on paper that can be rolled up.

Print the following Scriptures down the left-hand side of a piece of poster board. The people and place names are provided for your reference only. Make two columns next to the Scriptures. Label one column *Who*. Label the other column *Where*.

Genesis 13:3—Abraham from the Negev to Bethel and Ai

Genesis 39:1—Joseph to Egypt

Exodus 19:1—Israelites from Egypt to Desert of Sinai

Joshua 1:1, 2—Joshua and the people of Israel across the Jordan River

Ruth 1:1, 22—man from Bethlehem in Judah to Moab; Naomi and Ruth back to Bethlehem

Say: **We are going to make a map of places the people of Israel went in their travels. First, we are going to find out who traveled and where they went.** Assign students or pairs the Scriptures listed on the poster board. Ask them to find the Scriptures in their Bibles and decide who traveled and where they traveled. When the students are ready, have one student from each pair tell who traveled and where as you print the information on the poster.

Look at the masking tape shape on our classroom floor. This will be our map of places the Israelites traveled. We are going to show the places from our poster on the map. Ask the students to stand on the map and trace the place or route traveled. If you wish, have them place another marker on the floor map indicating the person involved.

When the students have completed the map, discuss travel in Old Testament times. **In Old Testament times, there were no maps to tell people where to travel like we have today. When God told Abraham to travel to a place that God would tell him, Abraham didn't know whether he would cross mountains or oceans, whether he would run into icebergs or waterfalls. He just had to follow God. Joseph, Moses, Joshua, Naomi, and Ruth were the same way. They didn't know where they were going—they had to have faith in God.**

Retrace the travels listed in the Scriptures by beginning in the Negev and walking from place to place.

We have already talked about Abraham, Joseph, Moses, and Joshua in our lessons. Let's learn some more about Ruth. In what division of the Bible do we find the book of Ruth? (History) The book of Ruth took place during the time of the Judges, such as Deborah and Gideon, whom the students learned about last week.

Assign students or student pairs the following six Scriptures from the book of Ruth. Students should find the Scriptures in their Bibles and practice reading it aloud. If you have more students who wish to read than Scriptures, divide some of the Scripture passages up even further. Scriptures follow: Ruth 1:1; Ruth 1:3-6; Ruth 1:15, 16, 22; Ruth 2:2, 3; Ruth 2:5, 6; Ruth 4:10, 17. When the students are ready, have them read the Scriptures in order as you record them onto the cassette.

How did Ruth show her faith in God? (She followed Naomi even though it meant leaving her home.)

How do you think Ruth felt when she went to Bethlehem? Had she ever been to Bethlehem before? (She might have been scared or nervous. She hadn't been to Bethlehem before.)

How did God care for Ruth and Naomi? (He provided grain for them to eat. He provided a husband and child for Ruth and a grandchild for Naomi.) You will need to explain that the child in Ruth 4:17 is actually the son of Boaz and Ruth.

If you have time, play the cassette recording back for the students and allow them to act out the story. Main characters: Naomi, Ruth, Orpah, Boaz. Other possible characters: Naomi's husband, foreman of the harvest, harvesters in the field.

▼ Responding to Study ▲

Materials
Bibles
sewing needle, 1" long
small bar magnet
small piece of cork
small bowl of water
compass

Before class, cut off a small circle from one end of the cork. Practice the compass activity described below so that you can successfully complete it with your students.

Ask students to find Psalm 100:2, 3 and Proverbs 3:5-8 in their Bibles. Read the verses aloud together. If you have time, work on memorizing the verses.

Who did we read about in the Bible today who allowed God to direct their paths? (Abraham, Joseph, Moses, Joshua, Naomi and Ruth) **Why did these Bible people allow God to direct them?** (They had faith that God knew the right way to go.)

We are going to make a compass. What is a compass? (It shows you which direction to go.) **What way does a compass always point?** (A compass always points north.)

To make your compass:

1. Run the magnet over the needle 25–30 times, ALWAYS in the same direction. This action "magnetizes" the needle to some extent.

2. Drive the needle through the cork, from one edge to the other so that the circle lies flat in the water and the needle does not touch the surface of the water. You can also tape the needle to the cork so the ends of the needle extend over the edges of the cork.

3. Float the cork and needle in the bowl of water so that the floating needle lies roughly parallel to the surface of the water.

4. Wait until the needle stops. The needle should point towards the nearest magnetic pole (North Pole).

5. Check your homemade compass with a real compass. Don't place the two compasses too close together or they will interfere with each other.

Say: **We trust a compass to tell us which way is north, even if we can't see which way we are going. Faith in God is the same way. We follow Him and trust Him to direct us even if we don't know which way we are going. The commands of God in His Word are our compasses to tell us which way to go.**

Ask: **When are some times when it is hard to follow God?**

Ask students to take turns holding the compass you brought as they tell a way they will have faith and follow God this week.

▼ Reviewing Study Skills ▲

Materials
Bibles
Bible Library (p. 296)
sets of *Bible Cards* used in the
    Building Study Skills step
Bible Atlas Map 1 (p. 305)
paper slips
tape
For the Record (p. 300)

Divide students into groups of 4–5. Give each group a set of shuffled *Bible Cards*, Genesis–Song of Solomon. Ask students to take turns drawing a book card from the pile and naming the book that comes before and after that book in the Bible. (For Genesis and Song of Solomon, they need only name the book after or the book before.) Students may refer to the table of contents in their Bibles or the *Bible Library* chart if they need help.

Play a Bible atlas game. Ask students to work in pairs. Give each pair a copy of *Bible Atlas Map 1* and a slip of paper with one of these Bible locations written on it:

Goshen	Midian
Nile River	Dead Sea
Red Sea	Sea of Galilee
Mt. Sinai	Zoar
Gaza	Joppa
Canaan	Jerusalem

At your signal, students should find the place listed on the slip of paper and tape it on the floor map.

Distribute the *For the Record* sheets and help students fill in the skills they have used today.

By Land or By Sea

1. Use 10 pieces of paper or candy to mark this page, five each of two colors.
2. Find Ephesus on *Bible Atlas Map 3*.
3. Pretend you are traveling from Ephesus to each of the places below.
4. If the shortest way from Ephesus to that location is by land, place one color marker on the box.
5. If the shortest way from Ephesus to that location is by sea, place the other color marker on the box.
6. When you are finished, what pattern do your markers make?

From Ephesus to Crete	From Ephesus to Lystra	From Ephesus to Alexandria
From Ephesus to Derbe	From Ephesus to Athens	From Ephesus to Iconium
From Ephesus to Paphos	From Ephesus to Phrygia	From Ephesus to Salamis

Lesson Aims

Students will
- Use a sample concordance to determine whether certain words are in the Bible
- Characterize the kings of Israel and Judah as good or bad depending on whether or not they obeyed God
- Choose to follow good leaders

Materials
Bibles
Set of *Bible Cards*, Genesis–Song of Solomon, for every 4–5 students (p. 297)
Bible division binders
Follow the Clues! (p. 71)
Sample Bible Concordance (pp. 303, 304)
poster board
markers
squares of paper
reusable adhesive or tape
beanbag, penny, paper wad, or small object that can be thrown onto a tic-tac-toe grid
masking tape

▼ Building Study Skills ▲

Make a tic-tac-toe game. Before class, print *X*s and *O*s on an equal number of squares of paper. Divide a sheet of poster board into nine sections to make a tic-tac-toe grid. In three of the spaces, print *Free Space*. In the other six spaces, print one of the following sayings, underlining one word in each as shown. The answers are provided in parentheses for your reference only.

A wise son heeds his father's <u>instruction</u>. (in Bible)
Cleanliness is next to <u>godliness</u>. (not in Bible)
God helps those who <u>help</u> themselves. (not in Bible)
A cheerful heart is good <u>medicine</u>. (in Bible)
If at first you don't <u>succeed</u>, try, try again. (not in Bible)
It is more blessed to give than to <u>receive</u>. (in Bible)

Set the tic-tac-toe grid on the floor or table. Make a masking tape line on the floor that the students must stand behind to play.

Have students work in groups of 4–5. Give each group a set of *Bible Cards*, Genesis–Song of Solomon. Have the groups try to put the cards in order from memory. If they need help, they may look at their *Bible Library* charts or in the table of contents in their Bibles.

Have the students place the Bible division binders in order on the shelf. They should be able to do this quickly by now. Have them say the Old Testament and New Testament divisions from memory.

Distribute copies of page 71 to the students. Have them work alone or in pairs and see how quickly they can discover the secret message by looking up the Old Testament Scriptures on the page and answering the clues. The message is: Follow leaders who choose to obey God.

Divide students into two teams—*X*s and *O*s. Give students the *Sample Bible Concordance*. Tell them that three of the sayings on the tic-tac-toe board are from the Bible. The other three sayings are not found in the Bible. They must use their Bible concordances to determine which sayings are in the Bible. Members from each team can take turns standing behind the masking tape line and throwing the beanbag onto the board. Teams must tell whether the saying on which the beanbag lands is found in the Bible or not. If they answer correctly or if they land on a free space, an *X* or *O* is attached to that space on the board.

▼ Using Study Skills ▲

Before class, make a poster titled *Kings of Israel*. See the illustration.

Print the following kings and Scripture references on paper strips, putting the matching name and reference together. The nations are provided for your reference only. The last four names in the list are false names.

King Asa—2 Chronicles 14:2, 4—Judah—did good
King Nadab—1 Kings 15:25, 26—Israel—did evil
King Pekah—2 Kings 15:27, 28—Israel—did evil
King Menahem—2 Kings 15:17, 18—Israel—did evil
King Manasseh—2 Chronicles 33:1, 2—Judah—did evil
King Ahaziah—2 Chronicles 22:2, 4—Judah—did evil
King Uzziah—2 Chronicles 26:1, 4—Judah—did right
King Amaziah—2 Chronicles 25:1, 2—Judah—did right, but not wholeheartedly
King Zechariah—2 Kings 15:8, 9—Israel—did evil
King Pekahiah—2 Kings 15:23, 24—Israel—did evil
King Abah—2 Chronicles 14:17
King Uriel—2 Kings 11:38
King Zittith—2 Chronicles 10:24
King Hariel—2 Kings 5:30

If possible, provide a Bible concordance for every 3–4 students in your class.

Say: **Last week we learned about a time when the nation of Israel was ruled by God through judges. This week we are going to talk about a time when the nation of Israel was ruled by kings. When these kings followed God, the nation of Israel followed God too. But when these kings disobeyed God, the nation of Israel disobeyed God as well.**

Show students the Kings poster you made before class. Ask: **What are the names of the first three kings of Israel at the top of the poster?** (Saul, David, Solomon) Divide students into three groups. Ask the groups to look up the Scriptures about Saul, David, and Solomon and read them together. They should decide from the Scriptures whether the king did good or evil in the sight of God. Write their conclusions by each king's name on the poster.

Say: **After Solomon died, the nation of Israel split into two nations—Israel and Judah. Each nation had a king. Let's put these kings in the correct place on our poster. Some of these kings are real kings. Some are names that were made up. You may look in your concordance to find out which names were really kings. Then look up the Scripture references and decide whether that king ruled over Israel or Judah.** Divide the students into groups of 3–4. Give each group a Bible concordance and several construction paper strips that were made before class. Ask each group to look up the names of their kings in the concordance. If the king is a real king, they should find the Scripture reference on their strip, decide if the king was over Israel or Judah, and tape the strip in the correct column on the Kings poster.

Say: **These are just a few of the kings that were over Israel and Judah. So many of these kings were evil that God eventually allowed people from both Israel and Judah to be captured by other nations and taken from their countries. This happened because the people followed their leaders when they disobeyed. Let's play a game to see how this might have happened.** Divide students into two teams. One team will be Israel and the other team will be Judah. Students will need their Bibles. Ask the teams to line up across the middle of the room. Teams will take turns choosing a king from the poster. They will look up the Scripture about the king and decide if he led the people to do good or to do evil. If the king did good, they will step forward one step. If the king did evil, they will step backward one step.

Which team ended up further back? (Israel) **Israel had more evil kings than Judah, and Israel was captured by enemies before Judah. But Judah continued to have more evil kings, and they eventually were captured too.**

Kings of Israel

King Saul (1 Samuel 10:1; 15:26)
King David (2 Samuel 5:4; 1 Kings 2:1, 3)
King Solomon (1 Kings 3:5-10)

Kings of Judah	Kings of Israel

▼ Responding to Study ▲

Materials
Bibles
large piece of material
dowel rod
yarn or string
glue
glitter glue pens, 1 for every 1
  or 2 students
markers

Before class, make a banner by gluing a piece of fabric to a dowel rod. Print a title in permanent marker or glitter glue: *Leaders We Follow*. Attach yarn or string to the rod for hanging.

Say: **Our memory verses remind us of ways we can obey God like the nation of Israel did when they followed godly leaders.** Review Psalm 100:2, 3 and Proverbs 3:5-8 with the students.

Why did the nations of Israel and Judah disobey God in our Scriptures today? (They followed leaders who disobeyed God.) **Israel and Judah got into trouble because they didn't have leaders who obeyed God. We will get into trouble too if we choose to follow leaders who disobey God. Who are some leaders we could choose to follow who do not obey God?** (Any person whose example we follow is a leader. That means friends, whether they lead us to do good or to do bad. Also, some leaders in our government may not be a good example to follow.) **Who are some leaders who obey God we can choose to follow?** (Parents, other family members, Bible school teachers, church leaders, and so on.) Ask students to use glitter glue to write names of godly leaders on the banner you made before class. If students have time, they can decorate the banner. Allow their work to dry, then display the banner in your classroom to remind them of godly examples they will choose to follow.

▼ Reviewing Study Skills ▲

Materials
Bibles
Bible Cards, Genesis–Song of
  Solomon (p. 297)
Bible Library (p. 296)
tic-tac-toe game used in the
  Building Study Skills step
Xs and Os for game
tape
paper
beanbag or other object used
  in the Building Study Skills
  step
markers
Sample Bible Concordance used
  in the Building Study Skills
  step
For the Record (p. 300)

Play a variation of the tic-tac-toe game played in the Building Study Skills step. Write the following words on squares of paper and tape them over the sayings on the tic-tac-toe grid: *mind, soul, doctrine, yesterday, beginning, sinned.* Divide students into two teams and have teams take turns throwing a beanbag at the grid from behind a masking tape line. Students must find a Scripture reference for the word in their sample concordances in order to place an *X* or *O* in the space.

Or have a reference relay your whole group will work together to complete. Students will need paper, Bibles, a *Bible Library* chart, and a set of *Bible Cards*. Call out a Scripture and have students complete the relay as follows. If you have more than seven students, have some students work in pairs to complete the tasks below.

Student 1: prints the Scripture on a piece of paper
Student 2: reads the reference from the paper
Student 3: takes the piece of paper and finds the book in the Bible
Student 4: finds the chapter
Student 5: finds the verse
Student 6: reads the verse
Student 7: tells in which division the reference is found

Once the students have found the first Scripture, have the first student in line move to the back and continue with the next Scripture. If you wish, time the students, and see if they can complete the relay more quickly with practice.
Scriptures: Proverbs 1:8; Deuteronomy 4:2; 1 Samuel 17:37; Psalm 91:15; 1 Chronicles 14:17; Job 38:4; Ezra 7:27.

Distribute the *For the Record* sheets to the students and have them fill in the skills they have completed.

Follow the Clues

Look up the Scriptures and answer the clues to find the main point of today's lesson.

[ ]	Find Psalm 119:166. Write the word that tells what I do to God's commands.
[ ]	Find Judges 20:2. Write the second word of the verse in the blank.
[ ]	Find Ecclesiastes 8:1. Write the first word of the verse in the blank.
[ ]	Find 2 Kings 10:3. Write the first word of the verse in the blank.
[ ]	Find Job 37:2. Write the third word of the verse in the blank.
[ ]	Find 2 Chronicles 14:4. Write the word that tells what Judah was to do to God's laws and commands.
[ ]	Find Nehemiah 1:5. Write the sixth word of the verse in the blank.

Read the words in order from top to bottom
to discover something you should do.

Write one way you can follow this advice.

LESSON 12 God Provides Leaders for His People

Esther 2; 4; 7; 8; Daniel 3

Lesson Aims

Students will
- Create a tableau based on research with a Bible dictionary
- Tell how Esther and Shadrach, Meshach and Abednego must have felt when faced with the life-and-death decision to be faithful to God
- Promise to obey God, even when it is hard

Materials
Bibles
Bible Library (p. 296)
Old Testament *Bible Cards* (pp. 297, 298)
Bible dictionary
Bible division binders
scissors
resealable plastic bags
permanent marker

▼ Building Study Skills ▲

Ask the students to put the Bible division binders on the shelf in order. Name the four divisions of the Old Testament aloud together. Ask: **What is the last division of the Old Testament?** (Prophecy) **What books are in the Prophecy division?** Students may look on their *Bible Library* charts to name the 17 books. **What did it mean to be a prophet?** Students may look in a Bible dictionary to discover what an Old Testament prophet was. **Look on your *Bible Library* charts. Why were some of the prophets called major prophets? Why were others called minor prophets?** (Major prophets have longer books; minor prophets have shorter books.) **Now you know about each division of the Old Testament. Let's work on naming the Old Testament books.**

Give each student a photocopied set of Old Testament *Bible Cards*. Ask them to cut the cards apart and shuffle them. Have them work alone or in pairs as quickly as they can to complete instructions you call out. They may use their *Bible Library* charts to help them.

1. Find the books of Law. Put them in order.
2. Find the books of History. Put them in order.
3. Find the books of Poetry. Put them in order.
4. Find the books of Prophecy. Put them in order.
5. Flip through your cards and say the books of the Old Testament as quickly as you can.
6. Choose a partner. Take turns saying as many books of the Old Testament from memory as you can.

Give students resealable bags to hold their *Bible Cards*. Print students' names with permanent marker on the outside of the bags.

When the students have completed their games, do another reference activity in groups of four. Students will need their Bibles, *Bible Library* charts, pencils, and paper. One student draws an Old Testament *Bible Cards* from the pile, such as Psalms. All students in the group find that book in their Bibles. Then the student who drew the card finds and calls out a reference from that book, such as Psalm 14:2. The other students write the reference on their papers and then find the reference in the Bible. Allow each student in the group to have a turn.

▼ Using Study Skills ▲

Before class make copies of the top half of page 75, enlarging each chart to fill an 8 ½" x 11" paper.

Gather props and costumes. For Esther, suggested items are a crown, necklace, ring, scepter, bracelets, beautiful robe, decree (rolled paper tied with ribbon). For Shadrach, Meshach, and Abednego, suggested items are robes, turbans, tie belts, and cloths to bind hands. Print the following Scriptures on separate slips of paper and number the slips so the students will know the order to read them. Scriptures from Esther: Esther 2:5-7, 17; 4:5, 7, 8, 15, 16; 7:1-4; 8:7, 8, 17. Scriptures from Daniel: Daniel 3:1, 12, 14-18, 26-28. Place each prop and a numbered slip of paper with a Scripture on it in a separate bag. Make a set of bags for Esther and a set of bags for Shadrach, Meshach, and Abednego.

Say: **Today we are going to talk about some leaders who helped God's people when they were in exile. What does it mean to be in exile?** (To *exile* someone means to send them away or throw them out.) **Remember the people of Israel followed leaders who disobeyed God and did evil. Enemies came in and captured their nations and took them away. Our stories today happened while the people of Israel were in captivity with their enemies. The names of our leaders were Esther and Shadrach, Meshach, and Abednego.**

Divide students into two groups. Give each group one of the reproducible pages prepared before class, a Bible dictionary, a large piece of roll paper, and markers or chalk. Ask the groups to read the Scriptures on their papers and look up the words in a Bible dictionary. Then they should use the information they learned to draw a large background picture of how it might have looked in the king's temple in Persia and where the image was set up in Babylon. They may include the kings in their pictures, but they should not include Esther or Shadrach, Meshach, and Abednego. Display their pictures on the wall.

Give one group the set of bags for Esther, and the other group the set of bags for Shadrach, Meshach, and Abednego. Each group should choose a student or students to be Esther or Shadrach, Meshach, and Abednego. The students should take turns choosing a bag, finding and reading the Scripture reference, then adding the costume part to their character(s).

When the groups have finished, bring the class together and have the characters stand in front of the backdrops as the students report on what they have learned.

Materials
Bibles
2 Bible dictionaries
Obeying in Exile (p. 75)
2 large pieces of roll paper
markers or chalk
props/costumes for Esther and Shadrach, Meshach, and Abednego
slips of paper
plastic grocery bags

▼ Responding to Study ▲

Ask: **Why was it hard for Esther to obey?** (She was afraid. She could have been killed. It would have been easier to say nothing.) **Why was it hard for Shadrach, Meshach, and Abednego to obey?** (They knew they would be thrown in a fiery furnace.)

Say: **Our memory verses remind us of ways we can obey.** Ask students to find Psalm 100:2, 3 and Proverbs 3:5-8 in their Bibles. **What ways to obey do we read in these verses?** (Worship God; sing to Him; trust Him; always rely on Him for help; be willing to learn; respect God.)

From your memory verses and your other Bible work, you know ways to obey. But when are some times when it is hard for you to obey? Distribute copies of the bottom half of page 75. Ask students to fill in specific times when it is difficult for them to obey. Direct them to color the border, cut out the page, and glue it to a sheet of construction paper.

In Bible times, leaders sealed their letters with their own special seals. When they sealed a letter, they were letting everyone know, "These are my true words, and I promise they are from me." Let's seal our papers too,

Materials
Bibles
I Will Obey (p. 75)
scissors
markers
glue sticks
construction paper
stickers

and show God that our words are true. Help students fold their papers in thirds and seal them with a sticker.

Let's promise God that we will obey Him this week even when it is hard.

Materials
Bible
Old Testament *Bible Cards* (pp. 297, 298)
Bible Library (p. 296)
timer
chalkboard or white board
chalk or dry-erase marker
For the Record (p. 300)

▼ Reviewing Study Skills ▲

Divide students into groups of four. Give each group one set of shuffled Old Testament *Bible Cards.* A dealer should deal five cards to each student. Place the remaining cards facedown in the center of the circle. The person to the left of the dealer starts playing. The "Genesis" and/or "Malachi" cards are played first. Other Bible books are played in order on top of those cards—going forward from Genesis and backward from Malachi. If a player has no card to play, he can draw a card from the stack in the center. The game is up when one player uses all his cards or when all the cards have been played. Students may use their *Bible Library* charts to help them with the order of the books.

Or divide students into teams of 4–5. Have teams sit in circles with their Bibles. Let each team take a turn choosing a one-point or two-point Scripture to look up. One-point Scriptures are easier to find. Two-point Scriptures are more difficult. Print each Scripture on the board for the students. At your signal, the team gets a chance to find the Scripture in the time limit. (Choose a time limit that is appropriate to the skill level of your class.) If any member of the team finds the Scripture in the allotted time, the team gets the correct number of points. One-point Scriptures: Psalm 1; Genesis 1:3; Deuteronomy 4:15; Joshua 1:8, 9; Proverbs 3:5-8; Exodus 20. Two-point Scriptures: Zephaniah 1:12; Hosea 5:4; Ezra 4:11; Jonah 3:6; Zechariah 2:10; Joel 2:28.

Distribute the *For the Record* sheets and help the students to fill in the skills they have completed. Any student who is ready may quote the History, Poetry, or Prophecy division books of the Bible to you. Praise the students for their continuing work.

Esther

Look up the following words in a Bible dictionary.

Xerxes

Persia

Look up this Scripture reference in your Bible. Use what you find to draw the palace where Esther lived.

Esther 1:5-7

Shadrach, Meshach, Abednego

Look up the following words in a Bible dictionary.

Babylon

King Nebuchadnezzar

Look up this Scripture reference in your Bible. Use what you find to draw the place where Shadrach, Meshach, and Abednego were told to worship the gold idol.

Daniel 3:1-6

I WILL OBEY!

It is hard to obey when my mom asks me to _____ .

It is hard to obey when my dad asks me to _____ .

It is hard to obey when my teacher asks me to _____ .

It is hard to obey when a kid in school _____ .

It is hard to obey when my brother or sister _____ .

LESSON 12 ▼ 75

Lesson Aims

Students will
- Research shepherds and sheep and identify ways that people are like sheep
- Paraphrase verses from the book of Proverbs
- Make a sheep as a reminder to follow Jesus, the Good Shepherd

Materials
Bibles
Old Testament *Bible Cards* (pp. 297, 298)
Bible Library (p. 296)
Bible division binders
Bible concordances
2 sheets of poster board
marker

▼ Building Study Skills ▲

Before the session, write the following information about sheep and shepherds on half of a large piece of poster board. Scriptures are provided for your reference only.
1. Sheep without a shepherd are harassed and helpless. (Matthew 9:36)
2. Sheep wander off. (Matthew 18:12)
3. Sheep listen to their shepherd's voice. (John 10:3)
4. The shepherd lays down his life for his sheep. (John 10:11)
5. The shepherd looks for lost sheep. (Matthew 18:12, 13)
6. The shepherd calls his sheep by name. (John 10:3, 4)
7. The shepherd leads the sheep to water. (Revelation 7:17)

Show students the poster you made before class. Say: **This poster has information that the New Testament tells us about sheep. What words could we look under in a concordance to find the Scripture references?** (sheep, shepherd) Divide students into groups according to the number of concordances you have. Ask them to look under the words *sheep* and *shepherd* to find New Testament verses that contain the information on the poster. Assign groups different sentences to find. The Scripture references listed with the poster information are one of several Scriptures the students may find. Ask the students to be prepared to tell their verse references and read their verses aloud. Print each reference on the poster as it is read.

▼ Using Study Skills ▲

Materials
Bibles
Finding Time (p. 79)
poster board used in the Building Study Skills step
poster board
markers
Bible dictionaries
dictionary
International Children's Bible
scissors
reusable adhesive
sheep pattern (p. 77)

Before the session, make several copies of the sheep pattern found on page 77. Print the following words from Psalm 23 on the other half of the poster board used in the Building Study Skills step: shepherd, rod, staff, quiet waters, pastures. On the blank poster board, draw or trace a simple figure to represent a shepherd. The figure should be large enough to write in. Leave room for the students to attach the sheep to the poster.

In the books of Poetry, the Bible gives us some very specific ways that we can follow God. Ask students to find Psalm 23 in their Bibles. Read the Psalm aloud together. **To what does this Psalm compare God? To what does it compare those of us who follow Him?** (a shepherd and his sheep) **Let's find what sheep are like and what a shepherd did.** Show students the words from Psalm 23 printed on the poster board. Assign groups or pairs the words *sheep* and *shepherd* to look up in a Bible dictionary. Ask groups to report back what they find.

We are going to make a poster that tells us about shepherds and sheep. What have we learned about shepherds? Ask student volunteers to come forward and print the information on the shepherd figure. Students should discover that a shepherd could use his rod or staff to direct or rescue sheep. A shepherd looked for calm, peaceful waters because rushing waters scared and confused sheep. Ask students to cut out their sheep and write a few of the characteristics of sheep on them.

Be sure the students know sheep need a shepherd because they are not smart enough to take care of themselves. Students can attach their sheep to the poster. If you have time, allow students to use markers to complete the poster scene with water, grass, trees, and so on.

Ask students to find Ecclesiastes 3:1-8 in their Bibles. Let the students take turns reading the verses aloud. **When is a time when you cried? Laughed? When were you born?** Allow students to share about some of the times in the verses they experienced. **The book of Proverbs is full of sayings that give us some wise advice about some of these times.** Ask students to work in pairs. Assign each pair one or more of the Scriptures from page 79. Ask them to find the Scripture in their Bibles and decide which time it describes. Then they should paraphrase the Scripture and write it on the lines. Also provide the *International Children's Bible* so that they can read the verses in simpler words. Matching verses follow.

1. A time to heal—Good news makes you feel better. Your happiness will show in your eyes. Proverbs 15:30

2. A time to keep—A person who gossips can't keep secrets. But a trustworthy person can keep a secret. Proverbs 11:13

Option
If you wish, provide encyclopedias or other reference books about sheep and shepherds to involve as many students as possible in the research

3. A time to keep—A foolish person loses his temper. But a wise person controls his anger. Proverbs 29:11

4. A time to speak—Whoever is careful about what he says protects his life. Proverbs 13:3

5. A time to speak—Speak up for those who cannot speak for themselves. Defend the rights of all those who have nothing. Proverbs 31:8

6. A time to be silent—Even a foolish person seems to be wise if he keeps quiet. He appears to have understanding if he doesn't speak. Proverbs 17:28

7. A time to love—Hatred stirs up trouble. But love forgives all wrongs. Proverbs 10:12

8. A time to love—A friend loves you all the time. A brother is always there to help you. Proverbs 17:17

9. A time to hate—If you respect the Lord, you also will hate evil. Proverbs 8:13

10. A time for peace—Peace of mind means a healthy body. But jealousy will rot your bones. Proverbs 14:30

▼ Responding to Study ▲

Materials
Bibles
shepherd and sheep poster picture made in the Using Study Skills step
cassette recorder
blank cassette
construction paper
glue
scissors
hole punch
spring links (available at hardware stores) or string

Ask students to take turns saying, "I am a sheep who follows Jesus" as you record them. When they are finished, rewind and fast forward the tape at random and play a short segment. Ask students to guess who is speaking. **Was it hard or easy to recognize the voices? How did you know who was talking?** (When we listen to someone a lot or know someone well, we are more likely to recognize his voice.) **How can we be like sheep when we follow Jesus?** (We can learn to know His voice.) **When you learn about the Bible and practice using the Bible, you are practicing listening to Jesus' voice. What other ways can we follow Jesus like sheep follow a shepherd?**

Allow students to take their sheep off the poster made in the Using Study Skills step. They may glue the sheep to construction paper and cut them out. Punch a hole in each sheep and put it on a spring link or tie string through the hole. Say: **You can hang this sheep on your locker, in your room, or on your book bag to remind you to follow Jesus, our Shepherd.** Ask students to share how they will follow Jesus this week. They can choose ways from the sheep poster or they can look at the Proverbs discussed in the Using Study Skills step.

▼ Reviewing Study Skills ▲

Materials
Bibles
Old Testament *Bible Cards*
   (pp. 297, 298)
For the Record (p. 300)

Play an action game with the students. Call out the following verses and ask them find them in their Bibles and perform the action mentioned in the verse. If you wish, have the students race to see who can be first. Scriptures follow. Actions are provided for your reference only.

Genesis 3:14—crawl on your belly
Mark 10:50—jump
Judges 2:22—walk
Judges 10:4—rode (donkeys)
Exodus 8:6—stretch out hand
1 Kings 19:18—bowed knees
Genesis 48:14—hand on head

Isaiah 57:4—stick out your tongue
Genesis 49:8—hand on neck
1 Samuel 18:7—danced
Psalm 107:29—whisper
Proverbs 16:30—wink eye; purse lips
Psalm 37:12—gnash (grit) their teeth

Do the *Bible Card* activity described in the Building Study Skills step. Distribute the cards in sections to the students and ask them to stand when their books are called. Have the students quote from memory as many of the books of the Old Testament as they can.

Distribute the *For the Record* sheets and ask students to fill in skills they have completed.

Finding Time

Find the verses in Proverbs. Decide which "time" from Ecclesiastes 3 each verse tells about. Write the verse in your own words.

1. A time to heal _____

_____

Proverbs 8:13
Proverbs 10:12
Proverbs 11:13
Proverbs 13:3
Proverbs 14:30
Proverbs 15:30
Proverbs 17:17
Proverbs 17:28
Proverbs 29:11
Proverbs 31:8

2. A time to keep _____

_____

3. A time to keep _____

_____

4. A time to speak _____

_____

5. A time to speak _____

_____

6. A time to be silent _____

_____

7. A time to love _____

_____

8. A time to love _____

_____

9. A time to hate _____

_____

10. A time for peace _____

_____

Prophets Reveal That God Does What He Says

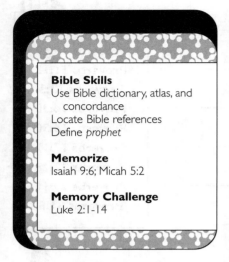

Bible Skills
Use Bible dictionary, atlas, and
   concordance
Locate Bible references
Define *prophet*

Memorize
Isaiah 9:6; Micah 5:2

Memory Challenge
Luke 2:1-14

Unit Overview

In a time when uncertainty and distrust permeate our society, this unit shows students that the Bible offers help and hope by assuring them that God can be trusted. They can depend on God. He always does what He says He will do. This unit shows the connection between the Old and the New Testaments and shows students that God included them in His promises and plan revealed in the Bible. Students will gain the assurance that they are never alone because God is always with them, loving them and working for them. Students will discover that God's promises, His plan, and the gift of His Son are reasons to celebrate. His gift is not a one-time gift, but an on-going gift to be celebrated daily. Offering His Son is God's greatest gift to us. Passing on the skills needed for personal study of God's Word is one of the greatest gifts a teacher can offer to students.

This unit provides activities to sharpen Bible study skills introduced in earlier units, to study the Bible, and to celebrate God's provision. It is important for every student to have a Bible and to have access to the Bible study tools. Competence with basic Bible skills allows students to develop a personal relationship with God through deepening knowledge of His Word. Prophecies of the events surrounding Jesus' birth and the fulfillment of those prophecies are the focus of the content of the five lessons. A unit bulletin board displaying the prophecies and fulfillment ties the lessons together as students add to the bulletin board throughout the unit. Students will become familiar with the books of Prophecy and the Gospels as they study and celebrate God's promises.

Instructions for Unit Bulletin Board

If you do not have a bulletin board in your classroom, attach a large poster board to the wall to serve as a bulletin board. Across the top of the display, use large letters to write "Books of Prophecy Point to Jesus." Divide the remaining area vertically into two sections, making the right side of the display larger than the left side. The left side will display pictures of prophets drawn and labeled by students. The right side will display pictures of the fulfillment of prophecies relating to the birth of Jesus. Students will draw these pictures and label them with captions and Bible references. Bible references to be used will be included within the lessons. From construction paper, make several wide arrows. Students will use these arrows to write the references for the Old Testament prophecy. The arrows will be added to the display to point from the picture of the prophet to the picture of the fulfillment. Have the background of the display and the arrows ready before Lesson 15 begins.

Summary

Lesson 14 introduces the Old Testament books of prophecy and shows that we can tell the difference between true and false prophecies.

Lesson 15 deals with the genealogy of Jesus and helps students to comprehend how God planned for Jesus' birth long before it happened.

In **Lesson 16** the students will investigate the messages of angels and prophets and learn to celebrate when God keeps His promises.

Students will learn in **Lesson 17** that godly people do as God instructs them to do.

Lesson 18 focuses on the fact that Jesus is the Son that God promised.

Bible Division Binder Activity Project

If you are continuing the Bible division binders, have the students use a Bible dictionary to discover information about prophets who wrote Old Testament books. Place their reports and original illustrations in the binder. Below are the recipients of some prophecies and the prophets who prophesied to them.

To Israel: Amos, Hosea
To Judah: Isaiah, Jeremiah, Joel, Micah, Habakkuk, Zephaniah
To Assyria: Jonah, Nahum
To Edom: Obadiah
To the captives in exile: Ezekiel
To Babylon and Persia: Daniel
To the returning captives: Haggai, Zechariah, Malachi

Ping-Pong Toss

Write the names of the eight divisions of the Bible on separate pieces of paper and tape them to eight plastic cups of various sizes and shapes. Place the cups in a line on a table so that the labels will be visible to the players. Tape the cups to the table so they will be stable. Place a strip of masking tape several feet in front of the table. This will be the line from which players will throw the balls.

Players will try to throw the Ping-Pong™ balls into the cups. If you do not have Ping-Pong™ balls, players can throw paper wads, pennies, buttons, or any other small object. When a ball lands in a cup, the player must name as many books in that division as possible. Players receive one point for each book named in order.

Matching Game

Using index cards and a marker, write the names of the divisions of the Bible and the related theme on separate cards. Place the cards facedown in four rows of four cards each. Create two teams of students. Choose one team to go first. A player picks up two cards. If a theme card corresponds to a division card, it is a match. The player keeps the cards for his team. Then a player from the other team chooses two cards. Continue until all cards have been matched. The team with the most matches wins.

Law	Helps us know what God is like.
OT History	Teaches us to obey God.
Poetry	Helps us worship God.
OT Prophecy	Points to Jesus.
Gospels	Help us to know Jesus.
NT History	Helps us tell the good news.
Letters	Help us love one another.
NT Prophecy	Points to Jesus' return.

Trust God's Message

Lesson Aims

Students will

- Find in the Bible the characteristics of authentic prophecy
- Use a time line to grasp the historical context of prophecy
- State ways they will show God they trust His Word

Materials
copies of the *Bible Library* (p. 296)
Bibles
Sample Bible Dictionary (p. 301, 302)
chalkboard or white board
chalk or dry-erase marker
a guest visitor
paper
pencils

Visitor Quiz
Here are some questions you may use for your quiz.
1. Our visitor's name was (supply a name).
2. Our visitor had dark brown hair.
3. Our visitor was not wearing glasses.
4. Our visitor was wearing black shoes.
5. Our visitor was carrying a Bible.
6. Our visitor was wearing a sweater.
7. Our visitor was wearing a ring.

▼ Building Study Skills ▲

Before class, arrange for a visitor to come to your room. Instruct the person to come into the room, introduce herself, wish the class "Merry Christmas," and then leave the room. She'll need to wait a few minutes after that, but you will need her only about 10 minutes.

When the session begins, give each student a copy of the *Bible Library* chart. Ask: **What is the last division of books in the Old Testament?** (the books of Prophecy) **How many books are in this division?** Ask a student to read the section about Prophecy in the *Bible Library* chart. Have students open their Bibles to Psalms and then turn past the books of Poetry to the first book of Prophecy, Isaiah. Say: **Now, find Malachi, the last book of Prophecy in the Old Testament.** Demonstrate by locating the books.

Give students copies of the *Sample Bible Dictionary*. Write the words *prophet* and *prophecy* on the board. **What is a prophet and what is a prophecy? Let's look in our *Sample Bible Dictionary* to find out. Use the guide words to help you.** Check to see that students have located the words. **God gave prophets messages to share with His people. He inspired prophets to give detailed information about the future.**

Say: **Now I would like you to meet someone.** Instruct the visitor to come in. After speaking to the children she should wait outside the door. Give your class a true/false quiz for fun. See the box in the margin for possible questions.

After the quiz is completed, ask the visitor to come back into the room. Have students check their answers by looking at the visitor.

Say: **We knew what was true because we had our visitor with us. Some people during the time of the prophets claimed to have messages from God, but they were not God's prophets. When a message was about the future, people could not see immediately if the message was true. Some people today claim to have messages from God that are not in the Bible. The Bible tells us how to know if prophecies are true or false.**

Write Deuteronomy 13:1-5 at the top of your board. Have students copy the reference onto their papers. Read the reference together. Ask a student to go to the board and write Deuteronomy 18:19-22. Have students copy the reference onto their papers. Read the reference together. Continue in the same way with Hebrews 1:1 and 2 Peter 1:19, 20.

▼ Using Study Skills ▲

If you have not already done so, copy the *Time Line Segments* on pages 309-314. Color the pages or ask students who arrive early to color the pages for you. Post the time line on a wall to use throughout this unit.

Ask for volunteers to work together to perform a skit based on Luke 1:5-25. Have them make signs showing the Bible reference for each scene. For example, a student will hold up the Luke 1:5-7 sign as two students act as Zechariah and Elizabeth and another student reads the verses aloud to the group. Provide props such as items for the temple and sheets or robes for costumes.

Ask for another group to read Mark 1:1-8, Malachi 3:1, and Isaiah 40:3. Have this group make posters with pictures illustrating prophets speaking and John the Baptist fulfilling the prophecies as recorded in Mark. Have them include the Bible references on the posters, showing that Mark 1:2, 3 come directly from Malachi 3:1 and Isaiah 40:3. When both groups finish, have each share its project with the other group.

If you have a small class, choose one of the activities for your students to do and then have students locate and read the Scripture references for the other activity. Help them see the fulfillment of the prophecies.

Ask: **Where did you find the prophecies that John the Baptist would be born?** (Students should answer by saying the references correctly: Mark 1:2, 3; Malachi 3:1; Isaiah 40:3; and Luke 1:13.) Students may not include Luke 1:13. If not, write the reference on the board and tell students to locate the verse. Ask a volunteer to read the verse and then explain that the words of the angel were also a prophecy from God.

Direct students' attention to the time line. Say: **This time line helps us understand the Bible by showing us when important events in the Bible took place and when people of the Bible lived. Find Isaiah on the time line.** Ask one student to point to Isaiah. **Between what years on the time line did Isaiah live?** (Between 930 B.C. and 722 B.C.) **We know that John the Baptist was born about six months before Jesus.** Point to Jesus, Mary, and Joseph on the time line. **Isaiah prophesied about the birth of John the Baptist almost 700 years before John was born. God told Isaiah to tell His people that He would send this messenger to prepare the way for Jesus.**

What other prophets are on this time line? (Elijah, Jeremiah, Ezekiel, and Daniel) Ask students to come to the time line and point out the pictures of the prophets. **Which of these prophets have books of the Bible named for them?** (Jeremiah, Ezekiel, and Daniel)

Materials
Time Line Segments (pp. 309-314)
reusable adhesive
Bibles
paper
pencils
various props for skit
large paper
markers

▼ Responding to Study ▲

Say: **God sent messages to His people through other prophets. Find these prophecies that are recorded in the Bible.** Give each student a copy of *Give Them This Message.* Have students locate and read the prophecies. Tell students to match the reference with the words of the prophets.

Ask: **What does the Bible say about God speaking to people?** (In the past, God spoke to people through prophets. Then He spoke to people by His Son.) **The words of God's prophets and of His Son are recorded in the Bible. We can know that these words are true. What can you do to show God that you believe His Word is true and that you trust His message?** Affirm the answers students give that indicate that they want to show God they trust in Him. Guide them to think of answers that lead to their learning all they can about God's Word by using Bible skills and Bible tools.

Pray for God to help each student trust His message in the Bible and believe that His Word is true. Ask God to help students learn to study His Word.

Materials
Give Them This Message (p. 85)
colored pencils
Bibles

Answers
Isaiah 9:6 connect to 4;
Micah 5:2 connect to 6;
Daniel 9:25 connect to 5;
Malachi 3:1 connect to 2;
Hosea 3:5 connect to 1;
Jeremiah 23:5 connect to 3

Materials
Bible Cards (pp. 297, 298)
Bibles
pencils
paper
For the Record (p. 300)

Say: **We are going to play a game to help us learn the order of the books of Prophecy. We will also practice finding verses in the books and learn more about what the books tell us.**

Using only the cards for the books of Prophecy, give each student a card. If you have a large number of students, plan to divide your class into groups of 17 or fewer. Before class, make enough copies of the books of Prophecy cards so that each group of students will have a set. For a small class, give students more than one card so that all 17 cards are being used. Make sure each student has a card, Bible, pencil, and paper. Say: **In your Bible, find the book of Prophecy named on your card.** Give students time to locate the book. Allow them to use the table of contents if necessary. **Choose a verse from your book of Prophecy and write the reference on your paper.** Have students randomly select a chapter and then choose a verse that they can understand and that has meaning to them. Younger students may need help with this decision. Play the game as described below.

Choose one student to begin the game. That student will place his card on a table at the front of the room and read the reference he chose to the rest of the class. The students will locate the reference. The first student to locate the reference will read the verse and then change places with the person in the front of the class. This student will place her card in correct sequence on the table, leaving space if books are missing in between. Continue the game until all cards are placed in order. If a student is first to find a verse but has already placed his card on the table, the student to his right will take his turn.

Say: **If we know the order of the books of the Bible, we can find verses faster and easier. When we know how to locate verses in the Bible, we can find God's truth for ourselves and we can help others learn about God too.**

After the game, give students time to demonstrate Bible skills listed on *For the Record* and to record their progress on the chart. As you begin this new unit, ask students who are progressing quickly in learning their skills to help younger or less experienced students to master their skills. This helps all students practice and use what they are learning.

Give Them This Message

God spoke to His people through prophets. The prophecies of God's prophets were always true. Locate the references in your Bible. Read the Bible verses. Match the correct Bible reference with the words of the prophet by drawing a line to connect the two. Use a different color for each prophet.

1
They will come trembling to the Lord and to his blessings.

2
The message of the covenant, whom you desire, will come.

Micah 5:2

Hosea 3:5

3
I will raise up to David a righteous Branch.

4
For to us a child is born, to us a son is given.

Malachi 3:1

Jeremiah 23:5

Isaiah 9:6

5
Until the Anointed One, the ruler, comes.

6
Out of you will come for me one who will be ruler.

Daniel 9:25

Genealogy of Jesus

Isaiah 7; Jeremiah 23; Matthew 1

Lesson Aims

Students will

- Use Bible dictionaries to locate specific information about Jesus
- Trace Jesus' "family tree" through history
- Grasp the significance of prophecy in God's plan to send Jesus

▼ Building Study Skills ▲

Materials

index cards, prepared in
   advance
Bible dictionaries
chalkboard or white board
chalk or dry-erase marker
lined paper
pencils
small slips of paper, 5 per group

Before class, write the letters J,E,S,U,S on sets of index cards, one letter per card. Prepare enough sets so that when students are divided into small groups during class, each group will have one set.

Write the word *Immanuel* on the board. Ask a student to read the word. Ask: **Have you heard this word before? Where have you heard this word? What do you already know about this word?** Students may have heard the word in connection with Christmas or in songs. Allow them to share what they know.

Say: **Let's see what the Bible dictionary says.** Guide students through the steps to locate *Immanuel* in the Bible dictionary. If any students are becoming proficient in using a Bible dictionary, allow them to lead the others in locating the entry. Have individual students or groups take turns sharing facts until all information has been shared. Be sure that the information students share includes "God with us" as the meaning of *Immanuel.*

Ask students to locate *Jesus* in their Bible dictionary. Ask: **What are the guide words on your page? Point to the entry on your page.** If students do not comment on multiple entries for *Jesus*, point out that most dictionaries will have more than one entry for *Jesus.* Help them see that the entry they want is for *Jesus Christ.* Because this entry is long, show students how to skim the entry for information they need.

Instruct each group to use their dictionaries to locate this specific information about Jesus: (1) meaning of the name, (2) names of parents, (3) place of birth, (4) the family line, (5) one additional fact or prophecy about the birth of Jesus. As each answer is found, have groups write the answer on a slip of paper, bring the answer to you for verification, and pick up a letter in the name *Jesus.* The first group to collect J-E-S-U-S from you wins.

Say: **We have learned from our Bible dictionaries that *Immanuel* means "God with us." We have also read some details about the birth of Jesus. Now let's see what the Bible says.**

▼ Using Study Skills ▲

Cut eight small crosses, about 1" x 2", from construction paper.

Give each student a paper, pencil, and markers or crayons. Tell students to fold their paper in half horizontally and then in half vertically to form four sections. Say: **We are going to write our Bible references on this paper so that we will know which verses to read. In the top left section of your paper, write**

Isaiah 7:14 and draw a picture of a sign under the reference you have written. In the top right section, write Jeremiah 23:5, 6 and draw a tree branch. In the bottom left section, write Matthew 1:1-16 and draw a tree. In the last section, write Matthew 1:18-23 and draw a cloud.

Make sure each student has a copy of the *Bible Library*. Ask: **In which division of the Bible will you find the books Isaiah and Jeremiah?** (the books of Prophecy) **Are the books of Prophecy in the Old or the New Testament?** (Old Testament) **In which Testament will you find the book Matthew?** (New Testament) **Matthew is one of the four Gospels.** Ask a student to read the section about the Gospels from the *Bible Library*. Ask students to recite the four Gospels in order. Say: **In Isaiah and Jeremiah, we will read prophecies about Jesus. In Matthew, we will read about Jesus' birth.**

Divide students into three groups to read Matthew 1:18-23, Isaiah 7:14, and Jeremiah 23:5, 6. If you have a small class, allow all students to work together.

As students read the verses with their groups, have them find words that might need explanation or that would have additional information in a Bible dictionary. Their words should include *Mary* and *Joseph* for Matthew 1:18-23; *Isaiah* and *Immanuel* for Isaiah 7:14; and *David* and *Branch* for Jeremiah 23:5, 6. Their information should include the following ideas:

Mary—family of David, virgin engaged to Joseph, mother of Jesus
Joseph—family of David, engaged to Mary, earthly father of Jesus
Isaiah—a prophet, gave many prophecies about Jesus
Immanuel—means "God with us," a name prophesied for Jesus
David—a good king, born in Bethlehem, a descendent of Jesus
Branch—a part of a family, Jesus is a righteous Branch of David's family

Say: **God sent messages to His people through Isaiah and Jeremiah. The messages we read today are about Jesus, though they were written hundreds of years before He was born. God was going to cause a woman to have a baby without a man as the father. God's Spirit would cause a special baby to grow within the woman's body. The baby would be born in the normal way. God would be the Father, and so the child would be Immanuel, which we know means "God with us." Mary was the woman chosen to be the mother of God's Son. Mary and Joseph were part of David's family. Jesus would be a Branch of King David's family.**

Ask for volunteers to take turns reading Matthew 1:1-16 one generation at a time. Help readers with the pronunciation of difficult names. As names are read, have students look at the time line to find the ancestors of Jesus who are included there. Ask volunteers to mark each ancestor with a paper cross. See the list in the margin.

Say: **We can see that God's plan to send Jesus to save people from their sins began thousands of years before He was born. The Old Testament tells how God chose a group of people, David's family, to obey and worship Him. God sent messages through prophets to help prepare these people for the coming of His son, Jesus.**

Ask students to look at the pictures they drew on their papers with the Bible references. Ask: **Why do you think we drew these pictures with our Bible references? Why did we draw a sign to help us remember what Isaiah 7:14 says?** (The Lord himself will give a sign.) **Isaiah wrote about a sign, a miracle that God would fulfill about 700 years later when Jesus would be born.**

Ask: **Why did we draw a branch to help us remember the prophecy in Jeremiah 23:5, 6?** (Jesus would be a righteous Branch raised up to David.) **Why did we draw a tree for Matthew 1:1-16?** (These verses tell about the family tree of David and Jesus.) **Why did we draw a cloud to remind us about Matthew 1:18-23?** (An angel of the Lord appeared to Joseph in a dream to tell him about Mary's baby, Jesus, who would save people from their sins.)

As we study the Bible, we can see that God has always been working for us, and we can count on Him to be with us.

Materials
paper
pencils
markers or crayons
Bible Library (p. 296)
Bibles
lined paper
Bible dictionaries
Time Line Segments (pp. 309-314) prepared before class
crosses cut from construction paper
reusable adhesive

Ancestors of Jesus
Abraham
Isaac
Jacob
Ruth
King David
Manasseh
Josiah
Joseph
Mary

Materials

unit bulletin board prepared
before class (see instructions
in Unit 4 Introduction, p. 80)
paper arrows
plain paper
markers and crayons
Bibles
Bible dictionaries
reusable adhesive, tape, or
stapler
The Divisions of the Bible (p. 89)

Answers to Books of Prophecy

Book that is not the name of a
prophet: Lamentations
Three books not included in
puzzle: Habakkuk, Zephaniah,
Zechariah

Materials

Books of Prophecy (p. 90)
pencils
Bible dictionaries
For the Record (p. 300)

▼ Responding to Study ▲

Direct students' attention to the unit bulletin board, *Books of Prophecy Point to Jesus.* Tell students that each week they will be adding prophecies and prophecy fulfillment to the display. Say: **The prophecies that were foretold hundreds of years before Jesus' birth came true. We are going to make a bulletin board to show how these Old Testament messages came true when Jesus was born in the time of the New Testament.** Ask some students to draw pictures to represent the prophets Isaiah and Jeremiah, and label the pictures with the prophets' names, which are also the names of books of Prophecy. Talk about the way prophets may have looked. Use pictures from the time line or from Bible dictionaries to give students ideas. Have other students write the Bible prophecy references on arrows that will point from the book of Prophecy to a picture of the fulfillment. Have some students locate the Scripture references and read the verses to the class. Ask some students to draw a picture of the fulfillment and label the picture with a caption and with the New Testament reference. Students may decide that some fulfillments need several pictures to show different scenes of the fulfillment. If students draw several pictures for Matthew 1:18-23, have them label each scene with the specific Bible reference the picture illustrates. Use these references: Isaiah 7:14 with an arrow to Matthew 1:18-23; Jeremiah 23:5, 6 with an arrow to Matthew 1:16, 17. Attach arrows and pictures to the appropriate places on the display. Refer to the instructions in the Unit 4 Introduction.

Ask: **How can you know that Jesus' birth was part of God's plan to save His people?** (God gave messages to prophets so that His people would know God had a plan. Prophecies were made hundreds of years before Jesus was born. People can see that God does what He says He will do because the prophecies came true.)

Give each student a copy of *The Divisions of the Bible.* Tell students that the words of the song are sung to the tune of "The Twelve Days of Christmas." Sing the song together as a class, or divide the class into eight groups and assign one division to each group. Each group will sing its division line whenever it comes into the song, and the whole class will sing the first and last line of each stanza. Say: **Knowing the divisions of the Bible will help us use our Bibles more easily. We can find Bible references to help us learn more about God's plan for us. Take this paper home with you and sing the song to help you learn the Bible divisions. Teach the song to some friends or family members so they will learn more about the Bible too.**

▼ Reviewing Study Skills ▲

Say: **The books of Prophecy help us know more about God's plan for His people. We can read God's messages that He sent through the prophets. This puzzle will help us learn more about God's prophets.** Distribute page 90. Make sure each student has access to the tools needed to complete the puzzle. Work on the puzzle together. Assign numbers to pairs or groups of students to find the answers in the Bible dictionary. Younger students may need help skimming through the information to find the specific answers needed. Ask for volunteers to give their answers so that students can check their work.

After students complete the crossword puzzle, allow time for students to demonstrate Bible skills listed on *For the Record* and to record their progress on the chart. Ask students who are progressing quickly in learning their skills to help younger or less experienced Bible students to master their skills.

The Divisions of the Bible

(Sing the words of this song to the tune of "The 12 Days of Christmas")

Oh, the Bible is divided to help us learn God's
    Word,
and His truth will endure for all time.

Oh, the eighth Bible division points us to Jesus'
    return;
  1 book of Prophecy
and His truth will endure for all time.

Oh, the seventh Bible division will help us love each
    other;
  21 books of Letters,
  1 book of Prophecy,
and His truth will endure for all time.

Oh, the sixth Bible division will help us tell good
    news;
  1 book of History,
  21 books of Letters,
  1 book of Prophecy,
and His truth will endure for all time.

Oh, the fifth Bible division will help us know God's
    Son;
  4 books of Gospels,
  1 book of History,
  21 books of Letters,
  1 book of Prophecy,
and His truth will endure for all time.

Oh, the fourth Bible division points us to Jesus
    Christ;
  17 books of Prophecy,
  4 books of Gospels,
  1 book of History,
  21 books of Letters,
  1 book of Prophecy,
and His truth will endure for all time.

Oh, the third Bible division will help us worship
    God;
  5 books of Poetry,
  17 books of Prophecy,
  4 books of Gospels,
  1 book of History,
  21 books of Letters,
  1 book of Prophecy,
and His truth will endure for all time.

Oh, the second Bible division will teach us to obey;
  12 books of History,
  5 books of Poetry,
  17 books of Prophecy,
  4 books of Gospels,
  1 book of History,
  21 books of Letters,
  1 book of Prophecy,
and His truth will endure for all time.

Oh, the first Bible division will help us learn of God;
  5 books of Law,
  12 books of History,
  5 books of Poetry,
  17 books of Prophecy,
  4 books of Gospels,
  1 book of History,
  21 books of Letters,
  1 book of Prophecy,
and His truth will endure for all time.

Books of Prophecy

The names of these 14 prophets fit into the crossword grid. Use a Bible dictionary to complete the puzzle. Then answer the questions.

Amos
Daniel
Ezekiel
Haggai
Hosea
Isaiah
Jeremiah
Joel
Jonah
Malachi
Micah
Nahum
Obadiah
Elijah

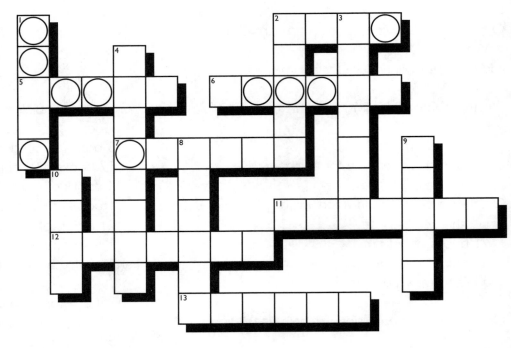

Across

2. spoke after an attack of locusts
5. lived and worked at the same time as Isaiah
6. taken captive to Babylon as a young man
7. prophet through whom God defeated the prophets of Baal
11. author of the last book of the Old Testament
12. prophesied about the destruction of the Edomites
13. prophet in Jerusalem after the exile in Babylon

Down

1. prophesied about the doom of Nineveh
2. swallowed by a great fish
3. prophesied to the Jews in exile
4. warned of the destruction of Jerusalem
8. gave many prophecies about the Christ
9. prophet to both Israel and Judah
10. a shepherd before he was a prophet

Unscramble the circled letters to discover the book of Prophecy that is not the name of a prophet. This book probably was written by Jeremiah. It expresses great sorrow about the destruction of Jerusalem. The name of the book is

— — — — — t — t — — — —

Name the three books of Prophecy that are names of prophets but not included in the crossword puzzle.

_____

_____

_____

 LESSON 15

The Angel's Announcement

Luke 1; Isaiah 9; Hosea 3

Lesson Aims

Students will

- Compare angels and prophets as messengers of God
- Match Old Testament prophecies with their New Testament fulfillment
- Celebrate God's promises

▼ Building Study Skills ▲

Say: **We learned last week that God gave messages to His people through some very special men. Who were these men?** (prophets Isaiah and Jeremiah) **What were their messages**? (Immanuel would be born. There would be a sign: a virgin would be His mother. He would be God's Son. Immanuel would be a righteous Branch of King David's family.) **Today we are going to learn about more messages from God.**

Write the word *angel* on the board so students can be sure of the spelling. Ask: **What is an angel?** Allow students to share what they think about when they think of an angel. **Let's look in a Bible dictionary to find information about angels.** Give Bible dictionaries to students and allow them time to turn to the correct page in the dictionary. If needed, review skills for using a Bible dictionary. Tell students to read through the entry and to raise their hands when they find information to answer the questions: What are angels? and What do angels do? Ask for volunteers to give answers. Write some of the answers on the board. Emphasize that angels are messengers.

Say: **We find angels in many places in the Bible. A Bible concordance will help us find all the verses in the Bible that include the word *angel*. The references in the concordance will show us where to look in the Bible to find the verses we need.** Review the skills needed for using a Bible concordance. Ask students who already are familiar with the process to help demonstrate using the concordance. Seeing their peers use a concordance will show younger or less experienced Bible students that using a concordance is helpful and is something they can learn to do. Have students locate *angel* in their concordance to see an example of different word form entries. Ask students to read the key word forms for *angel*.

Say: **We want to look specifically at the angel messages about the birth of Jesus. Which Bible division tells about Jesus' life and His teachings?** (Gospels) **What are the four books in this division?** (Matthew, Mark, Luke, John) **These books tell about Jesus chronologically or in the order that things happened in His life. The beginnings of the books tell about Jesus' birth or about the early part of His life. How can you know which references tell about the birth of Jesus?** (Look at the first few references for each Gospel book.) **Not all of the Gospel books tell about the same events in Jesus' life.** Give students time to discover which books tell about the birth of Jesus. Younger students may need help eliminating verses. **Which books have information about Jesus' birth?** (Matthew and Luke)

Have students close their concordances.

Say: **Sometimes finding the verse we need is like solving a puzzle. How**

Materials
chalkboard or white board
chalk or dry-erase marker
Bible dictionaries
Bible concordances
Bibles

would you solve this puzzle using only your Bible concordance? Find a verse about an angel's message that Mary's baby would be called the Son of the Most High. Allow students to brainstorm ideas about finding the verse. Steps to find the verse might include locating the word *angel* in the concordance and finding the entries about the birth of Jesus; locating the word *high* in the concordance and looking for a reference close to a reference in the listing for *angel*; references would need to be in a section of a book of the Bible that contains the birth of Jesus; other words to locate in the concordance might be *Son, baby,* or *Mary.* Decide on the reference that will solve the puzzle. The verse is Luke 1:32.

Say: **This verse is one of the verses in our Bible segment today. We will be reading about the angel's announcement to Mary in Luke 1:26-35, 38. We will also read God's messages in Isaiah 9:2, 6, 7 and Hosea 3:5.**

▼ Using Study Skills ▲

Read the references Luke 1:26-35, 38; Isaiah 9:2, 6, 7; Hosea 3:5 to students, giving them time to locate each Bible verse. Ask volunteers to read the Bible verses aloud. Ask: **In what division of the Bible are the books Isaiah and Hosea?** (Old Testament Prophecy) **Isaiah and Hosea were prophets of God. God sent messages about Jesus through these prophets.**

The book of Luke tells us about another of God's messengers. What is this messenger's name? (the angel Gabriel) **What is Gabriel's message in these verses?** (Mary is to be the mother of God's Son. He is to be named Jesus and He will be called the Son of the Most High. His kingdom will never end.) **Let's find out about Gabriel in our Bible dictionaries.** Have students find information about Gabriel and report what they learn.

Say: **Find Gabriel in your Bible concordance.** Ask different students to locate the verses about Gabriel. **What was Gabriel's message in Luke 1:19?** (Gabriel was sent to give the message to Zechariah that John would be born.) **Remember that John, the son of Zechariah and Elizabeth, was going to prepare the people for Jesus' coming. Where will we find other appearances of Gabriel?** (Daniel) **The message from Gabriel in Daniel 9 is about Jesus. What is the Bible reference in the concordance?** (Daniel 9:21) Have students locate and have one student read aloud Daniel 9:21. **This verse does not tell us what Gabriel's message is, but if we read more verses, we will see the message. Find and read Daniel 9:26.** Have one student read the verse aloud. **Do you know who the Anointed One is?** (Jesus) **Gabriel is telling Daniel that Jesus will come. Look for Daniel on the time line. Daniel lived several hundred years before Jesus.**

If you are keeping information in the unit binders, have students check the binders and review information recorded from the Bible dictionary about Jesus.

Say: **God sent many messages to His people about the coming of His Son, Jesus. Angels and prophets were God's messengers. God sent messages to His people through them. Sometimes He sent angels to give messages to the prophets, and then the prophets gave the messages to the people. We have seen that many of God's messages were sent hundreds of years before the event actually happened. Sometimes God gave messages through prophets in Old Testament times and then gave the message again through angels in New Testament times.**

Give students pencils and copies of *God's Messages Point to Jesus.* Tell students to use their Bible and Bible concordances to find the answers to the activities on the page. Allow students to work together in pairs or small groups to find the messages. When everyone has finished, ask students to share their answers.

Direct students' attention to the unit bulletin board, *Books of Prophecy Point to Jesus.* Tell students they will be adding prophecies to the display. Say: **The prophecies today come from Isaiah and Hosea.** Ask a student to draw a

Materials
Bibles
Bible dictionaries
Bible concordances
Time Line Segments (pp. 309-314) prepared from previous lessons
pencils
God's Messages Point to Jesus (p. 94)
unit bulletin board prepared before class (see instructions in Unit 4 Introduction, p. 80)
paper arrows
plain paper
markers and crayons
reusable adhesive, tape, or stapler

Answers for Activity 1:
1. Underline Luke 1:31 be with child and give birth to a s.
2. Underline Matthew 1:21 will give b. to a son

Answers for Activity 2:
BLESSED—Hosea 3:5, prophet; COUNSELOR—Isaiah 9:6, prophet; JESUS—Luke 1:31, angel; KINGDOM—Isaiah 9:7, prophet and Luke 1:33, angel; LIGHT—Isaiah 9:2, prophet; THRONE—Isaiah 9:7, prophet and Luke 1:32, angel

picture to represent the prophet Hosea and label the picture with the prophet's name. A picture for Isaiah should already be on the display from the last lesson. Have other students write the Bible prophecy references on arrows that will point from the book of Prophecy to a picture representing the verses in Luke. Ask some students to draw a picture to represent the verses in Luke and label the picture with a caption and with the New Testament reference. Use these references: Isaiah 9:7 and Hosea 3:5 with arrows to Luke 1:31-33.

▼ Responding to Study ▲

Ask: **Do you like celebrations? What are some things we celebrate? How do we celebrate? What kinds of things do we do to celebrate?** Allow students to respond.

Say: **We have a very important reason to celebrate. We have been learning about God's promises by using Bible dictionaries and concordances to study the Bible. We have seen in the Bible that God always keeps His promises. God's promises are not just for the people of the Bible. His promises are for us too. What are some ways we could celebrate God's promises to us?** Allow students to brainstorm ways to celebrate. Give students copies of *Make a Promise Box*. Tell students to take the papers home and make the Promise Box. Encourage them to choose a promise every day and honor God by celebrating His promises to them.

Materials
Make a Promise Box (p. 95)
God's Promises (p. 95)
apples, grapes, and oranges prepared in advance
napkins

▼ Reviewing Study Skills ▲

Say: **The messages angels delivered were often God's promises. People reacted in different ways to the angel messages. Some people obeyed the messages. Some people did not believe the messages. Some people celebrated when they heard God's message of promise. Use a concordance to help you find out about some of the messages angels delivered about the birth of God's Son, Jesus. We are going to send angel messages to each other to help us learn about God's promises.**

Give a paper and pencil to each student. Students will choose a reference in their concordance about an angel announcement concerning events related to Jesus' birth and will write the reference on the paper. After writing the reference, students will fold their paper into a paper airplane, and at your command, all students will fly their planes. When planes have landed, students will choose a flown plane, look up the reference written on the plane, and write what the verse says about the angel's message. The verse may tell what the actual message was, who received the message, or what happened as a result of the message. Students may need to read the verses around the selected verse in order to find the information. Students will then fly the planes again, choose a different plane, and read the message aloud.

After students complete this activity, allow time for students to demonstrate Bible skills listed on *For the Record* and to record their progress on the chart.

Materials
Bible concordances
plain sheets of paper
pencils
Bibles
For the Record (p. 300)

God's Messages Point to Jesus

Use a Bible concordance and your Bible to find the answers.

Activity 1:

Read Isaiah 7:14. Read the verses from the *Sample Bible Concordance* entries listed below for the New Testament prophecies. Underline the entries that match the Old Testament prophecy in Isaiah 7:14:

1. Key word: SON
Mark 1:11 "You are my *s.* whom I love;
Luke 1:31 be with child and give birth to a *s.*

2. Key word: BIRTH
Matthew 1:21 She will give *b.* to a son
Luke 1:14 many will rejoice because of his *b.*

Activity 2:

These key words or a form of the key word (blessed/blessings) are taken from God's messages written in Isaiah 9, Luke 1, and Hosea 3. Find the words in a Bible concordance. Check the concordance entry for each word to find the Bible reference for the message that contains the word. Is the message from a prophet or from an angel? Each message points to Jesus. When you find the Bible reference, write it beside the key word. Hint: Check the Bible references for all three books. Some words may be found in more than one message.

BLESSED

COUNSELOR

JESUS

KINGDOM

LIGHT

THRONE

LESSON 16

Decorate the outside squares. Cut on the solid lines to the center square. Fold in on the dotted lines around the center square. Fold the outside corner squares in to overlap the sides, and glue or tape the sides together to form a box. Put your Promise Box in a place where you will see it every day. Place your *God's Promises* strips inside the box.

God's Promises

Cut apart the promise strips below. Fold the strips and put them into your Promise Box. Each day, draw one of God's promises from the box. Find the Bible reference in your Bible, read the verses, and write God's promise on the strip. Choose a way to celebrate God's promise for the day. You might choose to sing a celebration song to God, pray, serve God in some way, tell others about God's promise, or find another way to celebrate!

Matthew 6:31-33
Luke 2:11
John 14:15-17
Romans 8:28
Philippians 4:19
1 John 1:9
1 John 2:24, 25

LESSON 16 ▼ 95

Mary and Joseph Go to Bethlehem

Matthew 2; Luke 2; Micah 5

Lesson Aims

Students will
- Use a location grid to find places on a Bible map
- Compare distances on several maps, ancient and modern
- Apply Bible prophecies and their fulfillment to God's plan of salvation

Materials
Index to Maps (page 308)
Bible Atlas Maps 1–3 (pp. 305-307)
lists of the Bible references for Lesson 17, prepared in advance

Materials
Bibles
paper
pencils
Index to Maps (page 308)
Bible Atlas Maps 1–3 (pp. 305-307)
Bible dictionaries
state or regional map of students' area
current map of lands around Mediterranean Sea (optional)
unit bulletin board prepared before class (see instructions in Unit 4 Introduction, p. 80)
paper arrows
paper
markers and crayons
Bibles
reusable adhesive, tape, or stapler

▼ Building Study Skills ▲

Before class, make lists of the Bible references for this lesson so that each group of three students will have a list. The list will include Micah 5:2; Luke 2:1-5; and Matthew 2:1, 2.

Say: **Last week we read the angel's announcement to Mary and to Joseph that Jesus, the Son of the Most High, would be born. Before the baby was born, though, Mary and Joseph took a trip. A Bible atlas will help us understand more about this trip.** Give students copies of the Bible maps and the index. **We want to find two towns in our atlas. The index to the maps will help us find the location of the towns. Look in the index for Nazareth. The places in the index are listed in alphabetical order. The number and letter beside the name of the place will help us locate the place on the map. This is the map and grid location. What is the map and grid location for Nazareth?** (2 B2) **The first number is the map number. We have three maps in our sample atlas. On which map will we find Nazareth?** (Map 2) **Each map has a grid. The grid is made of the longitude and latitude lines. Each column of squares in the grid is given a letter. Each row of squares is given a number. We will use this letter/number combination to locate Nazareth on the map. What is the grid location for Nazareth?** (B2) Demonstrate as you give each instruction. **Find Map 2. Find column B and row 2. Find the square where this column and row meet. Can you find Nazareth in this square?** Check to see that all students have located Nazareth. **Now use the same steps to find Bethlehem in this atlas.**

Divide students into groups of three. Give one student in each group the list of Bible references. Say: **The prophecy that Jesus would be born in Bethlehem was given by the prophet Micah. We will read in the books of Matthew and Luke that Micah's prophecy came true.**

▼ Using Study Skills ▲

Say: **Let's read our Bible segment for today.** Ask students with reference lists to read the references one at a time to a second student in the group. After that student locates a reference in the Bible, have him hand the Bible to the third member of the group who will read the verses to the group. Do this with each reference: Micah 5:2; Luke 2:1-5; Matthew 2:1, 2. After groups read the verses, have them make a list of all places that are named in the verses. Have students use the index to locate on the maps all places named in the Bible verses. Tell groups to record the grid location for each place on their lists. If the place is found on more than one map, have them locate the place on each map.

Ask: **How could we find out how far Mary and Joseph had to travel?** (Use a Bible dictionary. Read about the towns to find the distances between them.) Students should discover that Nazareth is about 100 miles from Jerusalem. Say: **From what you know about history, you know that Mary and Joseph did not have cars or buses to make such a long trip. People in Bible times walked or rode on animals to travel from place to place. Think about how difficult a trip from Nazareth to Bethlehem would have been for Mary and Joseph.**

Display a map of your area, perhaps a state or regional map. Compare distances between familiar places with the distance Mary and Joseph had to travel so that students will understand how long the trip was. They will also see that atlas maps are similar to other maps. If available, show students a current map of the area around the eastern Mediterranean Sea. They will be able to see that the places named in the Bible are real places and that many of the locations are still there today.

Say: **We have been reading prophecies about Jesus. Jesus is the fulfillment of the prophecies of the past. God planned very carefully for Jesus' coming to earth. Jesus brought God's plan of salvation. He is the hope for our future. The prophecies in the Old Testament that point to Jesus talk about our future. God's plan includes us.**

Micah's prophecy told where Jesus would be born. Ask a student to draw a picture to represent the prophet Micah and label the picture with the prophet's name, which is also the name of the book of Prophecy. Have another student write the Bible prophecy reference on an arrow that will point from the book of Prophecy to a picture of the fulfillment. Have a student locate the Scripture reference and read the verse to the class. **Luke tells us about the fulfillment of that prophecy.** Ask some students to draw a picture of the fulfillment and label the picture with a caption and with the New Testament reference. Use the reference Micah 5:2 with an arrow pointing to Luke 2:1-5. Attach the arrow and pictures to the appropriate places on the display. Refer to the instructions in the Unit 4 Introduction.

▼ Responding to Study ▲

Say: **We have been celebrating God's promises and now we can celebrate God's plan. We have been learning about His plan by reading the Bible and using Bible dictionaries, concordances, and atlases to help us understand His plan better. We can celebrate because God's plan includes us! It includes everyone! When visitors come to our class, we can celebrate because God's plan includes them too. Let's plan a welcome celebration for visitors and share God's plan with them.**

Have a brainstorming session to see how students would like to welcome visitors with a celebration. Include a way to put their plan into action so they can begin next week to welcome anyone who comes. Offer a suggestion for a welcome package to give to visitors. The package might include Bible stickers, pencils, bookmarks, snacks labeled with Scripture, and any other items students might want. Give students time to organize supplies, write notes, and prepare any other ideas they decide to incorporate. Encourage older students to use a Bible concordance to find Scripture references about God's love or God's salvation through Jesus. These references could be written on small papers and attached to the items in the welcome packages. Assign students specific jobs to do to welcome visitors. Throughout the planning, emphasize the celebration of God's plan.

When planning is completed, give students the reproducible *Celebration Calendar*. Say: **We're getting close to seeing God keep His promise to send a Savior to His people. The plan is coming into place. We're almost there. We**

Bible places
Syria
Nazareth
Galilee
Bethlehem
Judea
Israel

Option
You may want to have older students use a concordance or Bible dictionary to find other prophecies and fulfillment about Jesus' life on earth. Even though these references would not be about the birth of Jesus, they would still show that the books of Prophecy point to Jesus and that God planned for Jesus all along.

Materials
supplies such as stickers, pencils, bookmarks with Bible themes, ribbon, small boxes or bags
small prepackaged snack bags
Bibles
Bible concordances
paper
pencils
scissors
Celebration Calendar (p. 99)
scissors, glue, colored pencils, crayons (optional)

know from prophecies that Jesus is to be born in Bethlehem. We know what will happen when Mary and Joseph arrive there. We don't have to wait until Christmas to celebrate the birth of God's Son. Use this calendar every day to help you celebrate God's plan for you.** If there is time, have students assemble their calendars in class. If time is limited, tell students that the instructions are included on the paper, and they can assemble the calendar at home.

▼ Reviewing Study Skills ▲

Materials
balloons, prepared in advance
permanent markers
large trash bags
paper
pencils
Bibles
Bible Cards (pp. 297, 298)
For the Record (p. 300)

Before class, prepare sets of five balloons for each small group you will have in class. Inflate the balloons and use a permanent marker to write one of these Bible references on each balloon so that each group will have all five references: Deuteronomy 31:8; Hebrews 13:5, 6; Isaiah 9:6; Micah 5:2; and Matthew 1:21. Mix all the balloons into large trash bags until it is time to release them in your classroom.

Say: **Sometimes we celebrate with parties, and parties sometimes have balloons! Let's play a game with balloons to help us remember to celebrate God's plan.**

Divide students into small groups. Release the balloons into an area of the classroom that is an equal distance from all groups. Say: **On these balloons are five different Bible references that tell us something about God's plan for us. Send one person from your group to get a balloon and bring it back to your group. Read the reference on the balloon, write the reference on your paper, locate the verse in the Bible, read the verse, and write what the verse tells us about God's plan or how this verse applies to God's plan. After you write what the verse says about God's plan, send another group member to find a different balloon and do the same with the reference written on it. Continue finding balloons until you have found all five. The first team to complete all five, wins.** Begin the game. Encourage students to work together as a group to locate verses and decide how the verses apply to God's plan.

Possible answers:

Deuteronomy 31:8—The verse says the Lord will be with you, will never leave you nor forsake you. God's plan included sending Jesus. He will be with us forever.

Hebrews 13:5, 6—The verse says never will I leave you, never will I forsake you. God's plan includes us. He will always be with us.

Isaiah 9:6—The verse says to us a child is born, to us a son is given, Wonderful Counselor, Mighty God, Everlasting Father, Prince of Peace. God's plan was to give His Son to us to help us forever.

Micah 5:2—The verse says one who will be ruler whose origins are from ancient times. God's plan began thousands of years ago.

Matthew 1:21—The verse says He will save His people from their sins. God's plan is to save us.

After the activity, while some students are demonstrating Bible skills, give other students an opportunity to practice putting the books of the Bible in order by playing games with the *Bible Cards.* Students might make up their own games, or choose to play the following game: In pairs, students will shuffle cards and place them facedown in a stack. One player will draw the top two cards and show them to the other player. The second player will have to decide which book of the Bible precedes the other. If that player is right, she gets one point. If wrong, the other player gets the point. Players take turns choosing cards or guessing order. If there is a question about the order of the books, students may use the Bible to check their answers. Record any students' demonstrations of Bible skills on their *For the Record* charts.

Celebration Calendar

Color, then cut out the two large rectangles. For the rectangle with the Bible references, cut three sides of the small squares on the solid lines so that the square is still attached on the top side. Do not cut on the dotted lines. Glue the papers together, Scripture rectangle on top, with the printed sides facing up. Be sure the glue is only on the edges of the papers. Each day this week, read the Scripture on one square, fold up one square on the dotted line, and celebrate God's plan for us!

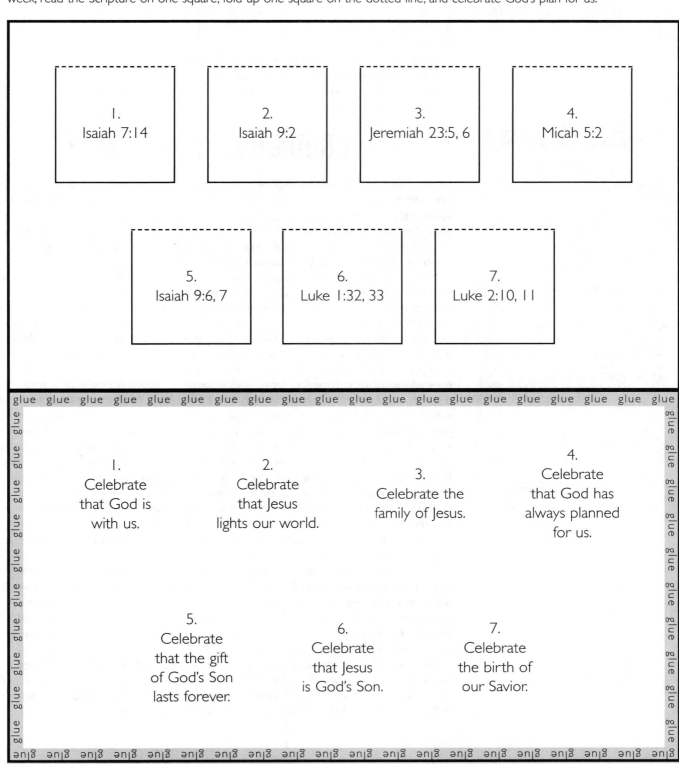

Lesson Aims

Students will
- Write step-by-step instructions for using a Bible tool
- Prepare and perform a dramatic reading of Luke 2
- Decide how to celebrate God's promises, God's plan, and God's gift

Materials
Bibles
Bible dictionaries
Bible concordances
pencils
paper
Scrambled Search (p. 103)

Answers to *Scrambled Search*
NBRO—born, Luke 2:6, 11
RAMNEG—manger, Luke 2:7, 12, 16
ROGLY—glory, Luke 2:9, 14, 32
ARVOIS—Savior, Luke 2:11
SEEDHSPHR—shepherds, Luke 2:8, 15, 18, 20
SIPNARGI—praising, Luke 2:13, 20
CEPAE—peace, Luke 2:14, 29
TIGLH—light, Luke 2:32
STAILVANO—salvation, Luke 2:30

▼ Building Study Skills ▲

Say: **Today is a special day. We will have even more reason to celebrate! We will be learning more about God's promises and plan for us. We will study His Word with the help of Bible tools that we have been learning to use. Are you able to use a Bible concordance and Bible dictionary to help you study God's Word? Could you teach someone else to use one of these Bible tools so that they could learn more too?**

Divide students into two teams. If you have a large class, divide students into an even number of teams with about five students on each team. If you have more than two teams, divide teams into pairs. Give a Bible concordance to one team in each pair and a Bible dictionary to the other team in the pair. Give these instructions to all teams. Say: **For whatever tool your team has, a Bible dictionary or a Bible concordance, you are going to write step-by-step instructions for using that Bible tool. Write very clear and detailed instructions, and include a Bible reference from a concordance or a fact about a topic from a Bible dictionary that the other team must find. After teams have finished writing instructions, your team will have a chance to give instructions to your partner team in using your Bible tool. You will read your instructions to the other team, and that team will follow your instructions exactly as you read them. If your team is receiving instructions about how to use a Bible concordance, you will pretend that you have never seen a Bible concordance before. If your team is receiving instructions about a Bible dictionary, you will pretend that you have never seen a Bible dictionary before.** Give students time to write their instructions, and then tell teams to teach each other how to use the Bible tools. See if they were able to follow the instructions and find the reference or fact.

Ask: **Do you feel confident about using a Bible concordance and dictionary to help you study the Bible? Let's use our Bible concordances to find these references.** Give students a copy of *Scrambled Search*. Tell students to unscramble the words and find the words in their concordances. Write all references for the words that appear in Luke 2:6-20 and Luke 2:25-32. Check answers after students finish the page.

Locate Luke 2:6-20 and Luke 2:25-32 in your Bibles. We read from the book of Luke last week. What did we read about? (Mary and Joseph traveled to Bethlehem.) **Look at the words you unscrambled. What do you think we will be reading about today?** (the birth of Jesus, the Son God promised)

▼ Using Study Skills ▲

If you have a large class, divide the class into groups so that more students may participate and have experience reading and locating Bible references. Have students read through the verses in Luke 2:6-20 and Luke 2:25-32 and divide the verses into sections to be read. Have students write the references for these sections: the narrative in each segment, the words of the angel, the words of the heavenly hosts, the words of the shepherds, and the words of Simeon. Before students begin writing references, explain that some of the verses will be divided into narration and spoken word. Tell students how to write the reference for the first part of a verse with a letter "a" and the second part of the verse with a letter "b."

Ask volunteers to read the following parts of the Bible segments as they would a skit: the narrative in each segment, the words of the angel, the words of the heavenly hosts, the words of the shepherds, and the words of Simeon. To include more students, have different students read parts of the narrative and include several students as shepherds and heavenly hosts. Have other students follow along in their Bibles.

Say: **Jesus is born! The prophecies have been fulfilled. Let's find out more about this great event. Use Bible dictionaries to find facts about shepherds, Jerusalem, light, and Simeon. Maybe you see other words that you would like to know more about. Look for those words too. Make a matching game with the facts you find in the Bible dictionary. In one column, number the words that you choose to read about in the dictionary. In another column, make a mixed-up list of facts. Use one fact for each word in your first column. Put a letter in front of each of the words in the second column so that the words and facts can be matched. Make sure you know the answers to your matching game.** Show students how to make an answer key for their matching game. Have students keep a record of the name of the Bible dictionary they used and the page numbers on which they found the facts that they included in their matching game. Have students put their names on their completed games and give their games to you. Redistribute the games so that no one gets their own game. Give students time to play the matching game you give to them. Allow students to use dictionaries to find the matches. Have students return the games to the original writer to have their answers checked. Discuss facts students learned about the words. Guide the discussion by asking questions. Ask them to tell you what they learned about shepherds. Ask what they learned about the use of the word *light* in reference to Jesus. Ask them to tell you about Simeon. Let students tell about any other words they studied.

Say: **The time was right for Jesus to be born. Everything was ready according to God's plan. God had prepared the people for the birth of His Son. The prophets and angels had delivered God's messages to the people. The books of Prophecy pointed to Jesus.** Give students paper and markers or crayons to draw pictures of the fulfillment of God's plan in Luke 2:6-20 and Luke 2:25-32. Have students label the pictures with a caption and with the New Testament reference for the scene they choose to draw. Attach the pictures to the display.

Say: **Jesus is the Son God promised. We celebrate Jesus' birth every Christmas. How did the heavenly hosts, shepherds, and Simeon celebrate Jesus' birth as God's promised Savior? We know that the Bible tells about the birth of Jesus in Luke 2, but let's use a concordance quickly to find the references for hosts, shepherds, and Simeon in Luke 2.** Have students find these three words in a concordance, locate the references for each word, and read the verses from their Bibles to find types of celebrations. Divide students into three groups to dramatize the celebrations. The heavenly hosts celebrated by praising God and saying, "Glory to God in the highest, and on earth peace to men on whom his favor rests." The shepherds celebrated by hurrying to see the baby and then spreading the word about what had been told to them about this child. Simeon celebrated by praising God and praying.

Materials
Bibles
paper
pencils
Bible dictionaries
unit bulletin board prepared
    before class (see instructions
    in Unit 4 Introduction)
plain paper
markers and crayons
reusable adhesive, tape, or
    staples
Bible concordances

Sections for Reading
For Luke 2:6-20
Narrative: Luke 2:6-10a, Luke
    2:13, Luke 2:15a, Luke 2:16-
    20
Words of the angel: Luke
    2:10b-11
Words of the heavenly hosts:
    Luke 2:14
Words of the shepherds: Luke
    2:15b
For Luke 2:25-32
Narrative: Luke 2:25-28
Words of Simeon: Luke 2:29-32

Option
If you have young or inexperienced students, you may want to prepare the matching game for them ahead of time rather than having the students make up the game.

▼ Responding to Study ▲

Materials
Celebrate! (p. 104)
gift wrapped box
Bible

Before class, gift wrap a box that has a removable lid. Wrap the box and lid separately so that you can remove the lid during class. Place a Bible inside the box.

Say: **The heavenly hosts, the shepherds, and Simeon celebrated Jesus' birth. How will you celebrate the gift of God's Son?** Have students suggest ways they want to celebrate. Have them think about the *Celebration Calendar* from Lesson 17. Ask them to share ways they celebrated God's promises and plan. Give students a copy of *Celebrate!* Say: **There are many celebrations recorded in the Bible. People have always had reasons to celebrate because of the great things God does for us. This week, read these Bible references that tell about celebrations. Decide how you will celebrate.** Send the papers home for students to use during the week to practice reading and locating Scripture references.

Place the gift box on the table. Say: **God's promises, God's plan, and God's Son are a gift to us.** Open the gift box and take out the Bible. **We learn more about God's gift as we study His Word. Our celebration of the gift of God's Son at Christmas only lasts a little while. We give gifts to others, and we receive gifts from them. We enjoy and use our gifts, but these gifts do not last forever. God's gift lasts forever. Every day should be a celebration that Jesus is God's promised Savior.**

▼ Reviewing Study Skills ▲

Materials
Bible concordances
Bibles
paper
pencils
chalkboard or white board
chalk or dry-erase markers
For the Record (p. 300)
several sets of *Bible Cards*
   (pp. 297, 298)

Say: **Memorizing God's Word is an important part of using our Bibles. When we memorize God's Word, we show God that His Words are important to us. Let's practice our memory verses now.**

Divide students into two teams. Have students locate the memory verses in their Bibles and choose key words from the verses. Use a concordance to look up each key word and write down the partial phrase as it is printed in the concordance. After finding several phrases, teams will take turns writing a phrase on the board for the other team to see. In turn, team members from the opposite team will recite the memory verse that includes the partial phrase. Team members may work together to recite the verse. For each correct verse recited, the team earns a letter to spell J-E-S-U-S. Keep score by writing the letters on the board as they are earned. The first team to spell *Jesus* wins.

After the game, give students time to demonstrate Bible skills listed on *For the Record* and to record their progress on the chart. While some students demonstrate skills, allow other students to play games with the *Bible Cards* to help them practice saying the Bible books in order. Students may make up games of their own, play the game described in the Reviewing Study Skills step of Lesson 17, or play the game described here: Students can play in teams or individually. Shuffle cards for the Old or New Testament. Place cards facedown in a stack. Begin play by turning over the top card and placing it on the table. In turn, players draw one card from the stack and place it in order with the other card or cards on the table. Another player may challenge the card if he thinks it is not in correct order. Players receive one point for each correct card. After a designated time, have students return to their seats.

Say: **We have been learning about God's promises and God's plan for us. We have been learning to use Bible tools to help us study God's Word. We have been learning books of the Bible and divisions of the Bible. We can use all we have been learning to help us live lives that are pleasing to God. We can live our lives in celebration for all God has done for us, especially for sending Jesus, God's promised Savior.**

End class by praying to thank God for sending His Son, keeping His promises, and always doing what He says He will do.

Scrambled Search

Unscramble these words from Luke 2. Find the words in a Bible concordance. Write all the references for the words that would be in verses in Luke 2:6-20 and Luke 2:25-32.

Scrambled Words:	Unscrambled Words:	References:
NBRO		
RAMNEG		
ROGLY		
ARVOIS		
SEEDHSPHR		
SIPNARGI		
CEPAE		
TIGLH		
STAILVANO		

Celebrate!

The Bible tells us about celebrations that took place in Bible times. Locate the Scripture references and read the verses in your Bible. One way to celebrate is already given for each verse. Can you find other ways that people celebrated in these verses? What were the reasons for their celebrations? Read the verses before and after the references to find out. We have many reasons to celebrate! Make a list of reasons you will celebrate, and tell how you will celebrate this week!

Psalm 126:1-3—Songs of joy

Acts 3:6-8—Jumping and praising

Luke 15:22-24—Put a ring on his finger

Luke 15:8-10—Call friends and neighbors together

John 2:2, 9—Wedding banquet

Philippians 4:4—Rejoice

1 Samuel 2:1—Prayed

God Planned, Promised, and Provided Salvation

Unit Overview

When we take both the Old and New Testaments as a whole, we begin to see that there's a plan from beginning to end. That plan was for God to provide salvation for His people.

Often children between the ages of 8 and 12 are becoming more and more ready to ask deeper questions about their relationships with God, and salvation is a big concern for them. Sometimes it is a matter of doing the right thing so that they will be able to go to Heaven. In these troubled days, when kids worry about guns at school, drugs on the streets, violence in their homes, and war, children often become concerned about Heaven. Other times, it is a matter of finding a strong relationship with God. Kids who face divorce, families that are torn apart and forced together, and moving from city to city as parents change jobs are hungry for stability in relationships. Finding that relationship with God becomes increasingly important, regardless of what's going on in kids' lives.

Regardless of the reasons why kids are interested in salvation, they need to know that God has planned for it, has promised it, and has provided it. From the very first instance of sin found in Genesis, God had a plan for saving His people. From before the first conversation with Abram, God promised salvation for His people. From the first prophecy about the defeat of Satan and sin, God provided the means of salvation through Jesus. The plan goes from the beginning of time in Genesis through the end of time in Revelation. The promise was for Adam and Eve and Abram and for people today and for people yet to be born. Jesus, the means by which salvation was provided, was a part of the creation of the world, came and lived in the world, died in the world, and eventually will come to destroy the world and redeem His people.

Bible Skills
Recite divisions of the Bible and their books
Use Bible concordance and atlas

Memorize
John 3:16, 17; John 20:31

Memory Challenge
Romans 3:23; 6:23; 8:37-39

The Eight Promises

During this unit students will learn the eight major promises of God. The promises are in chronological order and correspond to different eras in Bible history. At this point in the study the students will simply learn the promises in order and use sign language as a way to remember them. Use *The Eight Promises* (page 106) for your reference or as a study sheet for the students.

Summary

Lesson 19 introduces the eight promises and puts them in historical context.

Lesson 20 uses King Manasseh of Judah as an example to show that God will restore His people when they repent.

In **Lesson 21,** students will see Jesus as the center of God's plan of salvation.

Lesson 22 shows that God's promised salvation requires us to choose Him and reviews the steps in that process.

The Eight Promises

The Promise	What It Is and Who Received It	How God Kept the Promise
Hope	God promised Adam and Eve the hope of salvation.	When Jesus came, God kept His promise of salvation.
Nation	God promised Abraham he would be the father of a great nation and through him all nations would be blessed.	In Egypt, Abraham's family grew to several million people. The promised blessing came through Jesus who was a descendant of Abraham's family.
Land	God promised the Israelites a home in a new land.	Twelve tribes each received a portion of the promised land.
Deliverance	God promised the Israelites deliverance from their enemies.	God used the judges to deliver the people from their enemies.
Family	God promised David that Judah's everlasting king, the Messiah, would come from David's family.	Jesus, the Messiah, was a descendant of King David.
Restoration	God promised Judah He would bring them back home.	After 70 years in exile, Cyrus let Judah go home.
Salvation	God promised all people salvation from sin.	When Jesus died, He took our punishment for our sins so that God could forgive us.
Eternal Life	God promised all people eternal life.	At Pentecost, God first offered salvation through Jesus so that we can have eternal life with Him.

God Promised to Bless His People

Genesis 3; 12; Matthew 1; John 3

Lesson Aims

Students will
- Collect information on members of Jesus' family tree
- Participate in a skit on God's promises
- Sign (in sign language) the words *hope, nation,* and *land* as reminders of God's promises

▼ Building Study Skills ▲

Before class prepare the eight boxes. Wrap them with plain paper and attach one Bible division name to each box. Make sure the boxes each have an opening large enough to accommodate the *Bible Cards*.

In class shuffle the *Bible Cards* and distribute them to students as they arrive. Instruct students to sort the books according to their division by placing the cards in the correct box. Keep distributing cards until all students have arrived and all cards are placed in one of the eight boxes. When all cards have been sorted, gather students around the boxes and pull the cards from one box at a time. Determine if each card is in the correct box. Students may use their Bible's table of contents as needed. All cards placed incorrectly should be moved to the correct boxes per students' instructions. Then lead students to recite the Bible books one division at a time.

Say: **When we know how the Bible is organized, we will have an easier time using and understanding it. The books of the Bible are organized by their types. All the books that tell about the Law that God gave to His people are grouped together. Old Testament History books are together. Prophecy books are together and so on. Knowing how a Bible book is grouped helps us know what that book is about. For example, we know that History books tell us the history of God's people. We know that the Gospels tell us how Jesus came to earth to save us.**

Say: **Knowing the eight major promises that God kept and recorded in the Bible will also help us use and understand God's Word. We have already learned that the Bible tells us how God brought salvation to us. The eight promises help us follow God's plan for providing salvation.** Show cards as each one is mentioned. **God's promise was one of HOPE, specifically the hope of salvation through the Savior. From the beginning of time, God told people to expect Jesus. In order to bring salvation, God kept several promises. He promised to build a NATION of people who would love Him. He promised to give that nation a home LAND. He promised to DELIVER the nation from their enemies. He promised that one FAMILY in the nation would be the family that would bring Jesus into the world. He promised to RESTORE that nation to their homeland after they were captured and taken into captivity. All of these promises were fulfilled during the Old Testament days.**

God was not finished yet. He had prepared a nation so that He could bring salvation to people. When the time was right, God sent Jesus into that nation to be crucified and to be resurrected. Jesus was God's promise

Materials

Bibles
tape
Bible concordances
8 boxes that are similar in size (such as tissue boxes)
index cards with the 8 divisions and 8 promises (see p. 106)
paper
Bible Cards (pp. 297, 298)
index cards

of **SALVATION from sin. Everyone who takes God's offer of salvation through Jesus will receive God's promise of ETERNAL LIFE.** Lead students to repeat the eight promises in unison. Then move into the next activity.

Before class prepare index cards with names from Jesus' genealogy in Luke 3:23-35. Make enough cards with different names so that every student will have one card. In class divide students into groups, one group for each concordance. If you have enough concordances for each student, then groups are not needed. Group members are to share the concordance.

Distribute name cards, one card per student. Instruct students to locate the name in the concordance. The object is to identify the name of the person's father and to look for names of other people in the family. From the names given in the genealogy, students should choose the most important member of the family. In all cases, this will be Jesus. For those names with a lot of references in the concordance, tell students to choose the reference for the book of Luke. After reading the passage in the Bible, students should write the father's name above the name on the card. On the reverse side of the card, students should write the name of who they think is the most important person in that family. In order to discover this, students will have to read the genealogy. When everyone is finished, ask students to line up according to family order, from the latest ancestor (closest to Jesus) to the earliest. Say: **All of the names listed on your cards are members of the same family. Whose family is it?** Students turn over their cards to reveal the name *Jesus*. **All of these men were part of the nation and the family to which Jesus belonged.** If time permits or if needed to help students understand that these men were in Jesus' family, point out grandpa, great grandpa, great great grandpa, and so on.

Say: **Now let's go back in time to days when Jesus' greatest (oldest) grandpa was alive, Adam.**

▼ Using Study Skills ▲

Materials
Bibles
God Promised (pp. 110, 111)
table or desk for host
couch or chairs for guests and
   audience

Before class set up an area of the room to resemble the set of a talk show. Choose students or adults to play the host, Eve, and Abraham. Distribute the *God Promised* script to the people you have chosen. Those who don't have parts will be the audience. They are to hold their cards from the previous activity. When the audience is asked a question, they are to hold up the cards and shout "Jesus." Audience members will also need their Bibles.

▼ Responding to Study ▲

Materials
colored construction paper cut
   into half sheets
old magazine from which pictures can be removed
glue
file folders

During the next four weeks, students will complete a flip-style chart that explains the plan of salvation. Each week they will add more pages, which will be based on the lesson's topic. When the flip chart is completed, students may flip through the chart page by page and see the plan of salvation or share the plan of salvation with someone else.

Begin by explaining the following process to the students. Ask them to select three half-sheets of construction paper of the same or different colors. They are to write the message on the card, then draw original illustrations or search magazines for pictures that illustrate the message. Help students design the three cards. (See page 109 for messages.)

When students are finished, discuss the cards one by one with the group. Be sure they understand the meaning of each card. Look at Card 1 and read it together. Say: **We saw today from both Eve and Abraham how God planned to bless all people. From the moment that Adam and Eve sinned, God promised salvation through Jesus. Then God began to do what He prom-**

ised when He called Abraham to a new land to begin a new nation.

Look at and read Card 2. Say: **The Bible tells us who was in Jesus' earthly family. This passage shows how Jesus was a part of Abraham's family. Abraham was the father of the nation in which Jesus was born.**

Look at and read Card 3. Say: **These verses tell us why all people need Jesus. This was the case since Adam and Eve's first sin. Sin keeps us from God. God found a way to bring us back to Him through Jesus' death on the cross. Jesus paid for our sins. He is our Savior! All people need Jesus because all people have sinned.**

Have students place their cards in file folders and write their names on the outside. Store the folders so that they will be available again next week. Before moving to the Reviewing Study Skills step, lead the class in prayer: **Thank You, Lord, for giving us Your Word. Thank You for keeping Your promises. Thank You for the gift of salvation. In Jesus' name, Amen.**

▼ Reviewing Study Skills ▲

Before class practice the signs for hope, nation, and land of the eight promises so that you can demonstrate them for the class.

In class direct students in learning the sign language motions for hope, nation, and land. Practice each one several times separately and then together. Then have the class play this version of duck, duck, goose using the words *hope, hope, hope, nation, hope, hope, nation, land.* Seat the class in a circle. One player walks around the outside of the circle, touching each person on the head while saying "hope, hope, hope, nation," and so on, until he reaches the player he has chosen to race. He signals the race by saying the word *land.* Both players then run in opposite directions around the circle. The first one to return to the empty spot is awarded that place. The loser of the race becomes the person who walks around the outside of the circle. Students seated in the circle should perform the motions as each promise is spoken.

Materials
Promises Motions (p. 112)

Card 1
Message: From the beginning, God promised to bless all people.
God told Abraham, "All peoples on earth will be blessed through you" (Genesis 12:3b).
Illustration: the world, a globe, or a map.

Card 2
Message: Jesus is the blessing that God promised.
"A record of the genealogy of Jesus Christ the son of David, the son of Abraham" (Matthew 1:1).
Illustration: a cross or write the name Jesus in decorative letters.

Card 3
Message: All people need God's blessing because all people sin.
"There is no one righteous, not even one" (Romans 3:10).
"For all have sinned and fall short of the glory of God" (Romans 3:23).
Illustration: blackness. Draw a box and color it black.

God Promised

HOST: Good evening. Welcome to our show, *God Promised.* This show is about understanding God's promises. We have some wonderful guests for you tonight: Eve, the first woman, and Abraham, the father of many nations. Our musical guests are "The King's Family."

Tonight, we'll begin by looking at God's promise of hope. When we hope for something, we expect with confidence. God promised hope in the very beginning of time. We can be confident that what God promised will happen. Genesis 3:15 tells us about God's promise of hope. Let's all turn in our Bibles to Genesis 3:15. *(Audience finds and reads Genesis 3:15 silently, and then host chooses one person to read it aloud.)*

Our first guest tonight will help us understand the hope that God promises in this passage. Let's welcome Eve. *(Audience claps and Eve enters, shakes hands with the host, and sits in one of the chairs designated for the guests.)*

Welcome, Eve.

EVE: Thanks, it's good to be here.

HOST: Who is speaking in this passage? Who is saying "I will put—"

EVE: *(Interrupting)* God is speaking to the serpent.

HOST: Why is God speaking to a serpent?

EVE: Genesis 3:15 is part of God's judgment on the serpent for his role in the first sin. The serpent lied to me. I believed his lie and ate what God said not to eat. It was a very sad and hopeless time for us until God promised what He did in Genesis 3:15.

HOST: We already know that you are the woman that God mentions in Genesis 3:15.

EVE: Yes, that's right. The serpent is my enemy. The serpent is Satan. He is against all that God created. He wants to destroy all that God created, especially people.

HOST: Yes, but God promised something wonderful for people. What was it?

EVE: God promised hope. Genesis 3:15 says that a child of a woman will crush the serpent's head. Let's ask the audience. Audience, who is the child of a woman that Genesis 3:15 talks about? *(Audience should hold up their Jesus cards and say "Jesus.")* That's right. The child that God speaks of is His only Son, Jesus. The promise is that Jesus will defeat Satan.

HOST: This is a great promise. We all have trouble with the temptations that Satan tempts us with. This passage promises that Jesus will defeat Satan. That is a message of great hope.

EVE: God promised hope in the beginning of time. He kept His promise when Jesus died on the cross, was buried for three days, and then rose and ascended into Heaven. Jesus has indeed crushed Satan.

HOST: What does "you will strike his heel" mean?

EVE: This line is about Jesus' death on the cross. It was God's plan from the beginning that Jesus would bleed and die and take on all the sins of the world. This is what we would need in order to be forgiven for our sins. At the cross, Satan thought he was defeating the Son of God when, in fact, he was only striking Jesus' heel. Nothing was happening that God didn't plan. Jesus was the one defeating Satan!

HOST: Genesis 3:15 is certainly a great promise of hope. Now, it is time for us to bring in our second guest. Let's welcome Abraham. *(Audience claps. Abraham enters, shakes hands with the host, and sits in one of the chairs for the guests.)*

HOST: Abraham, you've been nicknamed "the father of many nations." How did you get such an honorable nickname?

ABRAHAM: In order to find the answer to that, let's turn to Genesis 12:1-3 in our Bibles. *(He instructs audience to do so. Audience finds and reads the passage silently, and then Abraham asks someone from the audience to read it aloud.)* I want you to notice two words in this passage: *land* and *nation*. God promised me both a homeland and a nation. First, He gave me the land. Then He went to work to make a nation. It took many years for this nation to grow and finally to take the land God gave to me to be our home.

I am the father, the one God called, to begin the nation of people who would be the nation of His Son, Jesus. This nation would be blessed because Jesus would be born into it. It was a nation God formed for the job of bringing up Jesus. The land He gave to us was to be the homeland of His Son, Jesus.

HOST: That tells us how you are the father of one nation, but what does many nations mean?

ABRAHAM: Genesis 12:3 says that all people on earth will be blessed through me. It wasn't just the one nation that God made from my family that was blessed through me. It was all people for all time. You are blessed because God chose me to father the nation for Jesus. You are blessed because of what Jesus did on the cross.

HOST: It is incredible how God planned for our salvation, how He promised to send Jesus, and how He provided the way for Jesus to come to earth. Abraham, you had a fascinating role in God's plan. Thank you for sharing that with us today. Audience, who was the blessing that God promised Abraham's nation? *(Audience holds up Jesus cards and shouts "Jesus.")* Not only did God promise the blessing to Abraham's nation, He promised it to all people for all time.

Anyone who takes Jesus as his or her Savior is a part of King Jesus' family. Our musical guests today are "The King's Family." That's you and me. Let's sing a song of praise.

(Have students sing "He Is Lord." Any song that honors the name of Jesus could be used.)

Have students create motions for each of the eight promises of God's plan. This page shows some suggestions based on sign language.

Hope

Cross fingers of both hands, holding them chest high with palms facing each other, left hand in front of the right hand.

Nation

Form the letter N with the right hand, tucking the thumb under the index and middle fingers but over the ring finger. The index and middle finger will stick out from the hand to indicate the letter N. Circle the N over the left fist and then place on back of the left fist.

Deliverance

Form the letter D with both hands by holding index finger up and form an O shape with the thumb, middle, ring, and little fingers. The shape will look like a D. Cross hands at wrists with palms facing you. Uncross and turn palms to face away from you.

Land

Form the letter L using the thumb and index finger of the right hand. Shape the thumb and index finger to look like an L. Circle the L over the open left hand with palm down. Circle counter clockwise from hand to elbow and back.

Family

Form the letter F with both hands by joining the thumb and index finger together to form an O shape. Keep the middle, ring, and little fingers up. Place hands in front of you so the index fingers touch. Move hands apart and circle until the little fingers touch.

Restoration

Form the letter R by crossing fingers of both hands. Point them toward each other. Circle alternately toward body.

Salvation

Form the letter S with both hands by making fists. Cross hands at wrists with palms toward you. Uncross and turn S hands to face away from you.

Eternal Life

For eternal, form the letter E with the right hand by bending fingers to make a partial fist. Tuck thumb across palm underneath the bent fingers. Fingers and thumb do not touch. With the palm facing away from you, circle the hand and then move it forward.

For life, spread fingers apart on both hands. Place hands about waist high with palms toward you. Move hands up to chest high while wiggling fingers.

LESSON 19

God Promised to Restore His People

2 Chronicles 33

Lesson Aims

Students will
- List events in the life of King Manasseh of Judah that indicate life changes he made
- Create flip chart pages to use for explaining the plan of salvation
- Play a promise game

▼ Building Study Skills ▲

Before class prepare index cards with division names and tape the division cards in a horizontal line on the wall. As students arrive, tape *Bible Cards* to their shoulders and upper arms. Use both arms. Divide the cards among the number of students. Distribute as many of the 66 books as possible, but give all students the same number of cards. Play this sorting game. At the signal, students race to tape their six cards under the correct division in the correct order on the wall. When finished, check students' work and move cards as needed to their correct divisions, or form teams and assign each team a division to check. Ask students to recite the names of the eight divisions in unison and then to recite the books of the Bible in unison. Point to the names as needed.

Help students memorize John 3:16, 17 and John 20:31 with the following activity. Before class write the words of John 3:16, John 3:17, and John 20:31 on poster board and display in the classroom. Inflate 18 balloons. Using a black marker, write the indicated phrases on separate balloons. Adjust the phrasing and the number of balloons to coordinate with the number of students in your class, one per student. Include the reference as one of the phrases.

Place all of the balloons in one area or container. Divide the students into two teams. At the signal, all students on both teams run to grab a balloon. Students are to read what is written on their balloons and decide to which of the three verses their phrases belong. Then they are to look for the other students who have phrases for the same verse. The first group to assemble all phrases for its verse, put them in order, and recite the verse receives five points for each player's team. For example, if the students who had the phrases for John 20:31 were the first group to assemble in order, then each person in that group would earn five points for his or her team. If two of the players were from Team A, then Team A receives 10 points and Team B would receive 20 points. Continue playing and keeping score as time allows. Have the black marker and extra balloons nearby so that any balloons that are popped may be replaced.

When the game is over, gather students in the lesson area. Distribute Bibles. Write 2 Chronicles 33:1, 3, 4, 9-13, 15, 16 on the chalkboard. Say: **Look at this reference. I'm going to ask you to read this aloud, but first I want you to read it silently.** After 30 seconds ask the class to read the reference aloud together. Correct any mistakes. Say: **Now, I want you to find 2 Chronicles 33:1 in your Bibles. Read verses 1, 3, 4, 9-13, 15, 16 silently.**

Materials
index cards
Bible Cards (pp. 297, 298)
tape
balloons
black marker
poster board

John 3:16
For God so loved the world
that he gave his one and only
  Son,
that whoever believes in him
shall not perish
but have eternal life.

John 3:17
For God did not send
his Son into the world
to condemn the world,
but to save the world
through him.

John 20:31
These are written
that you may believe
that Jesus is the Christ, the Son
  of God,
and that by believing
you may have life in his name.

▼ Using Study Skills ▲

Materials
brown, black, and white
   construction paper
chenille wire
black clothing
white clothing
scissors
poster board
marker
Turn Back! (p. 116)

Before class make three columns on the poster board. Label the left column "Before," the middle column "Turning Point," and the right column "After." Make a hook for Manasseh's nose by forming a circle with the chenille wire. Keep an opening in the perimeter of the circle so it can be placed in Manasseh's nose. Make two sets of shackles for his feet from the brown construction paper. Connect the shackles with a paper chain. Make crowns from the black and white construction paper.

Say: **Today's Scripture passage tells us about one of the kings of Judah. Look again at 2 Chronicles 33:1. What king of Judah is our lesson about?** (Manasseh) **How old was Manasseh when he became king?** (12) **How many of you are 12?** (Have students raise hands.) **How long was Manasseh king of Judah?** (55 years) **How old was Manasseh when his time as king of Judah was over?** (67)

Say: **Let's read our Scripture passage again. As we read, let's read to find out three things about Manasseh.** Pass out copies of *Turn Back!* Show the poster board. **First, we want to find out what Manasseh was like before his turning point. Second, we want to find out what his turning point was.** A turning point is an event that causes someone to change or to go in a different direction. **Third, we want to find out what he was like after his turning point.** Read the passage aloud as students read along or have students take turns reading.

Lead students in listing events or descriptions of Manasseh before his turning point, during his turning point, and after his turning point. Have students fill out their charts as the list is made on the poster chart. Suggestions follow.

Before: he built and rebuilt altars to idols, he worshiped the stars, he built altars to idols in the temple; he was evil; he led people astray (away from God); his nation was more evil than the nations before them; the nation did not listen to the Lord when He spoke to them.

Turning point: the army of Assyria came against the nation; Manasseh was taken prisoner; he was shackled, a ring was placed in his nose; he was taken to Babylon; he was distressed so he sought the Lord; he humbled himself before the Lord; the Lord listened to Manasseh's plea; the Lord restored Manasseh; He brought Manasseh back to Jerusalem and gave him back his kingdom.

After: Manasseh knew that the Lord is God; he got rid of the foreign gods (idols); he removed the idols from the temple; he restored the altar of the Lord and used it to praise and thank God; he told the people of Judah to serve the God of Israel.

Say: **Manasseh began as an evil king. His evil ways angered God, so God took Manasseh's kingship and kingdom away from him. When this happened, Manasseh took a serious look at himself and his evil ways. He looked to God for help. God listened to Manasseh and restored him. God gave Manasseh back his kingship and his kingdom. He let Manasseh go home.**

Divide the class into three groups: before, turning point, after. Each group is to choose one member to be Manasseh. The rest of the group will use the clothing available to dress their Manasseh volunteer to represent what he was like before his turning point, during his turning point, and after his turning point. The "before" group should dress their volunteer in black clothing and place the black crown on his head to represent evil; the "turning point" group can use the construction paper shackles and chenille wire hook to show Manasseh's captivity; the "after" group can use the white clothing and white crown to show his restoration.

When all three Manassehs are dressed, summarize the lesson. Say: **Manasseh was an evil king.** Indicate "before Manasseh." **Manasseh was taken prisoner by Assyria. He was removed from his throne. This led Manasseh to call out to the Lord and repent of his evil ways.** Indicate "turning point Manasseh." **The Lord restored Manasseh; he gave Manasseh another chance. He gave back to Manasseh what he had before he was a prisoner. Manasseh served**

the Lord for the rest of his life. Indicate "after Manasseh."

We have all been like Manasseh before he repented. Indicate "before Manasseh." **We have been evil because we have sinned against God. Some of us have had our turning points.** Indicate "turning point Manasseh." **They may not have been as dramatic as Manasseh's, but they helped us know that we need the saving grace of Jesus. If we have repented and Jesus is our Savior, He has restored us. He has given back what we lost because we were sinners.** Indicate "after Manasseh."

▼ Responding to Study ▲

Students will add three more pages to their flip charts that explain the plan of salvation. When the flip chart is completed, students may flip through the chart page by page and see the plan of salvation or share the plan of salvation with someone else.

Explain the process. Ask students to select three half-sheets of construction paper. They are to write the message, then search magazines for pictures that illustrate the message of each card. Help students design cards 4, 8, and 11.

When students are finished, discuss the cards one by one with the group. Read Card 4. Ask: **What happened to Manasseh because of his sin?** (He was taken prisoner.) **Manasseh was on his way to eternal death. But what happened to him?** (He turned away from his evil ways. He repented.)

Read Card 8. Say: **God restored Manasseh. What did Manasseh do after the Lord restored him?** (Manasseh lived for the Lord.) Read Card 11.

Be sure they understand the meaning of each card. Then have students place their cards in a file folder. Store the folders so that they will be available again next week.

Lead in prayer before moving to the Reviewing Study Skills step: **Father, we are all sinners. We have all treated You badly. Show us our sin, and lead us to repent. Lord, thank You for Your forgiveness and restoration. Help us always to live for You. In Jesus' name. Amen.**

▼ Reviewing Study Skills ▲

Before class, practice the signs for deliverance, family, and restoration of the eight promises so that you can demonstrate them for the class. (See *Promises Motions* on page 112.)

In class, direct students in learning the sign language motions for deliverance, family, and restoration. Practice each one several times separately. Review the signs for hope, nation, and land. Then practice the six signs in order. Encourage students to name the promise while they execute the sign.

When finished practicing the motions for the first six promises, play the following game. Print each promise on a separate index card. You will need one set of promise cards for each team. Place cards in order equal distances apart in the playing area. The path of the cards can follow a straight line, or it can zigzag. Place each team's first card, *hope*, at the starting line.

In class, divide students into teams of equal number, one team per set of cards. Give each team a ball. At the signal, each player takes a turn dribbling from card to card in their team's course. They must repeat the promises as they dribble each section of the course. For example, players begin with the word *hope*. Each time the ball hits the floor, the player must say the word *hope*. When the player reaches the second card, *nation*, the player starts saying the word *nation* each time the ball hits the floor. This continues for each player as he dribbles through the course. When one player finishes the course, he gives the ball to the next player in line. Let the winning team lead the class in reciting the eight promises while performing the motions for the first six promises.

Materials
flip chart items from Lesson 19
colored construction paper cut
   into half sheets
old magazines
scissors
notebook paper
glue
file folders

Card 4
Message: Sin is serious because
   sin brings eternal death.
"For the wages of sin is death,
   but the gift of God is eternal
   life in Christ Jesus our Lord"
   (Romans 6:23).
Illustration: handcuffs, someone
   being arrested, a coffin, a gun,
   or something that depicts
   punishment or death.

Card 8
Message: We must admit our
   sin and repent. God will forgive us and restore us.
Read 2 Chronicles 33:9-13.
Illustration: a picture of a person showing sorrow and a
   picture of a person showing
   joy and happiness.

Card 11
Message: We must live for Jesus.
"Do your best to present yourself to God as one approved,
   a workman who does not
   need to be ashamed and who
   correctly handles the word of
   truth" (2 Timothy 2:15).
Illustration: picture of a construction worker or someone dressed in a uniform.

Materials
index cards
marker
basketballs or other bouncing
   balls (one for each team)
Promises Motions (p. 112)

Turn Back!

In each of the columns below, read the Scriptures listed and write down the things that Manasseh and the people of Judah did.

Before	Turning Point	After
2 Chronicles 33:1, 3, 4, 9, 10	2 Chronicles 33:11-13	2 Chronicles 33:15, 16

Where do you fall in your own life? Are you before a turning point, at a turning point, or after a turning point? What can you do or have you done to repent of your own sins? Write a short prayer to God about which column you are in.

Dear God, _____

_____

_____

_____

_____

LESSON 20

Lesson Aims

Students will

- Mark key words in Scripture in order to see the relationship between them
- Add pages to their flip chart so they can share the plan of salvation
- Complete the series of sign language signs for the eight promises of God's plan

▼ Building Study Skills ▲

Before class make enlarged copies of the Promise Rhyme for students to read.

As students arrive, divide them into teams of four or five. Give the instructions for playing this game. Each team is given one ice cube. The first player holds the cube in his fist while reciting or reading John 3:16, 17 and then passes the ice cube to the next player. He does the same. This continues until the cube returns to the first player who holds it while reading or reciting John 20:31. Each player on the team does the same. This continues until the ice cube is melted. If the cube returns to the first player after both passages have been recited, he begins again with John 3:16, 17. The first team to melt the cube is the winner. If time permits, have students recite the books of the Bible while holding the ice cube. The first student names several books in order, then passes the ice cube. The next student starts where the previous student stopped and recites several more books. This continues until the ice cube is melted. The team that recites through the list of books the most times is the winner.

Distribute the Promise Rhyme to students. Read through the rhyme so students get a feel for it. Ask the winning team of the ice cube game to lead the group in reading the rhyme.

Explain each line of the rhyme. Say: "**God gave us HOPE since the time of Creation**" tells us that God promised to send Jesus from the moment Adam and Eve sinned. "'**Cause Jesus would be born to a faithful NATION**" tells us that God planned for Jesus to be one of us. He would be a part of a nation of people. God formed this nation at Mt. Sinai when He gave them the Ten Commandments. They are the Israelites.

"**The nation's LAND was Jesus' earthly home**" tells us that Jesus had a place to live, a homeland. God gave the Israelites a land flowing with milk and honey. This was the land where the Israelites moved after they left Egypt and wandered in the wilderness. What was the first city in the new land that God helped the Israelites take? (Jericho)

"**God's DELIVERANCE taught the nation not to roam**" tells us that the Israelites were not always faithful to God. They kept worshiping idols and getting themselves into trouble. When the people repented, God would deliver them from their troubles. He used judges like Gideon and Deborah to deliver the Israelites. This nation was not ready for the Savior yet.

"**Jesus' earthly FAMILY was fit for a king**" means that Jesus was born into a family of earthly kings. After the time of the judges, kings began to rule Israel. God promised that Jesus would be from the family of King David. King David was one of Israel's greatest kings. God was still preparing the way for Jesus, and the time was getting closer.

Materials
Memory verse posters made
   for Lesson 20
ice cubes
poster board
marker
Promise Rhyme (p. 120)

"RESTORATION to God made the nation sing" tells us that the Israelite nation didn't quite understand their role in providing an earthly nation and family for Jesus. The Israelites kept sinning and worshiping idols. God wasn't going to send Jesus until the idols were cleaned out and the nation was faithful to Him. In order to accomplish this, God sent the Israelites into captivity. During this captivity, the Israelites learned to worship only God. When God restored them to their homeland, the Israelites were no longer worshiping idols.

"When it was time, Jesus died for our SALVATION" tells us that the time finally came for Jesus to be born, to die, and to be raised again. When all of God's preparations were complete, Jesus came. Matthew, Mark, Luke, and John tell us about Jesus' life on earth. Jesus came to seek and to save the lost.

"Now ETERNAL LIFE is for every nation" tells us that God's work in Jesus is completed. Salvation is for all people. The disciples began the work of telling others about eternal life through Jesus. The apostle Paul was one of the first missionaries. We read about this in the book of Acts and in all the letters.

Have students sit in a circle with legs crossed and play this rhythm game. Students hold their hands about waist high with palms up. Each player's right hand should rest palm up on the palm of the student's left hand to his right. The first player lifts his right hand and slaps the left hand of the player on his right. Then that player does the same by slapping the palm of the player on his right. This is done to the rhythm determined by saying the Promise Rhyme. Players chant the Promise Rhyme while taking turns slapping hands around the circle.

▼ Using Study Skills ▲

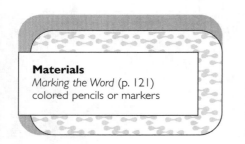

Materials
Marking the Word (p. 121)
colored pencils or markers

Gather students in the lesson area. Say: **We're going to talk more about the salvation that Jesus gives to us.** Distribute *Marking the Word* and pencils. Instruct students to read John 20:24-31 silently. After they have read the passage, instruct them to read through it again and draw a pair of eyes over each occurrence of the words *see* and *seen*. Then have them read the passage silently a third time and circle each occurrence of the words *believe* and *believing*. Write these words and symbols on the board for students to refer to as needed.

Ask: **What did Jesus say about people who see Him and believe that He is the Son of God?** (Indirectly, He said that it is easy to believe when you have seen.) **What did Jesus say about people who have not seen Him and believe that He is the Son of God?** (Jesus called them blessed.) **Which person are you? Have we seen Jesus' nail-pierced hands?** (no) **Then we are people who have not seen. Do you believe that Jesus is the Son of God? What did Jesus say about people who believe when they haven't seen?** (They are blessed.) **Why are they blessed?** (Because they haven't seen Jesus, yet they believe that He is the Son of God.)

Next, have students silently read Romans 3:10, 23; 6:23; 5:8. Then ask students to read through the verses again and mark the words *sin* and *sinners* with a frowning face. Draw a "no" symbol (circle with a slanted line through it) over the word combination of *no one*. Draw an *X* over the word *death*. Draw a box with a bow around the word *gift*. Draw an arrow from the word *gift* to the words *eternal life*. Draw a heart over the word *love*. Draw a cross over the words *Jesus* and *Christ*. Write each of these words and their corresponding symbols on the board for students to reference.

Ask: **Who is righteous?** (no one) **Who has sinned?** (all) **Does this mean that you are a sinner?** (yes) **What happens to sinners?** (death) **Does this mean that you will die?** (yes) **All people die. This is the bad news. That is why we marked the bad news with frowns, "no" symbols, and Xs. But there is good** news for those who have not seen Jesus but believe that He is the Son of God. Jesus has a gift for them. What is it? (eternal life) **What is eternal life?** (It is life forever with God after our physical death.) **Those who die a physical death without believing that Jesus is the Son of God will live forever without God.**

Next have students read Romans 10:9-11. Then as they read the passage again, have them draw a wavy line under what we must confess and a double line under what we must believe in order to be saved.

Ask: **What must we confess?** (Jesus is Lord.) **What do we do when we confess?** Discuss the idea that confession is both saying and agreeing. Say: **When we confess that Jesus is Lord, we tell someone that we believe Jesus is Lord, and we agree with God that Jesus is Lord. What must we believe?** (We must believe that God raised Jesus from the dead.) **Believing this and confessing that Jesus is Lord are two important steps in salvation.**

Say: **Let's read Romans 6:3-5 to discover another important step we take when we believe that God raised Jesus from the dead.** Read silently. When students finish, have them read the passage again. This time have them mark the words *baptized* and *baptism* with a wavy line to resemble waves of water. Mark around the words *dead, buried,* and *death* with a box. Mark the words *raised, new life* and *resurrection* with a butterfly shape. Again, write words and symbols on the board.

Ask: **What happens when someone dies?** (He is buried.) **How is he buried?** (He is placed underground.) **What happens when someone is baptized?** (He is taken under water.) **We could say that he is buried under water. Being baptized under water reminds us that Jesus died and was buried underground. In a way, we reenact what happened to Jesus. Jesus didn't stay in the ground. He was resurrected. He came up out of the ground. When we are baptized in water, we don't stay under the water. We come up out of the water. We reenact what happened to Jesus. If we join Jesus in His death through our baptism, then what happens to us when we join Jesus in His resurrection?** (We are united with Him; we will be with Him.) **What does being resurrected with Jesus mean?** (new life; eternal life)

Say: **We've talked about some important steps of salvation today. Let's review. Why is believing that Jesus is God's Son and that God raised Jesus from the dead important to salvation?** (It is Jesus who saves us through His death and resurrection. A relationship with God and His Son begins with believing that He exists and that He has done what He says He has.) **Why is knowing that we are sinners important to salvation?** (Without knowing our sin, we cannot realize our need for a Savior.) **Why is confessing that Jesus is Lord important to salvation?** (This shows what we believe enough to say so.) **Why is baptism important to salvation?** (We join with Jesus in His death and resurrection.)

▼ Responding to Study ▲

Students will add three more pages to their flip-style charts that explain the plan of salvation. When the flip chart is completed, students may flip through the chart page by page and see the plan of salvation or share the plan of salvation with someone else.

Explain the process as needed to the students. Ask them to select three half-sheets of construction paper of the same or different colors. They are to write the message on the card, then search magazines for pictures that illustrate the message. Help students design the following three cards: 6, 7, 9.

When students are finished, discuss the cards one by one with the group. Be sure they understand the meaning of each card. Then have students place their cards in a file folder. Store the folders so that they will be available again next week.

Lead the class in prayer before continuing to the Reviewing Study Skills step:

Materials
colored construction paper cut into half sheets
old magazines
scissors
notebook paper
glue
file folders
students' work from Lessons 19 and 20

Card 6
Message: God did His part through Jesus' death on the cross. He kept His promise to bless us.
"God demonstrates his own love for us in this: While we were still sinners, Christ died for us" (Romans 5:8).
Illustration: love. Draw a heart and color it red.

Card 7
Message: Now we must do our part. We must believe that Jesus is the Christ, the Son of the living God and that He died to save us.
"These are written that you may believe that Jesus is the Christ, the Son of God, and that by believing you may have life in his name" (John 20:31).
Illustration: a picture of an open book or a Bible.

Card 9
Message: We must confess (tell others and agree with God) that Jesus is Lord.
"If you confess with your mouth, 'Jesus is Lord,' and believe in your heart that God raised him from the dead, you will be saved" (Romans 10:9).
Illustration: a picture of two people talking together.

Father, You have shown us your great love by sending Jesus to die for our sins. Thank You. Please work in each of our hearts to bring us closer to You. Lead us to salvation and to eternal life with You. In Jesus' name, Amen.

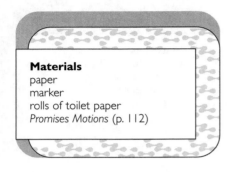

Materials
paper
marker
rolls of toilet paper
Promises Motions (p. 112)

▼ Reviewing Study Skills ▲

Before class practice the signs for salvation and eternal life from the eight promises so that you can demonstrate them for the class. (See *Promises Motions* on page 112.)

In class direct students in learning the sign language motions for salvation and eternal life. Practice each one several times separately. Review the signs for hope, nation, land, deliverance, family, and restoration. Then practice the six signs in order. Encourage students to name the promise while they execute the sign.

Before class write each of the eight promises on separate sheets of plain paper. In class assign eight students to each hold one of the signs. Scatter these eight students around the room in random order. If you don't have eight students, use chairs to hold the signs. Divide the rest of the students into two teams. Give each team several rolls of toilet paper, depending on how much area the eight promises cover. At the go signal, each team is to race to leave a trail of toilet paper from the first to the last promises in correct order. Players run to the first promise, hope, and wrap toilet paper around that person. While unrolling the paper and leaving a trail, players run to the second promise, wrap paper around that person, and continue until they reach the last promise, eternal life. The first team to have all players leave a correct paper trail wins. Ask the winners to lead the class in reciting the eight promises while performing the signs.

Promise Rhyme

God gave us HOPE since the time of creation.

'Cause Jesus would be born to a faithful NATION.

The nation's LAND was Jesus' earthly home.

God's DELIVERANCE taught the nation not to roam.

Jesus' earthly FAMILY was fit for a king.

RESTORATION to God made the nation sing.

When it was time, Jesus died for our SALVATION.

Now ETERNAL LIFE is for every nation.

John 20:24-31

24Now Thomas (called Didymus), one of the Twelve, was not with the disciples when Jesus came. 25So the other disciples told him, "We have seen the Lord!"

But he said to them, "Unless I see the nail marks in his hands and put my finger where the nails were, and put my hand into his side, I will not believe it."

26A week later his disciples were in the house again, and Thomas was with them. Though the doors were locked, Jesus came and stood among them and said, "Peace be with you!" 27Then he said to Thomas, "Put your finger here; see my hands. Reach out your hand and put it into my side. Stop doubting and believe."

28Thomas said to him, "My Lord and my God!"

29"Then Jesus told him, "Because you have seen me, you have believed; blessed are those who have not seen and yet have believed."

30Jesus did many other miraculous signs in the presence of his disciples, which are not recorded in this book. 31But these are written that you may believe that Jesus is the Christ, the Son of God, and that by believing you may have life in his name.

Romans 3:10, 23

10As it is written: "There is no one righteous, not even one; there is no one who understands, no one who seeks God. 23For all have sinned and fall short of the glory of God.

Romans 6:23

23For the wages of sin is death, but the gift of God is eternal life in Christ Jesus our Lord.

Romans 5:8

8But God demonstrates his own love for us in this: While we were still sinners, Christ died for us.

Romans 10:9-11

9If you confess with your mouth, "Jesus is Lord," and believe in your heart that God raised him from the dead, you will be saved. 10For it is with your heart that you believe and are justified, and it is with your mouth that you confess and are saved. 11As the Scripture says, "Anyone who trusts in him will never be put to shame."

Romans 6:3-5

3Or don't you know that all of us who were baptized into Christ Jesus were baptized into his death? 4We were therefore buried with him through baptism into death in order that, just as Christ was raised from the dead through the glory of the Father, we too may live a new life.

5If we have been united with him in his death, we will certainly also be united with him in his resurrection.

God Promises Eternal Life

John 3; Acts 16; 26; 1 John 5

Lesson Aims

Students will
- Locate cities related to this lesson's Scripture on a Bible map
- Demonstrate knowledge of the salvation process by identifying people who accepted God's gift of eternal life
- Express thanks to God for the plan of salvation

Materials

Bible Atlas Maps 1–3 (pp. 305-307)
Index to Maps (p. 308)
Bibles
memory verse poster boards used in Lessons 20 and 21
one object for passing per team

▼ Building Study Skills ▲

Post the memory-verse posters that were made for Lesson 20. Divide students into even teams and play this game. Give each team an object to pass such as a ball, a plate, a shoe, a broom, and so on. Teams line up in single file. Instruct teams how they will pass the object down the line. For example, the broom must sweep down the line. A shoe must be passed by the feet from foot to foot. A plate could be passed overhead and a ball between the legs. Players are to pass the object while quoting the memory verses. Everyone on the team recites the passage; the object is passed the entire time. When the object reaches the end of the line, it is to be passed back to the front of the line and so on until the complete verse has been quoted. Players who don't have the verses memorized may read from the posters. The winner is the team that passed the object through the most players. Play one round for each verse. This activity may also be used to review the books of the Bible.

Gather students together. Distribute Bible Atlas Maps 1–3. Say: **In today's lesson we will read about several Bible places. These places are Jerusalem, Caesarea, Damascus, and Philippi. We will use the atlas to find out where these cities are. Look at the Index to Maps. The names of the places on the maps are in alphabetical order. Let's begin with Jerusalem. What are the map coordinates of Jerusalem? There is one for each of the three maps. We are going to use Map 3. What are the map coordinates for Jerusalem on Map 3?** (C3) **Now find the grid on Map 3 where the column labeled C intersects with the row labeled 3. Put your finger on Jerusalem.**

Next have students locate Caesarea. Say: **The Caesarea listed in the index is Caesarea Philippi. This city is not the same as Caesarea. The Caesarea in today's lesson is on the coast of the Mediterranean Sea. It was a seaport town. It is found in the same grid as Jerusalem (C3) on Map 3. Look there to find it.**

Finally, assist students in locating Damascus (C3) and Philippi (A2) on Map 3. Say: **All four of these cities are mentioned in our Scripture text today.**

Distribute Bibles. Announce the following Scriptures one at a time; have all students locate the passages and read the verses to find these four cities. Use these verses: Acts 16:12 (Philippi); Acts 25:13 (Caesarea); Acts 26:10 (Jerusalem); and Acts 26:12 (Damascus).

Say: **Let's find out what happened in these cities.**

▼ Using Study Skills ▲

Distribute *He Who Has the Son Has Life.* Begin with the Philippian jailer. Find and read the Scripture passage and instruct students to place a check by each statement that describes the jailer. Some things are spelled out in the Scripture passage; some aren't. Discuss with the students what probably happened. Use what they know about the salvation process. The jailer asked, "What must I do to be saved?" Paul answered and spoke the word of the Lord to him. Did that include repentance and confession? Probably so. All the boxes in the first section of the jailer's could be checked, and the box next to "have God's gift of eternal life" should also be checked.

King Agrippa stopped listening to Paul tell about Jesus. He was almost persuaded to believe, but he choose not to believe. Only the first box in the first section should be checked along with "does not have God's gift of eternal life" in the second section.

When these two sections are completed, have students work silently on their own boxes. When they are finished, ask: **What do you need to do that you haven't done yet? What statements of yours are not checked? Which box did you check in the bottom section? Do you have life because you have the Son? Or do you need the Son?** Pray with the class or with individual students as you see the need.

Materials
He Who Has the Son Has Life
(p. 125)
Bibles
pencils

▼ Responding to Study ▲

Students will add the final three pages to their plan of salvation flip charts. When the flip chart is completed, students may flip through the chart page by page and see the plan of salvation or share the plan of salvation with someone else.

Explain the process as needed to the students. Ask them to select three half-sheets of construction paper of the same or different colors. They are to write the message of the card, then search magazines for pictures that illustrate the message. Help students design the following three cards: 5, 10, 12. (See page 124 for messages.)

When students are finished, have them discuss these cards. Read Card 5. Say: **Before any of us can believe that Jesus is God's Son, we must know who He is and what He did. We must hear about Jesus first. John 3:16, 17 tell us.**

Read Card 10. Say: **In our lesson today, we see that the Philippian jailer was baptized soon after he was told what to do to be saved. Jesus asks all of His followers to be baptized.**

Read Card 12. Say: **Jesus is the door to Heaven. There is only one way to Heaven and that way is Jesus.**

Have students add these three cards to the other nine cards and put the cards in order from one to twelve. Review the cards as needed with the group. Be sure they understand what each card teaches. If time permits, have students find a partner and present their flip charts to each other. Then have students place their cards in their file folders. Allow them to take the folders home this week. Encourage them to use their flip charts to share the plan of salvation with their friends and family.

Lead the class in prayer before continuing to the Reviewing Study Skills step: **Father, we thank You for the life You have given us through Your Son, Jesus. We ask Your help and blessing as we share these flip charts about Your plan of salvation with others. We pray for those who have not yet named You as Lord and Savior. Keep working in their lives and hearts that they may accept You. In Jesus' name, amen.**

Materials
colored construction paper cut
into half sheets
old magazines from which pictures can be removed
scissors
glue
file folders
students' work from Lessons
19, 20, and 21

▼ Reviewing Study Skills ▲

Materials
2 socks
dish towels, rags, or handker-
    chiefs for each student
16 plastic pop bottles or cans
index cards
tape
large playing area

Card 5
Message: Jesus died on the
    cross to save us from sin and
    eternal death.
"For God so loved the world
    that he gave his one and only
    Son, that whoever believes in
    him shall not perish but have
    eternal life. For God did not
    send his Son into the world
    to condemn the world, but
    to save the world through
    him" (John 3:16, 17).
Illustration: pictures with people
    from all walks and races of
    life.

Card 10
Message: We must be baptized.
Read Acts 16:25-34.
Illustration: picture of a body of
    water such as a lake or river.

Card 12
Message: God promised to
    bless us. His blessing comes
    through Jesus Christ who
    saves us from eternal death
    and gives us eternal life.
"And this is the testimony: God
    has given us eternal life, and
    this life is in his Son. He who
    has the Son has life; he who
    dies not have the Son of
    God does not have life"
    (1 John 5:11, 12).
Illustration: pictures of clouds,
    the sky, or something depict-
    ing Heaven.

Before class prepare the pop bottles by labeling them with the eight promises. Write each promise on separate index cards. Make two sets. Distinguish the sets from each other. For example, use all clear bottles for one and green for the other, or use two colors of labels. Attach the promises to the bottles.

In class have students play this version of Capture the Flag: Capture the Promises. Divide the playing area in half and divide the class into two teams. Assign each team one side of the playing area. Each team is to place its set of bottles in various locations within their territory. Each side determines an area for the jail. All players are to wear two flags (socks, handkerchiefs, etc.). These flags are to be tucked into their side pockets or into their pants, one on each side.

The object of the game is to capture all eight promises from the opposing team, to protect your own promises, and to snatch all the flags from the players on the opposing team. A promise is captured when a player crosses into his territory from the opposing team's territory with the labeled bottle. Players must wear flags. As long as a player has at least one flag, he is free from jail and can roam the entire playing area. Once both of his flags have been snatched, he must go to the jail area on the opposing team's side. A player can be freed from jail when his team has two flags from the opposing team to replace the ones that were snatched. Players are safe in their territory; their flags cannot be snatched.

Begin the game by having all players line up along the center line of the playing area. They are to recite the eight promises while performing the signs. After the group says "eternal life," play begins. When a team has captured all eight promises, that team is to put the promises in order, and recite them while performing the sign language motions. When finished, call the students together. Ask the winning team to lead the class in performing the signs and naming the promises one more time.

He Who Has the Son Has Life

"And this is the testimony: God has given us eternal life, and this life is in his Son. He who has the Son has life; he who does not have the Son of God does not have life" (1 John 5:11, 12).

Read about each person and check the boxes that describe each one. Who has the Son? Who has life? Who doesn't? Check the box beside each sentence that tells about each person.

Philippian Jailer
Read Acts 16:25-34

Did the Philippian jailer . . .
- ❏ hear the good news about Jesus?
- ❏ believe in the Lord Jesus?
- ❏ admit and repent from his sins?
- ❏ confess that Jesus is God's Son and his Savior?
- ❏ get baptized?

Did the Philippian jailer . . .
- ❏ have God's gift of eternal life?
- ❏ not have God's gift of eternal life?

King Agrippa
Read Acts 26:1-8, 12-16, 20, 22, 23, 27, 28

Did King Agrippa . . .
- ❏ hear the good news about Jesus?
- ❏ believe in the Lord Jesus?
- ❏ admit and repent from his sins?
- ❏ confess that Jesus is God's Son and his Savior?
- ❏ get baptized?

Did King Agrippa . . .
- ❏ have God's gift of eternal life?
- ❏ not have God's gift of eternal life?

Me
Read John 3:16, 17; 1 John 5:11, 12

Have I . . .
- ❏ heard the good news about Jesus?
- ❏ believed in the Lord Jesus?
- ❏ admitted and repented from my sins?
- ❏ confessed that Jesus is God's Son and my Savior?
- ❏ been baptized?

Do I . . .
- ❏ have God's gift of eternal life?
- ❏ not have God's gift of eternal life?

A Friend
Read John 3:16, 17; 1 John 5:11, 12

Has my friend . . .
- ❏ heard the good news about Jesus?
- ❏ believed in the Lord Jesus?
- ❏ admitted and repented from his sins?
- ❏ confessed that Jesus is God's Son and his Savior?
- ❏ been baptized?

Does my friend . . .
- ❏ have God's gift of eternal life?
- ❏ not have God's gift of eternal life?

Gospels Teach Us What Jesus Did

Bible Skills
Use Bible concordance and
   dictionary
Create a Gospel harmony

Memorize
Matthew 16:16

Memory Challenge
Luke 2:52; 12 disciples

Unit Overview

The word *gospel* means "good news." The books of Matthew, Mark, Luke and John are called Gospels because they tell the good news of Jesus' life, death, and resurrection. Matthew had been a tax collector. He and John, the fisherman, were companions of Jesus. Luke, the physician, traveled with Paul; Mark was a fellow worker with Peter. The book of Matthew, whose authorship is accepted but not stated in the book, emphasizes that Jesus is Messiah. Quoting from the Old Testament, Matthew's message was particularly helpful for those of Jewish heritage. Mark relates the events of Jesus' life. He seems more concerned with what the Son of God did than with what He said.

Luke carefully includes details that emphasize the human qualities of Jesus' life. Many believe that Luke's Gospel had particular appeal to the Greeks and that Mark's account met the needs of the Romans. Balancing the action-oriented book of Mark is the Gospel of John, which relates the conversations and discourses of Jesus.

Before Jesus began speaking for God on earth, John the Baptist was getting people ready to follow Jesus. He preached a baptism of repentance and told people that a mighty One was coming soon (Mark 1:1-8). Jesus had no sins to be forgiven, but He came to be baptized because He wanted to do everything that was right (Matthew 3:13-15). When Jesus was baptized, Heaven opened and the Holy Spirit descending like a dove, lighting on Him (Matthew 3:16). God himself spoke, saying that Jesus was His Son. God was pleased with Jesus' determination to fulfill all righteousness (Matthew 3:17).

Then came a time of testing (Matthew 4:1-11). This showed that Jesus really was the Son of God. He demonstrated His sinlessness as He faced temptation and did not give in. He could overcome the devil and his temptations because He knew Scripture (Matthew 4:4, 7, 10) and obeyed it. Knowing Bible verses is important in resisting temptations of the devil, but we must also obey. Even the devil knew Bible verses, but he failed to obey. Knowing and obeying the Bible helps us follow God rather than the devil and his desires.

Summary

Each of the lessons in this unit uses a harmony of the Gospels as a tool to show students the consistent similarities and subtle differences between the different Gospel writers' accounts of events in the life of Christ. In addition, the following concepts are presented:

Lesson 23 shows that Jesus relied on Scriptures to resist temptation.

Lesson 24 focuses on Jesus' disciples and how we need to become one.

Lesson 25 focuses on Jesus' authority to forgive sins, shown by His authority over this world.

Lesson 26 explains that God wants us to listen to Jesus and follow him.

Ancestors of Jesus

Mark the ancestors of Jesus on the *Time Line Segments* (pp. 309-314). Cut cross shapes from red construction paper. Attach them to the time line above the pictures representing Jesus' ancestors. Read the genealogy of Jesus in Matthew 1:1-17.

Point out that Jesus' genealogy is divided into three sections. Help students identify each section on the time line. From Abraham to King David covers the following eras: Patriarchs, Exodus and Conquest, Judges. From King David to after the exile covers these eras: Kings and Prophets and Exile. The final section covers ancestors from after the exile until the birth of Jesus. This includes the period of silence.

Ancestors of Jesus included on the time line are Abraham, Isaac, Jacob, Ruth, King David, Manasseh, Josiah, Joseph, and Mary.

Bonus: From the list of Jesus' ancestors, have students find the tribe from which Jesus came (Judah—Matthew 2:2). Help students recall that Jacob's sons were heads of the tribes of Israel. Judah was one of Jacob's sons. Judah was also the name that the tribes of Judah and Benjamin took when the nation of Israel split in two. God preserved the tribe of Judah because they were the tribe of Jesus.

Symbols of Miracles Treasure Hunt

John 20:30, 31 tells us that Jesus performed miracles so that we might believe that He is the Christ. Use this passage to introduce this project. Between the steps of the project, read or say the verse together again. By the end of project, ask volunteers to say the verse and to give examples of miracles Jesus did.

Begin by having students list miracles that Jesus did. They may recall His miracles, skim through the Gospels, or use a prepared list from a Bible study resource.

Next have students think of symbols for each miracle that would help them remember the miracle. For example, raising Lazarus could be a strip of cloth to represent the grave cloths in which he was wrapped. Make sure that the symbols can be easily obtained on the treasure hunt; that is, don't approve a symbol that would be difficult to find or unlikely for someone to give up for the hunt, such as a goldfish to represent the miraculous catch of fish from Luke 5. You may want to restrict symbols to items that would be found easily near your classroom. Have students write the name of each symbol on an index card.

When the symbols are prepared, divide the students into groups and divide the index cards equally among the groups. Set a time limit and have students find as many symbols as possible within that time limit.

When time is up and all students have returned, let the groups take turns showing a symbol and telling what miracle it represents. End the activity by having students restate John 20:30, 31 in their own words.

LESSON 23

Jesus Is Baptized and Tempted

Matthew 3, 4

Lesson Aims

Students will

- Write eyewitness accounts of an event and compare accounts with others
- Compare and contrast three Gospel accounts of Jesus' temptation
- Commit to fully rely on God (F.R.O.G.)

▼ Building Study Skills ▲

Materials
Bibles
Bible concordances
index cards
pencils

Divide the students into four teams. Put one team in each corner of the room. Arrange for a co-teacher or friend to come into the room at this point and give you an emergency phone message. Act, react as long as you wish, depending on class time available and tolerance level of your class! When the person leaves, explain to the students it was really a skit to test their powers of observation. Have each group take one minute and write down what happened. Let a spokesperson for each group read its account of what happened. Typically, there will be four varying accounts of the incident. Use this as a lead-in to a discussion of how all the Gospels are about the life of Christ, but from different viewpoints. Each writer witnessed the same life, but "saw" and was led by the Spirit to record different things.

Leave the students in teams. Have students open their Bibles, using the half trick to open to Psalms, then half the right half, which should put them in the book of Matthew. Have students find and read with a partner the Scriptures listed in Matthew 3. Give each team a concordance. Find other accounts of Jesus' baptism in the Gospels. Have each person write the other references on an index card. If time, find and read with a new partner the Scriptures listed in Mark. Find and read with a new partner the Scriptures listed in Luke. Call attention to the fact that Jesus' baptism is not recorded in John.

▼ Using Study Skills ▲

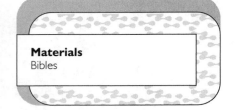

Materials
Bibles

Ask students to share their thoughts about what bread has to do with their study. As they discern that physical hunger was one way the devil tempted Jesus, lead them in discovering all the ways Jesus was tempted and how He responded. Have students find Matthew 4. Be a narrator (or delegate that task to one of your students) while reading verses 1-11.

Say: **The first temptation was to make bread of stones. After 40 days of fasting, Jesus had a real physical need. Jesus' answer was to quote Deuteronomy 8:3 and remain focused on God's purpose for Him. He had given up unlimited, independent use of His divine power in order to experience humanity fully. He resisted using His power to change the stones to bread. He had been in the desert to fast, not eat. He chose to wait for God's timing and trust that God would provide food at the best time for Him.**

The second temptation was to dare God to rescue Him. Note that the devil used Scripture, Psalm 91:11, 12, but misapplied it. Satan was using the real emotional need of security: will God protect, keep me safe? This

appealed to the weaknesses of pride, insecurity and a need to test God. Again, Jesus chose to answer by quoting Scripture, Deuteronomy 6:16, which told Him not to test God. He chose to obey and kept His focus on God's plan for His life.

The third temptation was to worship Satan! This was a combination of a real psychological need of power and significance and a possible doubt that in the end God will rule. This could have created an inappropriate desire for quick power, easy solutions, a need to prove equality with God, weaknesses we still face today. Once again, Jesus shows the importance of knowing and applying Scripture when tempted. He quotes the command of Deuteronomy 6:13 to worship and serve only God (knowledge). Rather than choosing earthly power and riches, Jesus chooses (action) to focus on the one and only true God, trusting God's plan and timing. Note that the devil left Jesus and angels came and attended Him.

For students who need more of a challenge, a concordance study of other times angels were involved in Jesus' life on earth could be done. Possibilities: announcing Jesus' birth to Mary, reassuring Joseph, naming Jesus, announcing Jesus' birth to the shepherds, protecting Jesus by sending his family to Egypt, ministering to Jesus in Gethsemane.

▼ Responding to Study ▲

Materials
Bibles
paper
pencils

Challenge the students to look up the temptation account in all of the Gospels, using header and footnote references given in their Bibles. Allow them to discover the temptations are only recorded in Matthew, Mark, and Luke (Matthew 4:1-11; Mark 1:12, 13; Luke 4:1-13). Say: **This account of Jesus' temptation is only in the first three Gospels. Matthew, Mark, and Luke are often called the Synoptic Gospels, meaning that they are written almost as if they were seen with the same eyes. There are some differences between these accounts, but that doesn't mean that one is correct and another is incorrect. Think about a group of people who are witnesses to a car accident. Each has his own perspective, and their stories may be different, but they're still talking about the same incident.** Divide the class into two teams, one with the assignment to come up with as many ways as they can think of that the accounts are alike, and the other to come up with as many ways as they can think of that the accounts are different. After a designated time, share their findings.

Ask: **Why do you think God would want to include in the Bible a story about Jesus being tempted by the devil?** (To show that Jesus was human, just like us; to show that Jesus was also God and not like us in how He responded to temptation.) Say: **When we read accounts like this in the Bible we see that temptation is common to all of us, even Jesus. However, we also see that with God's help, we can overcome temptation. These accounts also show us that God's Word is valuable for dealing with temptation and that if we know God's Word, we are better equipped to do God's will.**

Ask: **Why do you think God would want to give us three different accounts of this story?** (Allow students to share their thoughts.) **God knows that each of us are different; we have different ideas and opinions and ways we like to say and do things. Each of the writers of the Gospels had different audiences: Matthew wrote primarily for Jewish people, which is why he quotes so much from the Old Testament; Mark wrote mostly for Gentiles, people who aren't Jewish, and so he didn't quote any Old Testament Scriptures; Luke was writing for a specific person who needed to know the truth about what he was told about Jesus, so Luke focused on many details. It's better for us to have all three accounts so that we can see through the eyes of more people who knew and followed Jesus. It gives us a good idea of what kind of an example Jesus is to follow when we are tempted.**

▼ Reviewing Study Skills ▲

Materials
yarn
chalkboard or white board
chalk or dry-erase marker
poster board
die
pens
Fully Rely on God (p. 131)

Have students brainstorm ways they are tempted. Write temptations on the board or a large sheet of paper. Create a simple map on poster board with everyday locations on it: home, school, church, mall, sports field, car, movie theater, fast-foods places, and so on. A student rolls a die to move to a location, then shares a way he might be tempted at that location. Choose a topic that behavior represents, such as disobedience, stealing, cheating and look that word up in a Bible concordance to find out what the Bible has to say about it. Vary difficulty by working in teams or in pairs. Share findings with the group.

Say: **Pick a particular temptation you have in your life. Use the concordance to find Scriptures that would help you resist that temptation. Write one or more of those Scriptures on a card that you can carry with you in your backpack. When you find yourself confronted with that particular temptation this week, recall the Scripture and choose to act on it. Follow Jesus' example! Remember to pray each day for help from the Spirit to have the wisdom and strength to do what is pleasing to God. The devil would prefer we try to resist temptations alone with only our own power. Fully rely on God . . . F.R.O.G. Next time we meet, be prepared to share your frogs!**

Play a Books of the Bible game: Snap Concentration. Say: **When Jesus was tempted, He quoted Scripture from the Old Testament, the only Bible that existed at the time. Today, we have both the Old and New Testaments to help us when we are tempted. Jesus shows us that it is important to know the Scriptures so that's why we have been focusing on learning the books of the Bible and what each one says. Let's play a quick review game and see how well we remember the books of the Bible in order.**

Sit in a circle; pat both thighs twice, clap twice, snap the fingers on your right hand as you say "Genesis;" snap the fingers on your left hand as you say the name of the next spokesperson. That person continues in rhythm, on the right snap naming the next book of the Bible, on the left snap naming the next player. One misses when the next book is not said in rhythm. The object of the game is to see how many books can be named in order. Play until only one student remains. Or play a little less competitively by ending when you have been through the whole Bible, just the Old Testament, or just the New Testament. Vary according to the ability of your students and the time remaining.

Easier version: Pat, pat, clap, clap, right snap starts with Genesis, left snap says the next book of the Bible. Play continues around the circle instead of having to jump around naming the next player.

Whenever I am tempted to

_____,

I will remember to

Fully
  Rely
    On
      God!

Whenever I am tempted to

_____,

I will remember to

Fully
  Rely
    On
      God!

Whenever I am tempted to

_____,

I will remember to

Fully
  Rely
    On
      God!

Whenever I am tempted to

_____,

I will remember to

Fully
  Rely
    On
      God!

Whenever I am tempted to

_____,

I will remember to

Fully
  Rely
    On
      God!

Whenever I am tempted to

_____,

I will remember to

Fully
  Rely
    On
      God!

Whenever I am tempted to

_____,

I will remember to

Fully
  Rely
    On
      God!

Whenever I am tempted to

_____,

I will remember to

Fully
  Rely
    On
      God!

Jesus Called Disciples

Matthew 4, 9, 10

Lesson Aims

Students will

- Compare four different Gospels' accounts of the same event
- Define terms from today's Scripture
- Refute imaginary objections people might have for telling others about Jesus

---

Materials
Bibles
chalkboard and chalk or white board and dry-erase markers
Disciple Harmony Chart (p. 136)
pencils

▼ Building Study Skills ▲

Before class, create a *Disciple Harmony Chart* on the board.

The kids will work in teams to complete the chart. For your reference, see the *Sample Harmony* on page 133.

Say: **All four books in the Bible that tell the story of Jesus—Matthew, Mark, Luke, and John—stand alone, each emphasizing different things in Jesus' life and ministry. But when these are blended into one chronological account, or harmonized, we get a better understanding of Jesus' travels and appreciate the unity of their messages.**

Divide the students into four groups, one for each Gospel. Distibute a *Disciple Harmony Chart* to each team. Kids can work as a team, but for each question they must choose a different spokesperson for the group. When the group has decided on an answer, the spokesperson will stand to indicate to the class that that team has completed its task. Say: **Today we will explore the stories of Jesus calling the disciples. Each team will read the story from a different Gospel, and together we'll complete the harmony chart on the board.**

As time permits, continue until each team has shared their findings. Take time to compare and contrast the details introduced in the four Gospels.

Materials
Bibles
Bible concordances
Sample Bible Dictionary (pp. 301, 302)
paper
pencils

▼ Using Study Skills ▲

Let students work with partners. Pair strong Bible students with those needing extra help. Look up Matthew 9:35-38. If you have some students who can already look up Scriptures easily, give them the word *compassion* and tell them to use a concordance to find a story when Jesus had compassion for the crowds following Him.

Read the passage and have students look up the word *shepherd* in the *Sample Bible Dictionary* and answer these questions:

- **What guide words are on the page where you found the word *shepherd*?**
- **How many definitions of shepherd were given?** (three)
- **Write one new fact about sheep you learned from the dictionary.**

After a reasonable amount of time, ask pairs to share answers with another pair.

Say: **Jesus went throughout the villages and towns teaching in their synagogues, which were religious gathering places on the Sabbath and schools during the week. He preached that the kingdom of Heaven has come, that God is with us, and that He cares for us. He healed not only physical sickness, which authenticated His teaching and preaching, but also offered**

Sample Harmony

Matthew	Mark	Luke	John
Matthew 4:18-22	Mark 1:16-20	Luke 5:1-11	John 1:35-42
Jesus was walking beside the Sea of Galilee	Jesus walked beside the Sea of Galilee	Jesus was standing by the Lake of Gennesaret	
He saw two brothers, Simon	He saw Simon	He saw Simon	
and his brother	and his brother	and his brother	Simon Peter's brother
Andrew	Andrew	Andrew	Andrew
They were casting a net into the lake because they were fishermen	casting a net into the lake because they were fishermen	fishermen	casting a net into the lake because they were fishermen
Jesus said, "Come follow me. I will make you fishers of men."	Jesus said, "Come follow me. I will make you fishers of men."	Jesus said, "Don't be afraid. From now on you will catch men."	Jesus said, "You will be called Cephas."
They immediately left their nets	At once they left their nets		
and followed Jesus.	and followed him.		
Jesus went farther	When he had gone a little farther		
They were James and John, the sons of Zebedee	He saw James and John, the sons of Zebedee	James and John, the sons of Zebedee	
They were in a boat	They were in a boat	in the other boat	
They were preparing their nets	preparing their nets.		
Jesus called them	Jesus called them		
Immediately they left the boat and their father	They left their father Zebedee in the boat	left everything	
They followed Jesus	and followed him	and followed him	they followed Jesus

spiritual healing. Crowds began to follow Him. Jesus had compassion on them since many needed to be shown how to follow. There were only a few workers. Jesus instructed His disciples to pray for more workers, still good advice for today. The list of those who first chose to follow His call is found in Matthew 10:2-5, and it includes people from all walks of life: common people and uncommon leaders, rich and poor, educated and uneducated. God has a purpose for everyone, even those who seem small and insignificant.

Lead a prayer for God to send out more workers into His harvest field.

▼ Responding to Study ▲

Before class, prepare a "Fishing for Knowledge" center. Make fishing poles with magnets on the strings to snag, from a goldfish bowl or blue paper lake, fish-shaped cards with paper clips on the mouth. Prepare fish with words to look up from today's Scripture references (Matthew 4:18-22; 9:9-13, 35-38; 10:2-5). Put one word or phrase, such as fisherman, Pharisees, sinners, tax collector, righteous, synagogues, compassion, shepherd, disciples or apostles, and its Scripture reference on each fish. Put the fish in the lake you have created. When students snag a fish, have them write the dictionary definition of the word or phrase on it. Display the catch on the wall or bulletin board covered with a net for background. Refer to the definitions while doing the Bible story activities. Have several Bible dictionaries available.

Say: **Jesus called His disciples in different ways from different places, but the best example for us is when He called fishermen. In those days, fishermen were not very high in society; they worked hard both day and night; they probably smelled bad; and they probably didn't have much education. However, to show His power and the power of the good news, Jesus called simple fishermen and made them powerful disciples. We are supposed to do the same thing. We aren't supposed to go and find movie stars and millionaires; we're supposed to go and make disciples from among our friends and families and everywhere we go.**

Ask: **Do you think of yourself as a great leader or someone who can make lots of disciples for Jesus? Some people are really good at it. Others don't think they are because they think that maybe they aren't good at speaking in public or maybe they don't know enough about the Bible; others worry that people might know how bad they were before they became Christians. Jesus doesn't care about all that; He picked people nobody would have guessed would be great leaders, and they started the church. When we think about the disciples, we shouldn't just think of them as a list of names to remember; they are heroes of the Bible, of the church. When we remember their names, we remember the work that they did and how they followed Jesus.**

As a class, brainstorm to see how many of the 12 disciples they know. Use a concordance to find a list of all the 12 disciples (Matthew 10:2). Have the class use a Bible dictionary to find out some information about each one. Have the class write down what they learn about each one.

Materials
Bibles
Bible dictionary
fishing poles with magnets on strings
paper clips
paper fish
fish bowl or blue construction paper to make a lake
fishnet
goldfish crackers

Option
In keeping with the fisherman theme, enjoy eating goldfish crackers while searching! Or use individual packets of fish crackers as a reward for the top three fishermen, or top boy and top girl, since this age loves competition.

▼ Reviewing Study Skills ▲

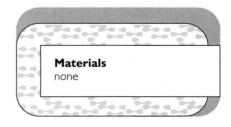

Materials
none

Say: **The disciples immediately left their boat and nets (material posses-
sions) and father (family) and followed Jesus. The Pharisees were sure
they were righteous (right with God) and had no need to follow Him. The
first step in following Jesus is acknowledging our need and admitting we
don't know all the answers. Jesus is concerned about reaching out to all
people: those who are living in sin and people who are more concerned
with appearing to be good than obeying God. What are some times or
places we might be like the Pharisees? like the disciples?**

Divide the class into groups of two or three. Assign each group one of the
groups of people mentioned in today's verses (Pharisees, disciples, fishermen, tax
collectors, etc.). Tell the students that everyone in their group is from the same
group they were assigned (everyone is a shepherd, etc.) and that everyone is a disciple of Jesus. One person in the group starts by saying what's bad about himself.
(Shepherds probably smell like sheep and so it's hard to get near people to talk to
them about Jesus.) Someone else then says a way that the negative can become a
positive. (If you smell bad, you could talk to farmers who work with manure or
talk to perfume salespeople at the mall.) Then that person says something negative and the other person turns it into something positive. Have each group go
through a few cycles like this.

Say: **Even though Jesus told His disciples to pray for more workers, He
wants us to know that we need to be prepared to be a worker. Many people
are ready to give their lives to Christ if someone would show them how.
What Scriptures would you share with someone like that?** Review the
Scriptures about salvation learned in Unit 5; then pray for more workers.

Disciple Harmony Chart

What Happened?	**Matthew** Matthew 4:18-22	**Mark** Mark 1:16-20	**Luke** Luke 5:1-11	**John** John 1:35-42
Where was Jesus?				
What was He doing?				
Who else was there?				
What were they doing?				
What did Jesus say?				
What happened then?				

  **LESSON 24**

Jesus Did Miracles Because He Is the Son of God

LESSON 25

Matthew 9

Lesson Aims

Students will

- Fill out a harmony chart for three Gospel accounts of the four friends who brought the paralyzed man to Jesus
- Express confidence that, because Jesus could perform miracles, He can forgive our sins
- Participate in a "memory verse auction"

▼ Building Study Skills ▲

As students arrive, distribute the paper and pens. Ask them to write down all of the instances of Jesus' miracles that they can think of. When everyone has arrived, divide the class into teams of two or three. Say: **Jesus performed many healing miracles. Some are recorded only once; others are recorded in two or more of the Gospels. Let's have a race to see how many different accounts of miracles we can find in the Gospels. Use your concordance to find the references to the stories you wrote down when you first arrived.**

When the students have had a few minutes to search the concordances and their lists of miracles, bring the class together and ask: **How many different accounts did you find? Did anyone find the account of the paralyzed man whose friends brought him to Jesus? In how many of the Gospels is the story of the paralyzed man recorded?** (three)

Have the students read the three accounts (Matthew 9:1-8; Mark 2:1-12; Luke 5:17-26). **Did you notice any differences between the three accounts? Why do you think there are differences included in the different Gospels? God included this story in these three Gospels so that the people reading the story would know about Jesus' power to heal and to forgive. The reason we see three different accounts of the same story is that there are three different authors who were writing for different audiences. Matthew, a disciple of Jesus, was writing primarily for the Jews; he included details that would matter to his Jewish audience. Mark was writing primarily for Gentiles, so he focused on details that would matter to them. Luke was writing to his friend Theophilus who wanted to know the details of what he had heard about Jesus, so Luke included many details that would have helped his friend believe. Let's take a few minutes to find the differences between the three accounts.**

▼ Using Study Skills ▲

Distribute copies of the *Healing Harmony Chart.* Say: **Jesus stepped into a boat, crossed over the Sea of Galilee, and returned to the town of Capernaum. He had gone there to live when He left Nazareth to begin His ministry, and in doing so He fulfilled prophecy. Jesus went throughout the region of Galilee teaching in their synagogues, preaching the good news of**

Materials
Bibles
Bible concordances
paper
pens

Materials
Healing Harmony Chart (p. 140)
Bibles

the kingdom and healing every disease and sickness among the people. News about him spread quickly. People brought to Him all who were ill and He healed them. Large crowds followed Him.

As Jesus came to His own town, Capernaum, some men brought to Him another man who was paralyzed. The crowds were so great, the only way they could get their friend to Jesus was to take out some of the roof and let him down in front of Jesus. When Jesus saw the faith of the friends and the man who was paralyzed, He first encouraged the man by giving him peace and assuring him of his spiritual well-being because of his faith saying, "Your sins are forgiven."

Some of the religious teachers there thought to themselves, *Forgiving sins is something only God can do*. They decided Jesus had committed a great crime, blasphemy, which was punishable by death (Leviticus 24:16). By telling someone his sins were forgiven, Jesus was claiming to be God. The teachers of the law refused to even consider that Jesus was Emmanuel, God with us.

Because Jesus *is* God's Son, He knew their thoughts! Jesus asked them why they entertained evil thoughts in their hearts. To show them He did have authority on earth to forgive sins, Jesus said to the man who was paralyzed, "Get up, take your mat and go home." The man did what Jesus said. The crowd was filled with awe, and they praised God. Matthew and the other Gospel writers recorded only a few of the people who were touched and healed by Jesus. Enough were recorded that we can be able to know Him and choose to be His disciples today. Miracles point people to God. They are acts of love by One who is love.

Divide the class into three groups. Assign one of the passages on the *Healing Harmony Chart* to each of the groups. Instruct the students to fill out the chart for their reference. When everyone has filled out their section, go over each section and try to compile one list that shows all the details and puts them into chronological order. Here is a guide for checking their work:

1. Jesus was in Capernaum (Mark 2:1).

2. Pharisees and teachers of the law were there (Luke 5:17).

3. There was no room to get in the house where Jesus was preaching (Mark 2:2; Luke 5:19).

4. The power of the Lord to heal was present (Luke 5:17).

5. Some men brought a paralyzed man with them on a mat (Matthew 9:2; Mark 2:3; Luke 5:18).

6. Four men carried their friend (Mark 2:3).

7. Because there was no room, they took the man to the roof, opened a hole in the tiles, and lowered the mat in front of Jesus (Mark 2:4; Luke 5:19).

8. Jesus saw the faith of the men (Matthew 9:2; Mark 2:5; Luke 5:20).

9. Jesus told the man, "Your sins are forgiven" (Matthew 9:2; Mark 2:5; Luke 5:20).

10. The Pharisees and teachers thought to themselves that Jesus had committed blasphemy (Matthew 9:3; Mark 2:7; Luke 5:21).

11. They thought, "Only God can forgive sins" (Mark 2:7; Luke 5:21).

12. Jesus knew their hearts and thoughts (Matthew 9:4; Mark 2:8; Luke 5:22).

13. Jesus asked them if it was easier to heal a man or to say that his sins are forgiven (Matthew 9:5; Mark 2:9; Luke 5:23).

14. Jesus said to them, "That you may know that the Son of Man has authority on earth to forgive sins . . ." (Matthew 9:6; Mark 2:10; Luke 5:24).

15. Jesus said to the paralyzed man, "Get up, take your mat" and walk/go home (Matthew 9:6; Mark 2:11; Luke 5:24).

16. The man got up (Matthew 9:7; Mark 2:12; Luke 5:25).

17. The man praised God (Luke 5:25).

18. The crowds were awed and amazed (Matthew 9:8; Mark 2:12; Luke 5:26).

19. The crowds praised God (Matthew 9:8; Mark 2:12; Luke 5:26).

20. The crowds said, "We have never seen anything like this!" (Mark 2:12).

21. The crowds said, "We have seen remarkable things today" (Luke 5:26).

▼ Responding to Study ▲

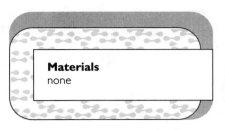

Materials
none

Say: **There are only a few differences between the stories. Most of the differences are a matter of having a few more details. None of the stories conflicts with each other. Isn't it amazing that three different accounts of the same story would support each other so well? These accounts help us in a number of ways. While they show that Jesus had the power of God to heal the sick, and while the miracle showed the Pharisees that Jesus had the authority to forgive sins, they show that and more to us. In addition to showing us that Jesus is the Son of God and therefore has authority to forgive our sins, these accounts show us that God's Word is trustworthy. If we are able to harmonize the accounts, show how they are similar and do not contradict each other, we can show others that God's Word can be trusted.**

Say: **Think about the fact that Jesus knew what the Pharisees and teachers were thinking. Jesus knows our thoughts, even if no one else does. We can't fool Him. He knew that they did not have faith in Him. Then think about the men who brought their friend. Even though there was no room to get into the house where Jesus was teaching, they didn't give up. They even dug a hole in the roof! When Jesus saw the man on a mat, lowered from the roof, He knew their hearts and that they had faith in Him. Sometimes we wonder why Jesus did all the miracles we read in the Bible. Jesus could have healed every sick person, but that wasn't His purpose. In this one instance of healing, Jesus revealed His whole purpose: to forgive sins.**

Divide the class into pairs. Have the students take turns answering the following reflective questions.

• **Why did Jesus heal people instead of telling them their sins were forgiven?** (He had the authority to forgive sins; He wanted people to put their faith in Him and not be looking for a "simple" thing like healing.)

• **Why did Jesus confront the Pharisees and teachers when they were thinking He had committed blasphemy?** (He especially wanted them to know who He was, since they probably should have had the faith the four friends exhibited; they had wrong ideas about who the Messiah was supposed to be and what He was supposed to do.)

• **What do you think this means for us?** (We should trust God to forgive our sins through Jesus; we should believe that Jesus has the authority and power to heal and to forgive sins; we can trust God's Word.)

▼ Reviewing Study Skills ▲

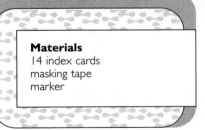

Materials
14 index cards
masking tape
marker

Before class, write each word of the memory verse and the reference on an index card. Tape each card in order upside down with a strip of tape across the top edge, so that it is "hinged" and so that, when the card is flipped up, it will be readable. Then roll a small piece of tape and place it on the back of the card so that, when it is flipped up, it will stick to the wall. Flip all the cards up so that the students will be able to read the verse.

Help the students remember the unit memory verse with a memory verse auction. Divide the class into two teams. Tell the class that the two teams will bid against each other for how many cards they can take away and still recite the memory verse. Tell them that they will get a point for every card that is hidden. However, if they make a mistake, the other team gets their points. Start the "bidding" by asking, **Which team can recite the verse with no cards showing?** Keep asking, adding a card, until one team signals that they can do it. If nobody responds, try going through the verse a few times as a group until someone feels he can start removing cards.

Using your Bible, try to show how each of the Gospel accounts of this story are alike and not alike. Read the questions. Find the answers to the questions for each Gospel account. Some of the Gospels may not have all the same answers; leave those columns blank.

What Happened?	Matthew 9:1-8	Mark 2:1-12	Luke 5:17-26
Where was Jesus?			
Who else was there?			
What was the problem?			
Who arrived?			
What did they do?			
What did Jesus say?			
What did the Pharisees and teachers think?			
What did Jesus know?			
What did Jesus say then?			
What did the man do?			
What did the crowd do?			

Jesus Showed God's Glory

Matthew 17

Lesson Aims

Students will
- State reasons why people choose to disobey God
- Write an informal harmony of three Gospel accounts of the transfiguration
- Grasp the significance of the transfiguration as proof that Jesus is the Messiah

▼ Building Study Skills ▲

Before class, create a center of all the ways we transmit messages today. Include as many as you have time and resources to collect. Some suggestions are cell phones, a TV, a radio, CDs, earphones, computers, stationery, and magnetic message boards.

As students arrive, distribute copies of the *Listen to Him!* page. Have students fill out the page. When all students have arrived and have had a chance to fill out the page, encourage the students to share their responses.

Ask: **How many of you have some of these objects at home? What is their purpose?** (to help us communicate with each other) **Why is it important for us to communicate?** (It helps us keep our relationships strong; it keeps us in contact with people we know and love.) **What would happen if this telephone started to ring? What would be the proper response?** (to answer it) **What would happen if I didn't answer it?** (You wouldn't know who was trying to call you; you wouldn't know why someone was trying to call you; it could have been important.) Say: **It's great that we have devices like telephones and cell phones to communicate with people all over the world, but if we don't use them correctly, they're useless; we can't communicate. The point is we have to listen with our ears or eyes for communication to take place.**

It's very much like how we are supposed to communicate with God. He has given us His Word in the Bible so that we would know what He wants us to say and do and how we can relate to Him better. The Bible is the most widely published book in all of history. There are millions of Bibles around the world. However, if we look at the TV or listen to the radio or read the newspaper, do we see a world that is listening to God? It's not enough to have the Bible or even to read it; we have to do what it says. We have to listen to God.

Ask: **Why do you think that, even though the Bible is so widely available, so few people do what God wants them to do?** (People choose to disobey; some people don't believe what it says.) **Why don't some people believe what the Bible says?** (They think it is made-up stories; they think that, because the stories happened so long ago, they don't apply to our lives today.) **These are some very common reasons why people don't listen to God. Today we are going to look at accounts of a time when God himself showed that Jesus is the Messiah and that we should listen to Him.**

Materials

Listen to Him! (p. 146)
pens
examples of communication devices: telephone, fax machine, computer, cell phone, CD player, radio, TV, stationery

▼ Using Study Skills ▲

Materials
Bibles
Bible concordances
Transfiguration Harmony Chart
  (p. 145)
pens

Have students turn to Matthew 17:1-13. Read the passage aloud to the class. Say: **This story is often called the transfiguration of Jesus. To be transfigured means to be changed in appearance, usually in a glorious way. In this account, we see that Jesus' appearance had changed. God was making a strong point to the disciples who witnessed the event. He was showing that Jesus was definitely the Messiah. About a week before this event happened, Jesus asked the disciples what the people thought about Him. The disciples told Him that the people thought that He was John the Baptist raised from the dead or Elijah or one of the other prophets. Then Jesus asked the disciples who they thought He was. Peter answered saying, "You are the Christ, the Son of the living God." Jesus told His disciples that this was the foundation of His kingdom. After this, Jesus predicted that He would die. Peter, thinking about the future kingdom that Jesus had spoken about, took Jesus aside and rebuked Him. He told Jesus that this would never happen to Him. Obviously Peter didn't understand what the kingdom was all about; Jesus tried to set him straight. Then we come to this account when Jesus took His three closest disciples with Him.**

Divide the students into teams of three. Challenge each group to discover how many of the Gospels record the event of the transfiguration. Since they already know it is in Matthew, each team could take one other Gospel to explore for the answer. Allow them to use the concordances to try to find some key words in the other Gospels, such as Peter, James, John, mountain, Moses, and Elijah. Lead them to find the accounts in Mark 9:2-12 and Luke 9:28-36. Pass out the *Transfiguration Harmony Chart* and allow each team to work on one of the passages, answering the questions and noting the verses in which the answers are found. Use the following list to check their work.

1. Six days after Peter's confession and the prediction of Jesus' death (Matthew 17:1; Mark 9:2).
2. Eight days after Peter's confession and the prediction of Jesus' death (Luke 9:28).
3. Jesus took Peter, James, and John with him to a mountain (Matthew 17:1; Mark 9:2; Luke 9:28).
4. They went to pray (Luke 9:28).
5. This happened while Jesus was praying (Luke 9:29).
6. Jesus' appearance was transfigured (Matthew 17:2; Mark 9:2).
7. His face shone brightly, like the sun (Matthew 17:2; Luke 9:29).
8. His clothes became bright white, as light or flashes of lightning (Matthew 17:2; Mark 9:3; Luke 9:29).
9. They saw Moses and Elijah speaking to Jesus (Matthew 17:3; Mark 9:4; Luke 9:30, 31).
10. Moses and Elijah spoke with Jesus concerning His departure, which would happen from Jerusalem (Luke 9:31).
11. Peter and the others were sleepy but became fully awake when they saw all this (Luke 9:32).
12. Peter spoke when Moses and Elijah began to leave (Luke 9:33).
13. Peter said to Jesus, "It is good for us to be here," and he offered to build three shelters (Matthew 17:4; Mark 9:5; Luke 9:33).
14. Peter and the others were frightened (Mark 9:6).
15. Peter didn't know what he was saying (Mark 9:6; Luke 9:33).
16. A bright cloud surrounded all of them (Matthew 17:5; Mark 9:7; Luke 9:34).
17. The disciples were afraid (Luke 9:34).
18. A voice spoke from the cloud (Matthew 17:5; Mark 9:7; Luke 9:35).
19. The voice said, "This is my son . . ." (Matthew 17:5; Mark 9:7; Luke 9:35).
20. The voice said, "Whom I love . . ." (Matthew 17:5; Mark 9:7).
21. The voice said, "Whom I have chosen . . ." (Luke 9:35).

22. The voice said, "With him I am well pleased" (Matthew 17:5).

23. The voice said, "Listen to him" (Matthew 17:5; Mark 9:7; Luke 9:35).

24. The disciples fell on their faces, terrified (Matthew 17:6).

25. Jesus touched them and said, "Get up. Don't be afraid" (Matthew 17:7).

26. They saw no one but Jesus (Matthew 17:8; Mark 9:8; Luke 9:36).

27. Jesus told His disciples not to tell anyone until the Son of Man had been raised from the dead (Matthew 17:9; Mark 9:9).

28. The disciples kept the matter to themselves (Mark 9:10; Luke 9:36).

29. They discussed among themselves what "rising from the dead" meant (Mark 9:10).

30. They asked Jesus why the "teachers of the law say that Elijah must come first" (Matthew 17:10; Mark 9:11).

31. Jesus said that Elijah does come (Matthew 17:11; Mark 9:12).

32. Jesus said that Elijah had come (Matthew 17:12; Mark 9:13).

33. Jesus said that the world did not recognize Elijah (Matthew 17:12).

34. Jesus said that the world did what they pleased with Elijah (Matthew 17:12; Mark 9:13).

35. Jesus said that the Son of Man would suffer in the same way (Matthew 17:12; Mark 9:12).

36. The disciples knew that Jesus was talking about John the Baptist (Matthew 17:13).

Say: **The Jews were waiting for the Messiah. He would finally fulfill the promises God gave Abraham. They were not sure when He would come, but the prophets had given them some clues. One is found in Malachi 4:4, 5.** Read the passage. Ask: **Does anyone notice anything similar about this Old Testament passage and the ones we've been studying today?** (They all include references to Moses and Elijah.) **The prophets said that the Messiah would come after Elijah; Malachi wasn't speaking about the real Elijah but someone who was like him.** Have a student look up and read Luke 1:11-17. **We saw that the disciples realized that Jesus was talking about John the Baptist when He was talking about Elijah coming and the world not knowing it was Him. This passage from Luke explains that John's ministry was prophesied to his father Zechariah, that it would be in the spirit of Elijah. Jesus confirms this. The reason why Moses appears in both the passage from Malachi and then in the transfiguration account is to show why the Messiah was to come—to restore the relationship between God and man that was broken because of our disobedience to the law.**

▼ Responding to Study ▲

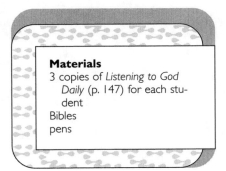

Materials
3 copies of *Listening to God Daily* (p. 147) for each student
Bibles
pens

Say: **When the disciples saw Moses and Elijah and heard the voice of God, they realized Jesus was more than a great leader, a good example, and a great prophet. He was God's Son. Their response to the realization of this profound truth was to fall down in worship, terrified. Israelites believed seeing God meant death (Exodus 33:20). Jesus came and touched them. He told them to get up and not to be afraid. Jesus knew they did not fully understand what they had seen and could not explain what they didn't understand. Peter, James, and John knew that Jesus was the Messiah, but they had much more to learn about the significance of His death and resurrection.**

This account of Jesus' transfiguration also teaches us the value of the whole Bible. The Jews often referred to their Scriptures as the "Law and the Prophets" because they relied on the law of Moses and the words of the prophets to remind them about God's holiness, His judgment, and His forgiveness. It is important for us to remember these things as well. These

writings were meant by God to show us that God has a plan and that, if we listen to Him, we will be able to accept that plan through Jesus. So, we must remember to seek His truth and listen to Him through His Word.

This week I'm going to challenge you to develop a regular habit of listening to God. One of the best ways is to read your Bible as often as you can. I have a guide that can help you do that. For the next three weeks, I want you to try to read your Bible every day and look for God's truth. Write down the verses that you read and the truths that you find in them. Then try to write down at least one specific way you can do something to show that you are listening to God. Let's start with the same verse. Distribute the copies of the *Listening to God Daily* sheet. Have students turn to Matthew 16:13-17. Instruct them to spend a few minutes reading the passage and filling in the blanks on "Sunday" of the first sheet. Ask students to choose one area to improve in their listening. Say: **Listen to God this week by reading His Word daily. If you do this before beginning the day's activities, in the evening you can reflect on how knowing those truths helped during that day. Write down what happened; be ready to share with the group next time we meet.**

Remember to do this yourself, so you can lead by example and share your story first when the class is back together again. Pray with the students: **God, show each of us this week the Scriptures, truths, words You want us to hear in Your Word. Help us listen to the Holy Spirit as to how we can use those truths each day. Help us to be willing to share and encourage each other with examples of how you are working in our lives. Thank You for Jesus. In His name we pray, amen.**

▼ Reviewing Study Skills ▲

Materials
masking tape
Bible Cards (p. 297, 298)
index cards
markers
beanbag

Before class, prepare eight index cards by writing each of the eight Bible divisions on them (four with the Old Testament divisions of Law, History, Poetry, and Prophecy; four with the New Testament divisions of Gospels, History, Letters, and Prophecy). Using masking tape, create a hopscotch board on the floor with eight squares. Label each of the squares by taping the index cards down.

Remind the students that the Bible has 66 books with one message: how God brought salvation to each of us. Say: **All the books of the Bible tell us something important about God's plan for our salvation. Bible scholars call this unity. The books of the Bible are arranged in two Testaments or agreements God made with man. The Old Testament tells us about God's old agreement with man, the agreement He made to send Jesus. The events in the Old Testament happened before Jesus was born. The New Testament tells us about God's new agreement with man, the agreement He made to save us through His Son, Jesus. The New Testament tells about the life and teachings of Jesus. It tells us about the growth of Jesus' church. It promises that Jesus will return.**

Using the *Bible Cards,* put one or two books from each section in their respective hopscotch squares. Put the remainder of the cards face up on the floor near the game board. Each player will take a turn throwing the beanbag marker to the next square, naming another book that belongs in that square before he can hop. Continue adding the cards to the game board until all are in their proper divisions. When a division has all its books, that will become a "free" square.

Transfiguration Harmony Chart

Compare the Gospel accounts of this event by answering the questions. Note the verse from each passage in which you find the answer.

What Happened?	Matthew 17:1-13	Mark 9:2-12	Luke 9:28-36
When did this happen?			
Who went, and where did they go?			
Describe Jesus' appearance.			
Who did they see with Jesus?			
What did Peter say?			
What surrounded all of them?			
What sound came from the cloud?			
What did the voice say?			
How did the disciples react to what they saw and heard?			

Listen to Him!

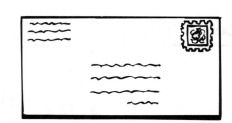

In the accounts of Jesus' transfiguration, God said that we must listen to Jesus. Even though Jesus lived on earth about 2,000 years ago, His disciples wrote down what He said and did so that we can obey Him even today. Choose two or three devices on this page and write down a way we can listen to God with each one.

LESSON 26

Listening to God Daily

Listening to God Daily

Each day when you read your Bible, write down the passage that you read. Then write down the truth you learned from God and the way you plan to listen to God and follow that truth during the week. Try to write down specific plans for at least one action each week.

Sunday
Bible verses I read: _____

Truth I learned: _____

How I plan to listen to God: _____

Monday
Bible verses I read: _____

Truth I learned: _____

How I plan to listen to God: _____

Tuesday
Bible verses I read: _____

Truth I learned: _____

How I plan to listen to God: _____

Wednesday
Bible verses I read: _____

Truth I learned: _____

How I plan to listen to God: _____

Thursday
Bible verses I read: _____

Truth I learned: _____

How I plan to listen to God: _____

Friday
Bible verses I read: _____

Truth I learned: _____

How I plan to listen to God: _____

Saturday
Bible verses I read: _____

Truth I learned: _____

How I plan to listen to God: _____

Bible Skills
Use Bible dictionary and
concordance

Memorize
Matthew 6:6-13

Memory Challenge
1 John 4:7-12

Unit Overview

Before the age of eight, most children exposed to a Christian environment have been presented basic Bible stories and probably some instruction on applying the stories to their lives. For the most part, they have been spoon-fed biblical knowledge but have yet to embark upon the rewarding adventure of studying the Bible for themselves. They have not had the opportunity to independently read a Bible passage and use study tools such as a dictionary and concordance to try to make sense of what God is saying to them. Equipping children with a basic working knowledge of the Bible, Bible study skills, and how to use study tools such as a Bible dictionary and concordance enables them to discover for themselves how to understand and correctly handle the Word of truth. While deciphering the Bible can sometimes be daunting to even the most mature Christian, developing these study skills as a child makes God's roadmap for life readily accessible and helps them to develop a deeper understanding of who He is and His will for their lives. Regular study will also give them an assurance of their salvation. Becoming proficient in the study of God's Word is a lifelong quest and requires time spent having hands-on experiences in the Word.

In this unit, students will dig into the Gospels of Matthew and Luke and learn basic truths of life from Jesus Christ, the master teacher himself. Specifically, they will be guided through hands-on Bible study drills that explore Christ's teaching the Beatitudes, how to pray, and parables. They will discover that Jesus taught by instruction, example, and in parables and how to apply His lessons to their lives. The skills emphasized will be how and when to use a Bible dictionary, memorization of Scripture, locating Scripture through the use of a concordance, and paraphrasing.

Summary

Students will learn in **Lesson 27** that we ought to rejoice and be glad in God's blessings and hope for our ultimate reward in Heaven.

Lesson 28 focuses on the Lord's Prayer. Students will look at how Jesus prayed and use the same elements in their own prayers.

In **Lesson 29** students will learn that spiritual growth involves hearing God's Word and doing what it says.

Students will celebrate God's love in **Lesson 30,** and express their love for Him through language and art.

Lesson 31 encourages Christians to show mercy to others as God has shown it to us.

Promised, Provided, Presented

This variation of the game "Rock, Paper, Scissors" helps your students understand and remember God's plan for salvation. The symbol for "God promised salvation" is to hold both hands out with just the index fingers extended, as if pointing to other people because God promised salvation to many people from Adam and Eve to Abraham to us today. The symbol for "God provided for salvation" is to hold one hand out with palm up and striking the palm with the other fist, as if pounding a nail into the hand which represents Jesus sacrifice on the cross. The symbol for "God presented salvation" is to extend both hands with palms up, as if offering a gift to someone.

Choose one student to be the leader. This student will say, "Promised, provided, presented" in three beats. On the third word and beat, the leader and students will extend their hands making one of the symbols. Each student who matches the leader's symbol gets one point. For every student who does not match the leader, the leader gets a point. Change leaders every round. After each student has had a turn to lead, tally the points. The student with the most points wins.

At the end of the game, lead the students through reciting the plan together as you do the hand motions.

Red-Letter Sword Drill

Divide the class into two teams. Give each team a concordance. Make sure each student has a Bible. Choose one person from each team to be the reader. Using a Bible with red letters that indicate the words Jesus spoke, locate a statement from Jesus in the Gospels and read it aloud to the class. Say "Go!" and have the class look in their concordances to locate the verse using key words from the verse. When a team thinks they have found it, they call out "Got it!" Their reader will then read the reference aloud and say, "Go!" Then each individual must search for the verse. The first person to find the verse reads it aloud. If the verse matches what was read, the team that found the reference in the concordance gets a point. If the verse does not match, everyone goes back to searching the concordance to find the correct verse. The team whose individual finds the verse in the Bible gets one point. Play 10 rounds.

God's Love Brings Blessings

Matthew 5

Lesson Aims

Students will

- Demonstrate the ability to use dictionary guide words to locate entries
- Brainstorm a list of questions to use in researching a Bible passage
- Play a concentration game to reinforce their knowledge of the Beatitudes

Materials
chalkboard or white board
chalk or dry-erase marker
Sample Bible Dictionary (pp. 301, 302)
highlight markers or pencils

▼ Building Study Skills ▲

Read aloud Matthew 5:1-12 from a *King James Version* Bible. Ask: **What does Jesus mean here? Have you ever had trouble understanding something you have read from a book?** Encourage the students to share. Ask: **What are some tools that we can use to help us understand what a book means when it uses words or phrases that we don't know?** (dictionaries, encyclopedias, the Internet) Say: **One of the best resources to use to understand words that you don't know very well is a dictionary. Most of us have used a dictionary before when trying to spell a word or learn what a new word means. There are also specialized dictionaries to help people with words and concepts that relate to a specific topic. What tool helps us understand words from the Bible that most regular dictionaries do not include, such as the names of people and places found in the Bible?**

Explain to the students that they are going to practice (review) using a Bible dictionary.

Pass out copies of the *Sample Bible Dictionary*. Review the use of guide words. They are located at the top of each page. Have the students highlight or circle the guide words on their handout. The word on the left matches the first word on the page, and the word on the right matches the last word on the page. Explain that the words listed between the guide words are in alphabetical order and will be found on the page if they are in the dictionary.

On the chalkboard or chart paper, write the following sample guide words and lists of entry words from a regular dictionary and Bible dictionary.

buzzard/caddy	**beatitude/betrothed**
brown	begotten
cake	Bethlehem
cabbage	bless
butterfly	believe
by	Bible
cactus	barren

Have the students decide which words would appear on a page with the given guide words. Cross out the words that would not appear on the page with the guide words *buzzard* and *caddy*. Continue completing both lists in the same manner. The words that would appear on the buzzard/caddy dictionary page include *cabbage*, *by*, and *cactus*. The Bible dictionary page would include *begotten*, *Bethlehem*, and *believe*.

Use the *Sample Bible Dictionary* handouts to give the students practice using this skill. Have them look at their handouts. Explain that you are going to play a game called "Where in the World." Take turns selecting an entry word that is found on their page and asking, "Where in the world is the word _____?" The students search their pages until they find the word's location and give a thumbs-up. The person who asked the question will then select someone to answer by telling what word comes before and after the word. Verify if the answer is correct. If correct, the student who gave the answer then asks the question using a different entry word from the page and selects someone else to answer. Continue the game until all words on the page have been covered. If you have access to a collection of Bible dictionaries, a good extension of this activity would be to play the game using multiple pages.

Pass out Bibles and explain that now that they are such Bible dictionary experts they will have the opportunity to put these Bible dictionary skills to good use by examining some of Jesus' teachings in the Gospels. Specifically, they will look at some of Jesus' instructions for us found in the Gospel of Matthew. Direct the students to open their Bibles to the book of Matthew and find chapter 5, verse l. Remind them that Matthew is the first book in the New Testament. Say: **Through the study of the first four books of the New Testament known as the Gospels of Matthew, Mark, Luke, and John, we learn that Jesus came to teach us and offer salvation. The word *gospel* literally means the "good news." This particular lesson taught in Matthew 5:1-12 is the first part of Christ's Sermon on the Mount. In it Jesus teaches what is often referred to as the Beatitudes. Now that you have mastered using an investigative tool such as a Bible dictionary, you are ready for the quest of discovering what lessons we can learn from God's Word today.**

▼ Using Study Skills ▲

Before class, print out Matthew 5:12 on large poster board.

Begin this part of the lesson with prayer asking the Holy Spirit to guide and reveal to your hearts what He wants you to understand in these Scriptures. (If you have the resources and want to add a sense of adventure to your lesson, casually put on a detective's hat and overcoat and grab a magnifying glass.) Looking at your open Bible, refer back to Matthew 5:1-12 and wonder out loud what this passage could possibly mean. (If playing the role of detective, use the magnifying glass to examine it.) Have the students take turns reading the verses. Explain that a good way to begin studying a passage is to act like a detective and use "asking" words. Ask the class to help you brainstorm a list of question words. Down the side of the chalkboard, write the words: *Who, Where, When, What, Why,* and *How* so that they will mirror the students' *Investigating with Questions* handout. Explain that when applied to the text, these questions are very helpful in uncovering the mysteries of the Scriptures. Say: **Some of the answers are easy to find in the Scripture themselves; however, some require more background knowledge. A Bible dictionary is a terrific place to find some of these unknown answers as are passages before and after the text being studied, chapter headings, and study helps found in some Bibles. Note, however, that just like in a real investigation, you will not always be able to find the answers to every question in a passage or through research, and that is okay. What God wants us to do is to spend time in His Word trying to understand its truths!**

Pass out the *Investigating with Questions* handouts and pencils. Explain that now they will put on the hat of a detective and investigate as a class some clues given to them in this passage. Start by brainstorming a title for Matthew 5:1-12. Guide them to look in their Bibles and ask if anyone has a chapter heading. Write the title on the chalkboard or chart paper and have the students do the same on their

Materials
chalkboard or white board
chalk or dry-erase marker
Investigating with Questions (p. 154)
2 poster boards
marker
pencils
Bibles
an assortment of Bible dictionaries
detective hat, overcoat, and magnifying glass (optional)

Note:
Investigating with Questions (p. 154) will be used again next week. You may want to make extra photocopies.

handouts. Tell them that as you are writing their discoveries on the board, they should also record the information on their handouts. Say: **Like a good detective, we will ask questions to get a better understanding of Matthew 5:1-12 and use the *Investigating with Questions* handouts to record our findings.**

Next explore the question of "who." Ask: **Who is speaking in Matthew 5:1-12 and to whom is he speaking?** (Jesus; speaking to the crowds) **Who wrote the book and what is the relationship with the speaker?** (Matthew; he was one of Jesus' disciples and an eye witness.) Tell students that sometimes to find the answers you have to look at the text leading up to the Scriptures and also after it. They may also look at their Bible study helps or marginal notes. Have the students look up Matthew in Bible dictionaries. Record their findings on the chart and have the students do the same on their handouts.

Proceed to the "where" question using the same investigative thought process. Matthew 5:1-12 has two primary locations mentioned. Ask the students to tell you what they are. On a mountainside is where the sermon took place. The kingdom of Heaven is the other location mentioned. Draw a box around this information on the Beatitudes poster and then record it on the chart. Remind the students that this passage is the first part of what scholars refer to as Christ's Sermon on the Mount. Have the students use their Bible dictionaries to look up *Sermon on the Mount* and to find extra details that are not specifically listed in the text. Record answers on the chart.

Continue with the "where" question by examining the kingdom of Heaven or Heaven and having the students look it up in the Bible dictionaries. Draw their attention to the cross references mentioned and explain that these are locations of other Scriptures where *Heaven* is found and that reading them will give them more information on the topic. Look Scriptures up in the Bible and read them to the class. Discuss findings.

Examine the "when" question. Ask: **When did the events happen?** (Early in Jesus' ministry; after Simon Peter, Andrew, James and John left home to follow Jesus; when Jesus was preaching throughout Galilee) Encourage the students to look back at Matthew 4:12-25 and the events leading to this passage. Keep in mind that being rewarded when we get to Heaven can also be interpreted as a "when" answer.

Have the students pose the "what" question. Encourage them by sharing that sometimes some questions in a Bible study are harder than others, just like in a real investigation. The "what" question is often one of those challenging questions. Write on the chart: "What is being talked about in the passage?" (Jesus is saying who are blessed.) Ask: **What is to be learned in the passage? To answer this, let's first look for any repeated words.** Refer to the Matthew 5:1-12 or the Beatitude poster and circle each *blessed* word. To find some of the answers to these questions, have the students look up the word *blessed* in a Bible dictionary. Explain that it means "made happy by God."

Next examine the "why" question. Ask: **Why did Christ say this?** Discuss any of these ideas: Beatitudes as a standard of conduct for believers, superficial "faith" of Pharisees vs. the real faith Christ wants, and kingdom values with eternal rewards vs. worldly values with earthly rewards. Look up *Pharisees* in the Bible dictionary. Say: **This was an influential group of Jews whose name means "separated ones." Sincere but misled, they believed that religious ritual and separation was the way to please God.**

From our study we have learned who God said will be blessed. Using the "how" question, list the ways in which certain people will be blessed. On both the chart and handouts, record the findings. Refer back to the Bible dictionary study done on the kingdom of Heaven while looking at the "where" question. Through discussion, lead students to understand that some answers can actually answer more than one question. Reassure them not to be intimidated by the process. Say: **Unlike some tests, Bible study is not for a grade but to get to know God through searching His Word. Do you remember the prayer we prayed at the beginning of this lesson?** Re-record the applicable "where" answers. Ask the students how they can be blessed according to the Bible. Spend time discussing the life application lessons from Matthew 5:1-12.

▼ Responding to Study ▲

Materials
large, unlined, white index cards
markers
rulers
pens/pencils

Say: **Through our study of the Beatitudes, we have discovered different characteristics in people who are blessed. What were the characteristics? How are they demonstrated? Do you know of anyone who has some of these characteristics?** Encourage the students to share names of people and why they believe these people have these characteristics. Lead students to think beyond their family and friends. Are there any acquaintances they know that seem to fit one of the Beatitudes? Say: **In 1 Thessalonians 5:11 Paul writes to the new believers in Thessalonica, "Therefore encourage one another and build each other up, just as in fact you are doing."** Everyone likes to be encouraged—even if it is with simple words such as "I admire you" or "I was thinking about you and praying for you today." Matthew 5:12 says, "Rejoice and be glad, because great is your reward in heaven." Although our true rewards will be in Heaven, encouragement on earth is a treat. We can be pure in heart and kind to others by writing notes of encouragement.

Have the students select at least three people that the Lord helped bring to their mind during this lesson. Pass out three or four blank index cards to each student and have him use a ruler to draw a line vertically down the middle of each card so that one side looks like the back of a postcard. Explain that the area to the right side of the line is to be kept blank and is for the person's name and address he is writing to. Show an example of a postcard if this concept is unfamiliar to the students. Encourage students to a write brief note to each person on their list. If they are having difficulty doing so, remind them that they can use their concordance to help them find an encouraging Scripture to share. After they are finished writing, instruct them to draw a picture on the front of their index cards. Send the students home with the postcards or to give to the person. Remind them to have their parents help get the addresses or they may be able to find them in a phone book—another investigative tool!

▼ Reviewing Study Skills ▲

Materials
Bibles
index cards
copies of *The Beatitudes*
(p. 155)

To practice the Beatitudes, Matthew 5:3-12, play Blessed Concentration. Before class, make copies of *The Beatitudes*, cut the squares apart, and put the first half of each beatitude on an index card and the second half on another index card. Then randomly number them on the back with the numbers 1-18. Make one set of cards for every four children. Lay the cards facedown on a table. As a warm-up, have the students read the entire passage from their Bibles. Have the students take turns turning two cards over at a time. If the two cards chosen are part of the Scripture that goes together the child may keep the cards and take another turn. When all the cards have been matched, have the students put the Scripture in the correct order to review the passage.

Title: _____

Scripture: _____

Who?
- **Who was speaking?** _____
- **To whom was he speaking?** _____

Where? _____

_____

When? _____

_____

What? _____

_____

Why? _____

_____

How? _____

_____

 LESSON 27

The Beatitudes

Blessed are the poor in spirit.	**for theirs is the kingdom of heaven.**	**Blessed are those who mourn,**
for they will be comforted.	**Blessed are the meek,**	**for they will inherit the earth.**
Blessed are those who hunger and thirst for righteousness,	**for they will be filled.**	**Blessed are the merciful,**
for they will be shown mercy.	**Blessed are the pure in heart,**	**for they will see God.**
Blessed are the peacemakers	**for they will be called sons of God.**	**Blessed are those who are persecuted because of righteousness,**
for theirs is the kingdom of heaven.	**Blessed are you when people insult you, persecute you and falsely say all kinds of evil against you because of me.**	**Rejoice and be glad, because great is your reward in heaven, for in the same way they persecuted the prophets who were before you.**

LESSON 28 — God's Love Meets Our Needs

Matthew 6

Lesson Aims

Students will

- Summarize a Bible passage using research from concordances and Bible dictionaries
- Make an acrostic on the word "part" as a pattern for prayer
- Create a prayer journal to use at home

Materials

Bibles
student and adult Bible dictionaries
chalkboard or white board
chalk or dry-erase marker
exhaustive Bible concordance
safari hat and backpack (optional)
Bibles

Beatitude

Poor in spirit
Those who mourn
Meek
Righteous
Merciful
Pure in Heart
Peacemakers
Persecuted because of righteousness

▼ Building Study Skills ▲

Open by saying: **Last week we used a Bible dictionary to help understand the Bible. We put on our "detective hats" and investigated Jesus' Sermon on the Mount and Beatitudes in Matthew 5:1-12. Now let's put on our "recall hats" and see what we can remember.** Write in large letters the word *Beatitude* on the board. Ask: **Can anyone recall what the word *Beatitude* means?** (Accept responses.) Verify the responses by having students recall how we find a word in a Bible dictionary. Model the process by looking up *Beatitude* in a student Bible dictionary. While flipping through the dictionary, stop and call out the guide words you are coming across on the pages. Turn the book so that the students can see the words. Ask if the word *Beatitude* comes before or after the guide words or if it would be on that page. Once you have located *Beatitude*, read the definition out loud. Write it next to the word *Beatitude* on the board or chart paper. Under the word *Beatitude*, make a brainstorm list of all those Christ called blessed in Matthew 5:1-12.

Say: **Throughout the Gospels of Matthew, Mark, Luke, and John, we see how Jesus gave many instructions on how to live. He also taught by giving examples of how we should do things. Today we will quest further in our attempt to get to know God our Father better by studying an example of prayer Jesus gave in the Gospel of Matthew. To go on this adventure, however, we will first need our collection of Bible study tools.** If you want to add some fun and drama to the lesson, put on a safari hat and grab a prepacked backpack stuffed with a Bible, a couple different Bible dictionaries, and an exhaustive concordance. Act like you are going on an archeological dig or adventure. As you continue the lesson, remove the books one by one from the backpack as you discuss the following. Hold up in front of the students a Bible. Flip to the back and wonder out loud if there is a concordance in it. If there is, say "check" and show it to the students. Ask: **Does anyone recall what a concordance is used for?** (A concordance is a reference book for finding Bible verses. It can be used when you want to study a Bible topic or person or when you know a few words of a verse but don't know the reference.) Think out loud that the concordance in your Bible might not be thorough enough for this quest, so show them an exhaustive concordance such as *The New Strong's Exhaustive Concordance of the Bible* (Thomas Nelson Publishers, 1990). Next show a few different types of Bible dictionaries and marvel at the differences among them. Explain that some Bible dictionaries have more information in them than others. Close the introduction by declaring that all the study tools for your next adventure are ready, and by inviting your students on the quest.

▼ Using Study Skills ▲

Materials
Bibles (preferably with a concordance or topical index in the back)
Bible dictionaries
chalkboard or white board
chalk or dry-erase marker
exhaustive Bible concordance for each group of students
Investigating with Questions handout (p. 154)
pencils
markers or crayons
poster with The Lord's Prayer written on it (optional)
A Prayer Pattern (p. 160)

At the top left hand corner of the chalkboard, write Matthew 6:6-13. Have the students open their Bibles to Matthew 6:6-13 and take turns reading the Scripture aloud. Ask the students what the main topic of the Scripture is. (Prayer) Write *PRAYER* in large letters at the top center of the chalkboard.

Have you ever had something that you wanted to talk to someone about— maybe a friend, a parent, a teacher, or your brother or sister—but you were not able to or were afraid what he would think about what you had to say? Discuss their responses. Say: **The good news is that you need not fret any longer over those times. In the Bible, Jeremiah 33:3 says, "Call to me and I will answer you and tell you great and unsearchable things you do not know." God is there to listen 24 hours a day, seven days a week and He wants you to call on Him. First Thessalonians 5:17 tells us to pray continually and Hebrews 13:5 says, "Never will I leave you; never will I forsake you." God doesn't want us to worry about things. "Do not be anxious about anything, but in everything, by prayer and petition, with thanksgiving, present your requests to God. And the peace of God, which transcends all understanding, will guard your hearts and your minds in Christ Jesus" (Philippians 4:6, 7). God loves you more than anyone in the world and that love will never change. So how can we communicate with God?** (Through prayer)

Have the students refer back to Matthew 6:6-13 and list words that may need to be defined: Father, heaven, hallowed, kingdom, forgive/forgiven, debts/ debtors, temptation, and deliver. Write the words to be defined on the board. (If using the Lord's Prayer poster option, draw attention to it and circle or underline the words to be defined.) Assign the words to students and have them look up definitions and share them with the class.

Say: **Like any good archeologist or detective, to find clues on what something means we must next ask questions to give us more knowledge on the subject.** Pass out the *Investigating with Questions* handouts and pencils. Have the students look at their handout and ask what they might title this passage. (The Lord's Prayer) Add the words *The Lord's* in front of the word *prayer* you have written at the top of the board. Ask them to share what question words are listed on the handouts. Record the question words under the title on the chalkboard or chart paper. Review each question word and what specifics it would reveal about Matthew 6:6-13. Divide the class into adventure groups. Have each group chose a recorder and reporter. Assign a question word or two to research.

Once the time you have allowed for the research is complete, have the group reporters share what their groups have discovered about the Bible passage. Record their findings on the chalkboard next to the question words. As a class, have students help formulate a summary of the passage. Write their summary on the chalkboard.

Write the words *A Prayer Pattern* on the chalkboard and number under it from one to six. Looking a little closer at the passage and all the research they have collected, have the students look for a prayer pattern by leading them verse by verse through Matthew 6:9-13 and asking the following questions: **What example is Christ setting in Matthew 6?**

1. Praise God our Father (Matthew 6:9)
2. Pray to grow His church (Matthew 6:10)
3. Show respect for His will (Matthew 6:10)
4. Ask Him for a need, prayer request (Matthew 6:11)
5. Ask for forgiveness, forgive others (Matthew 6:12)
6. Ask for strength and protection (Matthew 6:13)

Matthew 6:6-13
The Lord's Prayer—talking and listening to God
Who:
Where:
When:
What:
How:

Say: **To help us grow in our relationships with God we are to do our part of communicating with Him through prayer. One way to help remember how to pray as Christ taught in the Lord's Prayer is to think of the word** *part.* Distribute copies of *A Prayer Pattern,* and have the students fill them in as you explain. Say: ***P*** **is for** *praise.* **Start all prayers with praising Him.**
A **is for** *admit* **your sins. First John 1:9 says, "If we confess our sins, he is faithful and just and will forgive us our sins and purify us from all unrighteousness."** ***R*** **is for** *requests* **you have. James 4:2 says "You do not have, because you do not ask God." The next Scripture, James 4:3, reminds us, however, "When you ask, you do not receive, because you ask with wrong motives." God wants us to ask Him for the desires of our hearts but for His will to be done. It is always good to also ask Him to help you understand His answers when they are different from what you had hoped.** ***T*** **is for** *thanking* **Him. Thanking Him goes back to praising Him and showing respect for His will. More than anything, God just wants you to call on Him. Following a prayer pattern teaches you to call to Him not just for your wants and needs but to praise, honor, and respect Him as Christ instructed and modeled for us.**

▼ Responding to Study ▲

Use this activity to help students use what they've learned about the Lord's Prayer.

Give each student copies of the journal cover and journal pages. Have them fold the papers in half and put the pages inside the cover. Staple along the fold to make a book.

Have the students decorate their journals. Explain that each page is a place for them to record prayer thoughts to God. Say: **Using this journal will help you develop prayer patterns in your own prayers. In 1 Thessalonians 5:16-18, Paul reminds us to "be joyful always; pray continually; give thanks in all circumstances, for this is God's will for you in Christ Jesus." The more you pray and listen to God, the closer you will grow to Him and the better you will be able to be joyful always, give thanks in all circumstances, and understand His will for your life.**

Allow quiet reflecting time. To create a reflective environment, softly play a Christian CD or tape. Encourage students to write and date entries for each page. Share with them that they can use their journals as tools to help develop prayer habits and personal, active prayer with God. Once they fill their journals up, they may want to create another one at home or get spiral notebooks to divide into the P.A.R.T. segments. Close by giving the students the opportunity to use their prayer journals and to pray silently.

▼ Reviewing Study Skills ▲

Use one of the following activities to help students review skills and memorize the Lord's Prayer.

Prayer Mime: Explain to the students that they are going to be given time to look at the Lord's Prayer in Matthew 5:9-13 and to think of ways they could act out the words without saying anything. Tell them their actions may be literal or expressive and they don't have to be famous actors to express themselves through movement. After the entire class has practiced their movements and appears to be ready, have them stand up. Explain that they are all going to mime the Lord's Prayer at one time as you read it or play the song. Turn on the music and let the

Materials
My P.A.R.T. Prayer Journal cover (p. 161), one per student
prayer journal pages (p. 162), copied on both front and back, 2 per student
stapler and staples
pencils
markers, colored pencils, or crayons
Christian CD or tape that is suitable for quiet reflection
CD or tape player

Materials
instrumental CD or "The Lord's Prayer" song on CD
CD player

acting begin! For those who want to, allow them to act out their mime for the entire class.

Word Toss: Have the students sit in a circle on the floor and practice reciting the Lord's Prayer several times, referring to the board, poster, or chart paper as needed. Start the game by tossing the ball to a student and having him say the first word in the prayer, *Our*. Have that student then throw the ball to another student who has to say the second word of the verse, *Father*. Continue tossing the ball until all the words in the verse have been said. Students may refer to the written verse as they need help. Once they seem well versed in the Scripture, remove the posted words. Continue play having the students do it from memory. To perfect their memorization, have them see how quickly they can complete the verse. You may even want to time them!

Question Cube: Before class, copy the *Question It Cube Pattern*. Cut out the pattern, making sure to cut on the outside lines only. Fold inwards each dotted line so that the words are still facing out where they can be seen. Place a small amount of glue on each tab. Glue the tabs to the inside of the cube, so that they are hidden. When all the tabs are glued, reinforce the edges with clear tape. The finished project should look like a die with question words on each side. Another option is to find a small, square box and write one question word *(what, who, when, where, why, and how)* on each side.

This game is about recalling facts students have learned about the Bible story studied today. To help with the recall you may chose to let the students use their completed *Investigating With Questions* handout based on Matthew 6:6-13.

To play the game, divide the students in two teams. Have the teams line up shoulder to shoulder with their teammates and facing the opposing team. The first student in line from Team 1 will roll the cube and ask a question using the question word that is face up on the cube. (All questions must be based around the day's Bible lesson.)

Once the question has been asked, the first person on Team 2 answers the question. If Team 1 verifies the answer is correct, Team 2 will get a point. If the answer is incorrect, then the correct answer is given by Team 1. Continue the game by having the second person in line on Team 2 roll the cube and ask a question. Play continues until each person has been given a chance to answer a question, all questions have been exhausted, a point goal has been reached, or a time limit has been fulfilled.

Materials
The Lord's Prayer poster
a small rubber or soft ball

Materials
Question It Cube Pattern (p. 163)
  copied on cardstock
scissors
glue
clear tape
completed *Investigating With Questions* (p. 154)

Note
Question It Cubes will be used in the next session also. You may want to make several extra photocopies.

One way to remember how to pray as Jesus taught in the Lord's Prayer is to think of the word PART. Listen as your teacher tells you what each letter stands for. Then write an example of that kind of prayer next to each letter.

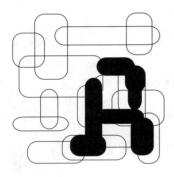

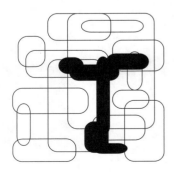

LESSON 28

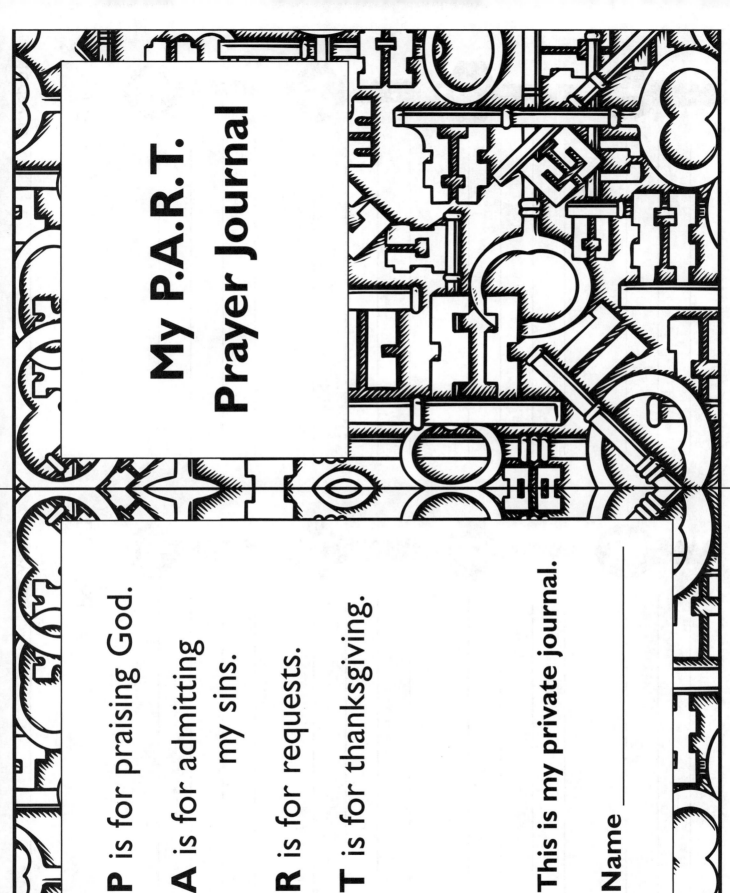

My P.A.R.T.
Prayer Journal

P is for praising God.

A is for admitting my sins.

R is for requests.

T is for thanksgiving.

This is my private journal.

Name _____

© 2004 Standard Publishing. Permission is granted to reproduce this page for ministry purposes only—not for resale.

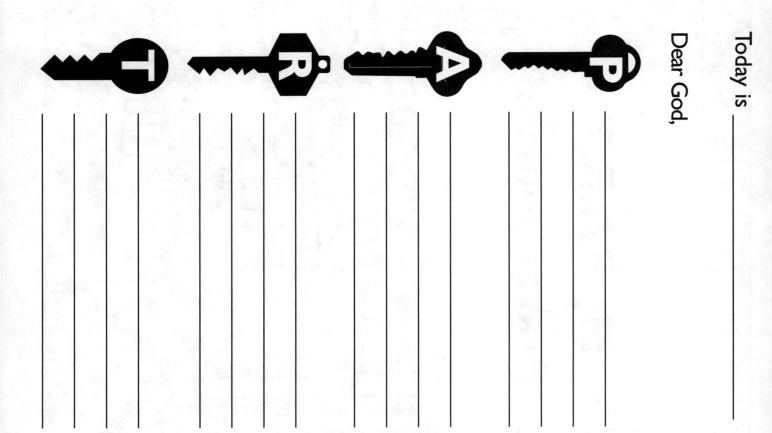

Today is _____

Dear God,

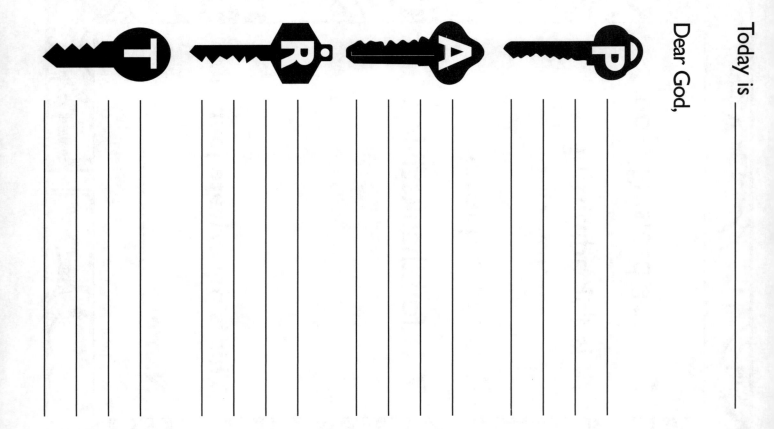

Today is _____

Dear God,

LESSON 28

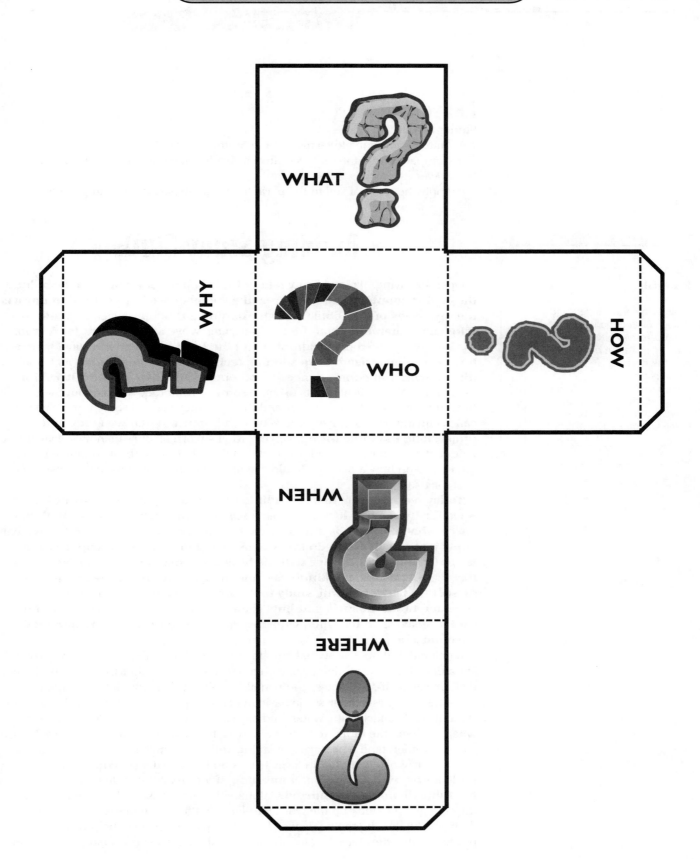

Godly People Grow in God's Word

Lesson Aims

Students will

- Match definitions to terms used in Matthew 13:1-23
- Compare and contrast three Gospel writers' accounts of the Parable of the Sower
- Apply the types of soil in the parable to real-life situations and people

Materials

Bibles
an assortment of student and adult Bible dictionaries
chalkboard or white board
chalk or dry-erase marker
self-stick notes
pens/pencils
exhaustive Bible concordance
farmer's straw hat, a bag to wear and hold seeds, and seeds (optional)

▼ Building Study Skills ▲

Open by saying: **Welcome my fellow Bible scholars! If you have been here these past couple of lessons you will remember we have started to unravel the mysteries of the Bible through examining Bible passages in Matthew. Who can remember what the two passages were about?** (Allow for responses.) **We've explored the Beatitudes and the Lord's Prayer and have learned how to use investigative questioning techniques and tools such as Bible dictionaries and concordances to gain understanding of God's Word for ourselves.** Allow the students to share some of what they recall about the Beatitudes and the Lord's Prayer and the tools they used to study them. See who can recite the Lord's Prayer. Ask: **Why is it important that we study and understand the Bible for ourselves?** (God's Word teaches us how to live. It is a guidebook for our lives. God planned that the Bible would be a complete book of guidelines on how a person should live his life. God created us and knows what is best for us.)

Today we are going to quest a little further to explore God's Word. Specifically, we will look at Christ's teaching through parables. We'll discover what a parable is and how we can understand its meaning so we can apply it to our lives. To do this we are going to take a road trip down on a farm. On this road trip we will see how godly people grow in God's Word through persistence, faithfulness, and study. As we continue to study and dissect God's Word using study tools, we will see how some events are repeated in the Gospels and how each telling of the story plays a part in God's speaking to us. Open your hearts and turn on your ears and let the adventure begin!

(Optional: Put on a straw hat and throw a seed bag with seeds in it over your shoulder). Have the students get with a partner. Pass out an assortment of Bible dictionaries, self-stick notes, and pencils. Explain that before a farmer plants a crop, he must first gather some basic information about what he is going to plant: What type of soil, climate, water, and care does the crop need? The same is true when studying the Bible. You need to have a basic understanding of words before you can understand a passage's meaning and then apply it with care to your life.

Write the word *PARABLE* in large letters on the board. Ask: **What Bible study tool can be used to find out a meaning of a word?** (Bible dictionary) **How is the Bible dictionary organized?** (alphabetical order) Next share that as a class they are going to look up the word *parable* in a Bible dictionary. Model and talk them through using the guide words at the top of the page to help with the process. Once they have located the word in their dictionaries, have them write the definition on a self-stick note. Ask a representative from each group to read their definition and come up to place it under the word *parable* on the board. If their dictionary doesn't have the word *parable* in it, have them select another dictionary or share with another group. Remind them that not all Bible dictionaries are all inclusive, and further investigation of other resources is sometimes needed. After hearing all the information on the word *parable* presented, ask if anyone can in their own words tell you what a parable is. (Parables are stories Jesus told to teach a lesson or spiritual truth.)

Explain: **Jesus, being perfect in all ways, was a master teacher. He often taught in parables to help make what He was going to teach clear and easy to understand. Of the approximately 30 parables He told, only two of them are fully explained in the New Testament—the Parable of the Sower and the Parable of the Weeds. Today we will examine the Parable of the Sower found in Matthew 13:1-23.**

▼ Using Study Skills ▲

Form four groups of students by combining pairs and have them look up the book of Matthew. (Each group should have at least one Bible for every two to three students.) Assist with the locating process by asking: **What part of the Bible is Matthew located in?** (New Testament) **How can you find that book if you do not know where it is located?** (Table of contents or finger tabs that are on some Bibles) Once Matthew is located, lead them to chapter 13. Read aloud Matthew 13:1-23 while the class follows in their Bibles. Remind them about farmers needing basic information before planting seed. Understanding definitions of words in the Bible are part of the process of becoming a Bible scholar. Once they understand the meaning of God's Word, then they can become a sower of it! Quote 2 Timothy 2:15, "Do your best to present yourself to God as one approved, a workman who does not need to be ashamed and who correctly handles the word of truth."

Pass out regular dictionaries, self-stick notes, and pencils, and write the following words on the board into four columns: *fulfill, perceive, scorched, sow/sown, crop, persecution, shallow, unfruitful, calloused, prophecy, sprang, withered, deceitfulness, produce, sow/Sower, yield.*

While writing, explain that all the words come from the Parable of the Sower in Matthew and that they might cause confusion if they are not understood. Ask students to look over Matthew 13:1-23 and see if there are any other words they might need defined to help understand the passage. Add any additions to the list. Explain that they are going to play a timed game called "What's the Meaning of It?" to see how masterful they have become at looking up words in the dictionary. Assign each group a column of words to define. Each group member will then write one of the words on a self-stick note. Explain that the team should work as a group to look up the word, read the definition, and dictate it to the "scribe." The person with the word being defined on his self-stick note is the scribe and writes down the definition. The scribe in turn selects a "runner" to put the self-stick note next to the correct word on the board.

If your class is small, each person should be given more than one word. Summaries of definitions may be given if it has been looked up in the dictionary and verified. Also, words such as "Sower" and "sown" may not be found in their dictionaries. For these words encourage the group to use the definition of the root word "sow" and the context of the Scripture to define the word.

Ask the class if they are clear on how to play the game. Begin timing when you say go. Each group will go through the process of looking up the definitions of the words, writing the definitions on the self-stick notes, and coming up to the board and placing the definitions beside each word. When a team has all of its words defined and posted, record its time above its column. Once all groups are finished, have them refer back to Matthew 13:1-23 in their Bibles and re-read it, applying the

Materials
Bibles
dictionaries (1 per group of students)
Bible dictionaries (1 or 2 per group)
chalkboard and chalk or chart paper and marker
self-stick notes
pencils
a watch or clock with a second hand
Digging for Details (p. 168)
red, yellow, and blue crayons or markers for each group

Answer Key
Digging for Details

1. blue	9. blue
2. yellow	10. yellow
3. blue	11. red
4. blue	12. red
5 yellow	13. blue
6. yellow	14. yellow
7. yellow	15. red
8. yellow	16. red

use of their defined words to the passage. When the entire class has finished, re-read the passage together and pause at each definition. During the pause, read the definition the group wrote and then continue and discuss the verse. Refer to the groups' recorded times and congratulate them all on a job well done!

To help students compare and contrast Matthew 13:1-23, Mark 4:1-20, and Luke 8:4-16, distribute copies of *Digging for Details.* Have the groups of students look at all three accounts of the parable. Suggest that three students each take one of the accounts, and one other student read the worksheet. The sheet instructs students to color each flower according to the Bible book from which it comes.

When groups are finished, have students hold up their sheets and compare the designs the colors make. Ask: **Why do you think Christ chose to explain this parable when He didn't others?** Remind students that everything Christ did had a divine purpose.

▼ Responding to Study ▲

Use one of the following activities to help students use what they've learned about the Parable of the Sower.

Picture It: To refresh the class's memory, ask if anyone can recall the definition of a parable. (A parable in the Bible is a story Jesus told to teach a lesson or spiritual truth.) Having a visual representation of a concept often helps people commit it to memory. Pass out paper, pencils, and some type of coloring medium. Ask: **What does the seed represent in the Parable of the Sower?** (the Word of God, Bible) To help the students commit the Parable of the Sower to memory, have each student draw a visual representation of the seed being God's Word. (If the students get stuck on this concept, brainstorm ideas with the class to help them get started.) Once the majority of the class has finished, allow those who want to share their drawings with the class. Another option is to hang the pictures for display.

Charades: To do this activity, have the students remain in their groups. Have someone from each group draw a slip of paper with the scenario written on it. Give each group time to meet and decide how they as a group will act out their scenario in mime. Everyone in the group must play some part. Once everyone is ready, have each group take turns performing its charades while the other teams guess the scenario. When someone guesses the scenario correctly, have the group acting stop and say: "Let he who has ears, let him hear!" Continue until all groups have had an opportunity to perform.

Note: People learn in different ways. Ensuring that a concept reaches all students means that various learning opportunities need to be presented. Having the students act out a part of the parable through mime/charades gives them yet another way to commit the parable to memory.

Cartoon strips: For this activity explain that students are going to make a comic or cartoon strip of the Parable of the Sower. Pass out *Cartoon Strips.* Have extras available.

Have the students use the top left-hand squares for their titles and bylines. Encourage them to think out their next cartoon squares and then begin drawing. Remind them to think of the beginning, middle, and end of the parable and to lay it out around those illustrations. (You may want to give them scratch paper to write or think it out.) If some students appear to get frustrated by the project, draw the chart on the board, talk them through the parable and give them ideas to illustrate along the way. Allow those who can work independently to do so.

As a closure activity, have the students swap cartoon strips with each other.

Materials
paper
pencils
markers, colored pencils, or
crayons

Materials
folded slips of paper with one
of the four scenarios of what
happened to the different
seeds (path/birds ate; rocky
places/sprang up, sun
scorched, and withered;
thorns/grew and choked
plants; good soil/produced
crop) written on them.

Option
To make the charade guessing
part more challenging, write
one of the scenarios on
more than one paper slip and
make the class aware of it.

Materials
Cartoon Strips (p. 169)
colored pencils, markers, or
crayons
pencils
rulers
paper

▼ Reviewing Study Skills ▲

If you still have the *Question It Cube* from Lesson 28, use it. You'll also need additional copies of the cube, one per group. Before class, copy the *Question It Cube* pattern. Cut out the pattern, making sure to cut on the outside lines only. Fold inward on each dotted line so that the words are still facing out where they can be seen. Place a small amount of glue on each tab. Glue the tabs to the inside of the cube so that they are hidden. When all the tabs are glued, reinforce the edges with clear tape. The finished project should look like a dice with question words on each side. Another option is to find a small, square box and write one question word *(what, who, when, where, why,* and *how)* on each side.

This game is about recalling facts students have learned about the Bible story studied today. To help with the recall you may chose to let the students use their Bibles.

Divide the students into groups of four or five. Have the students take turns rolling the cube and asking a question about the Parable of the Sower using the word that is face up on the cube. Players go around the circle, asking and answering questions. Play continues until time runs out.

Materials
Question It Cubes made in Lesson 28 or the *Question It Cube Pattern* (p. 163) copied on card stock
scissors
glue
clear tape

Digging for Details

Work in a group of three. Each person should choose a different Gospel: Matthew, Mark, or Luke. Read the Parable of the Sower. Look at the clues below. If the clue is from the parable as it appears in Matthew, color the flower red. If the clue is from the book of Mark, color the flower blue. If the clue is from Luke, color the flower yellow. Read carefully! The clues are tricky.

1 This account says that the thorns choked the plants so they did not bear grain.

2 This account does NOT say Jesus was sitting in a boat when He told the parable.

3 This describes the crop produced by the good soil as 30, 60, or 100 times what was planted.

4 This Gospel specifies that the Twelve asked Jesus for the meaning of the parable when He was alone.

5 This Gospel says the plants that grew in the rocky soil withered because of lack of moisture.

6 This describes the crop produced by the good soil as 100 times more than what was sown.

7 Jesus said, "The seed is the word of God."

8 "The devil comes and takes the word away from their hearts."

9 "As soon as they hear it, Satan comes and takes away the word."

10 "The seed on good soil stands for those with a noble and good heart."

11 The good soil produced a crop that was 100, 60, or 30 times what was sown.

12 Jesus said this prophecy was fulfilled: "For this people's heart has become calloused; they hardly hear with their ears ..."

13 The thorny soil is like "the worries of this life, the deceitfulness of wealth and the desires for other things."

14 The people who are like the rocky soil: "in the time of testing they fall away."

15 Jesus blessed His hearers and added, "Many prophets and righteous men longed to see what you see but did not see it."

16 "The evil one" comes and snatches away the seed on the path.

 LESSON 29

Cartoon Strip Patterns

God Loves Us and We Love God

Luke 15

Lesson Aims

Students will
- Paraphrase parables
- Rewrite a parable in first person
- Express God's love through words and art

Materials

Bibles
Bible dictionary
chalkboard or white board
chalk or dry-erase marker
paper
pencils
Parable Paraphrase (p. 174)
Once I Was Lost (p. 175)
something shaped like a heart
   (a heart cut out of construction paper or a heart-shaped
   helium balloon)
Valentine's Day decorations and
   valentine cards or boxes of
   candy hearts (optional)

▼ Building Study Skills ▲

Prior to class, cut three strips of paper large enough for a word to be easily read by the class but small enough to be hidden in the pages of the Bible you are using. On each paper strip, write with a marker in large print one of the following words: instruction, examples, and parables. On the strip marked "instruction" write the Bible references Matthew 5:1-12 in the bottom right hand corner. On the one marked "examples" write Matthew 6:6-13, and on the last strip marked "parables" write Matthew 13:1-9. Hide the strips in the Bible. To create a fun environment, decorate the room as if it were Valentine's Day using things such as streamers, balloons, Valentines or boxes of candy hearts with students' names written on them. Pass out the Valentines and candy hearts as the students arrive, being sure to have extra for visitors.

Excitement is contagious. Beginning class with an air of excitement over God's Word and His love will set the stage for a class full of excitement discovering life's truths found on each page of the Bible. Ask the students: **What if I were to tell you that I have discovered a book that holds all the true secrets to a life of love, peace, and happiness, and that this book clearly explains the perfect defense system to any attack you will ever have? Would you believe me?** Continue: **This absolutely amazing book is full of mystery, hidden meanings, intrigue, and revelations that show the true meaning of life, not only here on earth but beyond! It is so complex that scholars have devoted their entire lives to understanding it.** Ask: **Can anyone guess what book I am talking about?** As the answer, the Bible, is given, hold up a Bible. **Many people know who Christ is, but they do not know Him personally like a best friend. Reading the Bible and having a prayer time opens the lines of communication to God. The more time you spend getting to know Him, the more you will understand Him and love Him.** Pass out Bibles to those who do not have their own.

Remind the students that these past few classes they have learned about Jesus and how God sent Him as a teacher as well as a Redeemer. Share that Jesus was a master teacher. Because He was God, He knew exactly the best way to teach humans. He varied His methods or ways of teaching, and we find these lessons recorded in the Bible.

Write on a chalkboard the phrase "Jesus taught by . . ." See if any students can recall one or more of His methods we have studied in class (instruction, example, and parables). As the students recall, list the methods under the phrase "Jesus taught by." If they need some assistance give clues by writing the first letters of the words *instruction*, *example*, and *parables* under the phrase "Jesus taught by." To help continue jogging their memory, take out the strips of paper you placed in your Bible before class and pass them out to three volunteers. (If all three methods were recalled, still pass out the strips of paper at this time.) Have volunteers look up the Scriptures written on the paper.

Write these references on the board: Matthew 5:1-12 (Beatitudes), Matthew 6:6-13 (Lord's Prayer), and Matthew 13:1-9 (Sower and the Seed). Guide the class in locating the first Scripture. Have the volunteer with the Scripture read it out loud to the class. Ask: **Which teaching method did Christ use to teach this lesson?** Ask this after each Scripture is read. Verify the class's answers by asking the volunteers who have the strips of paper. Write Beatitudes, Lord's Prayer, and Sower and the Seed by the correct teaching method.

Springboard off the topic of parables. Write the word *parable* on the board. Share that in today's lesson they will be dissecting and celebrating the truths from the Bible in a parable that has to do with "this." Show the students some form of a heart. (It may be as elaborate as a helium balloon shaped like a heart or as simple as drawing a heart on the board. You may also draw their attention to the decorated classroom if you chose to decorate it.) Ask: **What does a heart represent?** (love) Say: **Though we often think of human love when we see a heart, God's love is so much greater. His love is amazingly patient, never ends, and is always welcoming no matter what we do wrong. It is this love, God's unconditional, never-ending love, that we will look at today by studying some parables. We will also learn how to draw meaning from the parables and paraphrase Scripture.** Pray with the students asking God to open their hearts, minds, and ears so they might hear what He has to say to them through His Word.

Have the students find a partner and locate the book of Luke and turn to chapter 15, verse 1. Once everyone has located Luke 15:1, ask them if their Bibles give a title of this section. Encourage them to share their titles (the Parable of the Lost Sheep). Brainstorm what they think the Bible passage is about and how it may be related to the theme of love.

Before you begin reading, remind the class that there are different versions of the Bible, and that although their Bibles might not have the exact words you are reading, the meaning is the same. Read Luke 15:1-7 aloud as the class follows along in their Bibles.

Distribute the *Parable Paraphrase* handout. Say: **Now that we have heard this parable, we are going to learn how to paraphrase a Bible passage in our own words. When we are able to retell a Bible story in our own words, it helps us to etch it into our minds and on our hearts so that we can go back to the story when we need its message to apply to our lives. Reading God's Word is one thing, but to be able to paraphrase passages helps with understanding them and remembering them.**

Demonstrate how to paraphrase by re-reading Luke 15:4-7 a few verses at a time and summarizing what it said. Continue this process, allowing the students to give more and more input as they catch on to the concept. Ask students to write their paraphrases on the sheep shape on page 174. Once all of the passages have been paraphrased, ask if someone could sum up the entire parable. Continue with a discussion on what they thought the parable meant. In summary re-read Luke 15:7 aloud: "I tell you that in the same way there will be more rejoicing in heaven over one sinner who repents than over ninety-nine righteous persons who do not need to repent."

Now that the students have the concept of paraphrasing, have them look at the next "lost parable" found in Luke 15:8-10. Ask someone to read the Parable of the Lost Coin aloud while the rest of the class listens carefully for the main points of the passage. After the passage is read, encourage the students to paraphrase the passage. They can write on the coin shape on page 174.

Introduce the last "lost parable" found in Luke 15:11-24 and distribute the *Once I Was Lost* handout. Allow students to pair up, and then go over the instructions on the handout with them. Students are to write the Parable of the Lost Son in first person—using "I." A couple of sentences are on the handout to get them started. Make sure the students can complete the assignment, and help them as much as necessary.

Discuss the similarities of the "lost parables" and why students think Christ chose to demonstrate His point in three different ways. Read John 3:16, 17. **God loves each one of us so much that He will wait patiently for us to call on Him no matter how or why we get lost. He will forgive us if we ask forgiveness. Christ's dying on the cross made that possible for us. Jesus wanted to reach everyone with this message. He used repetition and variation to re-emphasize His point that He wants none to perish.**

▼ Using Study Skills ▲

Tell the students that now that we have learned to paraphrase, we are going to look closer at the Parable of the Lost Son (Luke 15:11-24) and make a class crossword puzzle using words from the passage. Explain how every word in the Bible is God-inspired and is intentionally there, so it is important that we understand what it means. Read through the passage again as a class but this time locating and underlining key words and difficult words that they might not understand such as *estate* and *squandered*. As students identify words, write them on a chalkboard until the entire passage is covered. Encourage them to come up with a list of at least 15 words.

Pair students and assign them some of the words to look up in regular or Bible dictionaries and to record the definitions on their sheets of paper. Remind the students how dictionaries are organized in alphabetical order and that the guide words at the top of the pages guide you in knowing what words are on that page. Also remind them that not all words are found in Bible dictionaries so they may need to use traditional dictionaries. Once the majority of the class is finished with their definitions, have them report them to the class while you write them on the board.

Explain that the definitions will work as the clues to the crossword puzzle. Identify the longest word they came up with and write it in the center of the board. Assign its definition as number one across. Select the next longest word that has one of the same letters as number one across and connect it by writing it as number one down. Identify its definition as number one down. Continue the process as a class until all the words have been used. Add additional words and definitions if more are needed to make all the original words fit. Be sure to copy down the completed puzzle so that it may be used as a master. As an extension of this activity, make a blank copy of the puzzle with the definition clues and give it to the class to complete at the beginning of the next class.

▼ Responding to Study ▲

Use one of the following activities to help students use what they've learned from the Parable of the Lost Son.

Cards: Often times we wait until special occasions to tell others that we love them and have a particularly hard time witnessing to love ones who are "lost." Isaiah 55:11 says that God's Word will not return to Him empty and that it will accomplish what He desires. With this, we can be encouraged that our job is to share His Word (the Bible) with others and let the Holy Spirit take care of the rest. Encourage the students to think of others they care about and want to share God's love with. Have them use the craft materials and pictures from the *Express Your Love* page to make and decorate valentine-like cards with a Scripture on them. Direct them to the concordance of their Bible to help them find a verse on love to use. Encourage each to take his card home and make a point of giving it to that special someone this week.

Graffiti Board: Make a Perfect Love Graffiti Board by laying the bulletin board paper on the ground. Explain that this graffiti board will be used as a way to express our love for God and His love for us. Have students think of their favorite Scriptures on love or locate one by looking under the word *love* in a concordance. Once they have thought about what they want to write or draw, have them use the markers on the paper to express through writing phrases, Scriptures, and pictures their love for God and His love for us. If they wish, they can use pictures from the *Express Your Love* page. If there is not enough room for all the students to write/draw at one time, have them take turns looking up Scripture at their seats. Once the Graffiti Board is complete, hang it on a classroom wall.

▼ Reviewing Study Skills ▲

Have the students sit in a circle and hand the ball of yarn to one student. Explain this is a paraphrasing memory game and that you will tell them the title of a Bible story and that they will each have a turn adding one phrase to help tell the story. Once you have given the title of the Bible story, have the student with the ball of yarn start by telling one phrase about the beginning of the story. Once the "starter" is finished talking, have him hold the end of the yarn in one hand while rolling the rest of the ball across the circle to another student. That student then continues adding to the story retelling and rolls the yarn while holding a point of the yarn. This process will make a spider-like web. If a student who receives the yarn does not know what comes next in the story, he may pass and roll the yarn to another student. The process continues until the story is complete and the teacher stops giving new story titles. Close by noting that just like the web they have made with yarn, both the New and Old Testament are woven together to make a whole, and neither part is complete without the other.

Materials
Express Your Love (p. 176)
large piece of red, pink, or
  white bulletin board paper
bulletin board letters to spell
  "God's Perfect Love Is" or a
  title of your choice
markers
Bibles
Bible concordances

Materials
a ball of yarn

Parable Paraphrase

Write the parable of the Lost Son in first person.

I was the younger son, and I wanted the money I would someday inherit. I didn't want to wait.

Express Your Love

Use these pieces of art to create one or more cards to share God's love.

 LESSON 30

Godly People Show Mercy

Luke 10

Lesson Aims

Students will
- Evaluate the behavior of each character in the parable of the Good Samaritan
- Research the basic roles of priests and Levites
- Choose to show mercy in two different ways

▼ Building Study Skills ▲

Before class, arrange your classroom to accommodate a relay race. Place a pair of oversize shoes, a sweater, and a Bible at two stations, one for each of two teams. Write each Scripture reference on a slip of paper and place them in a location that is the same distance from each team's station.

When students have arrived, divide the class into two teams. Say: **You probably remember *Mr. Rogers' Neighborhood* from when you were much younger. What do remember him doing every show?** (He changed his shoes and sweater.) **Today we're going to talk about being a neighbor, but first, we're going to play a game to help us think about what God says about being a neighbor.**

Instruct the students that they will run a relay race in which they will first change their shoes, then put on a sweater, then grab one of the slips of paper. Then they will go back to the Bible, look up the Scripture verse that is written on the paper, and then read the verse from the Bible. When each player has read the verse, he must remove the sweater and shoes and run back to tag the next person on his team. Remind students that there are only eight slips of paper. The team with the most slips wins.

When the game is over, ask: **What does the Bible say about our neighbors?** (We should love our neighbors as ourselves.) **Why do you think God would want that command to appear so many times in the Bible?** (He wants us to love our neighbors.) **So who are our neighbors?** (friends, family, people we know and don't know)

Say: **The Bible includes a story about someone who asked that same question. In fact, someone read one of the verses from that passage of Scripture.** Find out who has the slip of paper with Luke 10:27 on it; have that person locate the passage. Ask him what story is found in that passage of Scripture. Say: **Jesus told the parable about the Good Samaritan in answer to the question, "Who is my neighbor?" This question was asked by a teacher of the Law, someone who probably should have known the answer to his own question, but Jesus decided to answer him with a story. This teacher of the Law wanted to show off how much he knew and try to get Jesus to say something wrong. Jesus told this story to show the man that even though he thought himself to be very religious and "right" before God, he still needed to change himself.**

Explain to the students why Jesus sometimes used parables. Say: **Even though this man thought he was righteous, Jesus wanted to show him that he was prejudiced against other people who were not like him. Because the man was a teacher of the Law, he was very important in the community, and**

Materials
2 pairs of oversize shoes or boots
2 cardigan sweaters
at least 2 Bibles

Scripture References
Leviticus 19:18
Matthew 19:19
Matthew 22:39
Mark 12:31
Luke 10:27
Romans 13:9
Galatians 5:14
James 2:8

telling him that he was not doing what God wanted could be a very touchy thing. Jesus wasn't afraid of telling people what they needed to hear, whether they liked it or not and whether they could harm Jesus because of what He said or not. However, because Jesus loved the man, even though he was wrong, Jesus taught him a lesson without ever having to say: "You are wrong!" A parable can teach people lessons by allowing them to hear the story and then figure out what it means. In fact, at the end of the parable, Jesus gave the teacher of the Law a "pop quiz," asking who he thought treated the beaten man like a neighbor.

Explain to the students that today they will be studying what it means to be a neighbor and to treat people with mercy.

Materials
Bible concordances
Good Neighbor/Bad Neighbor
  (p. 182)
pens/pencils

▼ Using Study Skills ▲

Distribute the *Good Neighbor/Bad Neighbor* handouts and pens to each of the students. Instruct the students to write down each character on one side of the fence and write the complete Scripture reference for the verse in which they are mentioned. Have a student or a few students read through Luke 10:25-37 aloud.

After the passage has been read aloud, ask the students to list the characters they noted on their handouts. Start with the Good Neighbor side. Ask: **Which of these people acted like a good neighbor?** (the Samaritan man; if there are any other answers, discuss whether the other students agree or disagree) **How can we judge whether they were a good or bad neighbor?** (by examining what they did when they saw the beaten man) **How do we know that those actions are right or wrong?** Say: **Sometimes we judge people by the way we feel when they say or do something that we like or don't like. If our friends invite us to go with their family to an amusement park, that would make us happy, and we'd say that they were a good friend. If our friends were to borrow something, like a game cartridge or a favorite book, and then destroy it, we might say that they were careless. If our friends were to spread untrue rumors about us, however, we would probably say that they were no longer our friends.**

Say: **Our actions often show exactly what we think about other people. If our actions are kind and thoughtful, other people will probably assume that we are kind and thoughtful by nature. If we act rudely or selfishly, other people will likely assume that we are rude, selfish people. Let's take a look at what the Bible shows us about how the people in the story treated the man who was beaten.**

Divide the class into as many teams as you have Bibles and concordances. Instruct the teams to locate Luke 10:25-37 in the Bibles. Have the teams look up the words *priest* and *Levite* in the concordances and Bibles; instruct them to write on the bottom half of their handouts the references to only those verses that give some explanation about what each does. The verses will explain that the basic role of the priests was to be a mediator between God and man, primarily offering sacrifices on behalf of the people. The basic role of the Levites was to provide support to the priests by working in the tabernacle and the temple. Have the groups share some of the verses that they found, noting that most of the references were from the Old Testament.

Say: **When God told Moses and the people of Israel to build the tabernacle, He wanted them to designate a place to worship God. God instructed that some of the people dedicate their lives to helping the people live right in God's eyes by offering sacrifices; these were the priests. God also instructed that some of the people should serve the priests by helping in the tabernacle and temple; these were the Levites. Both the priests and the Levites came from the same tribe, Levi; the priests were children of Aaron, Moses' brother, and the Levites were children from other clans in the** tribe. They were all cousins, of sorts, but some had greater responsibilities than others. Ultimately, however, they all had the same responsibility—to help the rest of the people maintain their relationships with God.

Say: **Throughout history, the priests helped maintain the relationship from the people to God, through sacrifices, and the Levites helped maintain the relationship from God to the people, mainly by explaining the Law and other Scriptures. That's why the person who asked Jesus the question was called a "teacher of the Law." Unfortunately, throughout history, the priests were so highly regarded by the people that sometimes both the priests and the people forgot that it was the priests' job to help the people relate to God and that it was the people's job to please God and not the priests. In the same way, sometimes both the Levites and the people forgot that it was the Levites' job to help the priests and to share the Word of God with the people and that it was the people's job to trust in God's Word and not simply in the Levites. Eventually, the priests and Levites became the most powerful people among God's people, so much so that the people worried more about the priests and Levites than other people, and sometimes God. This is exactly why Luke 10:29 says that the teacher of the Law "wanted to justify himself"; he was more concerned about whether he was right than how he treated his neighbor.**

Say: **Since it was the Levites' job to help the people understand God's Word, let's take a few minutes to see what God's Word says about how we should treat our neighbors.** Instruct students to stay in their groups and look up the word *neighbor* in the concordances and find at least two specific ways that God says we should treat our neighbors. Remind the students that the Bible could make reference to both good ways and bad ways that we can relate to neighbors. After a few minutes have the groups report some of their findings. Verses will likely include some of the Ten Commandments and other passages from the Old Testament.

Ask: **Why would God be concerned about how we treat other people?** (Because He cares for all of us.) **Why do you think the two most important groups of people in the nation, the people who were most concerned with how we relate to God, would not help the man?** Say: **Part of the reason was because the priests and Levites had specific rules about how they were to stay clean and what they could and could not do. One rule was that they were to stay away from dead bodies. Maybe they thought that the man was dead and they didn't want to risk touching him, just in case. Do you think that's a good reason for not helping the man?** (Maybe, if he was trying to be pure for God; not if he was more concerned about himself than someone else.) **It's not that easy to make such a decision, but Jesus seems to want us to be more concerned about each other than about the Law. The teacher of the Law knew everything there was to know about the Law. But Jesus showed him that if God wants us to love our neighbors, it's more important to show mercy than to expect perfection in regard to the Law. The priests and Levites had to be clean, according to the Law, but it wasn't just because they were supposed to be clean but because in their role of helping other people relate to God better, they had to set an example. If they were more concerned with doing exactly what the Law said and not why the Law said it, they were missing God's point. That is what Jesus meant with His parable.**

▼ Responding to Study ▲

Materials
What Can I Do to Help? (p. 183)
pens/pencils
brochures from local charitable
organizations

Before class, gather information about local organizations or agencies that help people in need (homeless, poor, hungry, sick, etc.). Bring these materials to class. If your church supports one of these organizations or does work similar to what they do, invite to class the person who knows about the agency or who runs the church's ministry and ask her to share with the class what she does. Encourage students to ask questions about how the agency shows love and mercy to other people.

Prompt discussion with questions like:
- How many people does your agency help each day, week, month, or year?
- What kind of help does your agency offer?
- What kind of spiritual help does your agency offer?
- Are there any opportunities for people to volunteer to help your agency?

After the guest has had an opportunity to share information about her agency, ask the students: **How does our guest and her agency help others and show mercy? Is this the only way to do that today? Can you think of other organizations or ministries that help people and show mercy in different ways? Does our church provide any other services or sponsor any other ministries that do this kind of work? Are any of you involved with these ministries? How do you think God wants us to show mercy to other people? Why do you think God wants us to show mercy to other people, even people we do not know?** Allow students to answer these questions and discuss them for a few minutes. Try to direct the discussion toward actions that show mercy and not simply providing free services and goods.

Say: **There are many organizations that provide services to people with different needs. Some provide food, others provide shelter, and others provide medicine and health care. Many of the people who need these services are poor, but some have simply made bad decisions in their lives and they are now facing some of the consequences. Regardless of why they are in their current situations, these agencies, including many churches and Christian ministries, help people with the simple goal of helping them. Have you ever thought about helping someone in need and then reconsidered because there was nothing in it for you? That's pretty common, but it's also the same reason why the priest and the Levite avoided the beaten man in Jesus' parable; they were more concerned about their own wellbeing than the man's.**

Ask: **What are some things that we can do to help check our attitudes about showing mercy to people?** (Remember that God has shown us mercy by forgiving our sins and that He wants us to do the same; we can read the Bible and learn more about what it means to show mercy; we can pray, asking God to help us overcome our attitudes about other people.) Ask: **Do you remember what it was that prompted Jesus to tell this story?** (The teacher of the Law asked Jesus what he needed to do to inherit eternal life.) **Why do you think Jesus told this story in response to a question about eternal life? Eternal life is not something that we can earn by doing good things, even obeying all the commandments, as the priest and Levite tried to do. It is a matter of God showing us mercy and giving us eternal life, even when we don't deserve it. That's called grace. When God gives us grace and offers us eternal life, even though we are sinners, He is showing us mercy. He wants us to do the same thing in our relationships with other people.**

Distribute *What Can I Do to Help?* handouts. Allow time for students to choose a category and write a way they can help and show mercy in that area.

▼ Reviewing Study Skills ▲

Materials
Bibles
Bible concordances
notebook paper
pens/pencils
What Can I Do to Help? (from
  previous step)

Distribute paper and pens. Say: **As we learn how to use the Bible, one of the most important skills we can develop is to be able to paraphrase Scriptures. A paraphrase is a shortened retelling of the verses in a language that most people will understand. Sometimes it includes explanation of concepts that people might not understand, like who priests and Levites were. The purpose of paraphrasing Scripture is to be able to know what the verses mean instead of simply reciting memorized verses. It shows that we understand the Bible. The priests and Levites memorized the Scriptures, but from Jesus' parable we can see that sometimes knowing what the Bible says and understanding what it means can be two different things.** Instruct the students to rewrite the parable in their own words. Tell them they may want to write it in a different context, such as a school. If you have time, you may want to have the students read their paraphrases aloud or even act them out. You may want to have the students work in small groups or pairs for the sake of time.

When all of the students have read their paraphrases, ask: **Why do you think it is important for us to be able to paraphrase Scripture? It is important for us to be able to retell God's Words to others so that they can also experience God's mercy. By telling people about how God is merciful to us by forgiving our sins and by explaining to others that the reason we are showing mercy to them is because of God's mercy to us, we are also helping them experience God's mercy.**

Say: **There's one final part of this story that we haven't discussed. Most people call this parable "The Good Samaritan." We don't think much about that, but when Jesus first told the story, He was probably making a few more people mad than just the priests and Levites. In those days, the Samaritans were hated by the Jews. Historically, they were sort of cousins, but the Samaritans did not worship God the same way the Jews did, and they had intermarried with people from other nations. The Jews looked down on the Samaritans. When Jesus told the story and the hero was not a Jewish priest or Levite but a Samaritan, Jesus was pointing out that everybody is supposed to show mercy to everybody else, regardless of their race, color, or religion. Jesus was saying that in order to please God, not only should we show others mercy, but we might have to change our own attitudes to do that.**

Instruct students to answer the final two questions on the *What Can I Do to Help?* page. As they think about their answers, close with a prayer thanking God for the parables of Jesus and for helping us to understand His mercy by showing us how to show mercy to others.

Good Neighbor/Bad Neighbor

Read Luke 10:25-37. As you find characters in the parable of the Good Samaritan, write them on the appropriate side of the fence. Near each person, write the complete Scripture reference for the verse where they are mentioned.

Good Neighbor   **Bad Neighbor**

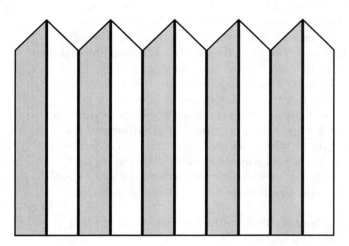

Look up the words *priest* and *Levite* in a concordance. Find Scriptures that tell what each one does. Write the Scripture references below.

 LESSON 31

Choose one or two of the categories below. Write one way that you can help in that area this week and one way that you can show mercy in that area.

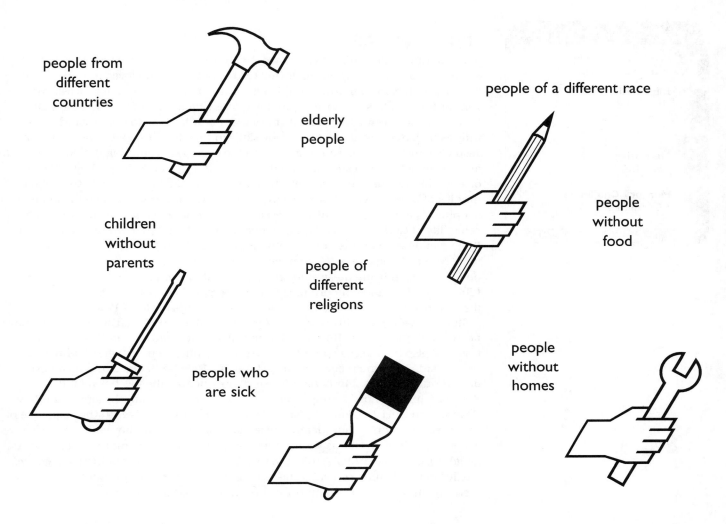

people from different countries

elderly people

people of a different race

children without parents

people of different religions

people without food

people who are sick

people without homes

What kind of attitudes do I have toward other people that might prevent me from showing them mercy?

What can I do to change those attitudes?

Gospels Teach Us That Jesus Is Our Savior

Lessons 32–35

Bible Skills
Use Bible dictionary and
   concordance
Gospel harmony

Memorize
John 11:25

Memory Challenge
1 Corinthians 15:3-8

Unit Overview

In the uncertain times in which we live, there is no greater assurance than knowing that there is a faithful, loving God at our side who loves us enough to send His only Son so that we could be forgiven of our sins and live forever with Him in Heaven. It is this loving, gracious, forgiving aspect of God's nature, and that of His Son, Jesus Christ, that your students will come to understand more fully as they exercise their Bible study skills in this unit, "Gospels Teach Us That Jesus Is Our Savior." As students explore the events surrounding the death, burial, and resurrection of Jesus through the eyes of the Gospel writers, they will discover how the various accounts complement each other. As they create Gospel harmonies of these texts and observe the many ways that Jesus fulfilled the ancient prophecies about the promised Messiah, their confidence in the accuracy and reliability of God's Word will greatly increase. Students will continue to use their Bible dictionaries in this unit to help them understand unfamiliar terms, and their concordances to help them locate specific Bible verses. As students' confidence builds in using these study tools, they will become more likely to use the Bible dictionary and concordance in their personal study time, thus enabling them to become more careful and accurate students of God's Word.

Students will begin this unit by discovering in Lesson 32 that Jesus is truly more powerful than death as He raises Lazarus from the dead. It is in this lesson that they will also hear Jesus speak the words of the unit memory verse, John 11:25: "Jesus said, 'I am the resurrection and the life. He who believes in me will live, even though he dies.'" In Lesson 33, students uncover the ties between the Passover and the Lord's Supper, as well as explore the establishment of the New Covenant in Christ's blood. Lesson 34 will acquaint students with the sequence of events surrounding Jesus' death, burial, and resurrection; they will use the account of these events, as well as the words of Paul in the unit memory challenge, 1 Corinthians 15:3-7, to come to a fuller understanding of the term *gospel*. Lastly, they will study several of Jesus post-resurrection appearances to see how Jesus' death and resurrection proved He was indeed the Messiah.

Summary

Lesson 32 encourages students to praise God for His power.

Lesson 33 helps students to remember the sacrifice that Jesus made on the cross.

Lesson 34 focuses on the resurrection of Jesus and how we should praise God for salvation through Jesus.

Lesson 35 examines the occasions when Jesus met different people after His resurrection.

Memory Verse Activities

Hot Potato: Have students form a circle. Using a small ball, have the students pass the ball around the circle. The first person to have the ball says the first word of the unit memory verse, then tosses it to the next person. The person who receives the ball says the next word. This pattern continues as the ball is passed around the circle until the whole verse has been recited. For variety, the ball can be passed across the circle in a random pattern, as opposed to the traditional format.

Mural: Write each word of the unit memory verse or phrase from the memory challenge on a separate piece of 9" x 12" white construction paper. As students finish early, they can take a word/phrase from the memory verse, illustrate it with crayons or markers, and then hang it on the classroom wall in the correct order. By the end of the quarter, you should have an illustrated version of the memory verse and the memory challenge hanging on the wall to which students can refer.

Challenge Station

You may also wish for students to continue working on their memorization of the order of the books of the Bible. To encourage this, have a challenge station set up with a copy of the *Bible Library* (p. 296), markers, scrap paper, stickers and/or small candy pieces. If students arrive early or have free time, they can go to this center alone or in pairs and work on reciting or writing the names of the books of the Bible or the sections of each Testament in order. Students can self-check their work using the *Bible Library* and reward themselves with a sticker or piece of candy for their efforts (limit one piece/sticker per visit to the center).

Review Bible Skills

If you have students who have just recently joined your class, are younger, or are simply less experienced at using their Bibles or the related study tools, you may wish to provide them some extra assistance in one or more of the following ways:

- Pair the less-experienced Bible student with a student who has more experience when using Bibles, study tools, or in completing activities.
- Give students a mini-lesson on how to use the Bible concordance or dictionary. You may even wish to have a more experienced student do this for you; sometimes students are the best teachers for other students!
- Acquaint newer students with the table of contents in their Bibles so that they know how to locate a particular book; briefly explain the chapter and verse system that the Bible uses.

No matter what level your students, it is imperative that they handle and use a Bible each week, and that there is a Bible dictionary and concordance available for each pair of students. You may wish to encourage your students to borrow a study Bible from a parent, as the concordances in the back of these are appropriate for use by this age level. Extra dictionaries and concordances can also be borrowed from families, church libraries, and the local public library. Just make sure that the concordances are referenced to the version of the Bible that you use in your classroom. The *New International Version* works well for this age group.

Lesson Aims

Students will
- Research background information on the raising of Lazarus
- Summarize and illustrate one of five Bible accounts of resurrections
- Choose one way that God shows His power, and express thanks to Him

Materials
chalkboard or white board
chalk or dry-erase marker
Bibles
Bible dictionaries

▼ Building Study Skills ▲

Write the word *resurrection* on the chalkboard. Ask: **What do you believe the word *resurrection* means? Have you ever heard of anyone being resurrected? Who? Do you know of anyone who has ever resurrected someone else? Who? How does someone get resurrected?**

Write students' ideas around the word *resurrection* in a web fashion on the board. Then tell students that today they are going to explore this word using their Bibles and Bible dictionaries so that they can get a better understanding of what it means.

Pass out Bible dictionaries to students, taking time to review with them briefly about the dictionary's function and use.

Have students look up *resurrection* in their Bible dictionaries, assisting as necessary. You may wish to pair students if your supply of Bible dictionaries is small. Have one or two students read the entry aloud while other students follow along. Look back to the web that students made to affirm any correct ideas that the students may have had. ***Resurrection* does mean to raise someone who was dead back to life. You were correct when you said you remembered that one of the prophets once resurrected someone.** Tell students that today they are going to use their dictionaries to explore several Bible resurrection stories that demonstrate Jesus' and God's power over death.

▼ Using Study Skills ▲

Materials
Bible Atlas Map 2 (p. 306)
Resurrection Report (p. 190)
2 9" × 12" pieces of construction paper
1 sheet of white paper
Bible dictionaries
Bibles
5 prepared index cards (see instructions)
pencils
markers or crayons
stapler

Before class, make a cover for the class book you will be making in this lesson by taking one piece of construction paper and writing on it "Alive Again: A Book of Bible Resurrections." Use the blank piece of paper to make the title page for the book; this page should again contain the title, the name of your class as the author, and the date on which the book was started.

Also, write one of the following names/references on each of the five index cards: the son of the widow of Zarephath—1 Kings 17:17-24; the son of the Shunammite woman—2 Kings 4:32-37; the son of the widow of Nain—Luke 7:11-17; Jairus's daughter—Luke 8:41, 42, 51-56; Dorcas—Acts 9:36-42. Later on, these cards will be passed out and used as research assignments for the class book.

Have students turn to John 11:17. Review the name of this section of the Bible (Gospels), and that John is the fourth Gospel of four. Tell the students that they will read the account of how Jesus raised His friend Lazarus from the dead. Have students look up *Lazarus* in their Bible dictionaries. Have the students read the entry silently, noting that it is the Lazarus of John 11, 12 and not the one in Matthew in which we are interested. Ask: **What information does the dictionary give you about Lazarus?** (He was a friend of Jesus, brother of Mary and Martha, and lived in Bethany.) Then have students find *Bethany* in their Bible dictionaries, having one student read this entry aloud. Assist students in finding *Bethany* in the Bible atlas, noting its proximity to Jerusalem (about two miles). **Now that we know a little more about who this story is about and where it is taking place, let's see how Jesus performed this amazing miracle.**

Direct students' attention to the text, calling on a student to read aloud John 11:17-22. Say: **Look at verses 21, 22. How was Martha feeling?** (upset that Jesus didn't come and heal her brother)

Explain to students that Mary and Martha had sent word to Jesus that Lazarus was sick, but that He had not come to heal him because He knew that God had even bigger plans in mind for Lazarus. However, the sisters did not know this, so they felt bad about Jesus not coming, but hopeful that Jesus could still do something about it.

Have another student read aloud verses 23-27. **What do you think Jesus meant when He said, "I am the resurrection and the life"?** (that He can give us eternal life with God if we believe in Him; that even though we die, we can live with Him in Heaven after we die)

Have students look up *Christ* in their dictionaries to discover the meaning of this term. **Martha believed Jesus was the one that God had sent to save His people; but she was hoping to get her brother back right away.**

Have a student read 11:32-37. **How did Jesus feel when He saw Mary and the others crying?** (sad; deeply moved, troubled) **Does it surprise you that Jesus cried? Why or why not?** (no, because He loves people; yes, because He knew He was going to raise Lazarus) **What were some of the people thinking?** (Why couldn't He have healed Lazarus?)

Have a student read verses 38-44. **Why did Martha not want Jesus to open the tomb?** (Lazarus had been dead four days and would smell pretty bad.) **Do you think she had any idea what Jesus was going to do? How did Jesus raise Lazarus from the dead?** (He thanked God and told Lazarus to come out.) **How do you think Mary, Martha, and the others standing around felt when they first saw Lazarus?** (excited, scared, amazed) **How do you think Lazarus felt?** (confused, wrapped up, happy) **Let's look to see now how people felt about Jesus after seeing Him raise Lazarus.**

Have students read verses 45, 46. **What do these verses say people did?** (Some believed in Him, others went to the Pharisees.) Have students look up *Pharisees* in dictionaries to see who they are. Explain to students how the Pharisees became very upset when people believed in Jesus because they thought His teaching about God's Law was wrong. Therefore, from this point on, they looked for a chance to arrest Jesus so that people would stop believing in Him.

Not only did the Pharisees set out to arrest Jesus, they also set out to kill someone else. Let's see who in John 12:10, 11. Have students read John 12:10, 11. **Who did the Pharisees want to kill? Why?** (Lazarus, since people were putting their faith in Jesus instead of following the Pharisees because of what they had seen) Explain to students that the Pharisees figured if they destroyed the "evidence" of the miracle, as well as arrest and kill the person who performed it, the excitement would die down, people would forget about Jesus, and life would go on as normal. **Little did they know that in just a few short days, after they did arrest and kill Jesus, God was going to resurrect Him, and that would cause more people than ever to believe in Him. But that's a story we'll save for a few weeks from now.**

Tell the students that the raising of Lazarus is only one of six resurrection stories we read of in the Bible where a person used God's power to raise another person from the dead. Explain to students that they are going to work in teams to make a class book that will help them learn about these other five resurrection stories. (Jesus' resurrection is unique in that God directly raised Him from the dead, and it is not included in this count. Inform students that they will explore this most important of all resurrection stories at a later time.) Divide students into five groups, giving each group a copy of *Resurrection Report* and one of the prepared index cards with their assignment on it. Model for them how to fill out the page by doing a sample page for Lazarus. Then give teams time to complete their pages, assisting them as necessary with finding their Scripture passages and filling out and illustrating their pages. When groups are finished, check their work (the on page 189 will assist you). Then allow them to put their page in appropriate chronological book order behind the title page that you prepared earlier. When all pages are in the book, use the stapler to attach the cover.

▼ Responding to Study ▲

Materials
completed class book
Time Line Segments (pp. 309-314)

Read "Alive Again" to your class, allowing each group to present their page, if desired.

As you read, briefly discuss each account using the following questions: **How is this resurrection story the same as the others we read? What makes it unique?**

When finished reading, ask students which account was their favorite and why. Then share the following: **Even though each one of these resurrection accounts was unique, they are all the same in that they remind us of something very special: God does have power over death, and Jesus is the "resurrection and the life!" As our new memory verse for this unit says, if we believe in Jesus, even though our physical bodies die, we will live forever with God in Heaven. But death isn't the only thing over which God has power.**

Direct students' attention to the *Time Line Segments* hanging up in the classroom. Challenge students to use the time line to think of an event they have studied this year that demonstrates God's power. Allow students who think of an idea to come up to the board one at a time and draw their ideas "pictionary-style." Other students in the class should try to guess what they are drawing. Play this as long as time allows, briefly discussing the way in which the event the student draws illustrates God's power (i.e., power over nature, sickness, etc.). At the conclusion of the game, discuss God's power as follows: **How does it make you feel to know that God and His Son, Jesus, are so powerful?** (safe and secure, amazed, a bit afraid, relaxed, etc.)

Say: **God deserves our praise because He is so powerful. What are some ways that we can show Him our praise for His power?** (praying, singing, living the way He asks us to, telling others about Him, etc.)

▼ Reviewing Study Skills ▲

Materials
index cards
markers
pencils
Bibles

Divide students into pairs, making sure to pair more experienced students with newer, less experienced students. Instruct pairs to work together to find John 11:25 in their Bibles. Then have each pair write each word of the memory verse on a separate index card. Have the pairs scramble their cards, and then attempt to put them back in order from memory. When they are finished, they can check their work using their Bibles, rearranging cards as necessary. After doing this two to three times, challenge one student in the pair to remove a few cards while his teammate isn't looking. The teammate should try to say the whole verse, even with the cards missing. Repeat this for as long as time permits.

Give each student an index card and a pencil. Challenge students to recall things over which God has power. Ask each student to pick the thing for which he or she is most thankful. Then encourage students to write a brief prayer (2–3 sentences) thanking God for His power and the way they most appreciate that He demonstrates it. Give students a moment of silence in which to say their prayers. Then close, thanking God for His tremendous power and particularly His power over death. Encourage students to place their cards in their Bibles or in a place in which they will see them throughout the week so that they can remember to praise God each day for what they have written.

Raised Person	Scripture	Miracle Done by	Location	Details
1. Son of widow of Zarephath	1 Kings 17:17-24	Elijah	Zarephath	Elijah took boy to upper room; laid on him three times and prayed; boy's life returned; widow believes that Elijah is a man of God.
2. Son of Shunammite woman	2 Kings 4:32-37	Elisha	Shunem	Elisha shut door; prayed to God; laid on boy two times; boy sneezed seven times and woke up.
3. Son of widow of Nain	Luke 7:11-17	Jesus	Nain	Jesus touched coffin; said "Young man, get up!" Man sat up/began talking; people filled with awe and praised God; said Jesus was a great prophet.
4. Jairus's daughter	Luke 8:41, 42, 51-56	Jesus	Jairus's house	Jesus took girl by the hand and said, "Child, get up!" Parents were astonished.
5. Dorcas	Acts 9:36-42	Peter	Joppa	Peter got on knees and prayed; said, "Tabitha, get up!" Many people believed in the Lord.

Resurrection Report

1. Who was raised from the dead? _____

2. Where is it recorded in the Bible? _____

3. Who performed the miracle? _____

4. Where did it happen? _____

5. What were the details? _____

_____

_____

_____

_____

_____

_____

_____

_____

_____

_____

_____

 LESSON 32

Jesus Does God's Will

Exodus 12; Luke 22; 1 Corinthians 11

Lesson Aims

Students will

- Create an imaginary invitation for a Passover dinner
- Reenact the last supper of Jesus and the disciples
- Compare three Gospel accounts of Jesus' prayer in Gethsemane

▼ Building Study Skills ▲

Before class, fold the 9" x 12" pieces of construction paper in half. On the front of the folded paper, write "You're Invited to the First Passover!" On the inside of each sheet, write the following headings, spacing them evenly apart:

Date:

Menu:

Dress Code:

Decorations:

Students will fill out these invitations later in the lesson.

Share with students that today's Bible story is found in Luke 22. Review with them in what Testament and division of the Bible this book can be found. **Is Luke in the Old Testament or the New Testament?** (New) **In what division of the New Testament is Luke found?** (the Gospels) **Do you remember what the Gospels tell us about?** (the life of Christ, the good news that Jesus died for people)

Then instruct students to work independently or in groups of three to do a "Fast Find" of Luke 22:7. (Students locate the Scripture as quickly as possible, and then help others around them to do the same if necessary.) Make sure to pair less experienced students with those who are more experienced in their Bible skills. When all students have located the passage, explain that what they are about to read takes place the night before Jesus went to the cross and features Jesus eating a very special meal with His disciples.

Say: **As we read this passage, see if you can discover the name of this very special meal.** Have a student read aloud Luke 22:7, 8. **What was the name of the special meal that Jesus wanted to eat with His disciples?** (Passover) **Have you ever heard of the Passover before? What do you know about it?** Allow students to share what knowledge they have about the Passover celebration and customs.

Then instruct students to use their Bible dictionaries to look up *Passover*. Read and discuss the definition given, making sure that students understand that the Passover occurred on the first night of the Feast of Unleavened Bread. It was a ceremonial meal celebrated by the Jews to help them remember their deliverance from Egypt and how the Lord "passed over" their homes with the plague of death because they were marked with the lamb's blood.

Divide students into groups of three if not done earlier, once again making sure that there is at least one experienced Bible student in each group. Distribute to each group a prepared Passover invitation.

To find out this invitation information, we are going to have to find the text that talks about the first Passover. Any ideas on how we could find this

Materials

Bibles

dictionaries

Bible concordances

9" × 12" light-colored construction paper (1 sheet per 3 students)

black marker

text? (Bible dictionary and concordance) Tell students even though the dictionary would be an excellent way to find this passage, today they are going to use their concordances to do so. Lead students to find the text that describes the first Passover by looking up the key word *Passover* in their concordances and finding the first text in chronological book order that mentions the Passover (Exodus 12:11). Have students turn to Exodus 12, and tell them that all the information they need will be located in verses 1-13. Instruct groups to read this passage and complete their invitations as directed. Allow students time to complete their invitations, assisting groups as necessary. When all groups have finished, allow students to share the information they have found, discussing its significance in commemorating Israel's slavery and release.

When was the Passover meal to be held? (on the fourteenth day of the first month of the year) Note for students that this usually occurs by our calendar in the month of March or April. **What foods were supposed to be eaten at this meal?** (roasted lamb or goat meat, bitter herbs, bread without yeast) Explain to students that the bitter herbs were to remind the Israelites of how hard and bitter their years spent in slavery were. The way the meat was prepared, as well as the eating of bread without yeast, symbolized the quickness with which the Israelites had to leave the country of Egypt in the middle of the night; there was no time to specially dress the meat or to let bread rise. Also note that by the time of Jesus, the Jewish people included four special cups of the fruit of the vine (wine) in their celebration of this meal—they will notice this when they read the account of Jesus' celebration of the Passover.

What was the dress code for this celebration? (cloak tucked into your belt, sandals on feet, staff in hand) Explain to students that this was the way a person would be dressed when prepared to travel or go out somewhere—this once again reminded them of how quickly they had to leave Egypt after the final plague of death hit.

The Passover had one very strange decoration. What was it? (the blood of the lamb or goat put on the sides and tops of the doorframes of the houses) Explain to students that this blood was a sign to the Lord that Israelites were in the house, and that the firstborn in that house should not be killed. The lamb or goat had been offered in sacrifice to God; it would take the place of the first born child/animal. But wherever the blood was not found, the firstborn son and animals of the house were killed. This was what caused the quick release of the Israelites.

Direct student attention to Exodus 12:17, having a student read this verse aloud, and other students to listen for why the Israelites were to celebrate this feast.

Why does this verse say that God wanted the Israelites to celebrate this feast? (to remember how He had delivered them from slavery) **This verse says that the Passover was to be "a lasting ordinance for generations to come"— it was something that the Jews were to celebrate once a year forever to remind them that they were God's chosen people whom He had set free to serve Him. In today's lesson, we are going to see how Jesus and His disciples kept this command of God to celebrate the Passover, and how Jesus gave parts of this meal a special, new meaning.**

▼ Using Study Skills ▲

Before class, set up some very low tables in a U-shaped pattern for students to use to reenact the last supper. Set a large goblet and a plate of unleavened bread (matzo) in the middle of the head table. If tables are not available, set out a large blanket with the goblet and bread placed in the middle. Have students pretend that a U-shaped table is in the middle of this area.

Also, on the blank piece of paper, use the marker to write the words "Mount of Olives." Choose a location somewhere in your classroom to represent the Mount of Olives, and post the sign you have made in that area.

Materials
large goblet
plate
unleavened bread (matzo)
low tables or a blanket
Bibles
completed Passover menus
Bible dictionaries
Bible Atlas Maps 1-3 (pp. 305-307)
paper
marker
Time Line Segments (pp. 309-314)

Have students turn in their Bibles once again to Luke 22. Instruct them to read verses 14-16 silently, paying special attention to what Jesus said and did.

Reenact the last supper with your students, explaining at each point what Jesus and the disciples were doing. Demonstrate how they would have reclined on their left sides with their heads near the table, and have the students join you. Then return to a sitting position.

Talk about how Jesus offered unleavened bread to the disciples. While this was traditional in the Passover meal, Jesus gave it new meaning and purpose: "This do in remembrance of me."

"After the supper" (verse 20), Jesus gave the disciples a cup of wine to share. While not a part of the original Passover, by Jesus' day Jewish people had added four "cups" to the meal, along with special prayers. As with the bread, Jesus gave a new meaning and purpose for the cup.

If you wish, allow the students to break matzos and drink grape juice as you reenact the last supper. Make sure, however, that none of your students have food allergies that would prevent them from doing so.

Ask: **What did Jesus mean when He said that the cup was a reminder of the new covenant in His blood? Let's use our Bible dictionaries to help us understand this.**

Have students look up the word *covenant,* making sure they understand that it is an agreement or promise between God and people. Draw attention to the *Time Line Segments,* pointing to the time of the Passover and to the giving of the Law on Mt. Sinai.

Explain that God made a covenant with Israel on Mt. Sinai: if they would keep the laws He gave them He would care for them, protect them, and not punish them for their sins. When the people of Israel celebrated the Passover each year they remembered God's covenant. Use the time line to remind the students that Israel kept their part of the covenant for a while, but then they broke it and were sent into exile as punishment.

Even though God's people had broken the covenant He made with them, He still loved them so He decided to make a new covenant, once and for all time. God sent Jesus, His only Son, to die and take the punishment for the sins of the whole world. That's the "new covenant" Jesus was talking about.

Explain to students that after Jesus and the disciples finished celebrating the Passover, they went to a place called the Mount of Olives to pray (Luke 22:39-42). Have students take their Bibles and move to the location you have labeled "Mount of Olives." They can define the term using their Bible dictionaries and locate the site on *Bible Atlas Map 2.*

> **Note**
> Be aware of your students' allergies before you allow them to eat.

▼ Responding to Study ▲

Explain to students that after Jesus died, arose, and went back to be with God in Heaven, His followers continued to celebrate the special meal of unleavened bread and fruit of the vine that Jesus had asked them to use to remember Him. Explain that this meal became known as the Lord's Supper and became a reminder to the believers of God's new covenant with His people, just as the Passover had been a special reminder of God's old covenant with the Israelites.

Why do you think it is important to remember that Jesus died for us and that God has forgiven us? (Allow students to respond.) **Believers in Jesus all over the world continue to remember Jesus' death by taking the Lord's Supper.**

Tell students that you are going to give them a chance to make a door hanger for their rooms that will also help them to remember Jesus' love for them and His death on the cross. Pass out the 4" x 9" pieces of construction paper, markers, and scissors to students. Instruct them to place a paper cup in the upper portion of the piece of construction paper and trace around it. Then have students cut from

> **Materials**
> 4" x 9" pieces of light construction paper
> 3 oz. paper cups
> scissors
> markers or crayons

one side of the construction paper to the circle they have drawn, cutting out the circle. Once students have their door hangers cut, have them label and decorate them as a reminder of Jesus' sacrifice or the new covenant. When students have finished, allow willing students to share with the rest of the class what they have drawn or written. **What have you included on your door hanger to help you remember Jesus' love for you? How do you think you will feel when you see your door hanger?**

▼ Reviewing Study Skills ▲

Review with students the definition and purpose of a Gospel harmony. (A harmony is a listing of texts found in the Gospels that all describe the same event. By reading all the texts listed in a harmony about one particular event, you can get a fuller picture of what really happened.)

Divide students into pairs, making sure to match more experienced students with those who may be less experienced. Assign each pair one of the following passages: Matthew 26:36-39; Mark 14:32-36; Luke 22:39-42. Instruct the students to complete the *Gethsemane Harmony* worksheets by reading the portions of the passages indicated and answering the questions.

Give students time to complete the harmony worksheet. When students have finished, lead students in checking their answers and filling in the rest of the worksheet for the two accounts they were not assigned. (Use the chart on page 195 to assist you.) As you go over the accounts, demonstrate to students how each writer contributes unique components to the story that harmonize together so the reader can get a more complete version of what actually happened.

When discussing question 1, explain to students that Mount of Olives and Gethsemane are both correct; Gethsemane is just more specific as it refers to a particular garden on the Mount of Olives. When discussing question 3, note that these two accounts are not in conflict; Jesus may have very well said both of these things to the disciples.

After answering questions 4, 5, and 6, ask students the following questions:

Does Luke tell us the information about Jesus' taking Peter, James, and John on a little farther and sharing with them how He was feeling? (no) **Why do you think this is?** (accept all reasonable answers)

Explain to students that each writer probably had to pick and choose which information he felt was most important to include in his retelling of the story.

We will never know for sure why Luke left this information out of his Gethsemane story—maybe he didn't think it was important, or maybe he didn't even know that part of the story. This shows us why Gospel harmonies are so helpful; they give us all the details instead of just one writer's version of the story.

After going over all answers on the chart, draw students' attention back to how Jesus willingly submitted himself to God's will.

Did Jesus want to die for us on the cross? What did Jesus say? (He told His disciples how upset He was; He asked God to make it possible for Him not to have to do it.) **What did Jesus mean when He said, "take this cup from me"? Was this the same cup as the Passover?**

Even though it meant that He would have to die a horrible death on the cross, Jesus told God that He would do whatever God wanted Him to do. Why do you think He did this? (because He loves God and loves us)

How does that make you feel to know that Jesus, God's perfect Son, was willing to die for you? (accept all reasonable answers)

Lead students in a closing prayer, thanking God for Jesus' willingness to die so that the new covenant would be possible. Also pray that God will assist your students in never forgetting Jesus' great love and sacrifice for them.

Materials
Bibles
Gethsemane Harmony (p. 196)
pencils

Question	Luke 22:39-42	Matthew 26:36-39	Mark 14:32-36
1. Where did Jesus go?	Mount of Olives	Gethsemane	Gethsemane
2. Who was with Jesus?	disciples	disciples	disciples
3. What did Jesus say to those who were with Him?	"Pray that you will not fall into temptation."	"Sit here while I go over there and pray."	"Sit here while I pray."
4. Who did Jesus take with Him from here?		Peter, two sons of Zebedee	Peter, James, and John
5. How was Jesus feeling?		sorrowful and troubled	deeply distressed and troubled
6. What did Jesus say to His friends?		"My soul is overwhelmed with sorrow to the point of death. Stay here and keep watch with me."	"My soul is overwhelmed with sorrow to the point of death. Stay here and keep watch."
7. What did Jesus do once He was by himself?	knelt down and prayed	fell with his face to the ground and prayed	fell to the ground and prayed
8. What did Jesus say in His prayer?	"Father, if you are willing, take this cup from me; yet not my will, but yours be done."	"My Father, if it is possible, may this cup be taken from me. Yet not as I will, but as you will."	"*Abba,* Father, everything is possible for you. Take this cup from me. Yet not what I will, but what you will."

Gethsemane Harmony

Directions: Use the Scriptures listed on the chart to help you answer the questions about the time Jesus spent in the Garden of Gethsemane with His followers.

Question	Luke 22:39-42	Matthew 26:36-39	Mark 14:32-36
1. Where did Jesus go?			
2. Who was with Jesus?			
3. What did Jesus say to those who were with Him?			
4. Who did Jesus take with Him from here?			
5. How was Jesus feeling?			
6. What did Jesus say to His friends?			
7. What did Jesus do once He was by himself?			
8. What did Jesus say in His prayer?			

LESSON 33

Jesus Is Alive!

Matthew 26, 27; Mark 15, 16; 1 Corinthians 15

Lesson Aims

Students will

- Make a chain showing the chronology of events surrounding Jesus' crucifixion
- Make a bracelet as an aid in telling the gospel message
- State in their own words why Jesus' death and resurrection is essential for people's salvation

▼ Building Study Skills ▲

Before class, write the following Scripture references on the board. Students will use these in creating their chain of events regarding the death of Jesus.

1. Matthew 26:36
2. Matthew 26:45
3. Matthew 26:57
4. Matthew 27:1
5. Matthew 27:2
6. Matthew 27:22
7. Mark 15:25
8. Mark 15:37

Materials
Bibles
2" x 12" strips of light colored construction paper
markers
glue sticks

Ask students to recall the topic of Lesson 33 (Jesus celebrating the Passover with His disciples; asking His followers to always remember His death, the new covenant, by using the Lord's Supper; Jesus praying in the garden of Gethsemane) **Today we are going to pick up the story right where we left off last week and take a look at the events that led to Jesus' death on the cross.**

Pass out a construction paper strip and a marker to each student. Direct attention to the Scripture references written on the board, explaining that each verse describes an event that occurred in the final hours before Jesus' death, and that the passages are numbered in the order in which they occurred. Explain to students that you will assign each of them a reference. If you have a large or less experienced class, you may wish to have students work in pairs; larger classes can also create multiple copies of the same chain if desired. They are to write the references on one side of their paper strips and find them in their Bibles. After reading the verses, they should write the main idea of the verse on the opposite side of their sentence strips. Then when all students are finished with their strips, they should use glue sticks to form the strips into a correctly ordered chain. Strips should be ordered by the number preceding the Scripture reference (1–8).

Before assigning Scripture references, briefly review the parts of a reference (book, chapter, and verse). Also review with students the location/classification of the books of Matthew and Mark (Gospels in the New Testament). Once you are sure all students understand how and where to find one of these references, assign each student a reference to write down on his strip and locate in his Bible. Allow students ample time to find, read, and summarize their verses on their paper strips, assisting with locating and understanding verses as necessary. Assure students that anything that they do not understand about their passages will be discussed in the next part of the lesson; their major focus at this point should simply be writing the major events that their verses describe on their paper strips.

As students finish their individual strips, guide the class to connect their strips into a properly ordered chain (passage 1 [Matthew 26:36] connected to passage 2 [Matthew 26:45], etc.). When the chain is finished, congratulate students on how well they used their research skills. Then tell students that they are going to use the chain they have created, along with their Bible dictionaries, to understand exactly what happened to Jesus during the last few hours of His life.

▼ Using Study Skills ▲

Materials
Bibles
Bible dictionaries
"chain of events" chain
modeling dough

Direct students' attention to the "chain of events" they have made, calling on the person/pair that completed Link 1 (Matthew 26:36) to read what happened first. (Jesus and His disciples went to Gethsemane to pray.) Remind students who were present for the previous lesson that this is the event for which they created their Gospel harmony. **What do you recall that Jesus and the disciples did in Gethsemane?** (Jesus prayed that God's will would be done; He was very troubled; the disciples waited for Jesus while He prayed.) Share with students that three times Jesus actually went off to pray by himself, asking His disciples to wait for Him and pray while He was gone. However, all three times Jesus came back and found His disciples sleeping.

This leads us to the next event on the chain. Who completed Link 2?

Call on the person who completed Link 2 to tell what happened in his verse. (Jesus found His disciples sleeping and told them it was time for Him to be betrayed.)

What does it mean to betray someone? (to give help or information to the enemy; to be disloyal) **Do you remember which of Jesus' disciples betrayed Him and turned Him in to the Jewish leaders?** (Judas)

Remind students that Judas had gone to the Jewish leaders and told them he would turn Jesus over to them for 30 pieces of silver. He arranged to do so on the night of the Passover, knowing that Jesus would go to the garden of Gethsemane to pray after the meal. He brought a large group of armed men with him (sent by the Jewish leaders) and showed them who Jesus was by kissing Him (a common greeting in Bible times). **It is at this point that the action in Link 3 takes place. Who completed this link?** Ask the person who completed Link 3 (Matthew 26:57) to tell what she wrote. (Jesus was taken to Caiaphas where the teachers of the law and elders assembled.) Have students use their Bible dictionaries to look up *Caiaphas* to find out who he was (the high priest at the time of Jesus). The elders (older men) and teachers of the law were the people who, along with the chief priests, made up the Sanhedrin. Have students look up *Sanhedrin* to see what the purpose of this group was (the high court of the Jews). Remind students that ever since Jesus had raised Lazarus from the dead, the Sanhedrin had been looking for a chance to kill Jesus because they thought He was teaching bad things and would cause trouble for them with the government. **The only thing that the Sanhedrin could find Jesus guilty of was saying the He was the Son of God. But that was all they needed to make their decision about what to do with Him. Let's see what happens next in Link 4.**

Call on the person who completed Link 4 (Matthew 27:1) to read what he wrote. (The chief priests and elders decided to put Jesus to death.) Then call on the person who completed Link 5 (Matthew 27:2) to read her link. (Jesus was bound and taken to Pilate, the governor.) **What does it mean to be bound?** (tied up with ropes, probably around the hands, arms and/or legs, like a prisoner)

Lead students to find out who Pilate was by looking up his name in their Bible dictionaries. Explain to students that the Sanhedrin was powerful, but they were not allowed to kill people for their crimes; only the Roman government was allowed to do that, and Pilate was the governor of Judea which was where Jerusalem was.

Let's see what the Jewish people asked Pilate to do with Jesus. Who completed Link 6? Allow the student who completed Link 6 (Matthew 27:22) to read it to the class. (The people asked Pilate to crucify Jesus.) Have students look up *crucifixion* in their Bible dictionaries to help them understand this form of death, noting that it was the worst of all the ways that the Roman government put people to death.

Did Pilate do what the people wanted? Let's find out by looking at Link 7. Have the student who completed Link 7 (Mark 15:25) read it aloud. (Jesus was crucified in the third hour.) Explain to students that Jesus was beaten after both of His trials; a crown of thorns was placed on His head (making fun of His charge that He said He was the "king of the Jews"); exhausted, He was forced to carry His heavy wooden cross to Golgotha, the place outside the city where the Romans crucified people; and then, at 9:00 A.M., they crucified Him by placing Him on the cross and driving the nails through His wrists and heel bones.

As He hung on the cross, many people made fun of Him and yelled insulting things at Him. But then, at 3:00 P.M., Link 8 takes place. Let's see what the final event in this part of the story is.

Have the person who wrote Link 8 (Mark 15:37) read it aloud. (With a loud cry, Jesus died.) **Jesus' long, terrible torture was over. Even though He had never sinned or done anything wrong, He died, taking the punishment for our sins, so we could be forgiven and live forever with God. How does this story make you feel so far?** (Accept all reasonable answers.)

Ask students to explain what they know about modern-day burial customs. **When someone dies today, what is usually done to the body?** (Accept all reasonable answers including body is prepared for burial, a visitation and funeral are held, body is buried, etc.) Share with students that after Jesus' death, a follower of His, Joseph of Arimathea, asked for His body. There was no time to properly prepare the body for burial because the Sabbath was about to begin at sundown; however, Joseph did wrap the body in linen with some spices and placed it in a tomb.

Invite students to learn more about Bible-times tombs. Have students choose partners and use their Bible dictionaries to look up the entry word *tomb*. Once they have read the definition, instruct the pairs to work together to build an appropriate "tomb" using modeling dough.

Allow students time to complete their research and build their tombs, assisting as necessary. When students have finished, allow them the opportunity to present their tombs, explaining the features they chose to include. Make sure students understand that all Bible-times tombs were cave-like structures with some sort of cover over the opening. Explain to students that the tomb that Jesus was placed in was new, and that Pilate had placed a guard in front of it so that Jesus' body would not be stolen by His followers.

All was quiet at the tomb of Jesus for the remainder of that sad Friday afternoon, as well as on the Sabbath (Saturday). But God had other plans for the third day after Jesus' death, Sunday, that no Roman guard could have stopped! Let's find out what happened!

Have students do a "Fast Find" in their Bibles of Mark 16:1. **It was early in the morning on Sunday, the first day of the week. Three women who were followers of Jesus were on their way to His tomb to finish the burial process. However, they knew they were facing a certain problem. Let's read verses 1-3 to see what this problem was.**

Have a student read verses 1-3 aloud. **What was the problem that the women faced?** (They were unsure of how they would move the stone in front of the tomb.) **Let's read on to see how this problem was solved.** Have another student read verses 4-7 aloud. **How was the stone problem solved?** (The stone was rolled away when the women arrived because Jesus had been resurrected.) Explain to students that Matthew tells us that the "young man" was actually an angel who had rolled the stone away.

What did the angel instruct the women to do? (Go tell Peter and the disciples that Jesus was going to meet them in Galilee.) **How would you have felt if you had been one of these women?** (Accept all reasonable answers, including frightened, excited, confused, etc.)

▼ Responding to Study ▲

Materials
chalkboard or white board
chalk or dry-erase marker
Bibles
leather or vinyl string (type used for making jewelry), cut into 12" lengths
small beads in the following colors (1 bead per color per child): red, gray, white, green
scissors

Remind students that the verses they have read that tell the story of Jesus' death, burial, and resurrection come from Matthew and Mark, two of the books we call Gospels. Ask students to name the other two books that make up the New Testament section we call the Gospels (Luke and John). Explain to students that the Greek word that we translate as *gospel* means "good news." Write on board: "Gospel = Good News."

Say: **Matthew, Mark, Luke, and John are called Gospels because each of these books contains the gospel message, or the good news, that Jesus died for our sins and then rose from the dead.** Explain to students that Jesus' death is good news for us because when He died, Jesus took the punishment for our sin so that we could be forgiven. Likewise, Jesus' resurrection is good news for us because it shows His power over death and demonstrates that we too can live forever with God in Heaven after we die.

Explain that the apostle Paul was one of Jesus' followers who told the good news of the gospel message all over the world. **Paul describes the gospel that he preached very well in the verses that we are using for our memory challenge in this unit. Let's take a look at these verses.**

Have students turn in their Bibles to 1 Corinthians 15:3-8. Give students time to read the passage silently, challenging them to pay special attention to what Paul says is included as part of the gospel message. Then call on one or more students to read the passage aloud. **What details does Paul list as part of the gospel message?** (Write these on the board as students share them: Jesus died for our sins; was buried; raised on the third day; appeared to several individuals/groups.)

Share with students that it is this message that Jesus has always asked His followers to share with others so that they can know about God's love and forgiveness for them. **Today we will make a bracelet that will help us remember the gospel message as Paul describes it here so we can remember these verses and share the good news about Jesus with others.**

Give each student a precut length of leather or vinyl string and four colored beads—one red, one gray, one white, and one green. Tell students that each bead stands for a part of the gospel message:

Red: Jesus' death (the color of His blood)
Gray: Jesus' burial (the color of stone)
White: Jesus' resurrection (the color of the angel's clothes)
Green: Jesus' appearances (the color of that symbolizes life)

Instruct students to tie a knot near the middle of their leather string, and then to thread each bead onto the string, tying a knot between each bead and after the last bead. When students are done making bracelets, assist them in tying them onto their wrists, and cutting off any excess string. Ideally, bracelets should be just loose enough to slip off and on without breaking or coming untied. After students have completed their bracelets, have them use their bracelets to practice telling the gospel message to each other. After all students have had time to practice sharing the message, discuss the impact that their knowledge of the gospel message has on them.

How does it make you feel to know that Jesus was willing to die so that you could be forgiven of your sins and live forever with God in Heaven? (Accept all reasonable answers; some answers may include: happy that He loved me that much; thankful that I don't have to be punished for my sins; excited to know that I can live with God forever; grateful that He took the punishment for me.) **What are some ways that we can show our thanks to Jesus for what He did for us?** (Believe in Him, do what He says, tell Him "thank You" in prayers and songs, tell others about Him, etc.)

▼ Reviewing Study Skills ▲

Give each student a copy of *Race to the Tomb* and a pencil. Read the directions on the page aloud to the students, making sure that they understand their task. Then give them the option of working by themselves or with a partner to complete the page. Remind students to check their answers when they are finished by looking up John 11:25 in their Bibles.

Allow students time to finish the page, assisting them as necessary. As students finish, encourage them to practice saying this verse to one another, reminding them that it is the memory verse for this unit. When all students have finished the page and most have had time to practice saying the verse, thank students for their hard work, and encourage them to continue working at home on memorizing this verse, as well as the unit memory challenge (1 Corinthians 15:3-8). Then ask students to reflect on the meaning of John 11:25.

Do you remember what it means when Jesus says that He is the "resurrection and the life?" (Accept all reasonable answers, leading students to see that Jesus means that His death gives us resurrection and life; even though we die, we will live eternally with God in Heaven because we have been forgiven.) Point out that this verse is just another way of stating the gospel, that is, the good news about Jesus. **Do you know of anyone else who can make this claim?** (no one but God and Jesus)

Lead students in a closing prayer, thanking and praising God for Jesus and for sending us the good news of forgiveness and eternal life through His death and resurrection. Pray that God will help your students see the importance of the gospel to their own lives, as well as give them the opportunity to share the message with others.

Materials
Race to the Tomb (p. 202)
Bibles

Answer to *Race to the Tomb*
Jesus said to her, I am the resurrection and the life. He who believes in me will live even though he dies.

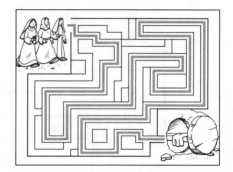

Race to the Tomb

Help the women find their way to the empty tomb by tracing the correct path. Number the letters from 1-20 in the order in which you come to them on the path. The first two are done for you. Then, use the numbered letters to crack the code below to see what Jesus says about His power over death. You can check your work when you are done by looking up John 11:25.

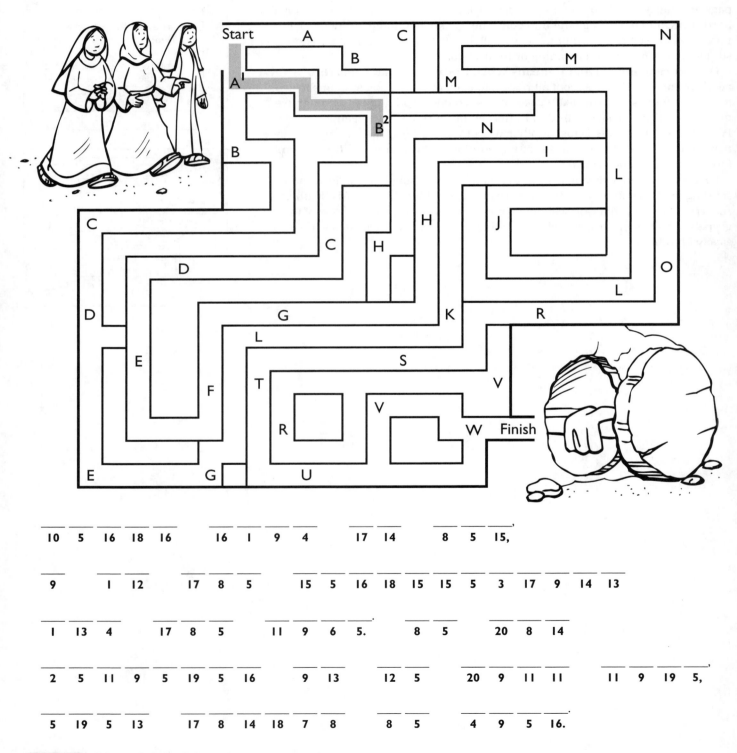

10	5	16	18	16		16	1	9	4		17	14

8 5 15,

___ ___ ___ ___ ___ ___ ___ ___ ___ ___ ___ ___ ___ ___ ___
9   1   12   17   8   5   15   5   16   18   15   15   5   3   17   9   14   13

___ ___ ___ ___ ___ ___ ___ ___ ___ ___ ___
1   13   4   17   8   5   11   9   6   5.   8   5   20   8   14

___ ___ ___ ___ ___ ___ ___ ___ ___ ___ ___ ___ ___ ___ ___ ___ ___
2   5   11   9   5   19   5   16   9   13   12   5   20   9   11   11   11   9   19   5,

___ ___ ___ ___ ___ ___ ___ ___ ___
5   19   5   13   17   8   14   18   7   8   8   5   4   9   5   16.

 LESSON 34

Recognize Jesus!

Luke 24; John 20

Lesson Aims

Students will

- Match Old Testament prophecies concerning the Messiah with their New Testament fulfillment in Jesus
- Report to the class on one of Jesus' post-resurrection appearances
- Thank and praise God for Jesus on a praise mural

▼ Building Study Skills ▲

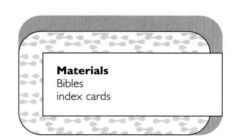

Materials
Bibles
index cards

Before class, write each of the following Scripture references on a separate index card. These cards will be used by students to play a matching game. The references are paired here for your reference:

Psalm 16:8-10; Luke 24:1-7
Psalm 22:7, 8; Matthew 27:43
Psalm 22:18; Matthew 27:35
Isaiah 53:5; John 19:33, 34
Isaiah 53:7; Matthew 26:62, 63
Isaiah 53:9; Matthew 27:57-60

Have students do a "Fast Find" of the unit memory challenge, 1 Corinthians 15:3-8. Review with students what Testament 1 Corinthians is found in (New) as well as in what division of the New Testament it occurs (epistles or Letters).

Do you remember what an *epistle* is? (A letter written by an apostle to a Christian or a group of Christians.) Remind students of the fact that this passage is one that describes the "gospel" or "good news" about Jesus' death for our sins and resurrection from the dead. Have all students read the passage aloud together.

Remind students that long before Jesus was born, God had told His people through His special messengers, the prophets, that He was going to make a new covenant with them and send them a Savior (one who would save them from their sins). God gave the prophets all sorts of information about this Savior, who was often called the Messiah, so that they could recognize Him when He arrived. Tell students that one way we know for sure that Jesus was God's promised Savior, the Messiah, is because He fulfilled or carried out so many of the Old Testament prophecies about the Messiah. (For example, the prophet Micah said that the Messiah would be born in Bethlehem; Jesus was.) Explain to students that this is what Paul means when he says that Jesus died for our sins and was raised on the third day "according to the Scriptures." The way He died and the fact that He was resurrected on the third day after He died was all predicted by the Old Testament prophets at least 400 years before Jesus' birth.

Today we will play a matching game that will help us become familiar with some of these Old Testament prophecies about the Messiah and see how Jesus fulfilled them.

Give each student one of the Scripture index cards you prepared before class. If you have a small class, use fewer passages; just be sure there is a New Testament match for each Old Testament passage you choose to use. If you have a larger class, have students work in pairs. Explain to students that some of them have Old Testament passages written on their cards and some of them have New

Testament passages. Say: **For each Old Testament prophecy there is a New Testament passage that shows Jesus' fulfilling that prophecy.** To play the game, each student should find and read his passage and then try to find the student who has the passage that matches his. To make sure students understand the game, demonstrate a matching pair for them using Isaiah 53:7 and Matthew 26:62, 63. Explain how the Matthew passage is the fulfillment of the Isaiah passage because it shows Jesus remaining silent in His trial when He was accused of wrong doing. Isaiah had predicted that the Messiah would stand silent before His accusers.

When you are sure that students understand their task, have them begin the game, assisting them in understanding and matching their passages as necessary. When all students have found their partners, allow pairs of students to share their matches by briefly summarizing their Old Testament prophecy and its New Testament fulfillment. The chart below lists the matching passages and a summary of the related content.

Psalm 16:8-10: Luke 24:1-7—The psalmist says God will not allow his "holy one" to see decay, nor will He abandon Him to the grave; Luke says Jesus is no longer dead, but is risen.

Psalm 22:7, 8; Matthew 27:43—The psalmist says that the Messiah was mocked and insulted; Matthew records that the Jews mocked Jesus using the very words of Psalm 22:8.

Psalm 22:18; Matthew 27:35—The psalmist says lots were cast for the Messiah's clothing; Matthew says the soldiers cast lots to divide up Jesus' clothing at His crucifixion.

Isaiah 53:5; John 19:33, 34—Isaiah says the Messiah will be "pierced for our transgressions"; John says Jesus' side was pierced after He died on the cross.

Isaiah 53:7; Matthew 26:62, 63—Isaiah says Messiah was silent before His accusers; Matthew says that during Jesus' trial, He remained silent.

Isaiah 53:9; Matthew 27:57-60—Isaiah says the Messiah was with the rich in His death; Matthew says Joseph of Arimathea, a rich man, buried Jesus in his own tomb.

When all students have shared their passages, direct student attention back to 1 Corinthians 15:3-8. Explain that Jesus not only died and was raised "according to the Scriptures"; He also proved He was alive by appearing to many people after He rose from the dead. Tell the students that today they are going to look at three of these post-resurrection appearances, all of which prove that Jesus was who He said He was, and that He was and is indeed alive.

▼ Using Study Skills ▲

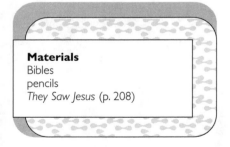

Materials
Bibles
pencils
They Saw Jesus (p. 208)

Divide students into at least three groups, limiting the size of each group to four students. Give each group a pencil and a copy of *They Saw Jesus*. (Groups may wish to choose one person to be the recorder for the group.) Tell groups that they are going to explore and report on one of three appearances that Jesus made after He was resurrected from the dead. (Make sure students are aware that Jesus made more than three resurrection appearances; today they will only have time to examine three appearances in-depth.) Assign each group one of the following passages, acquainting students with the people involved in each: Luke 24:13-35 (two travelers on the road to Emmaus); Luke 24:36-47 (the eleven disciples/those with them); John 20:24-30 (Thomas). Instruct groups to read their passages carefully and then answer the questions on the worksheet. Read each question aloud, making sure students understand what information is being requested. When you are sure students understand their task, allow groups time to complete their assignments, assisting them in understanding their passages as necessary. As you monitor each group's progress, make sure to encourage every group member to actively participate in the reading, research, and question-answer process.

When all groups have finished, call students back together. Share with groups that now they are going to get a chance to "teach" the class by sharing what they have learned with the rest of the class. Tell students that all of these passages occur after the first appearance of Jesus to the women outside of the tomb, and that they will look at them in the order in which they occurred. Beginning with the group that studied Luke 24:13-35, have each group read its passage aloud to the class while other students follow along in their Bibles. Then allow each group to share the answers to its questions, discussing/clarifying the information presented as appropriate. A discussion guide including the answers to each question is provided below.

Luke 24:13-35

1. **To whom did Jesus appear?** Two men that were walking together; one of them was named Cleopas.

2. **In what way did He make His appearance?** Jesus came up and walked along with them on the road; the two men didn't know it was Jesus until He broke bread with them later in the evening.

3. **Where did this appearance take place (city, location, etc.)?** On the road from Jerusalem to Emmaus and then in the village of Emmaus.

4. **What did Jesus say to His followers?** Before they recognized Him, He explained to them using Old Testament Scriptures ("Moses and all the Prophets") that the Christ (Messiah) had to suffer before He could "redeem Israel" and "enter his glory." Explain to students that most Jews mistakenly believed that the Messiah was going to be a great king who would help them conquer their enemies and then be their new ruler on the earth. They either overlooked or misunderstood the Old Testament prophecies that clearly state that the Messiah would have to suffer and die before He could deliver Israel from sin. These passages, such as those found in Isaiah 53 that students read earlier in the matching game, are probably the ones that Jesus helped these two men to understand.

5. **What, if anything, did Jesus do to convince His followers that He was really alive?** Talked with them, walked with them, broke bread and prayed with them—they clearly believed the person whom they were speaking to was a normal, living human being.

6. **How did Jesus' followers react to His visit?** They went back to Jerusalem, told the eleven disciples and the others with them that Jesus was indeed risen, and told all the details of their encounter with Him.

Pretend you are one of Jesus' disciples. Having heard the women's story about the empty tomb, as well as the report of Cleopas and his friend, how do you think you would be feeling about now? (Accept all reasonable answers including confused, frightened, hopeful that Jesus is alive, etc.) **Let's see what happens next from the group that researched Luke 24:36-47.** (Have a member of a group that researched this passage read it aloud to the class.)

Luke 24:36-47

1. **To whom did Jesus appear (see Luke 24:33)?** The eleven and those with them, including Cleopas and his friend. Remind students that the twelve disciples have now become the eleven because Judas, the betrayer, is no longer with them. The "others" simply refers to other followers of Jesus, mostly from Galilee.

2. **In what way did He make His appearance?** He simply appeared in the room in which they were meeting. Share with students that John says the doors of the room were locked which makes this appearance all the more miraculous.

3. **Where did this appearance take place (city, location, etc.)?** In Jerusalem, wherever the disciples were meeting. Remind students that this is where many of the Jews had gathered to celebrate the Passover and was also the site of Jesus' death, burial and resurrection.

4. **What did Jesus say to His followers?** Peace be with you; convinced them

He was a real man and not a ghost; asked for something to eat; explained to them how He had fulfilled the Old Testament prophecies about Him, especially those that said that the Christ (Messiah) had to suffer and die before He could bring repentance and forgiveness. Note that obviously the disciples too had not understood that part of being the Messiah was having to suffer and die. They clearly thought that Jesus' death meant that He couldn't possibly be the Messiah. However, Jesus had to explain to them the Old Testament Scriptures about himself so they could see that His death was a predicted part of God's plan for the Messiah, and not a sign of defeat.

5. **What, if anything, did Jesus do to convince His followers that He was really alive?** Showed them His hands and feet; invited them to touch Him to see that He had skin and bones; ate a piece of fish. **It was obviously important to Jesus that His followers understand that they were not seeing a ghost, but that God had given Him power over death and resurrected Him.**

6. **How did Jesus' followers react to His visit?** First they were startled and frightened because they thought they were seeing Jesus' ghost; then they still did not believe it was Him out of joy and amazement. **How do you think you would have responded to seeing Jesus? Would you have believed it was him? Why or why not?** (Accept all reasonable answers.)

Tell the students that John's account of this event tells us that one of the eleven, Thomas, was not present during this appearance of Jesus to His disciples.

It is not until a week later that Thomas finally gets to see Jesus for himself. Let's see exactly how that happened in the last of the three passages that we will look at today.

John 20:24-30

1. **To whom did Jesus appear?** His disciples, including Thomas.
2. **In what way did He make His appearance?** He just appeared among them, even though the doors were locked. Note that this is identical to the way Jesus had appeared to the disciples the week before.
3. **Where did this appearance take place (city, location, etc.)?** In a house in Jerusalem. Note that the disciples must have been in this same house when Jesus appeared the week before.
4. **What did Jesus say to His followers?** Peace be with you; told Thomas to touch him and stop doubting that He was really alive; said that those who believed in Him, even though they had not seen Him, would be blessed.
5. **What, if anything, did Jesus do to convince His followers that He was really alive?** He told Thomas to touch His hands (the nail prints); told Thomas, "Reach out your hand and put it into my side" (to feel where the sword had entered His body). **Jesus was obviously trying to convince Thomas it was really Him; He had the crucifixion wounds to prove it!**
6. **How did Jesus' followers react to His visit?** Thomas believed that it was really Jesus and said, "My Lord and my God!"

Considering all that you have heard that Jesus said and did in these three passages, do you think He was God's promised Messiah or not? Was He really alive, or was He just the ghost of a dead man? Accept all reasonable answers, guiding students to see that Jesus had to be the Messiah because of the way that His life and death fulfilled Old Testament prophecies. He proved He was indeed alive by showing His wounds, allowing people to touch Him, eating, and just acting normal.

▼ Responding to Study ▲

Divide students into pairs. Have them work together to find Deuteronomy 31:8, reminding them that this is our theme Scripture for this entire year-long study. Once students find the passage, ask all students to join together in reading this passage aloud.

What does this verse say that the Lord will do for us? Will not do? (goes before us and will be with us; will not leave us or forsake us) **Because we can be sure that God will always be with us, how does this tell us we do not have to feel?** (afraid or discouraged)

Direct student attention to the Bible time line displayed in the room. Remind students that from the beginning of their study until the present, they have seen God demonstrate His faithfulness to His people over and over again. Invite them to use the time line to think of some Bible stories in which God showed His faithfulness to a particular person/group of people, and encourage them to share their ideas. Some answers may include God's faithfulness in the covenant He made with Abraham, faithfulness in caring for Joseph, faithfulness in rescuing the Israelites from slavery, faithfulness to Joshua in conquering Jericho, faithfulness to Esther and Daniel in their specific circumstances.

God has always been faithful to His people over the course of history in more ways than we can count. But the ultimate example of God's never leaving us or forsaking us is found in His sending Jesus to save us from our sins and give us eternal life.

How does it make you feel to know that we have a God who loves us enough to send His only Son to die for us so that we can live forever with Him? (thankful, grateful, relieved, excited, etc.)

Tell students that you are going to give them an opportunity to thank and praise God for Jesus by creating a Praise Mural. Pass out markers and direct student attention to the roll paper mounted on the wall. Encourage students to draw pictures and/or write notes of thanks and praise for Jesus and His resurrection.

Materials
Bibles
Time Line Segments (pp. 309-314)
white roll paper
masking tape
markers (Test markers to make sure they do not bleed through the paper. Double layer the paper if necessary.)

▼ Reviewing Study Skills ▲

Share with students that they are going to use their concordances to complete a worksheet that will help them discover the names of several people to whom Jesus appeared after His resurrection. Divide students into pairs, giving each student a pencil and *Resurrection "Who Am I?"* and each pair a concordance. Read aloud the directions at the top of the sheet to students. Complete the example at the top of the page to make sure students understand their task. When you are sure students understand, instruct them to work as a team to complete the page. Assist students as necessary in looking up key words in their concordances that will lead them to the name of the person who fits the clues. When all students have finished, check the worksheet as a whole group, asking students who got the correct answers to share what key words they used to help them find their answers.

To close class, have students form a prayer circle. Tell students that you are going to give each of them the chance to say a brief sentence prayer in which they praise Jesus for something. After students have had a moment to choose something for which they are thankful or wish to express praise, invite students to bow their heads and join you in prayer. Close the prayer time by praising God for His faithfulness and for sending Jesus. Thank Him for making eternal life possible for us through Christ's death and resurrection.

Materials
Bibles
Bible concordances
Resurrection "Who Am I?" (p. 209)
pencils

Answers to Resurrection "Who Am I?":
1. Mary Magdalene (John 20:16)
2. Peter (Matthew 16:16)
3. James (James 1:22)
4. Saul/Paul (Acts 9:5)

They Saw Jesus

Read the Scripture passage your teacher assigns you. Then answer the questions. Be prepared to report what you learn to the class.

To whom did Jesus appear?

In what way did He make His appearance?

Where did this appearance take place?

What did Jesus say to His followers?

What, if anything, did Jesus do to convince His followers that He really was alive?

 LESSON 35

Resurrection "Who Am I?"

Jesus appeared to many people after His resurrection. Below you will find five riddles to help you figure out the names of five of these people. For each riddle, read the clues. Then look up in your concordance the underlined word to help you locate the quote given. Once you find the location of the quote, look it up in your Bible and see who said it. Then you will have the answer to your riddle!

Example:

I was one of Jesus' 12 disciples.

I wouldn't believe Jesus was alive until I actually saw the nail prints in His hands and put my hand in His side.

One time when Jesus wanted to travel to some dangerous territory, I said, "Let us also go, that we may <u>die</u> with him.

Steps to solving:

• Look up *die* in the concordance; try to find the quote referred to in the riddle. (Hint: it has to be in the New Testament because these are all riddles about Jesus.) It's John 11:16.

• Look up John 11:16. See who said this quote—it's Thomas! That is the answer to your riddle!

Answer: <u>Thomas</u>

1. I am a female follower of Jesus.

I was one of the women who brought spices to the tomb to help bury Jesus.

When Jesus appeared to me outside of His empty tomb, I cried out "<u>Rabboni!</u>"

Who am I? _____

2. I was a fisherman to whom Jesus appeared several times after He arose.

Once Jesus even appeared to me while I was fishing!

When Jesus asked us disciples who we thought He was, I said, "You are the <u>Christ</u>, the Son of the <u>living</u> God."

Who am I? _____

3. I was one of Jesus' half-brothers.

I did not believe that Jesus was God's Son until after He died and arose.

Later in my life, I wrote a New Testament book in which I said, "Do not merely <u>listen</u> to the word and so <u>deceive</u> yourselves. Do what it says."

Who am I? _____

4. Jesus did not appear to me until long after He had gone back to Heaven to live with God.

I used to kill Christians before I believed in Jesus.

When Jesus appeared to me and I asked Him who He was, He said, "I am Jesus, whom you are <u>persecuting</u>."

Who am I? _____

Acts Records How the Church Began and Grew

Bible Skills
Use Bible dictionary and
concordance
Use a map

Memorize
Matthew 28:18-20

Memory Challenge
Colossians 3:15-17

Unit Overview

In this unit, we will focus on the beginning of the church. Jesus had a mission for His followers: to tell the whole world that He had come to restore their relationship with God and that He had come to forgive them. The unit begins with the Great Commission and Jesus' ascension to Heaven. As the disciples stood there watching the clouds, angels had to prod them again: "What are looking for? What are you waiting for?" And soon after, on Pentecost, they got the power they needed: the Holy Spirit. The church started out with a small flame and grew in intensity.

This is a story that builds in excitement! Help your kids see the excitement of a band of fishermen and others who were suddenly on a mission from God. Help them see that the men who left Jesus later stood in the temple courts and preached His name. Help them grow in excitement with every convert, with every city lit by the light of the world.

Then turn it over to them. This story did not end with the death of the disciples. Help your students understand that the church they know exists because of the work done by the disciples in the first century church and by later disciples throughout history. Help your kids understand that the history of the church is like a relay race and that the baton has been passed to them. Give them the encouragement they need to run the race and press on toward the goal.

Summary

In **Lesson 36** students will investigate the post-resurrection appearances of Jesus and take a look at His Great Commission.

By locating significant places on a map, students will see in **Lesson 37** the worldwide impact of the gospel.

Lesson 38 explains that the church is for all who believe in Jesus Christ and introduces the first Gentile converts.

Saul's persecution of the church and his dramatic conversion is the focus of **Lesson 39.**

In one session, **Lesson 40,** students will trace three of Paul's missionary journeys in Acts.

A Worship Service

Acts 2:42 tells us that the early believers devoted themselves to the apostles' teaching, to the fellowship, to the breaking of bread, and to prayer. Set up a worship service with those four elements. Some suggestions follow. Students may want to dress in Bible-times costumes, and they may want to rearrange the room, perhaps putting the chairs in a circle or even moving them out altogether.

Apostles' Teaching: Have a student or several students read one of the following sermons: Acts 2:14-36; 3:12-26; 4:8-12; 13:16-41; 17:22-31.

Fellowship: Make this a time when students share how God is working in their lives or what they have learned recently about being a believer. If this is intimidating, assign each student one character from the book of Acts. Instruct each student to read about his character and to present a first-person monologue as that character. Students will tell how God worked in their lives. Possible characters include a person baptized on the day of Pentecost, Peter, the servant girl Rhoda,

John, Philip, Stephen, Cornelius, Paul, Dorcas, the Philippian jailer, Lydia, and Priscilla.

Breaking of Bread: Students may prepare unleavened bread for the service according to the recipe below. During the service, have students break off a bite-size piece. Also have small cups of grape juice prepared to drink with the bread. Have a student read 1 Corinthians 11:23-28. Lead the students in a prayer thanking God for Jesus' death on the cross.

Prayer: Have students write a prayer before the worship time. Then have them read the prayers aloud during the service. Encourage students to include things in their prayers that the early believers might have included in their prayers, such as the spread of the gospel, for the leaders of the country, for the people who might persecute them, and for people who are in need.

Unleavened Bread Recipe

Ingredients
1 cup flour
3 tablespoons oil
3 tablespoons water
rolling pin
electric skillet

1. Mix flour, oil, and water until the mixture forms a ball.
2. Divide the mixture in half.
3. Use a rolling pin to flatten the dough.
4. Cook the flattened dough in the skillet at 300–350 degrees for about two minutes on each side. The bread will look like a tortilla, and when it cools, it will be hard.

Jesus Plans the Church

Matthew 28; Luke 24; Acts 1

Lesson Aims

Students will

- Dramatize interviews as eyewitnesses of Jesus' post-resurrection appearances
- Identify individuals who believed and doubted the resurrection
- Write testimonies of why they follow Jesus

▼ Building Study Skills ▲

Materials
Eyewitness News Notes (p. 215)
Bibles
Bible concordances

Before class write the people and Bible references listed below on index cards or slips of paper. As students arrive, give each one an *Eyewitness News Notes* sheet and one of the index cards. Say: **This morning you are going to be interviewed by a reporter for TV station WORD. Using the Scripture reference I give you, research the facts associated with Jesus' appearance to the person named. Use the worksheet to take notes. For our TV news report you will pretend to be the person who saw Jesus, and you will tell from your point of view what happened. Some of you may end up being the same person, but that's OK. You'll be telling about different events in that person's life.**

If you have more than 10 students, assign pairs to research the Scripture. Then one student can be the person interviewed and the other student can be the WORD reporter asking pertinent questions. If you have fewer than 10 students, you may assign them more than one event (such as two of the appearances to the disciples), and you'll need to be prepared with the questions.

Mary Magdalene	Mark 16:9-11; John 20:10-18
The other women at the tomb	Matthew 28:8-10
Peter in Jerusalem	Luke 24:34; 1 Corinthians 15:5
The two travelers on the road	Mark 16:12,13
Ten disciples behind closed doors	Luke 24:36-43; John 20:19-25
All the disciples (excluding Judas)	Mark 16:14; John 20:26-31; 1 Corinthians 15:5
Thomas	John 20:24-29
Seven disciples while fishing	John 21:1-14
Eleven disciples on the mountain	Matthew 28:16-20; Mark 16:15-18
Those who watched Jesus ascend into Heaven	Luke 24:50-52; Acts 1:3-8

▼ Using Study Skills ▲

Materials
Bibles
completed *Eyewitness News Notes*

If you feel confident "ad libbing," prepare to do this part of the lesson as the WORD news anchor or reporter. For effect, hold a pretend microphone or wear a headset. If you are not comfortable making up the anchor part, follow the lecture below and stop at the appropriate times to let the students simply report on what they read in their Scripture.

Good evening, ladies and gentlemen. This is [insert name here] **with**

UNIT 9, LESSON 36

today's WORD up-to-the-nanosecond news. Today in various locations around Jerusalem we have heard reports of people who have seen Jesus of Nazareth risen from the dead. As you recall, Jesus was convicted of blasphemy and crucified. Many witnesses can attest to the fact that He was indeed dead. But now some other witnesses have come forward to say that they have seen Jesus alive! And your best news, up-to-the-nanosecond WORD news, will bring those witnesses to you. Let's go first to Mary Magdalene, who tells an astonishing tale . . .

Have the student who researched Mary Magdalene report. If you can, prompt the student with appropriate questions, such as "How did you feel when you told the others that Jesus was alive and they didn't believe you?"

Continue the "news report" with the other women at the tomb, then go on to the disciples. **The disciples were still together behind locked doors for fear of the Jews when Jesus appeared.** Have the student who researched Luke 24:36-43 and John 20:19-23 give an "interview" or do a report. **They saw and believed. A week later** (John 20:26) **Jesus appeared again when the disciples were meeting behind closed doors. This time, Thomas who had not been there the first time, believed when he saw** (Mark 16:14; John 20:24-31).

Seven of the disciples went back to the Sea of Galilee. Led by Peter, they returned to fishing (John 21:1-14). **They fished all night but caught nothing. Jesus called to them from the shore, but they did not realize it was Him. He asked if they had fish; they didn't. He directed them to let their net down on the right side. They obeyed and were unable to haul the net in because of the large catch—153 fish! Then John recognized Jesus, probably because Jesus had performed a similar miracle earlier** (Luke 5:1-11). Have the students who did this research report.

Eleven went to Galilee to the mountain as they were told by the women. When they saw Jesus, there were two responses: some worshiped Him, but some also doubted. Jesus gave them these last words of instruction: since they were under His authority, they were to make disciples of all nations; they were to baptize and teach people in the name of the Father, the Son, and the Holy Spirit; they were to teach the new disciples to obey everything Jesus commanded. But most important, Jesus would be with them always (Matthew 28:16-20; Mark 16:15-18). Allow the students to report.

Jesus appeared to the disciples in Jerusalem (Luke 24:44-49) **saying everything was fulfilled that is written about Him in the Law of Moses, the Prophets, and the Psalms. He opened their minds so they understood the Scriptures, that He was supposed to suffer and die, and to rise from the dead on the third day. He reminded them that they were witnesses of these things.** If students researched this passage, have them report.

Then Jesus led the disciples out to the vicinity of Bethany. He lifted up His hands and blessed them. He was taken up into Heaven as they watched. Suddenly two men, dressed in white stood beside them asking, "Why stand here looking into the sky? Jesus will return the same way He went." Then they worshiped him, returned to Jerusalem with great joy, and stayed continually at the temple, praising God (Acts 1:9-14).

If you are playing the news anchor, sign off with something like, **That's it for tonight's up-to-the-nanosecond WORD news. You get all the great news with WORD.**

Make sure you are out of character as you wrap up with comments such as these: **All of these appearances by Jesus helped His disciples understand the bigger purpose of his life, death, and resurrection. It wasn't just about bringing a new kingdom, which everybody wanted at the time. It was about bringing us all back into a better relationship with God. Every time He met with His disciples after His death, Jesus proved He was who He claimed to be, the Son of God.**

▼ Responding to Study ▲

Materials
Faith or Fear? game board
(p. 216)
set of *Faith or Fear? Cards* for
each group (p. 217)
coin for each group
small game token for each
student (buttons, pennies,
pieces of candy, etc.)

Break the class into groups of three or four. Give each group a copy of the *Faith or Fear?* game board, a set of *Faith or Fear? Cards,* and a coin. Give each student a game token. Tell the class that they are going to look at the responses of each person or each group to the appearances of Jesus (use the previous list for Scripture references). The game instructions are printed on the game board.

When each of the teams has had a chance to play for a while, ask: **Did everyone who saw Jesus alive after His resurrection believe that He was alive?** (Allow students to comment.) **Not everyone believed after Jesus appeared. Thomas had heard that the other disciples had seen Him, but he insisted that he would not believe until he saw Jesus himself. After he did see Jesus, he believed. However, Jesus told Thomas that while it was great that he believed when he finally saw Jesus, it would be much greater for those who would believe that Jesus rose from the dead even without seeing Him. After Jesus returned to Heaven, people simply had to believe that what the disciples told them about Jesus was true. The people of the church would have to have much faith to believe in Jesus when they were not able to see Him the way the disciples did.**

Ask: **Do you think that our church today is much like what Jesus intended it to be? What are some things that the church does today that are like what Jesus told His disciples to do?**

▼ Reviewing Study Skills ▲

Materials
inexpensive stationery pages
and envelopes
pens/pencils
Bibles
index cards

Before class, break Matthew 28:18-20 into short sections and write them on index cards. Tape the cards to the bottom of the chairs in the room.

Distribute the stationery and envelopes. Have one student look up and read John 20:30, 31. Say: **When John wrote his Gospel, he had a purpose. What was it?** (to convince the reader to believe in Jesus) **Jesus appeared to His disciples and did amazing things after the resurrection to prove to them that He was the Son of God and that they were following the truth. If Jesus commanded His followers to teach others to obey everything He commanded, what does that mean for us?** (As followers of Jesus, we also have the responsibility to teach others to follow Jesus.)

Ask: **Why do you believe in Jesus? How is your life different because you believe in Him? One of the best ways to tell others about Jesus and why they should follow Him is to share your testimony, which is a statement about why you follow Jesus and what He has done for you. Today we are going to write our testimonies, just as John wrote his Gospel. You are going to write your testimony to share with someone who doesn't believe.** Share your own personal story with the students, and help them verbalize how God is working in their lives now.

When everyone has had a chance to write a brief testimony, ask for volunteers to read theirs to the group. Encourage all the students to choose someone at home, school, or in the neighborhood with whom to share their testimony.

If you have time, practice memorizing Matthew 28:18-20. Tell the students that you have hidden the memory verse in the room. At the end of class, have them find the words under their chairs, and then take turns taping the words up in the correct order on the board or wall. Practice reading the verses as you take down a word or two each time until all the words are gone and the students are saying the verses from memory. Save the cards for another time as a table activity for the students to shuffle the cards and then put them in order.

Eyewitness News Notes

Using the Scriptures your teacher assigns you, answer the questions below to write a report about the appearances of Jesus after His death. Pretend you are an eyewitness, and a TV reporter is interviewing you about what you saw.

Who saw Jesus?

What did He say or do?

When did they see Him?

Where did they see Him?

How did the people respond to this sighting?

Where can we find more information about this story?

Faith or Fear?

How to play:
1. Every player needs a game token.
2. Each player flips the coin. If it is heads, move two spaces forward; if it is tails, move one space forward.
3. If a player lands on a "Faith or Fear" square, he must answer the question that another student will read from a "Faith or Fear?" Card. If he answers incorrectly, he must move back one space. If he answers correctly, he may move ahead one space. If the player chooses not to answer the question, he moves back two spaces.

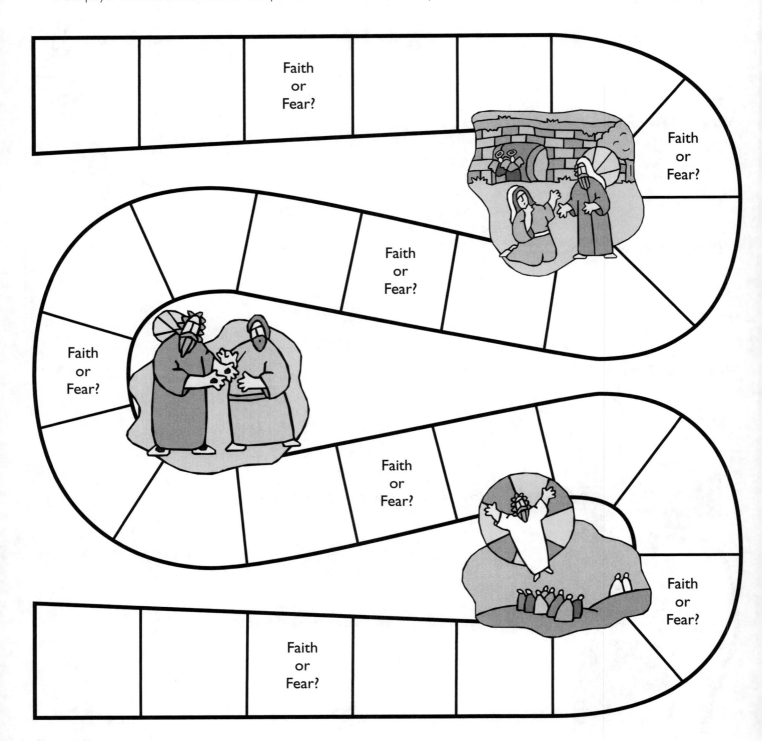

 LESSON 36

Who first saw Jesus outside the tomb? Mary Magdalene (Mark 16:9)	What did the other women (besides Mary Magdalene) do when Jesus met them at the tomb? clasped His feet and worshiped Him (Matthew 28:8, 9)	Where were the two travelers on the road going when Jesus met them? Emmaus (Luke 24:13)

What did Jesus say when He appeared to the 10 disciples behind closed doors? (choose one) Peace be with you
        I am here
        Greetings to you all
 	
Peace be with you (John 20:19)
	Name one of the 12 disciples who never saw Jesus after the resurrection.
	
	Judas
		What were the disciples doing at the Sea of Galilee when they saw Jesus?
		
		fishing (John 21:3)

Over how many days did Jesus appear to different people after the resurrection? 40 (Acts 1:3)	Name two things that Jesus told His disciples to do in the Great Commission. Go; make disciples; baptize; teach (Matthew 28:18-20)	What did Jesus' resurrection prove? that He was the Son of God
Why was it important for Jesus to appear to His disciples after the resurrection?	Describe one way you can help make disciples.	When Mary Magdalene first told the news that Jesus was alive, those who were mourning and weeping (choose one) did did not believe. did not (Mark 16:10, 11)

True or False: Jesus rebuked the 11 as they were eating for their lack of faith and stubborn refusal to believe those who had seen Him after He had risen.
 	
True (Mark 16:14)
	What was the name of one of the men on the road to Emmaus? (choose one)
	      Cletus
	      Cleopas
	      Clevon
	
	Cleopas (Luke 24:18)
		Who said he would not believe until he could see Jesus' hands and side?
		
		Thomas (John 20:24)

What meal did Jesus prepare and eat with the fishermen? breakfast (John 21:12)	When Jesus ascended into Heaven, what hid Him from sight? a cloud (Acts 1:9)	Fill in the blanks: Then Jesus came to them and said, "All ___ in heaven and on ___ has been given to me. Therefore ___ and make ___ of all nations, ___ them in the name of the ___, and of the ____, and of the ___ ___, and teaching them to ____ everything I have commanded you. And surely I am with you ___ to the very ___ of the age." (Matthew 29:18-20)

Lesson Aims

Students will

- Estimate distances from different Bible-times places to Jerusalem
- Compare practices of the early church with practices of the church today
- Review the Bible book divisions by playing a game

Materials
Bible dictionaries
Bible atlases that have distance scales
slips of paper
marker
pens
masking tape
yarn

▼ Building Study Skills ▲

Before class, collect reference materials for the students. You will need Bible atlases, though some may be able to use the maps in their Bibles. You'll also need Bible dictionaries, enough so that each student can have access to one.

Write the following words on small slips of paper:

Parthians	Phrygia
Medes	Pamphylia
Elamites	Egypt
Mesopotamia	Libya
Judea	Cyrene
Cappadocia	Rome
Pontus	Crete
Asia	Arabs

Some of these are names of places, while others are names of people groups. They are listed here as they appear in Acts 2:9-11.

When the students arrive, have each one pick a slip of paper and research the name on it. For the names of the people groups, students will begin by looking up the term in a Bible dictionary. Those choosing place names may start with an atlas.

Once students have found their assigned location on a map, have them estimate the distance from that location to the city of Jerusalem. You may need to instruct the students in using the distance scales printed on maps, or have the more experienced students help the less experienced ones.

After everyone has located his or her assigned place, have students take turns showing the class their locations. Have each one tell the approximate distance between the location and Jerusalem. Wrap up the discussion by saying: **Jews from many nations gathered in Jerusalem for the Passover each year. After Jesus was resurrected, those people were there for a historic event. We'll learn about that event today.**

Materials
Bibles

▼ Using Study Skills ▲

Ask a student to read aloud Acts 2:1-13. Explain what Pentecost is. Say: **Pentecost is the fiftieth day after the Sabbath of Passover. This feast, also called the Feast of Weeks, the Feast of Harvest, and the day of firstfruits, was related to the harvest and the Passover. In fact, Deuteronomy 16:10-12 makes a point to remind the people that they were slaves in Egypt. The sac-**

rifices and offerings made during these feasts were for the Lord, and they were to be remembered by everyone in the land, not just the Jews, but their servants and any foreigners as well. Jews from distant lands came to Jerusalem to celebrate the Passover and sometimes stayed until Pentecost. That's why there were so many people in Jerusalem that day.

The believers were all together, including the twelve apostles, as Matthias had been chosen to replace Judas (Acts 1:12-26). **Suddenly, a sound filled the whole house where they were sitting. What seemed to be tongues of fire separated and came to rest on each one of them; they were filled with the Holy Spirit and began to speak in other languages as the Spirit enabled them. The sound was heard by the people there for Pentecost. A crowd came together and was bewildered that each one heard them speaking the wonders of God in his own language. They wondered what it meant. Some scoffed and discounted the miracle, thinking the believers were drunk.**

Have a student read Acts 2:14-17. Explain: **Peter denied that they were drunk because it was early morning. He quoted from Joel 2:28-32 to explain what they were seeing and hearing. Look in your Bibles at Acts 2:22-36. Peter spoke to the crowd, in what has been called the "first gospel sermon." He drew on their knowledge of Jesus and the recent events: His death on the cross, His resurrection, His ascension. Using quotes from Psalms, Peter told them Jesus was the Messiah they were all looking for to come** (Psalm 16:8-11).

Upon hearing Peter's powerful, Spirit-filled message, the people were cut to the heart and asked, "What shall we do?" Peter instructed them to repent and be baptized for the forgiveness of their sins. Then they would receive the gift of the Holy Spirit. About three thousand accepted his message and were baptized that day. This was the beginning of the church. Because there were so many people from all over the world in Jerusalem for the Passover and Pentecost, Peter's speech was received by an international audience. Can you imagine what those people told their friends and families when they went back to their home countries? The result was new believers worldwide.

Ask: **Why do you think God chose the day of Pentecost on which to start the church?** (Allow students to reply.) **Perhaps it was the fulfillment of God's promise. God promised Abraham that he would be the father of a great nation and that his descendants would inherit the promised land. While the nation of Israel was in Egypt, they longed for the fulfillment of the promise. With Passover, the nation of Israel saw the way that God would fulfill the promise: He would establish a relationship based upon trust but purchased with a sacrifice. The Passover lamb was the way God determined whether the people trusted Him or not. Comparing it to Christianity, God evaluates whether people trust Him by the way they react to Jesus' death. Some accept it as a sacrifice for their own sins, and others do not. Pentecost is an appropriate celebration for the beginning of the church in that it is a remembrance of God's delivery through the actions of Passover.**

▼ Responding to Study ▲

Say: **We read in Acts, chapter 2 how the church began, and how the early Christians lived. Let's compare what the first Christians did with what we do today.**

Use a chalkboard, white board, or sheet of poster board to make a two-column chart. Label one column "First-century believers" and the second column "Believers today." Have students read Acts 2:42-47 and list in the first column characteristics and activities of the early church. (They devoted themselves to the apostles' teaching, fellowshiped, prayed, ate together, gave to those who were in

Materials
chalkboard, white board, or
poster board
chalk or markers

need, etc.) When a student makes a suggestion, you may want her to come up front and write it on the chart.

Then ask for ideas of how believers live today. Ask: **What do we do that is like the early church? What do we do differently? What does it mean to be a part of Christ's church in our time?** Accept all reasonable answers from the students, and have them write those things in the second column of the chart. As a transition to the next part of the lesson you may add: **One of the privileges we as modern Christians have is an abundance of reference materials. Not only do we have printed Bibles, but we also have the dictionaries, concordances, and other Bible tools we've been learning about using. Later we'll have another chance to demonstrate our Bible skills.**

▼ Reviewing Study Skills ▲

Materials
a *Bible Books Bingo* card for
   each player (p. 221)
pencils
Bible Cards (pp. 297, 298)
small container for the cards

Play *Bible Books Bingo* to review the books of the Bible. Give each student a copy of the bingo card from page 221, and have a complete set of *Bible Cards* face-down on the table.

Choose one student to be the caller. He will draw a card and name the book of the Bible. The students will choose an appropriate space on their bingo cards and write the name of that book in the space. They may choose any available space on the board. Each book must belong in the division(s) named at the top of the column.

Here are the different ways to win:

Blackout—Players must fill every space on the card.

Single row—Players fill all the spaces in one line, either horizontally, vertically, or diagonally.

Window—Players fill all the spaces along the border of the card.

Four corners—Players fill the four corners.

If you wish, you may offer a small treat to anyone who scores a "bingo," or continue to play until everyone has had a chance to win.

Bible Books Bingo

Bible Books Bingo

Law or Gospels	History	Poetry	Prophecy	Letters
		free space ★		

Bible Books Bingo

Law or Gospels	History	Poetry	Prophecy	Letters
		free space ★		

© 2004 Standard Publishing. Permission is granted to reproduce this page for ministry purposes only—not for resale.

LESSON 38 · The Church Accepts Gentiles

Acts 11

Lesson Aims

Students will
- Compare the distances and times of Bible-times travel with modern travel
- Recognize the gravity of Peter's decision to go with the gospel to the Gentiles
- Anticipate challenges they may face when people resist the gospel message

Materials
graph or drawing paper
rulers
pens
markers

▼ Building Study Skills ▲

As students arrive, distribute graph paper or drawing paper, pencils, rulers, and markers. Have them draw maps showing the routes they typically follow on an average day. This could include going from their homes to school, through the school building, from homes to church, or to their favorite place to hang out. Tell them to include streets, landmarks, and other geographical features to help someone else follow their routes. When everyone has had a chance to make their maps, have them take turns showing and explaining them to the class.

Ask: **Why is it important to have a map?** (Allow students to respond.) **Maps are important not only because they show where places are and how to get from one place to another, but they also give us an idea about what the place is like. In today's lesson, we are going to learn about a time when people traveled to different cities for the sake of the gospel. We'll discover that some of these people were far apart, not just geographically, but in what they believed.**

As an alternative to this activity, you may choose to have on hand maps of various kinds for the students to examine. They can find their streets, their schools, and your church on a city map. Then can identify states in which they have family or friends if you have a map of the United States. You may want to identify countries where your church has missionaries if you have a map of the world.

Materials
Bible atlas with a scale of miles
Bible Atlas Maps 1–3 (pp. 305-307) for each student
highlighters
rulers
one index card for each student

Answers
Caesarea (v. 11), map 3, C3
Jerusalem (v. 2), map 3, C3;
  map 2, C2; map 1, inset
Joppa (v. 5), map 3, C3; map 1, B2
Judea (v. 1), map 3, C3; map 2, C1-2

▼ Using Study Skills ▲

Before class, write the names of these places on the board:

Judea   Joppa
Jerusalem   Caesarea

Ask: **How many of you have ever planned a trip? What kinds of things must you do when you travel away from home?** (get a map, choose your route, figure out where you need to stay, figure out how much it will cost) Say: **These days it's not too difficult to plan a trip. You can go to the Internet, type in your starting point and your finishing point, and it will give you a map plus directions how to get from one point to another. There are books published to tell you what sites you can visit along the way and where you can get meals and find a place to stay as you travel.**

In Bible times, travel was far more difficult. Over land, most people walked from place to place. A brisk walk might be at a rate of three miles per hour; so a trip of 25 miles would take a full day of walking. Today, in a

car, we can go 25 miles in less than an hour.

Have several students read Acts 11:1-18 aloud. Say: **Peter had told the good news of Christ to Cornelius and his household. Cornelius, a wealthy Gentile military man, needed someone to teach him the way of salvation. Peter, a Jewish fisherman turned preacher, needed Cornelius's salvation experience to know that Gentiles were included in God's plan.**

Most Jewish believers thought God offered salvation only to the Jews, and in the past Jews had stayed completely away from Gentiles. Some Jews in Jerusalem believed Gentiles could be saved, but only if they followed all the Jewish laws and traditions. When Peter returned to Jerusalem, the Jews criticized him for going to Cornelius's house. They thought he should stay away from Gentiles as they always had.

Peter explained exactly how everything happened. He was in Joppa praying and had a vision in which he was instructed to eat animals that the Old Testament laws had called unclean, which the Jews were not allowed to eat. Peter refused. He had the same vision again, and a voice from Heaven said, "Do not call anything impure that God has made clean." He had the vision a third time, and right then three men came to the house where Peter was and asked him to go with them. In answer to Cornelius's prayer, the Spirit told Peter to go with them. Peter went and began to speak. "The Holy Spirit came on them just as He did us at the beginning," Peter told the Jews in Jerusalem. Peter reasoned that "if God gave them the same gift He gave us, who was I to think that I could oppose God?" When Peter told them this, the Jews had no further objections and praised God saying, "God has granted salvation even to the Gentiles." But joy over the conversion of Gentiles was not unanimous. It continued to be a struggle for some Jewish Christians in the early church.

Give students a Bible atlas that has a scale for miles. Have them figure how many miles it was from Joppa, where Peter was, to Caesarea, where Cornelius was. (about 30 miles) Compare the distances Peter and the men traveled to modern-day travel. If you used a map of your city in the Building Study Skills section you can indicate a location on that map that is 30 miles away. Say: **In a typical day, we might travel 30 miles to go school, shopping, to sports practice, and the library. How long would it take if you were walking? Would you do all of those things if you couldn't ride from place to place?**

Say: **Peter knew how important it was for people to be forgiven through Jesus. He also knew how important it was to obey God. God had given him a vision that made him question what he thought was important, like obeying the laws about the food he ate. He had to realize that God's message about salvation was more important than not eating certain food; it was important enough to spend a whole day or longer walking.**

Divide students into two teams. Each student is to choose one location from today's story and write that location on a separate index card. Teams trade cards. Each student should write the map number and grid numbers of that location on the card received. (There will be some duplicate locations. Then using a regular Bible atlas, have students identify the map and grid numbers for the location they have. Say: **In the index of your _Sample Bible Atlas_, find each place listed in Acts 11:1-18 and highlight the places on the page. Then, locate where Peter was and where Cornelius was. Put a circle on the town where Peter was and a star on the town where Cornelius was.**

▼ Responding to Study ▲

Help the students understand the significance of the first Gentile Christians. Ask: **Why did Peter need a special message from the Holy Spirit in order to take the gospel message to Cornelius? Why would he have avoided**

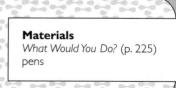

Materials
What Would You Do? (p. 225)
pens

Note
Read page 225 before you give it to your students and decide if it is appropriate for them.

Gentiles? (Jews avoided Gentiles originally out of obedience to God. It was also a long tradition, so Peter was going against social convention, and, he probably believed, against God.) **Yet Peter listened to God, went even though he did not fully understand, depended on God, and let God use him.**

What can we do to obey God and not depend on ourselves? Sometimes we know what we ought to do, but it's hard because it might make us unpopular or it might mean that we have to do something difficult. Let's look at some difficult situations that kids your age my face.

Pass out the *What Would You Do?* page. Divide the class into four groups. Assign each group one of the four situations and have students discuss them. Notice that the sheet asks the students to consider the pros and cons of acting in each situation. Some children may find it difficult because the situations don't have obvious answers. After they have had a few minutes to discuss their reactions, bring everyone back together to talk about the possible choices and the alternatives in each situation. Allow individuals to disagree.

Say: **When Peter was to go with the gospel to the Gentiles, it wasn't just something that was difficult or uncomfortable. He wasn't simply breaking a law about food. He was risking being labeled unclean. The Jews were God's chosen people, and the Gentiles were considered unclean and not part of God's promise. For Peter it was a decision to go against what he had always done. It was against what he had always been taught. If was different from what his friends thought, even different from what his teachers may have done. It was so different that God made sure to give him a special message instructing him to do it.**

When you are faced with difficult decisions, how does God direct you? The major way that God directs children is through their parents. Whenever you are faced with a difficult decision that makes you wonder if you should change what you think or believe, start by talking to your parents. They will direct and guide you, because that's the job God has given them. God will also speak to you through His Word, the Bible. That's why you've been learning how to use Bible tools and study the Bible for yourself. Sometimes you can't see your specific situation in the Bible, but you can learn overall principles that you can apply. The minister and leaders of the church can give you counsel also, and other Christian adults you know.

▼ Reviewing Study Skills ▲

Materials
local area road maps
memory verse word cards made in Lesson 36

Challenge the students to think about someone who lives within the same distance traveled in the story (30 miles). Ask: **Who do you know who lives within 30 miles of your home or this church?** Using the current area road maps, draw a circle representing 30 miles around your church or your town. Have students brainstorm as a group or with partners. **How can you share the gospel like Peter did with Cornelius with those who live in this circle? Peter listened to God's directions. How can you listen to God's directions? Peter took friends with him. Name friends you could take with you. Peter went even though he did not understand. He depended on God. How can you depend on God?** (be willing to change my agenda/schedule according to the opportunities God puts in my day, pray for wisdom and confidence to act) Share an example of this from your life. Challenge the students to live out what they have learned in this lesson.

If you have time, shuffle the memory verse word cards for Matthew 28:18-20.

Give each student a card until all the cards are distributed. Start the verse by calling for two words: *Therefore, go.* Lay them on the floor along a wall where they won't get stepped on. Instruct students to get up when their word is next and add it to the line of cards until the verse is completed. Time how long it takes. Reshuffle, play again and try to improve the time.

What Would You Do?

Read each of the following situations. Each one describes a time when someone your age might be tempted to disobey her parents or do something that she has been taught is wrong. Write down the reasons for the different choices the person might make.

1. Trina was walking home from the store. She had gone to pick up a few things for her mother for dinner. She had everything on the list and even had some change left over. At the corner she saw a woman standing. The woman looked cold and hungry, and she held a sign that read, "I need money for food."

Reasons Trina might give the leftover change to the woman:

_____

_____

Alternatives to giving her the money: _____

_____

_____

2. Joe was home alone after school because his mom was at work. She instructed him never to open the door to anyone if she wasn't home. But Joe's friend Stacey was standing outside the door crying. She said her brother had passed out and their parents weren't home.

Reasons Joe might open the door and let Stacey in:

_____

_____

Alternatives to opening the door: _____

_____

_____

3. Alicia was going to the movies with her parents to celebrate her eleventh birthday. The sign said tickets for children under 10 were half price. When it was their turn to buy tickets, the ticket seller asked how old Alicia was. Alicia was about to say "eleven," but her dad said, "She's nine." Alicia's parents teach her always to tell the truth.

Reasons Alicia might speak up and admit her age:

_____

_____

Alternatives to speaking up: _____

_____

_____

The Church Grows in Strength

Acts 9

Lesson Aims
Students will
- Identify the significance of the cities of Jerusalem and Damascus in the early history of the church
- Narrate the story of Saul's conversion
- Compare Paul's travels with those of modern-day missionaries

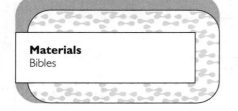

Materials
brochures, photos, and post-cards from a tourist attraction or historical site
Historical Site Marker (p. 229)
Bibles
Bible dictionary
pens

▼ Building Study Skills ▲

Have a collection of brochures, photos, guide books, or other information on tourist sites. As students arrive, have them look through the items and discuss their own trips to such places. Have students share stories about their trips, including funny or sad events. Ask them to talk about one event that they will never forget.

When all students have arrived, distribute the *Historical Site Marker* handouts and divide the class into two groups. Have one group write an imaginary historical marker for the city of Jerusalem using information from Acts 6:8-15; 7:51-60; 8:1-3. Have the other group write about what happened to Saul as he traveled to Damascus based on Acts 9:1-19. When the groups have completed their paragraphs, have them tell the whole class what they learned and wrote.

Say: **Even though the church began in Jerusalem, so did the persecution of the church. The man named Saul, who oversaw the stoning of Stephen, became very powerful in the persecution of the church. He was very zealous in his persecution, jailing Christians all around Jerusalem for their faith. He became so powerful and hateful in his persecution of the church that he got permission to pursue Christians to Damascus.**

Say: **When we travel, we often see plaques marking the sites of important or interesting events along our routes. When Saul was going to Damascus, he had a life-changing event happen to him. He met Jesus, the one whom he was persecuting. Today we are going to see how the church began to grow despite persecution.**

▼ Using Study Skills ▲

Materials
Bibles

Assign each student one or two verses of Acts 9:1-22, 26-28, 31 to read silently. Those who wrote a "historical marker" for Damascus in the first part of the lesson will have a slight advantage because they have already read part of the Scripture. Have the students prepare to narrate, that is, to say in their own words what they read. In this way they will tell the story of Saul as a group.

If you prefer, you may narrate the story yourself or use this narrative: **Stephen had just been stoned by angry Jewish leaders, while Saul watched, guarding the clothes the witnesses had laid at his feet. Fueling his zeal for his Jewish beliefs, Saul breathed out murderous threats against Jesus' disciples. He went to the High Priest, asked for letters to the synagogues in**

Damascus to enable him to take as prisoners any who belonged to the Way. Men or women, he intended to take them as prisoners to Jerusalem. On his journey, as he neared Damascus, a light from Heaven suddenly flashed around him. He fell to the ground and heard a voice: "Saul, Saul, why do you persecute me?"

Saul asked, "Who are you, Lord?"

"I am Jesus, whom you are persecuting. Now get up, go into the city, and you will be told what you must do."

Saul got up, opened his eyes—but could see nothing. His traveling companions, who had heard the sound, but did not see anyone, led him by the hand into Damascus. For three days he could not see and did not eat or drink anything.

In Damascus, a disciple, Ananias, had a vision. The Lord called "Ananias!"

He answered, "Yes, Lord."

The Lord told him to go to a specific house and to ask for Saul. As Saul was praying, God had given him a vision of Ananias placing his hands on him and restoring his sight. Ananias, knowing Saul's reputation and mission in Damascus, told God, "Saul has come to arrest all who call on Your name."

The Lord replied, "Go!" He told Ananias His purpose for Saul's life: "to carry my name before the Gentiles and their kings and before the people of Israel."

Ananias' response was obedience and trust—choosing to follow God's leading, even when it led to difficult persons and places. When Ananias placed his hands on Saul, something like scales fell from Saul's eyes, and he could see again. Ananias said, "Brother Saul, the Lord—Jesus who appeared to you on the road as you were coming here—has sent me so that you may see again and be filled with the Holy Spirit."

Saul could see again. He got up, was baptized, took some food, and regained his strength. Ananias had assumed Saul could not become a Christian. But, by Ananias' following where God led him, he showed love to Saul despite his feelings, and through him God's purpose for Saul's life was moved along.

When Saul had become a Christian, he immediately began preaching in the synagogues and proving that Jesus was the Messiah, but the Christians were afraid of him because of his past. Eventually they did come to trust him, but at first they did not. Even though he had a dramatic change in his life, others did not believe until they *saw* the change in his life. For a short time, Saul left the area and grew in his knowledge of Jesus. It is interesting to note that in Acts 9:31, it states that the church continued to grow and it lived in the fear of the Lord. Before that, it had lived in fear of Saul's persecution.

▼ Responding to Study ▲

Display a map of the world or have several world atlases available. Call students' attention to *Bible Atlas Map 3*. Say: **There's quite a distance between Tarsus, Saul's hometown, in the region called Galatia, and Jerusalem. How long do you think it took Saul to get there?** Allow students to guess, and help them to check the scale on a map to find out. **And there's quite a distance from Jerusalem to Damascus. Saul traveled that far to persecute the church.** Ask: **Would you be willing to walk that far for something you believed in?** Relate this to Paul's zeal for what he did.

Ask: **How far would you travel to tell someone the good news? Would you go to a different country—to a different continent, even? That's what missionaries to foreign countries do.** If you can, show students different places on

Materials
Bible Atlas Map 3 (p. 307)
map of the world
modern-day atlas with scales of distance

the world map where your church supports missionaries. If there's time, have the students use the distance scales on the maps to calculate how far the missionaries traveled to get from their hometowns to the countries they serve. Ask students to identify something that they might be willing to travel a long distance for. Ask them to share ways that they can show their faith without having to travel great distances.

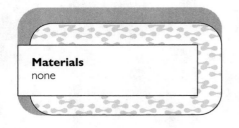

Materials
none

▼ Reviewing Study Skills ▲

Ask: **Who do you identify more with: Saul or Ananias? Do you need a flash of light and a voice from Heaven to change your life? Are you faithful enough to go a long distance for what you believe? Will you trust God to go into what seems like a dangerous situation like Ananias did?** Divide the class into two groups. Have one group brainstorm some ways a person could change in a dramatic way like Saul. Have the other group brainstorm people and situations in which they might be afraid to take the gospel. After several minutes, pull the groups together and compare ideas.

If you know of someone who had a drastic, life-changing conversion and who would have rapport with your students, consider asking him or her to come speak to your class. Sometimes a real-life example closer to home can help the students grasp the drama of the changes Christ brings to life.

Give the students two or three minutes of silence for individual prayer. Do not ask for group sharing. Lead a prayer at the end of the designated time, asking God to help all the students face their individual challenges, to change their lives as needed, and to be bold in sharing the gospel.

Historical Site Marker

Create a plaque for a historical site marker by writing a brief paragraph explaining what happened in each of the areas listed below. Use the Scriptures listed. If you need more background information, use a Bible dictionary.

Jerusalem
Acts 6:8-15;
7:51-60;
8:1-3

Damascus
Acts 9:1-22

The Church Has a Mission

Acts 13–28

Lesson Aims

Students will
- Find in Scripture the places Paul went on three missionary journeys
- Locate those places on a map and trace the routes of Paul's journeys
- Discuss the different responses people had to Paul's message, and anticipate responses they may receive

▼ Building Study Skills ▲

Materials
Paul's Journeys Map (p. 234)
Places Paul Went (p. 233)
Bibles
fine-tipped markers or colored pencils in red, green, and blue for each student

In this session, you and your class will cover a lot of ground—literally. You will look at three of Paul's missionary journeys in this one session! Remember that it is not important for your students to remember a lot of details. They are to get a broad overview of the travels of Paul, an impression of the scope of his ministry and his effect on the growth of the church. Of course these journeys lend themselves to a map study, so get the students involved as soon as they arrive.

Give each student copies of *Paul's Journeys Map* and *Places Paul Went*. Have students begin working right away on the first missionary journey. They will research Acts 13:1–14:28 and note verses in which each place is mentioned, and they will mark their maps with the route of the journey. Students with Bible experience may know right away that they can check the maps in the back of their Bibles to trace the journey. Congratulate their cleverness, and don't discourage them from doing so.

Tailor this activity to the skill level of your students. Allow them to work in pairs or groups if they need to. Stay close by to offer help and encouragement often. Keep the students from becoming overwhelmed with the scope of the assignment. Remind them that they're not required to know every detail of Paul's journeys.

▼ Using Study Skills ▲

Materials
Paul's Journeys Map (p. 234)
Places Paul Went (p. 233)
Bibles
fine-tipped markers or colored pencils in red, green, and blue for each student

Go over the following background information and be prepared to interpret it for your students. As you guide them in completing the second and third missionary journeys on their reproducible sheets, fill in with some of this information.

After Saul's conversion he began to preach the gospel in the synagogues. Acts tells us that some of the Jews wanted to kill Saul. In Acts 13:9 we learn that Saul was also known as Paul. Paul was a Greek name; Saul, Hebrew. This is sort of a clue to God's plan for Saul/Paul's life. Even though Saul was a Jew, he was also known by a Greek name. Even though he began his career as a Jewish Pharisee, he became a missionary to the Gentiles as Paul.

In Acts 13, Luke shifts his focus to Paul's ministry. Set apart by the Antioch church for a missionary tour (13:1-3), Paul and Barnabas took the good news to Cyprus and south Galatia with great success (13:4–14:28). On this journey they met Elymas (Bar-Jesus), the sorcerer who opposed them and was blinded as a result (Acts13:6-12). They healed a man who was disabled and were hailed as gods in human form (Acts 14:8-13). But the Jewish-Gentile controversy still was unresolved. With so many Gentiles responding to Christ, the disagreement threatened to divide the church. A council met in Jerusalem to rule on how Gentile Christians were to respond to the Old Testament laws. After hearing both sides, James, Jesus' brother who was a leader in the Jerusalem church, resolved the issue. Messengers were sent to the churches with the decision (15:1-31).

The second journey began after the council, when Paul and Silas preached in Antioch. Then they left for Syria and Cilicia as Barnabas and Mark sailed for Cyprus (15:36-41). On this second missionary journey, Paul and Silas traveled all through Macedonia and Achaia, establishing churches in Philippi, Thessalonica, Berea, Corinth, and Ephesus before returning to Antioch (16:1–18:22). It was on this journey that they met Lydia of Thyatira (Acts 16:13-15), and converted the Philippian jailer (Acts 16:16-34).

On Paul's third missionary journey, he traveled through Galatia, Phrygia, Macedonia, and Achaia. As he encouraged and taught the believers (19:1–21:9), Paul felt the need to go to Jerusalem. He was warned of impending imprisonment (21:10-12), yet he continued in that direction.

While in Jerusalem, Paul was attacked in the temple by an angry mob. He was taken into protective custody by a Roman official (21:17–22:29). Paul was put in prison and brought to trial before the Jewish Sanhedrin (23:1-9), Governor Felix (23:23–24:27), and Festus and Agrippa (25:1–26:32). Each time, Paul gave a strong and clear witness for Jesus. Because Paul appealed to Caesar, he was sent to Rome for the final hearing of his case. On the way, there was a shipwreck, and the sailors and prisoners had to swim ashore. Even in this circumstance, Paul shared his faith (27:1–28:10). After three months, the journey continued and Paul arrived in Rome. There he was held under house arrest while awaiting trial (28:11-31). Even so, Paul had freedom to talk to visitors and guards. Boldly and without hindrance, he preached the kingdom of God and taught about Jesus (28:31).

When the students have completed the reproducible sheets, say something like this: **Wow! That was an ambitious assignment, but I'm glad you stuck with it. Do you see how far Paul traveled around the world? What motivated him to put up with the challenges and hardships of traveling? What was the result of his ministry?** (Allow students to respond and discuss.)

▼ Responding to Study ▲

After Paul's life changed, he changed the world. Distribute *Name Change* to the students. **And in the process, his name was changed from Saul to Paul. Others in the Bible had name changes. Abram became Abraham in the Old Testament, and Jesus changed Simon to Peter in the New Testament.**

How has your life changed since you've known Jesus? What would you tell someone about the change in your life, or about what Jesus means to you? Use your favorite instant messaging script to write your thoughts to a friend. Let the kids have fun creating imaginary instant messages on *Name Change.* Have them follow the directions on the worksheet, including trading sheets and replying to each other.

Materials
Name Change (p. 235)

▼ Reviewing Study Skills ▲

Say: **We have a choice: to believe—or not to believe—Jesus is God's Son who came to earth, lived a perfect life, died on a cross for our sins, and rose again so we can have the gift of eternal life with God. If, like Paul, we do believe, we will want to follow the Great Commission of Jesus to go into all the world and make disciples.**

Materials
Bibles
chalkboard or white board
chalk or dry-erase markers

However, we need to be prepared, as Paul was, for people who reject the message. Paul converted many people who heard his message, believed, repented, and were baptized. Can you name some of them? But people also heard Paul's excellent and compelling preaching and refused to believe the truth.

As time permits, begin in Acts 13 and skim over the stories, noticing the ways people responded to Paul's message. Have a class recorder write them on the marker board as you go. For example, in Acts 13:6-8, the proconsul, an intelligent man, wanted to hear the word of God, but Elymas the sorcerer opposed Paul and Barnabas and tried to turn the proconsul from the faith. In Acts 13:43-45, Jews in Antioch believed Paul's message and followed him, but others were filled with jealousy and talked abusively against what Paul was saying. In Iconium (Acts 14:1-7), "a great number of Jews and Gentiles believed," but some unbelievers stirred up a plot to mistreat or execute Paul.

Some people want to hear, but others reject the gospel. And some will not only reject it, but will want to keep others from hearing. That happened to Paul, and it may happen to you. Have you ever encountered people who wanted to hear the gospel? Have you ever encountered those who don't want you to pass it on? How did Paul handle it when people rejected his message? How can you handle it when people reject yours? Have the students discuss in pairs or as a group situations in which people have rejected the gospel message or wanted to prevent others from sharing the good news. Close with prayer asking God to help the students in their efforts to share Christ.

Answers for *Places Paul Went* (p. 233)

Journey 1 (Acts 13:1–14:28)		Journey 2 (Acts 15:36–18:22)		Journey 3 (Acts 18:23–21:17)	
Antioch	13:1	Derbe	16:1	Antioch	18:22
Selucia	13:4	Lystra	16:1	Ephesus	19:1
Cyprus	13:4	Troas	16:8	Philippi	20:6
Salamis	13:5	Samothrace	16:11	Troas	20:6
Paphos	13:6	Neapolis	16:11	Assos	20:13
Perga	13:13	Philippi	16:12	Mitylene	20:14
Antioch	13:14	Amphipolis	17:1	Kios	20:15
Iconium	13:51	Apollonia	17:1	Samos	20:15
Lystra	14:6	Thessalonica	17:1	Miletus	20:15
Derbe	14:6	Berea	17:10	Cos	21:1
Attalia	14:25	Athens	17:15	Rhodes	21:1
		Corinth	18:1	Patara	21:1
		Cenchrea	18:18	Tyre	21:3
		Ephesus	18:19	Ptolemais	21:7
		Caesarea	18:22	Caesarea	21:8
		Antioch	18:22	Jerusalem	21:15

Places Paul Went

The book of Acts tells about the beginning of the church. Read the sections of Acts indicated to discover the places Paul went on his missionary journeys. In the blank next to each place, write the chapter and verse where you find the place mentioned in Acts. One has been done for you.

Journey 1 (Acts 13:1–14:28)

Antioch _____
Selucia _____
Cyprus _____
Salamis _____
Paphos _____
Perga _____
Antioch _____
Iconium _____
Lystra _____
Derbe _____
Attalia _____14:25_____

Journey 2 (Acts 15:36–18:22)

Derbe _____
Lystra _____
Troas _____
Samothrace _____
Neapolis _____
Philippi _____
Amphipolis _____
Apollonia _____
Thessalonica _____
Berea _____
Athens _____
Corinth _____
Cenchrea _____
Ephesus _____
Caesarea _____
Antioch _____

Journey 3 (Acts 18:23–21:17)

Antioch _____
Ephesus _____
Philippi _____
Troas _____
Assos _____
Mitylene _____
Kios _____
Samos _____
Miletus _____
Cos _____
Rhodes _____
Patara _____
Tyre _____
Ptolemais _____
Caesarea _____
Jerusalem _____

Paul's Journeys Map

Draw the route of Paul's first missionary journey in **green**. Draw the route of the second missionary journey in **red,** and the third in **blue**.

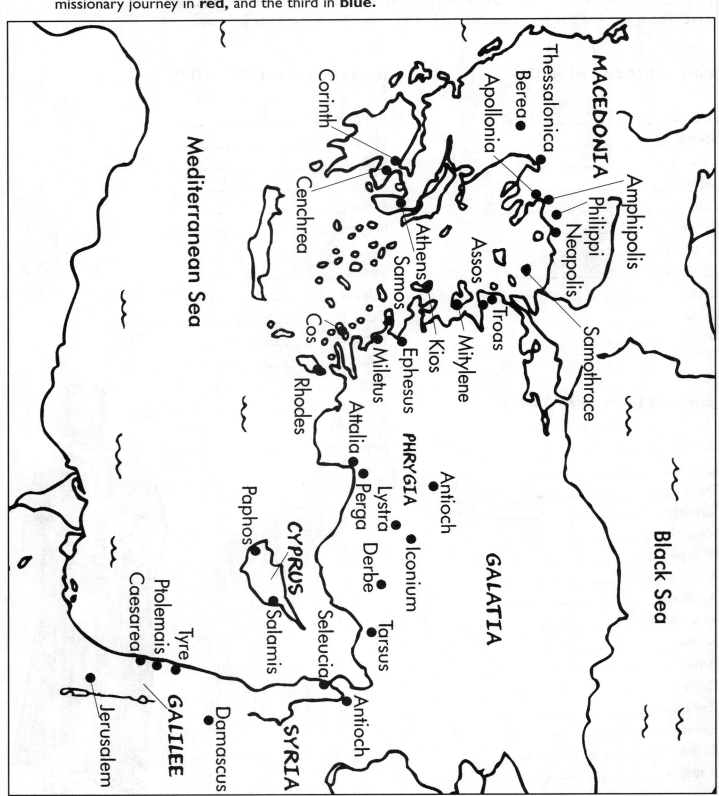

LESSON 40

Name Change

Acts 13:9 says that Saul was also known as Paul. This different name is a clue to what God's plan was for Saul/Paul. He was a changed man with a changed name and a changed message. Pretend you are online with a friend and you want to instant message her about the change Jesus has made in your life. What would you say? Write out your message using numbers in place of words (8 for *ate,* 2 for *to,* etc.), replacing words that sound alike, or leaving out vowels altogether.

For example:

I cnt W8 2 teL U bout d change n my Lyf!
Jesus iz soo kewl!

Now exchange with a partner. Let her read your message and send one back to you.

Letters Instruct the Church in Right Living

Bible Skills
Use Bible dictionary and atlas
Recite books of the New
  Testament
Paraphrase Scriptures

Memorize
Ephesians 5:15-17

Memory Challenge
1 Corinthians 13:4-7; Galatians
6:22, 23; Ephesians 6:10, 11;
James 2:17

Unit Overview

The New Testament Letters provide guidelines for righteous living. God wants our lives to be characterized by unconditional love, just as He loves. He wants us to exhibit evidence that we have been changed and that the Holy Spirit lives in us. This evidence, the fruit of the Spirit, is characterized by righteous behavior: love, joy, peace, patience, kindness, goodness, gentleness, faithfulness, and self-control.

God wasn't saying that trusting Him would remove the consequences of sin from our lives. God wants us to have a realistic approach to life, and that includes understanding the need to defend ourselves against the attacks of Satan. In light of that, God has provided the resources and strength to stand against the devil's attacks. In addition to defending against attacks, God also wants His people to live life deliberately. Not only should we read and understand God's Word, but we should do what it says.

Share these thoughts with your students throughout this unit. Once they have a solid background in God's plan of salvation, they need to accept the plan and make wise decisions to live for Him. This is perhaps the most crucial time in your students' lives for making decisions about following Jesus. They will be making a transition from simply learning the material by rote to applying it to their lives. Help them to see that the Bible is the guide that helps them live their lives as God intended.

Summary

In **Lesson 41,** students will see the differences between the world's definition of love and God's definition.

The emphasis of **Lesson 42** is the contrast between the works of the sinful life and the fruit of the Spirit.

In **Lesson 43,** students not only identify the armor of God, but apply it to situations they face.

Lesson 44 highlights active faith, as opposed to faith without works.

Memory Challenge Dominoes

Before class, write each word of a memory passage on index cards. Have students place the cards facedown on the table. Have each student draw three cards, keeping them hidden from the other players. The student who has the first word of the passage starts the game by placing the word face up on the table. The next person places a card if he can continue putting the words in order. If not, he passes to the next player. Play continues until the verse is completed. Any player who cannot place a card must draw a new one until there are no cards left.

As an alternative, have the first person place any word from the verse face up on the table. Then the play can proceed, with other players placing words before or after the face-up card. When the whole verse is completed, have the students recite the verse together.

Unconditional Love

1 John 4:7-11, 1 Corinthians 13:4-8a

Lesson Aims

Students will
- Identify words as synonyms for love
- Define love in terms used in Scripture
- Recognize love as action as well as feeling

▼ Building Study Skills ▲

Write the following words on small slips of paper:

charity	kindness	adoration	worship
affection	attachment	regard	admiration
fondness	devotion	concern	enthusiasm
liking	passion	attraction	benevolence

Before class, hide the slips of paper in different places all around the classroom. When the students arrive, announce that you're having a "love hunt." Instruct the students to look all around the room to find "love."

Perhaps the students will ask how it's possible to hunt love. As soon as one or two students have found slips of paper, someone may come up with the idea that the words on the slips of paper are all synonyms for *love.* If none of the students make the connection, explain.

Hold up a thesaurus and say: **Do you know what a thesaurus is?** Allow students to answer. **You use a thesaurus to find words that mean the same as a given word. All the words written on the slips of paper are words found in the thesaurus for the word *love.* For a definition we could also look in a dictionary or a Bible dictionary. One Bible dictionary defines *love* as "the expression of the essential nature of God; the attitude of God toward His Son and toward the human race." What kind of definition do you think you would find in a regular dictionary?** Allow students to answer. Probably they'll assume that a dictionary definition doesn't include God's character. (*Love* in modern dictionaries includes the elements of lust and sexuality.)

Help your students understand that the Bible concept of love is far greater and richer than what the world knows.

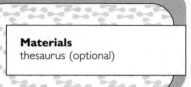

Materials
thesaurus (optional)

▼ Using Study Skills ▲

Pass out copies of *The Meaning of Love* and ask students to turn in their Bibles to 1 John 4:7-11. Introduce the activity: **We looked at synonyms for love, and now we'll look at how the Bible describes and defines love. Look in your Bible and on your worksheet. Follow the directions to complete the statements about love.**

In 1 John we are told many things about love. What did John say about love? (that love comes from God) **How does John describe love?** (God loved us and sent His Son as a sacrifice.) **What is significant about that?** (We did not do anything to deserve it.) **That is the ultimate example of unconditional love. In**

Materials
The Meaning of Love (p. 239)
Bible
pencils

your life has there ever been a time when you did something for someone because you loved her even though she did not deserve it?

If you read verses 7 and 8, what do you notice? (If you love you are of God, and if you do not love then you are not.) **That is a good reason to show love to others. There is an even better reason in verse 11. What is it?** (Since God loved us we are to love others.)

Unconditional **is one word that is often used to describe the kind of love the Bible talks about. What is unconditional love?** (Loving someone who has done nothing to deserve it, loving others who do not love in return.)

Open your Bibles to 1 Corinthians 13:4 and listen while I read some of Paul's words about love. (Read 1 Corinthians 13:4-8a.) **What were some ways Paul described love? How does this compare to what John said?**

Notice in these verses that love isn't described as a feeling. Love involves action. For example, Paul says that love always perseveres. What does it mean to persevere? (to continue doing something, to last in spite of obstacles) **Perseverance is an action, not a feeling.**

Paul says love does not envy. If you envy, of what are you guilty? (being jealous of what someone else is, or has) **How do you know that love does not envy?** (You can't love someone and want what's best for him if you are jealous, or if you want something he has.)

Since we are to love others we must strive to love as God does. God's love is action. In what actions does God love? (He cares for us, provides for us, guides us. He gave His Son as a sacrifice for our sins.) **God's love embodies all of those actions we just read about. It may seem impossible to actually succeed in every one of those actions. Why is it hard to succeed in the actions of love?** (Because we are fallen, sinful people; Satan tempts us to hate; loving others unconditionally is hard!) **That is why we turn to God for help. With God's help all of those actions are possible.**

▼ Responding to Study ▲

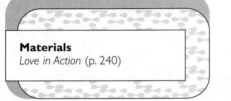

Materials
Love in Action (p. 240)

Before class make copies of *Love in Action*. Distribute the activity sheet and say: **We talked about how love is active, but how do you "do" love? This activity sheet has examples of situations in which active love is shown. Match the characteristic of active love to each expression of love.**

After students complete the activity, discuss each situation. Allow the students to express both their triumphs and frustrations in showing love to people who don't deserve it and don't return it.

▼ Reviewing Study Skills ▲

Materials
concordances

To give the students practice in using a concordance, assign each student one of these phrases, and have him locate the phrase in Scripture. Most of these phrases can be found in several places. The last three phrases are not found in the Bible. Let students take turns reading the Scriptures about love that they correctly locate.

"showing love to a thousand generations of those who love me and keep my commands"

"love the Lord your God"   "love one another"

"his love endures forever"   "greater love has no one than this"

"slow to anger and abounding in love"   love conquers all

"love your enemies"   love at first sight

"love your neighbor as yourself"   love is blind

The Meaning of Love

Read 1 John 4:7-21. Match each question to its answer by drawing a line to connect them.

Who should we love? •	• one another
Where does love come from? •	• sent His Son for our sins
Who knows God? •	• those who don't love
Who does not know God? •	• He sent His Son.
God is _____. •	• everyone who loves
How did God show His love to us? •	• love
This is love, that God loved us and _____. •	• ought to love one another
Since God loved us, we _____. •	• God
We know and rely on _____. •	• fear in love
Whoever lives in love _____, and God in him. •	• lives in God
There is no _____. •	• hates his brother
Perfect love _____. •	• the love God has for us
We love because _____. •	• He first loved us
If anyone says, "I love God," yet _____, he is a liar. •	• casts out fear
Whoever loves God must also _____ •	• love his brother

LESSON 41 ▼ 239

Love in Action

Read each of the situations below. Imagine the person involved is your friend. How could you help your friend understand love in action? Write the number of the statement from 1 Corinthians 13 that could help your friend. One has been done for you.

1. Love is patient.
2. Love is kind.
3. Love does not envy.
4. Love does not boast.
5. Love is not self-seeking.
6. Love is not easily angered.
7. Love keeps no record of wrongs.
8. Love does not delight in evil.
9. Love rejoices in the truth.
10. Love always hopes

_____ Jamal said, "I hate having to wait all the time for my little sister. She eats slow, moves slow, reads slow. I wish she'd just hurry up!"

_____ "Sure, I'm glad to see you," Katie told her grandpa. "Did you bring me a present?"

_____ "That's the third time this week you've lied," Madison said. "And I haven't forgotten that you took my pencil without asking that time, and you cheated on that spelling test back in second grade."

__10__ "It's no use," Shelby said. "My dad will never change. He'll never be the dad I want him to be."

_____ "My mom said I couldn't come over today, so I just told her I was going to the library."

_____ "You'll never be as good a student or as talented an athlete as me," Martin said.

_____ Ashley is jealous of Brianna's clothes, her intelligence, and her happy family.

_____ "You broke my CD player!" Austin screamed at Kyle, and raised his fist.

_____ "So what if Julia's the only girl in the class we're not inviting to the party? I don't like her."

_____ "I didn't ask him if it was stolen. It may have been, but I'm just glad he lets me play with it."

LESSON 41

Fruit of the Spirit

Galatians 1, 5

Lesson Aims

Students will
- Exhibit understanding of the conflict between good and evil by naming some classic enemies from literature or history
- Become familiar with definitions of sinful acts, in contrast to the fruit of the Spirit
- Interpret the fruit of the Spirit in a skit

▼ Building Study Skills ▲

Write the following pairs of fictional characters on the board:

      Peter Pan and Captain Hook
      Little Red Riding Hood and the wolf
      Road Runner and Wile E. Coyote
      Aslan and the White Witch
      the Dalmatians and Cruella DeVil
      Spiderman and the Green Goblin
      Yoda and Darth Vader
      Gandalf and Sauron

When the students arrive, ask them what these pairs of characters have in common. (They're famous enemies. One is good, the other bad.) Talk about how the struggle between good and evil is a classic theme in literature. Ask students for other examples of good/evil pairs—in history, the Bible, or fiction. Introduce today's session by saying: **We all understand the conflict between good and evil. We read about it in books, see it on TV and movies, and hear about it in history. But we also experience the struggle between good and evil in our lives every day. How?** Let students respond. **Let's see what the Bible says about the struggle between good and evil.**

Materials
none

▼ Using Study Skills ▲

Have students turn to Galatians 5:16-18, and ask one student to read it aloud. **This is the essence of the fight we experience every day. This Scripture introduces the two enemies—the Holy Spirit and the sinful nature. "They are in conflict," Paul says in verse 17.**

Do you know what it's like to want to do something right and yet you do something wrong? You have experienced temptation and know that it's hard to resist. You're being pulled in two directions and you must decide whether to obey God or to refuse.

The "bad guy" in this battle is the sinful nature that every person has. Paul lists these acts of the sinful nature in verses 19-21: sexual immorality, impurity, debauchery, idolatry, witchcraft, hatred, discord, jealousy, fits of rage, selfish ambition, dissensions, factions, envy, drunkenness, and orgies. Do you know what all those words mean?

Materials
Bibles
Bible dictionaries
regular dictionaries
The Everyday War (page 244)
photocopies of the crossword
   grid on page 243 (optional)

Stop and give the students Bible dictionaries in which to look up the terms from Galatians 5:19-21. Because not all Bible dictionaries list all of the terms, you may also want to provide regular dictionaries. In order to save time, and especially if you feel it is more appropriate for your students, have them work out the coded words on the reproducible, *The Everyday War.* As the students decode the words, they will become familiar with the definitions of the different terms.

When all your students have decoded the terms, continue with the Bible study. **If the "bad guy" in the fight is the sinful nature, who is the "good guy"?** (the Holy Spirit) **Paul contrasts the acts of the bad guy with the acts of the good guy. He calls the good acts** *the fruit of the Spirit.*

Have a student read aloud Galatians 5:22, 23. Ask: **Why would Paul call good acts "fruit"?** Allow students to share ideas. Some possible answers: fruit is evidence of what a plant is, and that it is healthy and growing; fruit is the product of the work of the plant; the fruit is good and is essential to bearing seeds for new plants.

To give the students additional exposure to the vocabulary of the fruit of the Spirit, provide copies of the crossword grid on page 243. Students can work in pairs to fit the nine words into the grid using the number of letters in each word and the intersecting letters. As they work or after they finish, discuss the terms to be sure that the students know what all the words mean.

Ask: **What part does the Holy Spirit play in the fruit of the Spirit? Why doesn't Paul call these good acts "fruit of hard work," or "do-it-yourself fruit"?** (We need the Holy Spirit's help to resist temptation and do right. If we try to do it ourselves we will fail. The Spirit guides us to do right and gives us strength. It is the power of God's Spirit in us that transforms our hearts and helps us show outwardly who lives in us.)

In the rest of Galatians 6 Paul tells us why we live by the Spirit. Have a student read Galatians 5:24-26. **If we crucify something, what does that mean?** (We kill it; it is dead.) **So if we crucified the sinful nature, then it should be dead to us. How do we "keep in step with the Spirit"?** (We are ready and willing to be led by God; in our everyday activities we look for opportunities that God gives us to follow Him, get involved in people's lives, and show His love by caring; we not only read His word and pray, but we're ready to use what we learn to love others; God's Spirit is working within us.) **When you keep in step with the Spirit, you know what the Lord's will is. That reminds us of the memory verse for this unit, Ephesians 5:15-17.** If a student is able to recite the Scripture, have him or her do it now. Otherwise, spend some time memorizing the verses using your students' favorite method.

▼ Responding to Study ▲

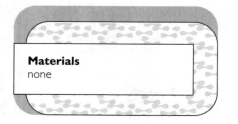

Materials
none

Since we now know the fruit of the Spirit, we are going to see how well we can put them into action.

Divide students into pairs or groups of three. Assign each group one "fruit" and instruct them to make up a skit to act out. The rest of the class will try to guess what the fruit is. In their skit, the pair or group can exhibit the fruit and show the positive results of doing so, or they can act out a negative situation, in which a character needs to show that fruit.

After each group presents, ask some of the following questions: **How easy was it to come up with your skit? How did you decide what to show? Do you think it would be easy to make that choice in real life? How can you be prepared for situations like that?**

▼ Reviewing Study Skills ▲

Assign each student one of the fruit of the Spirit to find in a concordance. Have her find other uses of the word, particularly instances in which the word is used to describe a characteristic of God. Make sure the concordances you are using are consistent with the Bibles the students are using. Otherwise, you may need to make some adjustments (such as looking up *temperance* for *self-control*). Have the students read the verses that they locate. As an alternative activity, assign the following Scriptures to students to read:

Romans 12:9 (love)
James 1:2 (joy)
1 Corinthians 7:15 (peace)
Ephesians 4:2 (patience)
Colossians 3:12 (kindness)
Galatians 6:9 (goodness)
3 John 3 (faithfulness)
Philippians 4:5 (gentleness)
1 Peter 5:8 (self-control)

Materials
Bibles
concordances

Fruit of the Spirit Crossword

Fit the nine words for the fruit of the Spirit in this puzzle grid. Look at the number of letters per word and the ways the letters intersect to figure it out.

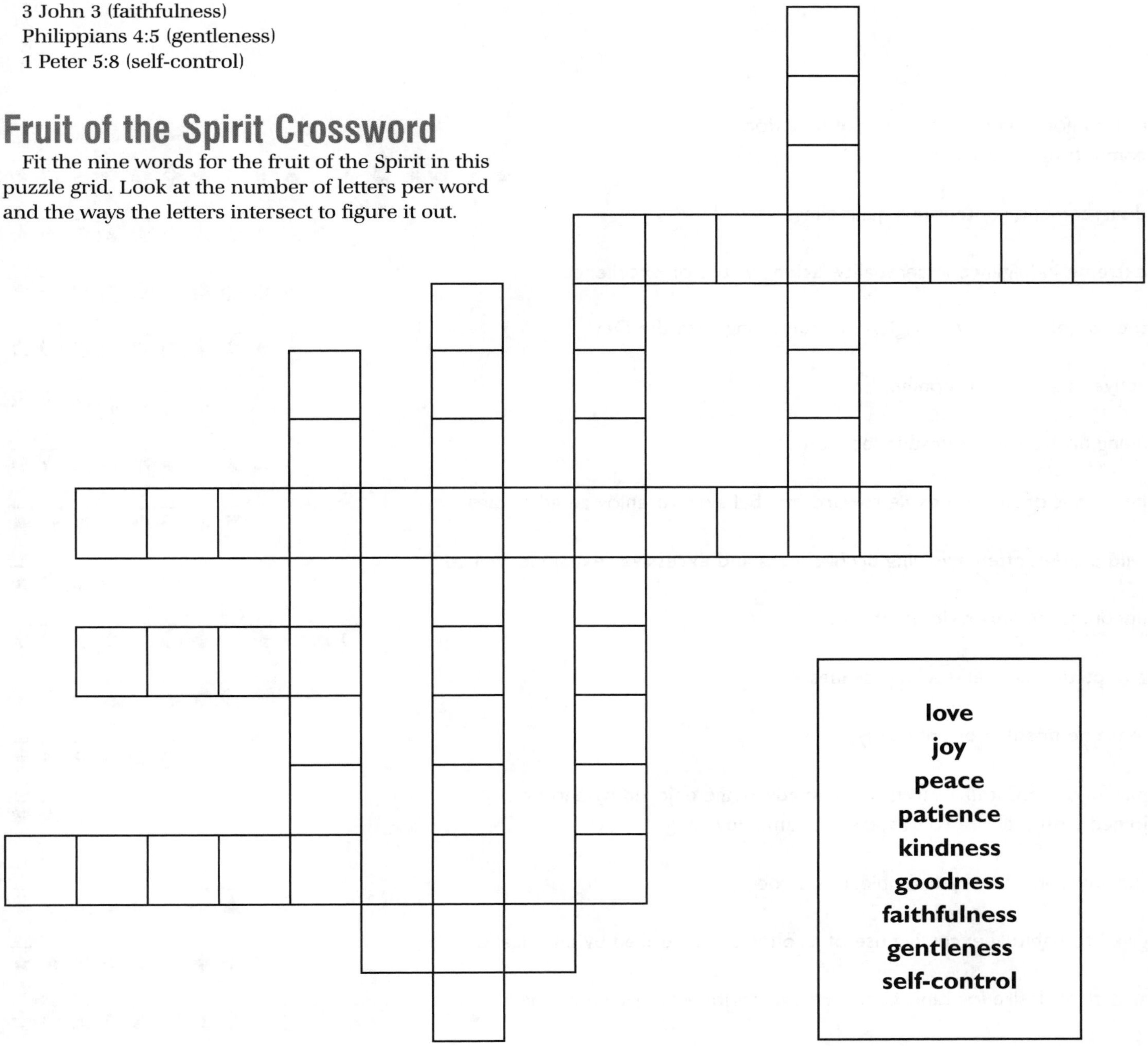

love
joy
peace
patience
kindness
goodness
faithfulness
gentleness
self-control

Every day there's a war within you. Your sinful nature fights against the Holy Spirit to tempt you to do wrong. What are the actions of the sinful nature? Read the definitions below. Use the code to discover the words from Galatians 5 that fit the definitions.

A B C D E F G H I J K L M N O P R S T U V W X Y

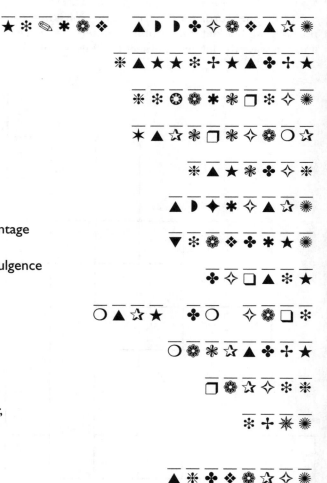

not conforming to good rules of behavior, committing sexual sins

disagreement, contentious quarreling, discord

extreme indulgence in sensuality, lacking virtue or excellence

the use of sorcery or magic; communicating with the Devil

active quarreling or conflict

being unclean, immodest, indecent

intolerant of rivalry, hostile toward one believed to enjoy an advantage

wild parties, often involving drunkenness and excessive sexual indulgence

uncontrolled anger, violent wrath

groups that are self-seeking, cliques, divisive

extreme hostility or animosity

painful or resentful awareness of an advantage enjoyed by another, joined with a desire to possess the same advantage

the worship of a physical object as a god

given to habitual excessive use of alcohol, characterized by intoxication

an ardent desire for rank, fame, or power without regard for others

LESSON 42

Armor of God

Ephesians 6:10-18

Lesson Aims

Students will
- Make paper armor
- Write short descriptions of the armor of God
- Apply the armor of God to real-life situations

▼ Building Study Skills ▲

As students arrive, direct them to tables where you have art materials ready. Assign each student one of these pieces of equipment for a soldier: breastplate, shield, helmet, belt, sandals, sword. Instruct the students to make their piece of armor from the supplies.

Here are some ideas for each piece: For the breastplate, put rectangular pieces of cardboard together with straps to make a sandwich board that fits over the shoulders. For the shield, cut a large circle or oval of cardboard and attach a couple of strips of paper to the back for a hand grip. For the helmet, use the bottom of a plastic milk jug. For the belt and sandals, use cardboard with yarn or strips of paper to tie them. For the sword, use a long, thin piece of cardboard. Students may cover their pieces with aluminum foil if desired.

Give the students enough time to make one piece of armor. Have Bible dictionaries or other reference books available that have illustrations of first-century armor. Make sure you have one complete set of armor for a student to put on during the Using Study Skills section.

Materials
sheets of cardboard or poster
    board
masking tape
white glue
scissors
yarn
stapler
aluminum foil
construction paper or craft
    paper
markers

▼ Using Study Skills ▲

Last week we talked about the war between good and evil. As soldiers in that war, we need to be prepared to do battle with the enemy, Satan. Satan is always looking for ways to tempt a Christian to sin against God. We need to protect ourselves against his attacks.

Paul tells us how to be prepared for Satan's attacks in Ephesians 6:10-18. Have several volunteers read the verses aloud. **Paul advises us to protect ourselves with the armor of God. We have to be equipped to fight, just as a soldier in today's army.** Ask for a student volunteer to stand in front of the class. As you mention each piece of armor, have the student put it on.

The first piece of armor Paul mentions is the belt of truth. We are to stand firm with the belt of truth buckled around our waist. We know the gospel is true and that we can trust what God says. As Christians we know the truth and we can be confident to tell the truth of God's Word.

The breastplate is the armor that covers the chest and back, protecting vital internal organs. Without the breastplate the warrior is vulnerable to a lethal blow to the heart. God is righteous, and so as His servants we want to do everything right and please God. Satan will try to turn our hearts to do wrong. Seeking righteousness helps us protect our hearts.

Materials
armor made in Building Study
    Skills

A soldier of God must have his feet fitted with the readiness that comes from the gospel of peace. The word "fitted" means equipped with a pair of shoes. Christians should not pick fights, and should try to make peace whenever we can. The gospel is all about peace, about reconciling people to God and restoring the relationship ruined by sin.

A shield is carried over the arm, and is used to deflect the enemy's blows. We must have faith in God and not doubt His promises. We can face temptation with confidence that God will do what He says, even if we can't always see His work.

The helmet of salvation protects your brain, the control center of your body. Our salvation is what defines our relationship with God. We must remember that Jesus saved us from death and we will live in Heaven for eternity. We must be prepared to tell others of His salvation.

The sword is the only offensive weapon in the armor. The sword of the Spirit is the Word of God, the Bible. When we are faced with temptation, we must know what God's Word says in order to know what choice to make. If you have Scripture memorized you will be well armed against Satan's attacks.

The war against Satan has eternal consequences. If we give in to him, we'll be in trouble. If we choose to fight Satan by putting on the armor of God, we will win the spiritual war.

▼ Responding to Study ▲

Seeing the armor you made is a good reminder of all the things we need to do to resist Satan. Let's look again at the elements of the armor and what the Bible teaches.

Distribute copies of *The Armor of God.* Have the students follow the directions to write a short description of each piece of the armor. They will use a concordance to locate similar verses. (Example: belt of *truth;* look up *truth* to find 2 Timothy 2:15 or another verse in the Letters about truth.) If you want to save time, or if you would prefer that students not use the concordance for this activity, give them the following Scripture references to match with parts of the armor in the chart: Hebrews 12:14; Colossians 3:9, 10; Hebrews 11:1; 1 Timothy 6:11, 12; Romans 1:16; Psalm 119:11.

If you have time, informally quiz the students to check their understanding of the armor of God. Then move on to Reviewing Study Skills.

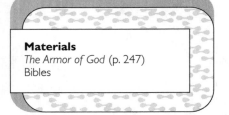

Materials
The Armor of God (p. 247)
Bibles

▼ Reviewing Study Skills ▲

Being able to name and describe the armor of God is a start, but it's better to be able to apply what we know about the armor in our lives. Distribute the *Gear Up* handout. Students will match the different pieces of armor with real-life situations. Talk about each situation together.

Then close with prayer: **Dear God, we thank You for equipping us to resist the devil. But even more, we thank You for Your Holy Spirit living in us and guiding us each day. Help us to use the armor when we need to, and to know when we need to. In Jesus' name, amen.**

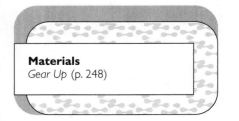

Materials
Gear Up (p. 248)

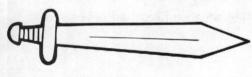

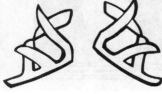

Name each piece of the armor of God. Then write how each piece is used. Finally, use a concordance and your Bible to locate a verse in the New Testament Letters on the same subject.

Gear Up

Choose one of the parts of the armor of God to apply to each situation below.

1. **belt of truth**
2. **sword of the Spirit**
3. **shield of faith**
4. **breastplate of righteousness**
5. **shoes of peace**
6. **helmet of salvation**

_____ Mitchell and his friend Thomas were playing their favorite trading card game. When Mitchell went home, he discovered that he had the most powerful card from Thomas's deck in his deck. He wasn't exactly sure how it got there. Mitchell really wanted that card. Thomas would just think he lost it, and he wouldn't blame Mitchell. Mitchell must decide whether to keep the card or return it to Thomas.

_____ Terry said, "My uncle told me that there's no such thing as Heaven or Hell. He said he doesn't need Jesus to save him, because there's nothing to save him from." Terry needs to know what to tell her uncle.

_____ Dina usually did her homework, but this one time she didn't. When her teacher asked her the next day, "Did you do your homework?" Dina was tempted to say, "Yes, I did it, but I left it at home. Can I turn it in tomorrow?" She was fairly sure her teacher would believe her because Dina had never lied to her before.

_____ "I believe some of the Bible, but not all of it," Alex said. "I believe the things I can see or prove myself. I don't believe what I can't see."

_____ "I don't understand your religion," Ari told Ben. "In our holy book it says you have to fight those who refuse to believe—go to war, even. Why is your Jesus called the Prince of Peace?"

_____ "I can watch whatever TV show or movies I want," said Crystal. "There's nothing in the Bible that says I can't."

LESSON 43

Faith in Action

James 1:22; 2:8, 14-24

Lesson Aims

Students will

- Act on their faith in adult volunteers
- Reconcile the apparent differences in Scriptures dealing with faith and works
- Locate heroes of the faith from Hebrews 11 in a concordance

▼ Building Study Skills ▲

For this first activity, you will need to recruit some other adults to help you. You may also need to go to a different room, or even outside. Say: **Today's lesson is on faith. One way to understand faith is to experience it firsthand.**

Have one student stand on a platform. A sturdy chair or table may work, as well as a stage, or a low set of steps. Have the adult volunteers stand in two lines facing each other with arms extended toward the other line. It may help to have adults lock their arms with each other for support. Have the student turn his back to the adults. Then on the count of three, have the student fall back into the arms of the adults. Have as many students do this as want to, and then return to your classroom.

Have dictionaries ready in the classroom when you get back. Instruct the students look up the word *faith* in both the Bible dictionary and a regular dictionary. Have them compare and contrast the definitions they find.

Say: **Now that you have experienced putting your faith in someone, how did it feel? Was it scary, fun, exciting? Were you nervous before you did it? Would you do it again? How does that compare with putting faith in God? How easy was it to put faith in another person? What about putting faith in God? Is it easier or harder to put your faith in God, whom you cannot see, or other people, whom you can see?**

Whether or not you realize it, you put faith in people all the time. When you get into a car you put faith in the person driving, the people who built it, and other drivers on the road. Can you think of other areas of life in which you exercise faith? Let kids respond. **You may be thinking that those things just require *trust*. What is the difference between faith and trust?** Have students look up *trust* and compare it to the definition of *faith*. **Faith is an important topic in the Bible. We are going to focus on what James had to say about it in his book. Let's turn to James, chapter 1.**

Materials
Bible dictionaries
regular dictionaries

▼ Using Study Skills ▲

Before class write the references for short sections of the lesson Scripture, James 1:22; 2:8; 14-24, on small slips of paper. Put the slips into a bowl, hat, or other container, and have three students each choose one. Ask them to be ready to read their verses in order. When prepared, have students read the Scripture. Ask: **What was James trying to say about faith in these verses? What do deeds have to do with anything?**

Materials
slips of paper with Scripture references
What Can Faith Do? (p. 252)

When in your life have you had to prove that something you said was true? Faith is something that at sometime you may be required to defend. You can tell people that you have faith, but they may not believe you unless you show it. According to James, what do you do to prove your faith?

What is the relationship between faith and works? Let's read some other Scriptures that address this topic. Ask a couple of volunteers to read Romans 3:28 and Galatians 2:15, 16. What do these verses say that we are saved by? (faith) Do the other verses contradict James? Allow some time for discussion, but keep a tight rein on how far the discussion goes. Don't allow any student to be intimidated by a more forceful or articulate student.

According to James 2:19, can we simply say that we believe, but not act on it? Demons believe—they know who Jesus is and what He has done—and yet they don't submit to His authority. And their actions certainly prove that they have no respect for Jesus. They try to get Christians to disobey Him!

So you know you are saved by faith, and you know that you may have to prove it. You also know that you prove your faith by your actions. But what actions? Have students look back at the James passage. (Actions that show you know and do/obey God's Word.)

Let's take some time now to look at some of the things that our faith does. Distribute *What Can Faith Do?* Give students time to look up each verse and complete the page. Talk about the importance of faith in a person's life.

There is also an opposite to all this. What about people who simply go through the motions—who do good deeds, but who have a crummy attitude? Some people do good things, but they do so only because of what it will get them? How can you tell the faithful from the fakers? Show the students a piece of real fruit and a piece of artificial fruit. One of these is real and one is fake. Can you tell them apart just by looking at them? Pass both pieces of fruit around. Now can you tell them apart? How is touching the fruit different from just looking at it? Let students respond. Just like with the fruit, sometimes the only way you can tell if someone's faith is real or not is by getting up close. Have you ever been fooled by someone's insincere faith? Allow students to answer briefly.

Hebrews, chapter 11 has been called the "heroes of the faith" chapter of the Bible. Let's look there to find out who the heroes of the faith are. Instruct the students to skim-read the chapter to find names of Old Testament people who acted in faith.

While the students skim the chapter, divide the chalkboard or marker board into two columns. Have one student at a time come up to the board and write the name of one of the heroes in the first column. In the second column, she should write a phrase or two describing what the person did that exhibited faith. Encourage students to request help from the rest of the class.

Let's think about the passage we started with in James. What was his point? What is more important, faith or deeds? How do we show that we have faith? What two verses talked about being saved by faith? How does the teaching in James and Hebrews 11 work together? (Let students respond. Suggest that faith in God is the basis for our actions; faith in who God is and His promises is the reason to act and show others who we trust. If we don't act on our faith, do we really have faith?)

Materials
notebook paper
pens/pencils
white board or chalkboard
dry-erase markers or chalk

▼ Responding to Study ▲

Before class write the following questions on the board.
• What will happen if you drop a quarter?
• What will happen if you shut a door really hard?
• What will happen if you flip a light switch?

• What will happen if you put your hand on a hot stove?

The questions may seem simple, but they are significant. Make sure the students take them seriously. Ask: **How do you know the answers to these questions?** Probably the students will say something about the laws of nature and their previous experience.

Ask: **Do you have previous experience with faith in God? Have you backed up your faith with actions?** Allow students to respond. **We can gain confidence as we act on our faith, as we experience firsthand how God always does what is best, and how He always keeps His promises. We can encourage each other to have faith as we tell each other about how we see God at work in our lives, and how He answers our prayers.**

▼ Reviewing Study Skills ▲

We talked earlier about the heroes of the faith listed in Hebrews 11. Let's find their stories in the Bible.

Distribute the concordances again. Divide students into groups. Have each group use the concordance to locate Old Testament accounts of the people listed in Hebrews 11. Use the chart that you made in the Using Study Skills step. As students locate the Bible accounts, ask them to add the Bible book and chapter under the appropriate name on the chart.

Evaluate the students' abilities to use the concordance with some of the following questions: **How easy was it to locate each of these people and the event in the concordance? Did you already know where some of them would be?**

Close the session with prayer: **Our dear God, please help us to have real faith that proves itself with action. As we see You at work in our lives today, make our faith grow stronger. In Jesus' name, amen.**

Materials
Bible
concordance
paper
pens/pencils

What Can Faith Do?

Look up the following Scriptures and fill in the words that tell what faith can do. As you write each word, cross off the letters of the word at the bottom of the page. After you have crossed off all the letters, the remaining letters will spell out the answer to the question at the bottom of the page.

Matthew 9:22—Faith can ____ ____ ____ ____

Romans 10:17—Faith comes from ____ ____ ____ ____ ____ ____ ____ the message

Galatians 2:15, 16—Faith ____ ____ ____ ____ ____ ____ ____ ____ ____

Hebrews 11:3—Faith gives ____ ____ ____ ____ ____ ____ ____ ____ ____ ____

Luke 7:50—Faith ____ ____ ____ ____ ____

2 Corinthians 1:24—By faith you ____ ____ ____ ____ ____ firm

2 Corinthians 5:7—We live by faith, not by ____ ____ ____ ____ ____

Ephesians 2:8—by ____ ____ ____ ____ ____ you have been saved through faith

A A A A A A A
C C
D D D
E E E E E
F
G G G
H H H
I I I I I I
J
L
N N N N N
O
R R R
S S S S S S S
T T T T
U U
V

How is true faith shown? Through ☐ ☐ ☐ ☐ ☐ ☐ ☐

 LESSON 44

Old Testament People and Events Prepare for God's Plan

Unit Overview

This unit is meant to be a review of the entire Old Testament, particularly how it fits into God's plan. Many Christians view the Old Testament as God's "Plan A" and the New Testament as "Plan B." The biggest reason for this is a misunderstanding of the role of the Old Testament in God's overall plan. Some view the Old Testament as being a record of a time when people were judged by the Law and the New Testament as being the time when people would be judged according to God's grace. Perhaps we could summarize this as the difference between faith and works, faith meaning a relationship with God that is based on trust and works meaning a relationship with God based on the good or bad things we do. The memory verse for this unit, Hebrews 11:1-3, 6, shows that faith is also the core of the relationships many people in the Old Testament had with God.

Clearly God always intended for our relationship with Him to be based on faith and not on simply following a list of rules and regulations. The writer of Hebrews goes on to list people from the Old Testament who are considered to be faithful examples: Abel, Enoch, Noah, Abraham, Isaac, Jacob, Joseph, Moses, and more. Throughout the books of the Old Testament, we can read the stories about these faithful people and see that they did not always do what God wanted them to do. And yet, they are counted among the righteous, the faithful.

It is easy to teach the Old Testament and focus on the Law. The stories are stark examples of God's holiness and justice and man's sinfulness and guilt. For children who are very much aware of the consequences of disobedience, the stories serve as clear reminders to seek God's will and do it. However, since hindsight is 20/20, consider the words of Hebrews and try to help your students understand that while it is great to memorize the Ten Commandments and other Scripture verses, it's more important to trust God to fulfill the promises He made long ago in history to Abraham and others.

Help students to remember the details about the stories many of them have heard from when they were toddlers, but help them also to understand how those details point to God's ultimate plan to save His people from their sins.

Bible skill
Recite the books and divisions
  of the Old Testament
Old Testament chronology

Memorize
Hebrews 11:1-3, 6

Memory challenge
Deuteronomy 31:8

Summary

Lesson 45 helps students see that sin has consequences but that we can still live in faith after sin.

Lesson 46 shows that even when things do not seem to be working out quite right, God is still faithful in His promises.

Lesson 47 demonstrates God's power to fulfill His plan despite our own weakness.

Lesson 48 explains that God's ultimate plan is far better than any kingdom of this earth.

Time Line Review

Using the *Time Line Segments*, pages 309-314, review what part each of the following people or events had in God's plan of salvation.

Find Adam and Eve on the time line. Ask students to tell what God did with Adam and Eve to prepare for salvation through Jesus.

Answer: Adam and Eve received the promise that Jesus would come and defeat Satan (Genesis 3:15).

Find Abraham on the time line. Ask students to tell what God did with Abraham to prepare for salvation through Jesus.

Answer: God promised Abraham that all people would be blessed through his descendants because Jesus would be born from his family (Genesis 12:3).

Find the Passover on the time line. Ask students to tell what God did in the Passover to show what salvation through Jesus would be like.

Answer: The Passover shows how the blood of Jesus, the Lamb of God, saves people from death (Exodus 12).

Find Gideon on the time line. Ask students to tell what God did with Gideon to show what salvation through Jesus would be like.

Answer: When the people cried out in repentance, God delivered them because Gideon trusted and obeyed God. In this way, Gideon is like Jesus (Judges 7).

Find David on the time line. Ask students to tell what God did with David to prepare for salvation through Jesus.

Answer: God promised that Jesus, the King of kings, would come from David's family (2 Samuel 7:16).

Find Isaiah and Jeremiah on the time line. Ask students to tell what God said through these prophets to prepare people for salvation through Jesus.

Answer: Isaiah prophesied that God's Son, Jesus, would be born (Isaiah 7:14; 9:6, 7). Jeremiah foretold that God would forgive people because Jesus came (Jeremiah 31:31-34).

Find Cyrus on the time line. Ask students to tell what God did through Cyrus to provide for salvation through Jesus.

Answer: Cyrus allowed the people of Judah to return to the land where Jesus was to be born (Ezra 1:1-4).

Find Jesus' crucifixion and resurrection events on the time line. Ask students to tell what God did in these events to provide salvation through Jesus.

Answer: In the crucifixion, Jesus took our punishment so God could forgive us (Colossians 2:13, 15; 2 Corinthians 5:21). In the resurrection, Jesus overcame the power of death to offer us eternal life (1 Corinthians 15:53-57).

Find Pentecost and Peter & Cornelius on the time line. Ask students to tell what God did through Pentecost, Peter, and Cornelius to offer salvation through Jesus.

Answer: At Pentecost, God spoke through Peter to offer salvation to all who would believe in Jesus (Acts 2:38, 39). God showed through Peter and Cornelius that salvation was offered to everyone (Acts 10:34, 35).

Adam and Noah See the Effects of Sin LESSON 45

Genesis 1–10

Lesson Aims

Students will

- Recognize God's eternal plan from the time of the Garden of Eden through the great flood
- Consider the consequences of disobedience
- Express thanks for God's gift of salvation that He planned from the beginning

▼ Building Study Skills ▲

Before class, arrange sugar cookies, icing, knives, plates, and napkins so that students can start decorating the cookies when they enter the classroom. Prepare at least one cookie to look like Earth. As students arrive, tell them to decorate the cookies as if they are planet Earth with oceans and land. When all students have arrived and have decorated at least one cookie each, have each student show off the cookie he decorated.

Have one student read Genesis 1:27-31. Say: **Every time God created something from day 1 through day 6, He said the same thing, that it was good. Take a look at the cookies we decorated. They look pretty good, don't they? Good enough to eat? Of course, that is exactly why they were made, to be eaten. When God made Adam and Eve, He looked at everything that He had made and said that it was very good. When He made Adam and Eve, He had fulfilled the purpose of the earth. It was for Adam and Eve. And their purpose was to enjoy God's creation and work within it to please Him. However, things didn't stay good for long.**

Take one of the cookies you prepared before class and show it to the students. Ask: **Who wants to eat one of these cookies?** Take out the jar of pickles and place a couple of pickles on the cookie. Ask: **Now who wants to eat the cookie?** Even though you may have a few students who would dare eat the cookie, don't allow them to eat it. Say: **Even though we might dare eat a cookie covered with pickles, that isn't exactly how it's supposed to be, is it? Cookies are supposed to be sweet and taste good, but a cookie covered with pickles will not likely taste that good. That's just not how it was supposed to be. Even if we were to eat the cookie, it wouldn't taste as good as one without pickles. Even if it didn't make us sick to try it, it might make someone else sick just to watch. Even if nobody ever eats this cookie, I might get a few strange looks from your parents when they hear that we had cookies and pickles. Why is that?** (because they just don't go together; it's not the way they are supposed to be) Say: **That's right; because it just isn't natural to put those things together. Someone might wonder what is wrong with me for even trying it. There are consequences to putting together things that shouldn't be together, such as pickles and cookies and God's good creation and sin.**

Allow the students to eat their cookies. While they are eating, read Genesis 3:22-24. Say: **After Adam and Eve sinned, God couldn't allow them to stay in the garden any longer. God cannot coexist with sin because He is perfectly good, just as He had made His creation. Sin caused a separation between God and people. And it didn't get any better.**

Materials
prepackaged sugar cookies
blue and green icing tubes
plastic knives
paper plates and napkins
jar of dill pickle slices
Bible

Today's lesson is about how sin messed up God's creation. Just like putting pickles on a cookie just seems wrong, a waste of a perfectly good cookie, so is sin in God's "very good" creation. It wasn't meant to be that way. Today we're going to look at what happened to God's creation and His perfect plan because of sin.

▼ Using Study Skills ▲

<table>
<tr><td>

Materials
Sin Keeps Growing and Growing
  (p. 259)
Bibles
pens/pencils
</td></tr>
</table>

Distribute the *Sin Keeps Growing and Growing* handouts. Break the class into three groups. Assign each group one of the three passages listed on the handout. Say: **Throughout the Bible, we see many people sin, from Adam and Eve through the kings of Israel. Even from the beginning, we can see that sin has terrible effects upon the people who sin and upon others. Even though it was Adam and Eve who sinned first, their children were not able to live in the garden.**

Instruct the students to read the assigned passage and fill out the handout as a group, leaving the final three questions blank until later. When all the groups have finished their sections, bring the class together and go over what each group found. Instruct everyone to fill in the remaining sections of the handout as the other groups share their information. If the students do not have complete answers for each column, instruct them to go over the passage aloud with the rest of the group and encourage the whole class to figure out the answers. It is possible that the passage doesn't mention specific consequences. Ask the students if they know the consequences to each story. (Adam and Eve were driven from the garden; Cain was cursed and sent away; the people and the earth were destroyed by the flood.)

Say: **Each of these stories involves serious consequences for sin. Adam and Eve were placed in a perfect garden, a place where they could walk with God every day. They only had one commandment, "Don't eat from the tree of the knowledge of good and evil." But they disobeyed, and God punished them. Cain did not present a sacrifice that was acceptable to God and he became jealous when God accepted Abel's sacrifice, jealous enough to kill him. And God punished him. The people of the earth had gotten so far from God that every thought they had was only about something evil, and they did this all the time. They were so wicked that God regretted making people and decided to destroy them.**

Ask: **Have you ever tried to plan something, like a party or a vacation or a day trip, and have it turn out all wrong?** Allow students to share their experiences. Say: **It is a terrible feeling when you spend a lot of time planning a really cool trip or event and then have something go wrong to spoil the whole thing. It makes us sad and angry. It's really not much different with God. He had created a perfect place and expected His people to obey Him, but they didn't. He created a family and expected them to love each other, and they didn't. He eventually became so angry with people that He decided to destroy the whole earth. The flood was the ultimate expression of anger and disappointment by God. However, that wasn't the end of every story.**

Say: **Even though there were terrible consequences for sin, God still had a plan to forgive His people. In Genesis 3:15, God places a curse on the serpent and says that there would be someone to come from the woman who would crush the serpent's head, even though the serpent would strike His heel. This is the first reference in the Bible to Jesus. This kind of statement is a prophecy. The ones about Jesus before He was born are called messianic prophecies, because they are about the Messiah. Even after the very first sin by man, God shows that He had a plan for dealing with it. Think about it. What did God tell Adam and Eve would happen if they ate from the tree?** (They would die.) **Did they die right away after they ate? No,** but they did die eventually. From this, we can see that God was already sharing some of His grace with His people. Even though God told the truth about their death, He had sort of given them a second chance.

We can see this in their children. When they left the garden, Adam and Eve did not completely forget about God. When we see Cain and Abel offering sacrifices to God, we can assume that God had given them directions for doing so and that they were encouraged or taught by their parents to do so. Even after Cain killed Abel, God did not kill him right away, but He sent Cain away. Cain said that this was too much for him to bear; he did not want to be sent away from God's presence, and God said that He would not allow anyone to kill Cain.

Even later, when God saw that people were only thinking and doing evil things all the time and decided to destroy the whole earth, He still found favor with Noah. Even though all of God's "very good" creation was ruined by people's sin, God still found favor in some of it, and He decided to protect part of it with Noah and his family. After the flood, God promised to never destroy the world with a flood. After all the bad things that happened within His creation, God showed that He had a plan to protect and save His people.

▼ Responding to Study ▲

Have the groups separate and instruct each student to read through the final questions on the handout and answer them individually. Remind them about God's perfection and that the creation was called "very good" when He had made Adam and Eve.

When the class has had a few minutes to answer the questions, discuss their answers. Ask: **Why do you think God designed the world so that there would be consequences to sin?** (If there were no consequences, there would be no reason to obey.) **What do these consequences cause us to do?** (They cause us to consider carefully whether we will choose to disobey God or obey Him.) **What should they cause us to do?** (They should encourage us to choose to obey God rather than disobey.)

Say: **The consequences that God set up for when we disobey Him are designed to balance with the blessings of obeying Him. God truly wants us to have a choice in whether we obey Him. If we didn't have a choice, then we wouldn't really be loving God the way He loves us. If we think about the amazing things God created for us in the garden and in the world, we can see that God has an amazing plan for us. The plan includes a relationship in which we can love God because He loves us. Even when we mess things up with sin, God loves us enough to provide a plan to deal with sin, even from the very beginning.**

Ask: **How can we see God's plan to save His people in all of these stories?** (God prophesied about the Messiah in His curse upon the serpent; God didn't kill Adam, Eve, or Cain outright when they sinned; God spared Noah and his family when He destroyed the earth with the flood.) Ask: **What are some ways that we can express our love for God, even though we continue to sin?** Have the class discuss ways that we can show God that we love Him. Talk about how we relate to others, especially our families. Remind the students about the bad family relationship that Cain and Abel had and that even after Cain killed Abel, God still offered to protect Cain from others. Talk about how our thoughts and actions anger God. Remind students about how the people of Noah's day thought and did only evil things all the time and how God promised never to destroy the earth again with a flood.

Materials
Sin Keeps Growing and Growing
(p. 259)

▼ Reviewing Study Skills ▲

Bible Words
16 index cards
marker
God Created People & People Sinned (p. 260)

Before class, break down the memory verse into 16 sections and write each section on an index card. You will use these sections to help the students memorize the verse. Save these cards for future use.

Say: **From the very beginning, God had a plan. Despite the sin that was brought into the world by Adam and Eve and despite the fact that God had to destroy the whole earth in Noah's day, God still had a plan. The plan had a promise. What was the promise that God gave Adam and Eve after they sinned?** (He promised them salvation; that the offspring of Eve would crush the serpent.) **The most important thing Adam and Eve had to do was to trust God. He told them not to eat from the tree, but the serpent came along and confused things. If they had just trusted God, things may have turned out better for them. God told Noah to do something outrageous. What was it?** (to build a boat and to gather his family and at least two of every animal onto the boat) **That's a pretty big order for an old man to fill, but Noah trusted God; that's why Genesis says that Noah found favor in God's eyes. Now we're going to look at our memory verse for the unit. The memory challenge comes from Deuteronomy 31:8, which says, "The Lord himself goes before you and will be with you; he will never leave you nor forsake you. Do not be afraid; do not be discouraged." This promise from God is huge. Our memory verse states that the "ancients" took God at His word and trusted Him. Who are the ancients from the lesson?** (Adam, Eve, Cain, Abel, Noah) **Of all of these people only a few trusted God, and our memory verse remembers them.**

Lay out the cards in front of the students and have them recite the verse. When they have read the verse once or twice aloud, take away the last card. Have them recite the whole verse again without the last card. Repeat the procedure until they have taken away all the cards and can recite the verse from memory.

When the game is over, distribute the *God Created People & People Sinned* handouts. Say: **This handout begins the outline of God's plan through the Old Testament starting with His creation and ending at the Tower of Babel. Study this handout on your own and look for points where God is actively preparing people for His Messiah, His Son, Jesus. Next week we'll see how God continues His plan through Abraham.**

At the end of the session, lead the class in a prayer thanking God for His promise of hope and salvation, which He planned from the beginning. Thank Him for never forsaking us, even when we choose to disobey and not trust Him.

Sin Keeps Growing and Growing

Read each of the following passages and place the correct information in the appropriate columns below.

Scripture	Who is involved?	What was their sin?	How did it grow?	What were the consequences?
Genesis 3:6-24				
Genesis 4:1-12				
Genesis 6:1-7				

Why do you think God designed the world so that there would be consequences to sin?

What do these consequences cause us to do?

What should they cause us to do?

Creation

The first words recorded in the Bible—"In the beginning, God created the heavens and the earth"—help us understand that nothing in this world exists without God. From the story of creation, we learn that God gave us everything we need—companionship, food, beauty, work. It helps us understand that we were created for fellowship with God.

Adam & Eve

God put Adam and Eve in charge of the Garden of Eden. Here, they could eat fruit from any tree except the tree of the knowledge of good and evil. Adam and Eve could choose to obey God, or they could choose to disobey God. As long as they obeyed, they had fellowship with God. If they disobeyed, their fellowship would be broken. After being tempted by Satan (who was in the form of a serpent), Adam and Eve ate from the forbidden tree. Sin entered the world. Fellowship with God was broken.

Garden of Eden

Adam and Eve's lives changed when they sinned. They were banished from the Garden of Eden. God put an angel and a sword of fire by the garden to keep people away. Outside the garden, Adam had to work hard to grow food. Eve had great pain when giving birth to her children. The moment that Adam and Eve disobeyed God was the moment that human beings needed a Savior. And it was then that God promised to send Jesus.

Noah

Years passed, and the children of Adam and Eve were wicked, corrupt, and violent. They had forgotten God, and God was sorry He had created them. One man found favor in God's eyes: Noah. God decided to destroy the wicked people and start again with Noah and his family. Noah followed God's instructions and built an ark that was large enough for Noah's family and for at least two of every living creature. When every creature and person were safely inside, God shut the door and sent the rain. It rained for 40 days and nights until the earth was completely covered with water. After the flood, God placed a rainbow in the sky as a symbol of His promise never again to destroy the earth with a flood.

Tower of Babel

After the flood, God told the people to scatter and fill the earth. Instead, they settled together and began to build a tower to reach the heavens. They wanted to stay together. Since they all spoke the same language, they could easily build a tower. So God confused their language, and the people could not understand one another. The people scattered over the earth. This was the beginning of languages and nations.

Lesson Aims

Students will

- Exercise self-control in waiting to eat candy as an object lesson on waiting for God's timing
- Trace the movements of Abram on a map to appreciate the extent of his faith
- Consider ways to make their faith more active

▼ Building Study Skills ▲

As students arrive, give each one a small handful of candies and tell them not to eat them. When everyone has arrived, say: **Last week we talked about the beginning of the world and the effects of sin on the world. After the flood, people began to multiply on the earth and move around. There were people moving all around the world, sort of like the little groups of candies you have in your hands. Spread the candies out in front of you and then look around the table. Your handful isn't much different from the rest. What if I promised you more? Would you like more? Of course you would. What if I promised that you could have as many candies as the stars in the sky or grains of sand on the beach?**

This is exactly what God did after the flood. When people began to increase on the earth, God chose one man and called him from among His small handful of people on the earth. Choose one student to give you one candy. **God called Abram and promised him that he would be the father of a great nation. Abram didn't have a family, but he trusted God. This was a great decision, because God did bless him because of his faith.**

Today we are going to look at how putting our faith into action pleases God and how it fits into His plan. Remind students that they must not eat their candies as you go into the next part of the lesson.

Materials
large bag of candy-coated chocolates

▼ Using Study Skills ▲

Distribute the maps. Instruct students to choose one candy from their handful and use it in this activity. Tell them that the candy represents Abram and they should use it to trace Abram's travels on the map. Begin by having a student read Genesis 11:27-32. As you come to a place name (Ur, Haran, Canaan) tell the students to move their candy from place to place. Have a student read Genesis 12:1-3.

Say: **We see in these verses that Abram was a man who moved a lot. However, now he was faced with a problem. God asked Abram to leave his extended family and homeland and follow Him to a new land. God also promised that He would make Abram the father of a great nation and that Abram would be a blessing to all people. That's a big promise, and Abram trusted God enough to follow Him away from his family.**

Have a student read Genesis 12:4-9. Help your students follow along on the map with their candies. Say: **Here is the final part of God's promise to Abram. God**

Materials
Bibles
candies from previous activity
Bible Atlas Map 1 for each student (p. 305)

promised Abram that he would be the father of a great nation (in verse 2), that he would be a blessing to all people (in verse 3), and that God would give Abram and his offspring all the land in Canaan (in verse 7).

Have another student read Genesis 12:10. Instruct the students to move their candies there. Say: **Now we have seen Abram travel through all the lands of the Old Testament. His travels went from the far east between the Tigris and Euphrates Rivers, to the far north in Haran, to the far west in Canaan and Egypt, and the far south in the Negev.**

Say: **Now Abram had seen all the land that God had promised to his offspring. He had to be pretty excited about all the things God had promised, at least enough to follow Him all around the world. What Abram didn't fully understand was that God had also given him a preview of his entire plan. When God promised that Abram, an old man at the time, would be the father of a great nation, Abram surely didn't fully understand that he would be a patriarch of the 12 tribes of Israel, God's chosen people. At the time, he didn't even have one child. When God promised that Abram's offspring would inherit the land, Abram surely didn't understand it completely, since he was constantly moving from place to place. When God promised that Abram would be a blessing to all people, he surely didn't understand it with all the trouble he faced throughout his life. And still he trusted God. He just had a small taste of what was to come.** Allow your students to eat the one candy that represented Abram.

Say: **However, Abram didn't fully trust God. He tried to force God's promise to come true by taking matters into his own hands. But God was faithful. Eventually, Abram did have a son, Isaac.** Read Genesis 25:19, 20. **Isaac became the father of Esau and Jacob, and Jacob became the father of the 12 tribes. But Abraham died before that came to pass. He had only a taste of what God promised.** Allow students to eat another candy.

Explain to your students that Abraham had faith in God, but it was an active faith. Say: **Abraham could have sat back and said, "OK, God, I trust You to fulfill Your promises. Let's have it." But he didn't. When God told him to follow, Abraham did. When God told Abraham to sacrifice his only son, Isaac, Abraham was fully prepared to do so, expecting that God would raise him from the dead. Even though Abraham wasn't perfect, just as we are not perfect, he still trusted God. His faith in God allowed God to continue His plan for His people by providing for the Messiah. The great nation that was promised was the nation of Israel, and the blessing to all people was Jesus, who was a descendant of the nation of Israel.**

Say: **God also revealed part of His plan through another individual who had an active faith: Joseph. Joseph was a son of Jacob, the son of Isaac. He had 11 brothers, and as you can imagine, there was some trouble among the brothers. It didn't help matters that Jacob showed he loved Joseph more than the rest of his sons. So, Joseph's brothers sold him into slavery, and he ended up in Egypt. Even though Joseph faced many hardships in his life—sold by his brothers, life as a slave, wrongly imprisoned—he still remained faithful to God. In fact, he relied on God to get him out of his situations, and eventually he became second-in-command over all of Egypt. That allowed him to save his family, and therefore God's chosen people, from a famine.** Have someone read Genesis 45:4-7.

Say: **Because of his faithfulness, God rewarded Joseph with a position that allowed him to save his family and the line that would lead to the Messiah. Joseph brought his family to Egypt, and, eventually, they did become slaves to the Egyptians. But God raised up a deliverer in Moses, who led millions of God's people from slavery back to the land that God promised to Abraham.** Have someone read Hebrews 11:8, 13. **Abraham never saw all of this, but he did have a small taste.** Allow students to eat another candy.

▼ Responding to Study ▲

Materials
candies from previous activities
additional candies or another
larger prize for each student

Ask: **Are you enjoying your candy? Why or why not?** (Allow a few responses.) **What if I were to tell you that you will get a greater reward at the end of class? Would that make it any easier to eat your candy?**

Say: **God made a promise to provide for salvation back in the beginning when sin first became a problem for man. Adam, Eve, Abel, Cain, Noah, and everyone still died; they did not see the promise fulfilled. However, Noah and Abraham trusted God and hoped for the fulfillment of the promise, and the Bible says that it was credited to them as righteousness. By being saved through the flood, Noah had a small taste of God's salvation. By seeing his son born, Abraham had a small taste of the promise fulfilled.**

Say: **I'll give you a choice right now. You can choose to eat the rest of your candies right now, or you can choose to wait until the end of the lesson for the greater reward. If you eat it now, that will be your reward.**

Say: **Some people think that becoming a Christian means that you can't have "fun" anymore. That usually means that you probably shouldn't be doing what some people call fun. However, even if bad things happen, just as it did with Noah and Abraham, you can still have an active faith and trust God. The reward is not here. So what are you going to do?**

Allow students to discuss why they will or will not eat the candies. Ask them to share why Christians can look forward to Heaven and why it might be difficult to make that decision, even though the rewards are greater. Encourage them to think about ways that they can make their faith more active.

▼ Reviewing Study Skills ▲

Materials
God Began a Nation (p. 264)

Say: **Even though the church begins in the New Testament, God's plan begins in the Old Testament. Throughout the Old Testament, we read about people who had active faith and who did amazing things like Abraham and Joseph. God gave us the Old Testament to help us see the examples of how people before us tried to live out their faith in Him. In order for us to understand why God had to prepare the world to accept salvation through Jesus, we need to understand the Old Testament. So to help us remember more about the Old Testament, we're going to play a review game.**

Have the class sit in a circle facing each other. Explain to the students that they will be playing a rhythm game to help them remember the books of the Old Testament. Show the class a rhythm of slapping their legs, clapping their hands, and snapping their fingers in the following sequence: slap, slap, clap, clap, snap, pause, snap. Instruct the students that you will start by saying a book of the Old Testament on the first snap and then someone else's name on the second snap. The person named will then follow suit. For example, a sequence would start as follows: slap, slap, clap, clap, Genesis, pause, Jennifer, slap, slap, clap, clap, Exodus, pause, Jeff, etc. If a person misses either the book of the Bible or the rhythm, the game starts again and that person begins with Genesis. The game is over when you make it through the whole Old Testament.

When the game is over, distribute the *God Began a Nation* handouts. Say: **This handout continues the outline of God's plan through the Old Testament starting with Abraham and ending with the exodus of the nation of Israel from Egypt. Study this handout on your own and look for the points where God is actively preparing people for the Messiah, His Son, Jesus.** Close with a prayer thanking God for showing how He prepared for salvation throughout the Old Testament and asking for help to have an active faith.

And don't forget: before you dismiss the class, reward those who chose not to eat their candies with a generous portion, or some other wonderful surprise.

Abraham

Many of the world's nations began at the Tower of Babel. But one nation—the nation of Jesus—began because God told it to begin. This nation was to be trusted with the law of God, the word of God, and the Son of God. God called Abraham to move from Ur to Canaan. God gave the land of Canaan to Abraham and his descendants. God promised Abraham that his descendants would be a great nation through which the whole world would be blessed. Abraham's descendants became the Israelites, the Jews. Jesus was born to this nation.

Isaac

Isaac was a child of promise. God promised Abraham and Sarah a son. Isaac's birth was a miracle because Sarah had been unable to have children. God gave Abraham and Sarah a son when she was too old to have children. God spoke the same promise to Isaac that He spoke to Isaac's father, Abraham. God continued building a nation through which the whole world would be blessed. Isaac married Rebekah, and they had twin sons, Esau and Jacob.

Jacob

Jacob dreamed of a stairway reaching to Heaven. In this dream, God spoke the same promise to Jacob that He had spoken to Jacob's father, Isaac, and to Jacob's grandfather, Abraham. Abraham, Isaac, and Jacob are called the Patriarchs (fathers) of Israel. The descendants of Abraham, Isaac, and Jacob are called the children of Israel. This name comes from Jacob. Jacob's name was changed to Israel after wrestling all night with God (Genesis 32:28). The leaders of the 12 tribes of Israel came from Jacob's 12 sons.

Joseph

Joseph was one of the 12 sons born to Jacob. He was favored by his father but not liked by his brothers. Joseph's father gave him a coat of many colors. His brothers sold him into slavery. Joseph was taken to Egypt where he eventually became second-in-command to Pharaoh. Joseph was in charge of Egypt's food. During a famine, Joseph's brothers came to Egypt to buy food. Soon Joseph's entire family moved to Egypt where they were saved from starvation. God used Joseph to protect the growing nation of Israel.

Slavery in Egypt

Abraham's descendants had lived in Egypt since Joseph moved them there to protect them from famine. When a pharaoh came to power who did not know Joseph, he forced the Israelites to become slaves. The slavery and hardships placed on them by Egyptians helped the children of Israel grow strong. God was preparing them to move to the promised land.

Moses

From the time Moses was born, God protected him and prepared him to lead the children of Israel to the promised land. During his 40 years in Pharaoh's house, Moses learned how to lead people. When Moses left Egypt, he spent 40 years getting to know God. Then God spoke from a burning bush and called Moses to return to Egypt and lead the children of Israel to the promised land.

Passover

God showed His mighty hand to Pharaoh and all those in Egypt. Of the 10 plagues, the last—the death of the firstborn—was the most powerful. The night of this plague, each Israelite family put the blood of a lamb on the tops and sides of their doorframes. They ate a meal of unleavened bread, roasted lamb, and bitter herbs. That night as God moved through Egypt, He passed over the houses where He saw the blood of the lamb. The firstborn sons of Egypt died, but the firstborn sons of those in the blood marked houses were saved.

Exodus

During the night of the Passover, Pharaoh gave the Israelites permission to leave Egypt. So they began their journey to the promised land. God guided them by day with a pillar of cloud and by night with a pillar of fire. God parted the water of the Red Sea, and the children of Israel crossed on dry ground. God gave them manna and quail and water as they traveled. They camped at the foot of Mt. Sinai where God gave them the laws that would govern them and set them apart as a holy nation.

Joshua, Deborah, and Gideon Trust God's Power

Joshua, Judges

Lesson Aims

Students will

- Reenact the conquest of the promised land through a Bible quiz
- Recall facts in the accounts of Joshua and Caleb, Deborah, and Gideon
- Solve problem situations, trusting in God's power

▼ Building Study Skills ▲

Before class, make 12 squares on the floor with masking tape. These squares represent the promised land that will eventually be divided among the 12 tribes.

When all students have arrived, tell them that today they will have an Old Testament conquest quiz. Divide the class into two teams. One team will represent the Canaanite nations of the promised land, and the other team will represent the nation of Israel. Give each student a couple of index cards and a pen. To begin, have the Canaanites stand in the boxes. Have the Israelites stand facing the Canaanites. Using the Old Testament side of the *Bible Library*, ask a question about either the divisions or the books of the Old Testament, focusing on which books are in each division and the chronology of the books. Have the first two students facing each other write down their answers and hold them hidden until both are ready (you may need to have a time limit). When both are ready, have the two students show their answers. If the Canaanite is wrong and the Israelite is correct, the Canaanite steps out of the box and the Israelite moves into that box. If the Canaanite is correct and the Israelite is wrong, the Canaanite remains in the box. If both players are wrong, the Canaanite moves out of the box leaving the box empty. If both players are correct, nobody moves.

After the Israelites have totally displaced the Canaanites, or after about 10 minutes of play, bring the students together and discuss the conquest. Say: **Even though it was possible for the Israelites in our game to never enter the promised land, the real nation of Israel did enter the promised land and began to conquer it. However, it wasn't on their own strength. They had to rely on God. Forty years before, God had led them right there; unfortunately, they didn't trust God and were scared away by the sight of the Canaanites. So God let them wander in the wilderness for 40 years. Today's lesson is about trusting God's power to accomplish His plan.**

> **Materials**
> *Bible Library* (p. 296)
> index cards
> pens
> masking tape

▼ Using Study Skills ▲

Say: **God led the descendants of Abraham to Egypt where they were able to increase in number and grow strong. In Egypt, this family was saved from starvation during a terrible famine. Their descendants, the Israelites, became slaves in Egypt, but they also grew strong and began to work together as a nation. Can you think of a reason why slavery actually helped the nation grow together?** (They all wanted to be free; they all knew the promises of God to Abraham and were united in that hope.)

> **Materials**
> Bibles
> *God Gave a Home to the Nation* (p. 269)

Say: **God called Moses to lead Israel out of Egypt and to bring them to the promised land. During the exodus from Egypt, God gave the nation the Law. By trusting God and obeying His law, the nation of Israel would show that it was a faithful nation. Eventually, they did make it to the promised land.**

Give students copies of *God Gave a Home to the Nation* and refer to it as you talk. Have a few students read Numbers 13:1-3, 17-20, 31-33; 14:1-4, 11, 12, 20-23. Say: **Even though the Israelite spies saw an amazing land, they convinced the people that the Canaanites were stronger than they were. They were so scared that they wanted to go back to Egypt. Because of their lack of faith, God wanted to destroy them, but Moses asked God to forgive them. God did forgive them, but He still punished them, not allowing anyone to enter the promised land who did not trust Him.**

However, there were two spies who did trust God, Joshua and Caleb; both were allowed to enter the promised land. Moses himself was not allowed to enter the promised land, though God did let him see it from a mountain. When Moses died, Joshua led the people into the promised land. Why do you think God allowed Joshua and Caleb to enter the promised land? (Because they had faith in God.)

Say: **We always have to remember that even though God gave the nation of Israel the Law, He was more interested in the people's faith in Him. Joshua and Caleb both saw the giants of Canaan, but they also saw that God's power was greater. As the nation entered the promised land, they first encountered Jericho, a walled city. Who knows what happened at Jericho?** (The nation of Israel did not have the weapons needed to destroy the wall, but God instructed them to surround the city. On the seventh day, they circled the city seven times and then blew their trumpets and shouted. The wall fell. The whole time they circled the city of Jericho, they were following the priests who were carrying the ark of the covenant; they were following God—they trusted God.) **With every city they encountered and when they trusted God, they were victorious, but when they did not trust God and tried to do things their own way, they were defeated.**

When the nation had mostly occupied the promised land, they started to forget God again. God had instructed them to kill everyone and destroy everything. This was because the Canaanites were idol worshipers. Why would God want the idol worshipers completely destroyed? (If they did not get rid of the idol worshipers, the Israelites would be tempted to follow false gods.) **It's easy to figure out why idol worship was so inviting; idol worshipers could actually see their gods. The Israelites had to trust a god they could not see. And even though God gave them victory, the people still did not completely trust Him. So God allowed the remaining Canaanites to attack and rule His people. Every time another group of Canaanites defeated the Israelites, the Israelites turned back to God, but every time God delivered them, they turned away again. After Joshua, God sent judges to lead His people.**

Deborah was a prophetess who judged Israel. Who knows the story of Deborah and Barak? (At one time, when the Israelites were being ruled by a Canaanite king, Deborah called a man, Barak, and told him that God wanted him to take an army and defeat the king. Barak said that he wouldn't go unless Deborah went with him. God was angry with Barak, but he still defeated the enemy, but not with an army. While the commander of the Canaanite army was fighting, God caused a rain that made the enemy chariots sink in the mud. Not wanting to be stuck in the mud and killed, the enemy commander, Sisera, fled from the battle. Eventually, he had to stop for a rest, and he asked someone he thought was an old friend to hide him. Instead, the woman, Jael, killed Sisera as he slept. The enemy was defeated, not by the might of the army but by the hand of a woman.)

Have the students read aloud Judges 6:1-6, 14-16; 7:2-4, 7, 16-21. Say: **With Deborah, the people seemed to trust just a little, but when Barak wouldn't go without Deborah, it was clear that they did not trust God completely.**

In this case, with Gideon, the Israelites counted on their own strength to defeat their enemies, and God knew it. The nation of Israel was really hurting at this point; the Midianites were oppressing the people into starvation. The Israelites had a lot of motivation to want to fight back, but they were nearly beaten already. Gideon himself was hesitant to fight; he even tried to make the excuse that he was the weakest man of the weakest family of the weakest clan in his tribe. This is probably intentional by God. Since God stated that He wanted to make sure that the people knew that He alone defeated the Midianites, it makes sense that He would choose someone who wasn't superior in strength or leadership qualities.

▼ Responding to Study ▲

Do you ever try to take care of your own problems? Does it always work? Where can you go for help? (parents, ministers, other Christians, the Bible, pray to God) These are all excellent answers, but the most important one to remember is to go to God, whether it is through the Bible, through prayer, or to go through people. God used all these ways to help His people throughout the Bible. Even at times when it seems impossible for things to work out, we need to trust God's power. Abraham was promised he would be the father of many nations when he was an old man; that seemed impossible, but God made it happen. Joseph had all kinds of terrible things happen to him, but God used them for good. The people of Israel needed to be delivered from 400 years of slavery in Egypt, and God delivered them. The promised land was populated with people, seemingly giants, that the Israelites feared, but God led them into the land and delivered it to them. Every time the people trusted God, He showed them His power to overcome.

Ask: What kind of troubles do you face? Are they as great as some of the problems that the Israelites faced? Sometimes our problems seem smaller than what the Israelites faced, sometimes they seem bigger. Do you ever forget to trust God because you think that the problem is small enough for you to handle? God doesn't care how big or small our problems seem to be to us; His power can handle it all.

Distribute the *Big Problem or Small?* handout. Divide the class into three groups. Have each group take one of the situations on the handout and discuss it. Have the students answer the questions at the bottom of the page on their own. Close with a prayer asking God to help us to trust His power in all situations.

Materials
Big Problem or Small? (p. 268)
pens/pencils

▼ Reviewing Study Skills ▲

Divide the class into two teams. Tell them that they will be competing in a Bible drill. Explain that each team will look up the words *power* and *trust* in their concordances. Each team will then choose one verse for the other team to look up. The first person in each team will hold the Bible ready. When both people are ready, one team will read the reference to the other team; then the other team will read their reference to the first team. On a signal, the Bible readers will race to find the Scripture verse. Continue finding verses as time allows.

Materials
2 Bible concordances
2 Bibles

Big Problem or Small?

Consider each of the situations below. Decide whether you think each is a big problem or a small one. Discuss with your group how you think the people in the situations could trust God's power.

Situation 1

Denise's parents have just told her that they are getting a divorce. Denise's mom is moving out of the house and to another city with a man she met on a business trip. Denise is angry with her mother for what she is doing. She worries about what will happen to her, her younger brother and sister, and their dad. Denise is afraid that her dad's anger will get worse than it has been the past few months.

Is this a big problem or a small one? What can Denise do to trust God's power in this situation?

Situation 2

Rafael stayed up late last night watching a movie. He forgot that he had a big math test today. He didn't study as much as he knows he should have. Halfway through the test, Rafael's teacher stepped out of the classroom to speak with another teacher. As soon as the door closed, a few of his classmates started asking each other for answers. Rafael knows that he really can't afford to do poorly on the test. There were only a couple questions that he was struggling with; the rest seemed to be pretty easy. It would be easy to get the answers he needs, and then he could just go ahead and finish the test on his own.

Is this a big problem or a small one? What can Rafael do to trust God's power in this situation?

Situation 3

Chris was walking home from school one day when he saw a group of kids gathered around what looked like a fight. A few of the troublemakers in class had gathered to torment Ahmad, the new student from the Middle East. The bullies were making fun of his name and where he came from. Then they started pushing and hitting him. Some of the other kids told them to stop, but others screamed for them to hit Ahmad again.

Is this a big problem or a small one? What can Chris do to trust God's power in this situation?

Questions for You

Have you ever faced a situation that seemed like there was no way to win?

Did you have a choice between an easy solution that disobeyed God and a tougher solution that obeyed Him?

What could you do in a situation like that to make the right choice?

Twelve Spies

When the Israelites reached the promised land, 12 men—one leader from each tribe—were sent to explore it. The spies brought back large clusters of grapes. Two spies, Joshua and Caleb, believed that God would give them the land. Ten spies were afraid and said that they would not take the land. The people followed the 10 spies and wanted to return to Egypt. As a result, God told them that anyone 20 years or older who grumbled against God would not enter the promised land.

Israel Wanders

The children of Israel wandered in the wilderness for 40 years. When everyone who had grumbled against God had died, God led the children of Israel back to the edge of the promised land. Moses climbed Mt. Nebo where God showed him all the promised land. Moses died there, and God buried him. Joshua took leadership of Israel.

Joshua

Joshua led the Israelites to take possession of the promised land. He led the people to faithfully serve God. At the end of his life, Joshua led the people to renew their covenant with God. He said, "Choose for yourselves this day whom you will serve. . . . As for me and my household, we will serve the Lord." And the people answered, "We will serve the Lord our God and obey him" (Joshua 24:15, 24).

Jericho

When it was time for the Israelites to enter the promised land, they gathered at the Jordan River across from Jericho. God held back the waters of the river, and the Israelites crossed through it into the promised land. Then the army and priests conquered the city of Jericho by marching around it once each day for seven days. On the seventh day, they marched around the city seven times. The Israelites shouted, and the walls fell down. God gave them victory, and the conquest of the promised land began.

Promised Land

God had instructed the Israelites to rid the promised land of all idol worshipers. If the Israelites were to remain holy and faithful to God, they could not live among idol worshipers. The land was divided among the 12 tribes. Each tribe was to keep its area free of idol worshipers. Instead of doing this, they settled among the idol worshipers. As a result, they forgot they were a holy nation, and they began to worship idols.

Deborah

Because the children of Israel chose to worship idols, God allowed them to be ruled by their enemies. When the Israelites were ready to return to God, He used judges to deliver them. Deborah was a prophetess who judged Israel under the Palm of Deborah. For 20 years, the Israelites had been ruled by Jabin, a king of Canaan. Sisera was the commander of Jabin's army; he had 900 iron chariots. But with God, the children of Israel could defeat any army. God told Deborah and Barak to gather 10,000 men at Mt. Tabor. When Sisera heard that an Israelite army had gathered at Mt. Tabor, he took his 900 chariots to meet them. During the battle, God confused Sisera's army. He caused it to rain; Sisera's iron chariots sunk in the mud. Jabin was defeated, and Israel lived in peace for 40 years.

Gideon

Sadly, the children of Israel began to worship idols again. This time the Midianites attacked; they destroyed Israel's crops; they took their animals; they left them nothing to eat. God called Gideon to deliver Israel. Gideon gathered 32,000 men to fight the Midianites. God said that was too many men. God used Gideon, 300 men, and 300 trumpets, jars, and torches to defeat the Midianites. After this, Israel lived in peace for 40 years.

Samson

The cycle continued. This time, God allowed the Philistines to rule over Israel. God raised Samson to deliver Israel from the Philistines. Samson was strong, and God was with him as long as he didn't break his vow with God by cutting his hair. When the Philistines learned Samson's secret, they cut his hair and captured him. But his hair began to grow back. When the Philistines gathered to celebrate, they called for Samson to entertain them. Samson stood between the two support pillars of the Philistine temple. He prayed, and God gave him the strength to push the pillars. The temple fell and killed Samson and the Philistines.

Lesson Aims

Students will
- Guess the identity of objects without seeing them (as an object lesson on faith)
- Survey Old Testament history during the periods of kings and exile
- Express thanks for God's mercy and hope for the future

Materials
blindfold
can opener, videotape, stapler, or other objects that might be hard to describe but easy to identify if held

▼ Building Study Skills ▲

Choose a volunteer to be blindfolded. Tell the volunteer that you will describe an object for him to guess. Do not use words that will give it away (for example, don't describe a videotape as something you put in a VCR); you want to be descriptive but vague. Give the volunteer a half dozen or so guesses or wait until he is completely stumped. Then give the item to the person and let him guess again. Go through each of the items you have brought with different volunteers.

Ask: **Why was it difficult to guess what the object was?** (The description gave only a partial idea of what it could be.) **Why was it easier to guess when you could hold it?**

Say: **Sometimes descriptions are enough to explain what an object is, but it usually takes direct contact before we truly understand. It's the same thing with spiritual matters. Back in Genesis, God promised Abraham that he would be the father of a great nation. Abraham probably had a good idea what that could mean, but not until he actually held his son Isaac in his arms did he fully understand what it meant to be a father. The nation of Israel was told about the promised land when they were delivered from Egypt. But they didn't fully understand until they saw the huge grapes collected by the 12 spies or until they actually set foot in the promised land.**

Say: **Part of that promise to Abraham was that there would be a great nation. But when the Israelites began to occupy the land, they started looking at the nations they were defeating that had kings. The people eventually started to complain that if they were to be a nation, they needed a king. Today we are going to look at the significance of the kingdom of Israel in God's plan.**

▼ Using Study Skills ▲

Materials
Bible concordances
Bibles
Bible dictionary
pens
paper
God Gave Leaders to Deliver the Nation (pp. 274-277)

Give copies of pages 274-277 to the students and call their attention to the continuing story of God's people. The handout begins with Ruth in the time of the judges and transitions with Samuel into the time of the kings. Divide the class into two groups. Give one group a Bible dictionary to look up the word *ark*. Instruct the group to find out all they can about the ark described in Exodus. Help them discover the difference between Noah's ark and the ark of the covenant. Give the other group some Bibles and at least one concordance. Tell them to find a few references explaining how the ark helped the people of Israel. Have both groups write down notes so they can share what they discover with the rest of the class. After five to ten minutes of research, have the groups report.

Say: **The ark of the covenant was carried into battle by the Israelites because it represented their trust in God's power. But when we get to 1 Samuel 4, we see that the nation of Israel once again forgot about God.** Have a student read 1 Samuel 4:1-3. Say: **First, we see that the people simply did not trust God, which is very likely the reason why they were defeated by the Philistines. Next we see that they trusted the ark more than God himself. They were treating it like an idol, just like the pagan nations they were fighting had idols. Because of their lack of faith, the Israelites were defeated and the ark was captured by the Philistines. Even though the ark was eventually returned to Israel, the people still did not completely trust God.**

Have a student read 1 Samuel 8:1-9. Ask: **Did you ever ask your parents for something because your friends had it? Did that always get you what you wanted?** (Allow students to respond.) **Even though the nation did reject Samuel's leadership, it ultimately rejected God. This time, God gave them what they asked for, even though it was not necessarily good for them. Why would God do that?** (to teach the nation a lesson about trusting his power) **Saul was the first king of Israel.** Have someone read 1 Samuel 9:1, 2, 17. Say: **Here is someone that many people would look to as king. He was a "man without equal," and he was taller than anyone else. Do you think those are good characteristics for a king?** Have someone read 1 Samuel 9:21. **Does it sound like Saul thought of himself as a king? Does his excuse sound familiar?** (Gideon made the same excuse.) **It doesn't sound like he was very willing. In fact, when Samuel went to present Saul to the people, Saul hid from the people. God had to tell Samuel where Saul was hiding.** Have someone read 1 Samuel 10:23, 24. **Once again, it seems that the people made a decision without trusting God. And Saul's reign is characterized by bad decisions and a lack of trust in God. Eventually, God rejected Saul as king and appointed David as king.**

Most of us know a few stories about David. (Have a few students tell what they know about David.) Continue by saying: **Much of David's reign as king was characterized by success in battle. However, David did not always have success in his personal life. He lied, committed adultery, and even had a loyal servant killed to cover up his sin. Again, David's problems began when he trusted his own power and abilities rather than God's. Perhaps the best thing we can know about David is that he was "a man after God's own heart." Even though David sinned, as we all do, he still tried to seek and do God's will. The book of Psalms includes many songs about David's successes and failures in seeking God, and it includes many descriptions about the blessings of living faithfully under God's reign.**

David's son Solomon tried to follow in his father's footsteps. As Solomon began his reign, he made a great decision. Have a student read 1 Kings 3:5-14. **Solomon recognized that his abilities were far weaker than God's and that his own wisdom was far less than God's. So he asked God to give him wisdom to rule God's people correctly. In this, Solomon did two important things: first, he recognized that the kingdom was God's; second, he asked for God's direction instead of power and wealth for himself. Because of this request, God blessed Solomon with what he asked for and the wealth and power as well. It was under Solomon's reign that the nation of Israel reached its largest area. God's promise to Abraham about the promised land was finally fully realized.**

Unfortunately, even that did not last long. Solomon's own sons rebelled and ended up dividing the kingdom into two kingdoms. After that the kings of Israel and Judah, the new kingdom, led the people through cycles of obeying God and disobeying. Just as He had in the garden, in conquest of the promised land, and during the time of the judges, God punished His people for their disobedience and lack of faith. Throughout the times of the kings, God raised up prophets to preach God's word to His people. The

messages of the prophets often focused on three basic themes: first, the nation has not trusted God; second, God will judge the nation; and third, God will restore the nation. This three-part message is the core of God's plan from the beginning.

One prophet in particular, Daniel, summed up everything that had happened in Israel's past. Have someone read Daniel 9:4-19. **Daniel summarizes the history of Israel, including its sins. He confesses the sins of God's people and praises God for His righteousness. He also praises God for His mercy and begs for forgiveness.**

Here was a man who truly understood God's kingdom. At the time Daniel prophesied, God's people were in exile in Babylon. Even though Daniel prayed along with all of Israel to return to the promised land, he knew exactly why they were in Babylon—they had disobeyed God. Daniel was certainly a man who trusted God. Most of us know the story about when Daniel was thrown to the lions because he remained faithful to God, despite the decree of the king; God protected Daniel because he was faithful. This is exactly what God expected from His people.

▼ Responding to Study ▲

Materials
Praying for God's Kingdom
(p. 273)
pens

Distribute copies of the *Praying for God's Kingdom* handout to the students. Say: **When Daniel prayed for the restoration of God's people, he understood that the people did not deserve to be forgiven. Daniel also understood that God offered mercy. This was God's plan from the beginning. Even though we often choose to not obey God, we still have the same opportunity to accept God's plan.**

It is sort of like the objects you tried to guess at the beginning of the lesson. You had a fairly good idea of what was being described, but until you actually held it, you didn't know what it was. Just as the people of Israel continued to sin, we continue to sin today, but God still offers us a taste of His kingdom that is yet to come when we become Christians. However, that is a choice that each of us must make on our own. Let's look at Daniel's prayer for forgiveness and see how our own lives compare to the people of Israel.

Allow students time to examine Daniel's prayer and then answer the questions at the bottom of the handout. When everyone has had a chance to finish the page, say a prayer thanking God for His mercy and for giving us a taste of His kingdom.

▼ Reviewing Study Skills ▲

Materials
God Gave Leaders to Deliver the Nation (pp. 274-277)
Bibles

Break the class into two groups. Tell the students to use the handout and their Bibles to make up questions about this period in Israel's history. After they've prepared a list of questions, have the teams take turns asking one question of the other team. The team that answers the most questions correctly wins.

Praying for God's Kingdom

Read Daniel 9:1-19. In the columns below, list the things that Daniel said the nation of Israel had done wrong, the things that happened to them as a result, and the things that Daniel hoped would happen.

What They Did Wrong	What Happened Because of It	What Would Happen in the Future

What kinds of things do you find yourself doing wrong?

What consequences of sin (your own or other people's) have you suffered?

What do you hope will be different in God's kingdom?

Ruth

Ruth lived during the time of the judges. She was not a judge, but she is well-known because she became the great-grandmother of King David. Ruth was from the country of Moab, but she married an Israelite. When both her husband and father-in-law died, Ruth moved with her mother-in-law to the promised land. Ruth gathered grain in the fields of Boaz. Soon Ruth and Boaz were married. Their son Obed was the father of Jesse who was the father of David. Jesus was born into the family of King David.

Samuel

Samuel was a prophet-judge. He led Israel during the transition from the era of the judges to the era of the kings and prophets. Samuel was a special baby—a gift from God to his mother, Hannah. In response to God's kindness, Hannah gave the young boy Samuel to God. Samuel lived and served with Eli the priest in the temple. When Israel asked for a king, it was Samuel who anointed Saul. Then under the Lord's direction, Samuel anointed Saul's successor, David.

Saul

By the end of the era of the judges, the children of Israel were in despair. They cried out to God for a king. Other nations had kings. Instead of looking to God to lead them, they wanted a king. God allowed this, and Saul was anointed king. He began to finish the conquest of the promised land and to lead people in the ways of God. Then Saul began to disobey God. He looked for help in evil places. God took the throne of Israel away from Saul and his family.

David

Although David sinned, the Bible says that David was a man after God's own heart. As a shepherd, David killed the giant Goliath. He played his harp in the palace of King Saul. David wrote many Psalms. David was God's chosen replacement for King Saul. King David led the people to finish conquering the promised land. He drove out all the evil nations and evil influences. His reign was a time of peace.

Solomon

David's son Solomon was the third king of Israel. Solomon was the wisest man who ever lived. In a dream, God told Solomon to ask for anything he wanted. Solomon humbly asked for wisdom to rule God's people. God gave Solomon wisdom. He also gave Solomon riches. Solomon's job as king was to build a more permanent temple to God. This temple would replace the tent-like temple the people had built during their trip from Egypt to the promised land. The temple took seven years to build.

Divided Kingdom

War and division took over the land when Solomon died. The nation was split into two nations, and each nation crowned its own king. Ten of the 12 tribes remained together under the name Israel. Two of the 12 tribes—Benjamin and Judah—split from the 12 and took the name Judah.

Ahab & Jezebel in Israel

From the time the kingdom divided until the time it was taken captive, the tribes that kept the name Israel had no godly kings. All of them were evil and turned the people from God. Ahab and Jezebel killed the prophets of God, built temples to the false god Baal, and set up poles to the goddess Asherah. Ahab "did more to provoke the Lord, the God of Israel, to anger than did all the kings of Israel before him" (1 Kings 16:33).

Elijah and Elisha in Israel

Elijah was God's prophet during the reign of Ahab and Jezebel. Elijah announced that there would be no rain or dew except at his word. Elijah challenged the false prophets to a contest with God. That day, fire from the Lord came down and consumed Elijah's sacrifice to God while the sacrifice to Baal remained untouched. At the end of his life, God sent a chariot of fire to Elijah, and he went to Heaven in a whirlwind.

Elisha followed Elijah as God's prophet in Israel. God showed this by giving Elijah's cloak to Elisha. Elisha showed the kindness and grace of God. Elisha was the prophet who told Naaman to dip seven times in the Jordan River to rid himself of leprosy.

Isaiah in Judah

Isaiah was a prophet in Judah at the time when Assyria scattered Israel. He spoke for God from the time of King Uzziah until the reign of King Manasseh. Isaiah is called the gospel prophet because he spoke about Jesus and salvation. He told the people that salvation is from the Lord. Seven hundred years before Jesus was born, Isaiah told about Jesus' birth (Isaiah 7:14). Isaiah also wrote about Jesus' death (Isaiah 53:5).

Assyria Scatters Israel

For 200, God allowed the idol worshipers in Israel to remain a nation. Finally, the Assyrians marched on Israel and destroyed the nation. The people were scattered all over the world. The 10 tribes of Israel were no more.

Manasseh in Judah

On the other side of the division, Judah was still teetering between God and evil. Some kings were godly, but most were evil. Manasseh was 12 when he began to rule Judah. He did evil in the eyes of the Lord. God's anger burned against Manasseh. God announced His judgment on Judah. He would destroy Jerusalem and turn the people over to their enemies (2 Kings 21:10-15). Even though Manasseh later repented and was forgiven by God (2 Chronicles 33:10-13), God's judgment stood.

Josiah in Judah

Josiah was the grandson of Manasseh. He began to rule in Judah when he was 8 years old. He did what was right in the eyes of the Lord. During Josiah's reign, the temple was repaired, God's law was rediscovered, the covenant with God was restored, and Josiah got rid of the idols. "Neither before nor after Josiah was there a king like him who turned to the Lord as he did—with all his heart and with all his soul and with all his strength" (2 Kings 23:25).

Babylon Seizes Jerusalem

Josiah was a godly king, but God did not turn away from the judgment on Judah and Jerusalem that he had announced while Manasseh was king. More evil kings followed Josiah. Jehoiakim was king in Judah when Nebuchadnezzar, king of Babylon, marched to Jerusalem and seized it. This was the first of three attacks Babylon made on Jerusalem. Nebuchadnezzar left Jehoiakim on the throne but Judah was under Babylonian rule. Along with some of the articles of the temple, Nebuchadnezzar took captives to Babylon. Among them were Daniel, Shadrach, Meshach, and Abednego.

Jeremiah in Judah

Jeremiah is called the weeping prophet because he wept for the fate of Jerusalem and Judah. He was God's prophet in Jerusalem from the time of King Josiah until some time after the city was destroyed. Jeremiah urged the people to repent and return to God. Later he urged the people to surrender to Babylon. God instructed Jeremiah to write down His messages. When the king read the words of Jeremiah, he cut the scroll into pieces and threw them into the fire. So Jeremiah wrote God's messages again. Jeremiah's message was not popular, and Jeremiah was beaten, imprisoned, and thrown into a cistern. God always protected and delivered Jeremiah.

Many from Judah Taken to Babylon

Jehoiakim's son, Jehoiachin, became king, and he rebelled against Babylon. Babylon seized Jerusalem for the second time. This time Babylon removed all the treasures from the temple and the palace. Ten thousand people of Judah were taken captive including the officers, fighting men, craftsmen, and artisans. Only the poorest people were left in Jerusalem. Jeremiah remained in Jerusalem. Zedekiah became king over Judah.

Ezekiel in Babylon

Ezekiel was one of God's prophets during Judah's exile. He was taken to Babylon with the 10,000 captives after Babylon's second attack on Jerusalem. Ezekiel spoke God's Word to the captives. He told them that Judah would be judged because of her unfaithfulness and that God would restore her. Ezekiel's vision of the valley of dry bones showed that God would restore Judah.

Babylon Destroys Jerusalem

While Ezekiel was reminding the captives of God's judgment, King Zedekiah was rebelling against Babylon. So Babylon returned to Jerusalem a third time and laid siege to it. For almost two years, the Babylonian army camped outside the city. No one could come in and no one could go out. When famine overtook the city, Zedekiah and his army broke through the wall and tried to escape. They were captured, and the city of Jerusalem was destroyed. The Babylonian army tore down the walls and set fire to the city. They took the people who were still living in Jerusalem to Babylon. All of Judah was in exile.

Fiery Furnace

By now, Daniel, Shadrach, Meshach, and Abednego were serving in Nebuchadnezzar's court. When Nebuchadnezzar ordered them to bow down and worship a statue, Shadrach, Meshach, and Abednego refused and were thrown into the fiery furnace. Another person joined them in the fire, and they stood there unharmed. God showed the Babylonians His power, and God showed His children that He would protect and deliver them.

Cyrus Lets Judah Go Home

God told the children of Israel that they would be captives for 70 years. After 70 years, God raised up a ruler who would allow the people of Judah—the Jews—to return home. God could not find such a ruler among the Babylonians. So God gave Babylon to the Medes and Persians. One night, while the king of Babylon was having a feast, a hand appeared. It wrote: "Mene, Mene, Tekel, Parsin" on the wall. Daniel was called to read the writing. Daniel told the king that the Babylonian empire would come to an end and the Medes and Persians would take over. The prophecy came true that very night. God moved the heart of the new ruler, Cyrus, to release Judah from her captivity.

LESSON 48

Zerubbabel Rebuilds the Temple

Judah was taken captive in three stages, and the people returned to their homeland in three stages. Zerubbabel led the first group of captives back to Jerusalem. Their task was to rebuild the temple. King Cyrus returned the articles of the temple that Nebuchadnezzar had taken. About 50,000 people returned.

Daniel

Daniel was one of God's prophets during the 70 years of exile. Daniel's message to the captives was that God had not forgotten them, and he admonished them to continue to trust God. Daniel served God faithfully during his entire life. His faithfulness was shown as he prayed to God even though that choice could be punished by death in a den of lions. Daniel was thrown to the lions for praying, but God delivered him by shutting the lions' mouths.

Esther

Esther was God's agent of protection for Judah during the captivity. After Esther became queen, she revealed a plot to destroy the Jews and persuaded her husband, King Xerxes, to preserve her people, the Jews.

Ezra Rebuilds People

Ezra led the second group of captives back to the promised land. Ezra read from the book of the law, and God's laws were renewed among the children of Israel. They began again to obey God's laws. This obedience made them the holy nation God had called them to be. Thus, the people were restored.

Nehemiah Rebuilds the Wall

Nehemiah led the third and final return to the promised land. His task was to rebuild the walls of Jerusalem. Because Jerusalem was the center of Judah's worship, it needed walls of protection. God showed His power, and He showed His presence with the children of Israel when the people rebuilt the walls in just 52 days.

400 Years of Silence

God called the children of Israel to be faithful to Him. He called them to worship only Him. All of Israel's history shows God working patiently with them to teach them to worship only Him. When the nation continued to be unfaithful by worshiping idols, God sent them away from the promised land. When God brought Judah home from captivity, they stopped worshiping idols and worshiped only God, but they were still not ready for the Savior. The prophet Malachi tells us that the people of Judah needed to grow up. They no longer worshiped idols, but they still had many sins and practices that made God unhappy. Judah needed to learn how to obey God. Four hundred years of prophetic silence followed Malachi. John the Baptist broke the silence when he began to prepare the hearts of the people for Jesus.

New Testament People and Events Spread God's Plan

Bible Skill
Recite the books and divisions of New Testament
New Testament chronology

Memorize
Philippians 1:4-6

Memory Challenge
Hebrews 13:5, 6

Unit Overview

The Old Testament set the stage for God's plan to unfold. From the very beginning, God made it clear that He had a plan for relationships with His people and for saving them despite their sins. Even though the Law seemed to set up a system in which people were doomed because of their sin, there was still a continual underlying theme of grace. Every time the people of God sinned, from Adam through the kings of Israel, they were punished, but there was also a time of reconciliation. Through this repeating cycle, we can see God's grace over and over.

In the New Testament, however, we see the inner workings of God's plan. While the Old Testament prophecies laid the ground work and prepared God's people for salvation, the birth, life, death, and resurrection of Jesus were the foundations of how God's plan would actually work. In the Old Testament, God prepared His people for His plan of salvation. In the Gospels, God provided for that salvation through His Son, Jesus Christ. Through the rest of the New Testament, God presented the plan for all people who would believe. This is the story of the church and how Jesus' followers planted the church by spreading the gospel about Jesus and salvation found through Him.

This is a time of transition for many children ages 8 through 12. It seems that children get older faster than ever before. Problems that once were for adults to deal with became the problems of teens, and now tweens and even younger are facing issues that shake adults to their core. Because of this transition and because of the life-changing issues that kids today face, helping them understand God's plan and how they can fit into it and take hold of the salvation that He offers is more important than ever before.

By helping kids understand the chronology of the New Testament and how it relates to the Old Testament, you will be preparing them to understand exactly what Jesus did in His life and death and resurrection for them as individuals. Having seen the examples of sin and its consequences throughout the Old Testament and having little "tastes" of God's grace and mercy throughout history, kids will come to appreciate the value of God's plan and the enormity of Jesus' sacrifice to provide salvation for that plan.

Summary

The concept of active faith is introduced in **Lesson 49** with the lives of Zechariah and the Roman centurion.

Even though they did it in different ways, both Peter and Paul had a global impact on the spread of the gospel. This is the main idea of **Lesson 50.**

Lesson 51 examines the active faith of some of the lesser known people from the book of Acts: James the brother of Jesus and Dorcas.

While the book of Revelation is intimidating even to some adults, **Lesson 52** makes it accessible to students.

Lesson Aims

Students will

- Pantomime different Bible characters when they showed great faith
- Recall their experiences as eyewitnesses
- Compare the faith shown by Zechariah and the centurion

▼ Building Study Skills ▲

Before class, write each of the following phrases on an index card: Noah builds an ark; Abraham travels to Canaan; Joseph is a ruler in Egypt; Moses parts the Red Sea; Joshua and the nation march around Jericho; David kills Goliath; Solomon builds the temple; Esther bows before the king and saves her people. As students arrive, give each one a card. Ask each student to silently act out the phrase so that everyone can guess what his card says. When everyone has arrived, continue to act out the cards for a few more minutes.

Say: **Can you guess what the common theme was for these scenes? All of the scenes were times when God's people actively lived out their faith in Him.**

Let's think back over some of these scenes. Why would it have been difficult for Noah to trust God? (All the other people around him were not trusting in God.) **How did Abraham express his faith in God?** (He left his country to follow God to another country; God made big promises about land, a nation, and a blessing. Abraham took Him at His word, even though he didn't see all of the promises fulfilled in his lifetime.) **What did Moses do that showed he had an active faith in God?** (He confronted Pharaoh and led the people from Egypt, even though he didn't think he was a good speaker or leader.) **Joshua trusted God through the conquest of the promised land. And David actually fought a giant, even though the army was afraid of him. Solomon showed his faith in God by building a temple to God. Esther risked her own life to try to save her people from an evil plot from an evil man.**

Just as it wasn't easy to act out the scenes without speaking, it wasn't easy for each of these people to follow God in each of these situations. Today we're going to look at a few people who also had to express their faith in God in a difficult situation.

Materials
index cards
pen

▼ Using Study Skills ▲

Have a student read Luke 1:1-4. Discuss the importance of getting the facts straight. Ask: **Have you ever been in a situation where you had to give an account of something you saw or did? Have you ever witnessed an accident or had to explain to your parents where you went and how you spent your time? Why is it important to give an accurate account?** (If you don't give accurate details, then the police won't know what really happened at the accident scene; maybe your parents won't believe you.) **In this passage of Luke, he is writing to a friend, trying to explain the details of the stories his friend had**

Materials
Bibles
Bible dictionary
Bible concordance

heard about Jesus. It is likely that Theophilus is a new Christian or some-one whom Luke is trying to convince to become a Christian. **Why do you think it is important for Luke to tell his friend that he spent a lot of time investigating the details?** (So that his friend would know that the stories are true and that he can believe in Jesus.) Say: **There are many stories in the Bible. God gave us the Bible so that we would know that what He promises He will do. Apparently, Luke's friend had heard many things about Jesus, but he wanted to make sure that they were true. So Luke wrote his account of Jesus' ministry; he researched and examined the facts, and he wrote them so that Theophilus would be certain about the things he had been taught before. Our faith is often built upon an examination of the facts. Sometimes it is built upon what we experience.**

Have different students read parts of Luke 1:5-25 and 57-66. Say: **Zechariah was doing his priestly duties, offering incense on the altar when he was visited by an angel, Gabriel. Gabriel told Zechariah that God had heard his prayers and would answer them. Zechariah and his wife, Elizabeth, had never been able to have children, and now they were too old, but they prayed that God would give them a child. However, Zechariah did not believe Gabriel. For this reason, Zechariah was unable to speak until his son was born. Most people wanted to name the baby after his father, Zechariah, but the angel had told Zechariah that he must name the boy** *John.* **When Zechariah wrote down, "His name is John," he was immediately able to speak again. Even though he did not trust God's message at first, he acted faithfully and did as the angel of God had commanded him, and at that moment, he was able to speak.**

The boy grew up to be known as John the Baptist, the man who preached to the nation to repent because God's kingdom was soon going to be revealed. He was also the man who baptized Jesus. Zechariah's life of faith helped prepare the way for Jesus and His ministry. This story leads us to the next example of a man who had an active faith in God.

Have a student read Luke 7:1-10. Have another student look up the word *centurion* in the Bible dictionary and summarize the entry. Say: **Zechariah was a priest, someone who knew the power of God from the stories he was told from his childhood; the centurion knew only what he heard from others about Jesus. The centurion did not have the history that Zechariah had, but he still had faith. He knew enough about Jesus to send for Him; he probably heard the stories about miracles and healings. He may have even heard Jesus speak or seen how Jesus interacted with the crowds that followed Him. Whatever it was he knew about Jesus, it was enough to convince him that Jesus had the power to heal his servant. He knew that Jesus had authority greater than his own.**

The centurion was different from what we normally think the Romans were like. He cared that his servant was sick and paralyzed. He knew the elders of the Jewish people, who also spoke well of him to Jesus. Even though he was a soldier sent to keep the peace among the conquered Jews, he was different.

Jesus knew that he was different too. Give the concordance to a student and have the student look up instances of the word *centurion.* Instruct other students to look up the passages from the concordance and determine whether it is related to this story. When you find it, have a student read Matthew 8:10-12. **Jesus made a really big statement, which was recorded by both Matthew and Luke, that the centurion had more faith than anyone in the nation of Israel. Even though the Jews were God's "chosen people," Jesus was stating that their faith, in general, was less than that of a Gentile.**

Remember that part of the promise given to Abraham was that he would be a blessing to all people. We know today that this was a reference to Jesus, that through Abraham would come the Messiah who would bless all people. The centurion, just like Abraham, however, received only a small

taste of the blessing. His servant was healed as Jesus spoke the words. But that little taste was based upon a little bit of faith from someone who didn't have a whole lifetime of history of God's promises to His people. He heard about Jesus and responded to Him.

▼ Responding to Study ▲

Distribute *What Do You Know?* sheets. Say: **Zechariah knew about God's past interaction with the nation of Israel, and even though an angel brought him a message from God, he didn't believe it at first. He had to experience God's direct influence on his own life, and then he couldn't speak until his son was born. The centurion knew only what others told him, and yet he acted out of faith in what Jesus could do for his servant. Today, we have the Bible accounts written by people such as Matthew and Luke. Just as Luke had written to his friend in order to convince him to believe in Jesus, the rest of the Bible is written so that we might believe.**

Say: **Let's take a brief test on what we know about Jesus. Take your *What Do You Know?* sheets and fill out the things you know about Jesus in the first column. In the second column, write how you know that information. Use a concordance to find Bible verses that support what you know about Jesus.**

When students have had a few minutes to write down some things that they know about Jesus, help them find verses about those things with the concordances. Distribute the *God Sent Jesus* handouts to give students an overview of major events in Jesus' life. Say: **Even though you know these things to be true, sometimes we need to know where the information comes from, in case we have a friend like Theophilus. What do these things you know about Jesus cause you to do to respond to Jesus? Take the next couple of minutes to think about how you can respond to Jesus based on what you know about Him from the Bible, from your parents, and from your Christian friends.**

Materials
What Do You Know? (p. 282)
God Sent Jesus (pp. 283, 284)
pens
Bibles
Bible concordances

▼ Reviewing Study Skills ▲

Before class, tape two sheets of aluminum foil or roll paper together to form a rectangle that is about 2 feet wide by 3 feet long. This will be a shield. Then with a permanent marker write the names of the New Testament books in three columns. Mount the shield on a wall in the classroom.

Say: **The Roman centurion was familiar with a shield. What would he use it for?** (to protect himself in battle) **Ephesians refers to our faith as a shield. Our faith can protect us from all kinds of spiritual attacks. Where do we learn about faith?** (from what other people tell us and from the Bible) **Let's review the books of the New Testament so that we can learn more about God's Word.**

Give each student about twelve inches of masking tape and instruct him to ball it up so that he has a sticky ball of tape. Have the students line up facing the shield. The first person in line must throw the tape ball at the shield. The tape should stick to the shield on one of the books of the New Testament. The student must then recite the books of the New Testament starting at the book where his tape ball stuck. Continue until all the students have had at least one turn.

Close with a prayer thanking God that He has given us the Bible to show examples of how we can live with an active faith.

Materials
aluminum foil or roll paper
black permanent marker
masking tape

Fill in the chart below with what you know about Jesus. In the second column next to each statement of what you know about Jesus, write how you know it (for example, read it in the Bible; heard a friend's testimony; experienced it firsthand). Write Scripture references where appropriate.

What I Know About Jesus   **How I Know It**

Jesus, Mary, and Joseph

When the time was right and when God's preparations were complete, Jesus was born. God chose Mary to be Jesus' mother and Joseph to be Jesus' earthly father. He was born in a stable. He slept in a manger. Magi followed the star that announced His birth and came to worship Him.

Jesus' Baptism

When Jesus was 30 years old, He was ready to begin His ministry. He was baptized. The spirit of God came down on Jesus like a dove. After this, Jesus went into the wilderness to be tempted by Satan. Jesus was tempted by Satan many times during His life, just as we are. But Jesus never sinned.

Jesus Calls Twelve Disciples

Jesus called 12 men to follow Him. Jesus taught these men about salvation, forgiveness, eternal life, and many other things of God. Jesus taught them so that after He returned to Heaven, they would continue to take God's offer of salvation to people all over the world.

Jesus Feeds 5000

Jesus performed many miracles, wonders, and signs to show people that he was from God. Jesus fed more than 5000 people by multiplying five loaves of bread and two small fish. Not only did Jesus meet the physical needs of many people, but He did so in a way that showed them that He was God's Son and that God cared for them.

Jesus Walks on Water

Some of Jesus' miracles were done for the sake of His closest followers, the disciples. When Jesus walked on the Sea of Galilee, He wanted His disciples to know with absolute certainty that He was who He claimed to be: the Son of God, the Messiah. Jesus showed that He had ultimate authority, not just in His teachings but even over creation itself.

Peter's Confession

One day, Jesus asked His disciples, "Who do you say I am?" Peter answered, "You are the Christ, the Son of the living God" (Matthew 16:15, 16). Peter's answer is very important to Christians. Anyone who follows Jesus must believe that Jesus is the Christ—the one God sent to die for people's sins. And anyone who follows Jesus must believe that Jesus is God's Son.

Transfiguration

Jesus took Peter, James, and John up on a mountain to pray. While Jesus was praying, His clothes and face became as bright as the sun. Moses and Elijah appeared with Jesus, and they talked about Jesus' departure. Jesus had given up His heavenly glory to come to earth as a man. At Jesus' transfiguration, the disciples saw Jesus' true heavenly glory.

Triumphal Entry

The triumphal entry marks the beginning of the last week of Jesus' life on earth. One Sunday, Jesus entered Jerusalem knowing that He would be crucified that very week. The crowds greeted Jesus with shouts of praise. They waved palm branches and put their coats in the road as a carpet of honor for Jesus as He rode into Jerusalem on a donkey.

Last Supper

Jesus was in Jerusalem to celebrate Passover—the feast when Jews celebrated their deliverance from slavery in Egypt. On Thursday, Jesus met with His disciples to eat the Passover meal. He told them to break the bread and drink the cup to remember His body and His blood—His sacrifice for sinners on the cross of Calvary. We call the bread and the cup the Lord's Supper, or Communion. Later that night, Judas, one of the twelve disciples, betrayed Jesus and handed Him over to soldiers to be tried and crucified. Jesus was celebrating the Passover meal when He ate the Last Supper with His disciples. This event helps us understand that Jesus is our Passover lamb. Just as the blood of the lamb saved the Israelites from the death of their firstborn, the blood of Jesus saves us from spiritual death.

Crucifixion and Burial

After a night of questioning, Jesus was sentenced to die by crucifixion. He was beaten and mocked and then nailed to the cross. It was 9 A.M. on Friday. By 3 P.M., Jesus was dead. He had been crucified. He was taken down from the cross and buried in a new tomb. The tomb was sealed, and soldiers stood by it to guard it.

Resurrection

God raised Jesus from the dead. This is another important truth that anyone who follows Jesus must believe. On the morning of Jesus' resurrection, three women went to Jesus' tomb. Instead of finding Jesus' body, they found two angels who said, "He is not here; he has risen!" (Luke 24:6). It was Sunday, one week after Jesus' triumphal entry. Over the next 40 days, many people saw Jesus alive (Acts 1:3). Jesus had been crucified, but now He is alive!

Go and Tell

Great Commission

Forty days after Jesus was raised from the dead, he ascended into Heaven. Just before he left, he gave his disciples an important command: "Go and make disciples of all nations, baptizing them in the name of the Father and of the Son and of the Holy Spirit, and teaching them to obey everything I have commanded you. And surely I am with you always, to the very end of the age"" (Matthew 28:19, 20). God's second stage was complete. Salvation through Jesus had been provided. Now it was time to offer salvation through Jesus.

LESSON 49

Peter and Paul Spread the Gospel

Acts; Paul's Letters; Peter's Letters

Lesson Aims

Students will
- Review important events in the life of Peter
- Compare the far-reaching ministries of Peter and Paul
- Name two things they can do to spread the gospel

▼ Building Study Skills ▲

Write the following Scripture references on slips of paper and hand them out to students as they arrive: Matthew 16:15-19; Luke 9:28-36; Mark 14:66-72; John 21:15-19; Acts 2:37-41; Acts 3:1-10; Acts 4:13-20; Acts 12:1-11. Have the students read the Scriptures and be prepared to tell the class what they learn about the life of Peter.

Say: **We've met Peter in previous lessons. What do you remember about him?** (He was a fisherman, called by Jesus to be an apostle.) **Let's listen as our friends remind us of some of the major events in Peter's life.**

After the students report, ask: **How do you think Peter's experiences prepared him to spread the gospel? Today we'll look not only at Peter's life, but his words.**

Materials
Scripture references written on slips of paper

▼ Using Study Skills ▲

Say: **Last week we talked about having an active faith in what God promises. This week we're going to look at Peter's active faith.**

We know that Peter did not always show an active faith. We know that he denied Jesus three times during Jesus' trial. We also know that after Jesus rose from the dead, He confronted Peter and told him to "feed my sheep," that is, Jesus told Peter to share the good news with people. After Jesus returned to Heaven, Peter did just that.

When Peter preached on the Day of Pentecost, 3000 from all over the world became Christians. In preaching to this crowd, Peter was basically preaching to the whole world. As these people left Jerusalem to go home, they took the gospel with them. This is a picture of how the gospel spreads when just one person does his part for the Lord right where he is.

Peter also wrote two of the Letters in the New Testament. Through his writing he did the job Jesus gave him: He fed the sheep. Let's look together at Peter's letters.

Have a student read 1 Peter 5:1-4. **What did Peter tell the elders to do?** (Be shepherds of the flock; serve the Chief Shepherd.) Have another student read 2 Peter 1:16-21. **What event does Peter recall in this passage?** (the transfiguration) **What does Peter say about the reliability of Scripture?** (God spoke through men by inspiration of the Holy Spirit.) **Peter himself was inspired to write; he knew that he wasn't making up anything and that he was being obedient to God.**

Materials
Bibles

Let's read some more of Peter's best-known teaching. Have several students read these passages. The descriptive phrases are for your reference:

1 Peter 1:13-16	Christians must be self-controlled and holy
1 Peter 2:4, 5	all Christians are priests, "living stones" in God's spiritual house
1 Peter 2:9	Christians are a chosen people, holy priesthood, royal nation
1 Peter 3:15, 16	Christians should be prepared to explain their faith
1 Peter 5:8, 9	the devil prowls like a "roaring lion"
2 Peter 3:8, 9	God wants all people to come to repentance

Paul also had global impact but in a different way. Paul's influence on the world was accomplished by actually traveling around the world preaching the gospel. The Letters of the New Testament that were written to churches in specific cities were written by Paul. Can you name them? Have students name those letters: Romans, 1 & 2 Corinthians, Galatians, Ephesians, Philippians, Colossians, 1 & 2 Thessalonians. **After Paul left a city he knew that he couldn't simply leave them without some sort of helpful advice.**

Peter made the first convert among the Gentiles when he shared the gospel with Cornelius. Paul's mission from the beginning was largely for the Gentiles (Acts 9:15). **Again think about God's promise to Abraham. He told Abraham that he would be a blessing to all people. This was Peter's and Paul's message: even though God began with His "chosen people" to make known His plan of salvation, God wants everyone to come to Him.**

▼ Responding to Study ▲

Say: **As we studied the Old Testament, we learned that God had planned for our salvation from the very beginning. In the Gospels, we saw how God provided our salvation. In the rest of the New Testament, we see God's plan for presenting the gospel. Basically, it's a matter of sharing the good news where you are or going where God sends you with the gospel. Peter's sermon started the church in Jerusalem but it also had global impact. Paul traveled around the world preaching the gospel.**

We have the same responsibilities as Peter and Paul. That sounds kind of scary, doesn't it? What kinds of things can we do to share the gospel in our homes? Let students respond. **What about in our schools? How about in our town or city or nation? Do you know anyone who has gone on a short-term mission trip or became a full-time missionary?** Let students respond, but be prepared to talk about opportunities your congregation provides or missionaries they support. **Even though it might be difficult, people take short missions trips all the time. Sometimes it is to another country, but many times it is someplace that needs the gospel and where there are few churches or Christians to help people get to know Jesus.**

Distribute copies of the *God Began Jesus' Church* handouts. Say: **Here is the basic timeline of how the church began and the things that Jesus' followers did then to spread the gospel. Read through these descriptions, then draw your picture and fill in your name on page 289. Write down at least two things that you think you could do to help spread the gospel in your own way.**

Materials
God Began Jesus' Church
(pp. 288, 289)
paper
pens

▼ Reviewing Study Skills ▲

Earlier in the lesson the students mentioned the letters of Paul that were written to churches in specific cities. Have the students take turns finding each New Testament Letter in the Bible dictionary. They are to discover to whom the book was written. Then have them locate on a map or in a Bible atlas the place where each letter was sent. If there is time, have the students find out the major themes or messages of each of the books.

Close with a prayer something like this: **Thank you, Father, for Your plan of salvation. Thank You for Your servants of the past who spread the gospel, and for those who made it known to us. Please help the missionaries of today to tell Your message boldly. And help us to do the same. In Jesus' name, amen.**

Materials
Bibles
Bible dictionaries
Bible atlas

Pentecost

Ten days after Jesus went to Heaven, people from all over the world were gathered in Jerusalem to celebrate Pentecost. God's Holy Spirit came upon the apostles and gave them the ability to speak in languages that they had not studied. Everyone heard God's offer of salvation in his own language. Peter told the people about Jesus. Three thousand people were baptized that day; Jesus' church began.

Peter and John Heal a Lame Man

One day when Peter and John went to the temple to pray, they met a crippled man who asked them for money. Peter said, "Silver or gold I do not have, but what I have I give to you. In the name of Jesus Christ of Nazareth, walk" (Acts 3:6). The man got up and walked! Many people were amazed. Nonetheless, Peter and John were arrested, and they boldly spoke God's message of salvation to the Sanhedrin.

Stephen Stoned

The church continued to grow. Stephen—a man full of faith and the Holy Spirit—was one of seven men chosen to distribute food to widows. He did great wonders and miracles among the people. Stephen was arrested and taken before the Sanhedrin. Stephen told them about Jesus. This angered them. They dragged Stephen out of the city and stoned him. A young man named Saul watched.

Philip and an Ethiopian

After Stephen's death, Saul began to persecute Jesus' church. Many believers left Jerusalem and scattered throughout Judea and Samaria. They took the good news of Jesus with them. Philip proclaimed Jesus in Samaria. Then the angel of the Lord called Philip to go to the road leading to Gaza. There, he met an Ethiopian who was reading God's Word but didn't understand it. Philip told the Ethiopian about salvation through Jesus. When they came to some water, the Ethiopian was baptized, and he went on his way rejoicing.

Saul's Conversion

Meanwhile, Saul left Jerusalem to arrest believers in Damascus. On the road to Damascus, a bright light flashed around Saul, and he fell to the ground. Jesus spoke to Saul and told him to go into Damascus to wait for further instructions. When Saul God up, he could not see. Later, Ananias spoke to Saul, and Saul was baptized. Saul began to share the good news of Jesus.

Peter and Cornelius

Jewish law forbade Jews from visiting Gentiles. Cornelius was a God-fearing Gentile. An angel appeared to Cornelius and told him to send for Peter. Meanwhile, God spoke to Peter in a vision. God told Peter that it was all right to visit Gentiles. So when Cornelius' messengers arrived, Peter went with them to Cornelius' house. There, Peter spoke the good news of Jesus to Cornelius' household. The Holy Spirit came upon everyone who heard Peter's message, and those who believed were baptized.

 LESSON 50

Paul and Barnabas

The church in Antioch was growing fast, so the church in Jerusalem sent Barnabas to Antioch. Barnabas went to Tarsus to get Saul. Together they met with the church in Antioch for a year. Believers were first called Christians at Antioch. The Holy Spirit called the church at Antioch to set apart Barnabas and Paul (Saul) for missionary work. Thus, Paul and Barnabas began the first missionary journey.

Paul, Silas, and Timothy

Paul and Barnabas returned to Antioch when they finished their first journey. Paul prepared to travel again. This time Silas and Timothy were his partners. During this second journey, they visited Philippi where Paul and Silas were put in jail for freeing a slave girl from an evil spirit. At midnight, they were praying and singing praise to God when an earthquake freed them. Instead of leaving, they stayed to tell the jailer and his family about Jesus.

Paul

During Paul's third missionary journey, he revisited many churches. During this visit to the city of Ephesus, many believers openly confessed their evil deeds. Those who had practiced sorcery brought their scrolls together and burned them. Paul ended this journey in Jerusalem.

Paul's Journey to Rome

In Jerusalem, Paul was arrested. Paul told the good news of Jesus to the leaders in Jerusalem. He was taken to Caesarea where he told the good news of Jesus to rulers of the Roman government. During his trials, Paul appealed to Caesar, the Roman emperor. On the way to Rome, Paul and his companions were shipwrecked, but no one died. When Paul reached Rome, he lived by himself with a soldier to guard him. He welcomed all who came to see him, and he told them the good news of Jesus.

John

As Paul traveled, he also wrote. Many of the books in the New Testament were written by Paul to encourage believers. The apostle John also wrote a book to encourage believers. John wrote Revelation when he was exiled on the island of Patmos. Revelation is a book of prophecy. The book encourages Christians because it tells them about Heaven—God's reward for those who accept his offer of salvation. It tells believers what will happen when the time for God's offer of salvation ends.

Name _____

Lesson Aims

Students will
- Act as partners to accomplish a task
- Research the ministries of James and Dorcas
- Identify areas of ministry in which students participate

Materials
2 old extra-large buttoned
  shirts
2 old extra-large pants
2 cards on which Philippians
  1:4-6 is written

▼ Building Study Skills ▲

When students have arrived, divide the class into two teams. At the end of the room, place the shirts and pants. On your cue, the first person on each team will run to the clothes and bring them back to the second person and help him put the clothes on. When the second person has the shirt and pants on, he must read the unit memory verse (Philippians 1:4-6) from one of the cards. The first person must then help the second person remove the clothes and then run them back to the other end of the room. When they return to the line, the second person repeats the process with the third person, and so on. The first person in line will actually be the last person to dress and read the memory verse.

Say: **This unit's memory verse talks about partnering in ministry. Sometimes we forget that it's not just the ministers or leaders of the church who are supposed to do the work within the church. All Christians must take on their own ministries within the church and partner with other Christians to make sure that we are all working toward the same goal: to make disciples. Today we're going to talk about two people in the early church who we don't talk about a lot but who had a great amount of impact on the early church: James and Dorcas.**

Materials
Bibles
Bible concordances

▼ Using Study Skills ▲

Distribute Bibles and concordances. Tell the students that they are going to be looking for a missing person. Say: **When we read through the New Testament, we read about a few different men named James. There were two men named James among Jesus' disciples, and there's one who is the brother of Jesus. We're going to look for references regarding James, the brother of Jesus, to see if we can figure out a few things about him.** Pair up students and ask them to look up the name *James* and determine whether the verse is about a disciple or the brother of Jesus. When the class has found a few references, have the pairs share their verses and work together to figure out who James was.

Say: **The first reference we found for James was in Matthew 13:55 where it lists four brothers of Jesus; this list is repeated in Mark 6:3. The next reference, even though it doesn't mention him by name, is in John 7:2-5.** Have a student read these verses. **In this passage, it seems that James does not believe in Jesus or understand His ministry. The next reference is found in Acts 12:17 when Peter tells about how God released him from**

prison. Apparently, James has become a leader in Jesus' church. He has apparently gotten over whatever misunderstandings he had about who Jesus really was. Throughout the rest of the references, we find that James has truly accepted Jesus and is working hard to make the church succeed. In Acts 15, where we find a major concern of the church, how to accept Gentiles into the church, James makes a bold statement: "It is my judgment, therefore, that we should not make it difficult for the Gentiles who are turning to God" (Acts 15:19). Throughout the rest of the New Testament, we find a constant struggle between Jews and Gentiles. Here James is making an argument that the church should help the Gentiles enter the church and become part of God's family, according to His promises to Abraham.

Say: **Dorcas, on the other hand, was not a leader the way James was. Dorcas was a believer who did whatever she could to help other people. Acts 9:36-42 shares her story.** Have the students read through this story aloud. Ask: **What kinds of things did she do to serve in the church?** (doing good; helping the poor; making clothing for people) **Are these the kinds of things that we typically think of the church leaders doing?** Usually, we expect leaders to do things like preach and teach and run programs and "big" things like that. However, the Bible tells us that when Dorcas died, the church in Joppa sent for Peter. When he arrived, he found many people who had been helped by her. That so many people were saddened by her death indicates that she was truly a leader in the sense that she was an excellent model for other people to follow.

▼ Responding to Study ▲

Say: **Even though you are younger than most members of the church, you should never feel that you cannot help the church. You should never feel that your contributions are less than those of anyone else in the church. Another person we don't often focus on in our study of the New Testament is Timothy. He is often referred to as Paul's "son in the faith." In 1 Timothy 4:12, Paul tells Timothy, "Don't let anyone look down on you because you are young, but set an example for the believers in speech, in life, in love, in faith and in purity." It's in 1 Timothy and Titus where Paul gives instructions about the qualifications for elders and deacons in the church; Timothy was an evangelist who was busy setting up churches and appointing leaders to help them continue to grow.**

Discuss some of the ways that the students are involved and how they can get more involved. Distribute the *What Can I Do?* page. Instruct the students to follow the directions on the page and fill in the chart.

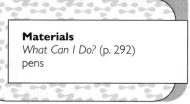

Materials
What Can I Do? (p. 292)
pens

▼ Reviewing Study Skills ▲

Divide the class into two teams. Have each team prepare to present the unit memory Scripture, Philippians 1:4-6, to the other team. They may choose any method, but if you wish, you may suggest these: play charades, make a poster, do a choral reading, use sign language, or sing an original song.

Close with a prayer thanking God for giving us examples of people who use their talents and faith to serve the church and asking God for guidance and encouragement to help us use our own talents to serve His church.

Materials
various, depending on method
students choose

What Can I Do?

Listed below are a few different areas of ministry within the church and outside the church. Choose one or two areas and list at least two different ways in each that you can make your faith active and serve the church.

Child Care

Cleaning

Cooking

Singing

Benevolence (giving/sharing)

Encouragement

Visiting Others

Prayer

LESSON 51

John Encourages the Church

1, 2, 3 John; Revelation

Lesson Aims
Students will
- Imagine what Heaven is like
- Discover how John describes his vision of Heaven in Revelation
- Express to God their feelings about Heaven

▼ Building Study Skills ▲

Before class, arrange the art materials on the tables so that the students can begin working right away. As students arrive, have them construct a picture of what they think Heaven will be like.

Say: **The Bible gives us a beautiful picture of what Heaven will look like and what it will be like to be there with God. Some of the pictures it describes are a bit confusing, like a description of a rainbow that is like an emerald. In Revelation, John uses figurative language to describe what he saw in a vision. If we read the first chapter of Revelation, we have a big picture of a spectacular view. In your pictures, you are interpreting for someone else what you see in your mind. John wrote down what he saw, but you can imagine that it was far too amazing to describe with words. Heaven could look like a number of different things, but regardless of how it is described, God is preparing it to be more wonderful than we can imagine.**

When all students have had a chance to finish their pictures, have them explain what the pictures show and what feelings they experience when they think about Heaven.

Materials
paper
markers
glue
glitter
cotton balls
Bibles

▼ Using Study Skills ▲

Tell students that they will need to follow along in their Bibles. Whenever you read a Bible reference have someone read it aloud. Say: **Revelation, the last book of the Bible, records special visions given by God to the apostle John.** Have a student read Revelation 1:9-11. Ask another student to locate the cities of the seven churches on a Bible map.

Next, have a student read Revelation 1:8. *Alpha* and *Omega* are the first and last letters of the Greek alphabet. Jesus is the greatest, the Almighty God. **One of the major themes of the book of Revelation is that Jesus is triumphant over Satan and over all the bad things in this world. When John tried to describe in words the fantastic visions he had, he pictured evil as horrible destructive beasts. But in the visions, Jesus always won over evil. The message of Revelation is that we can be confident that Jesus has always, and will always, win.**

Refer students to the reproducible page, *Visions of Heaven*. Have them follow the instructions to learn how John described Heaven in the book of Revelation. Students may work individually or in groups. Give them at least ten minutes to work on the top half of the page.

Materials
Bibles
Bible atlas
Visions of Heaven (p. 295)

After the students are finished, lead them in discussing what they found out. Wrap up by saying: **Another major theme of the book of Revelation is that Jesus will come back. No one knows how soon Jesus is coming. A time we think is long may seem short to God** (2 Peter 3:8), **but Jesus will return swiftly and suddenly. People will be surprised** (Matthew 24:36-44). **Those who follow Him will be happy because they will be ready to welcome Jesus whenever He comes; others will try to hide because they are not ready.**

Jesus will bring a reward for those who have done right and punishment for those who have done wrong (Matthew 25:31-46). **At the end of the book of Revelation John says, "Amen. Come, Lord Jesus" asking Jesus to come as He promised.**

We can depend on God's promises. We shall see Him (Revelation 22:4). **God will end all of our grief, and there will never be anything to make us sad again. God told John to write it down for everybody to read.**

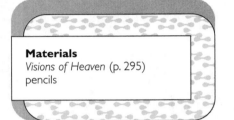

Materials
Visions of Heaven (p. 295)
pencils

▼ Responding to Study ▲

Say: **For many people, Revelation is very confusing, but that was not God's point. He wanted to encourage people that He would keep His promise, no matter how awful the world would get. He wants His people to know that He is always in charge. He also wants us to know that the final blessing, the final answer to His promise to Abraham, is eternity with Him in Heaven. It is a promise to restore the same kind of relationship that Adam and Eve had in the garden before they sinned. We will be in direct contact and relationship with God for the rest of eternity.**

Earlier in this session you made a picture of what Heaven may look like, and we talked about our feelings when we think of Heaven. At the bottom of page 295 is a place for you to respond to God about Heaven. Take a few minutes to write your thoughts and feelings directly to God.

▼ Reviewing Study Skills ▲

Materials
66 spring clothespins
fine-tip marker
half sheet of poster board
stopwatch

Before class, write the name of each of the books of the Bible on a clothespin. On the poster board, write the words "Pin Down the Bible" across the top. Divide the board vertically down the center. Write "Old Testament" on one side of the line and "New Testament" on the other side.

Say: **Whenever we look forward to Jesus' return, we are counting on God to keep a promise He made. God made many promises to people throughout the Bible, and if we know more about the Bible, we can look for those promises whenever we need encouragement. The best promise was first stated in Genesis; it was a promise to destroy Satan. When Jesus returns at the end of time, Satan and His angels will be cast into a lake of fire for eternity, but everyone who trusted in God to keep His promise, from Adam to Zechariah, will be with Him in Heaven. Let's practice reciting the books of the Bible in order.**

Divide the class into teams of two or three. Have them work together to race the other teams in placing the clothespins on the poster board in the correct order.

Close with a prayer thanking God for giving us hope through His Word and thanking Him for keeping His promises throughout the Bible.

Visions of Heaven

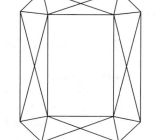

In the book of Revelation John calls Heaven "the New Jerusalem." Read the Scriptures listed to discover how John describes Heaven.

1. Revelation 21:11—in John's vision the city shined like
a light   a star   a precious jewel

2. Revelation 21:12—the city had this many gates
12   3   24

3. Revelation 21:15—the city was this shape
circle   rectangle   square

4. Revelation 21:18—the city was made of
brick   glass   pure gold

5. Revelation 21:19, 20—the foundations were made of all these things EXCEPT
sapphire   emerald   topaz   turquoise   amethyst

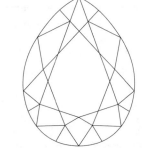

6. Revelation 21:21—each gate was a
diamond   pearl   ruby

7. Revelation 21:21—the great street of the city was made of
silver   platinum   gold

8. Revelation 21:4, 23-27—these things will NOT be in Heaven (cross out all that apply)
death   mourning   crying   pain   light
sun   moon   night   glory   honor
anything impure   locks on the gates

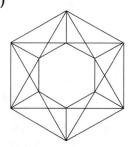

In My Own Words

When you read John's descriptions of Heaven, how do you feel? Write your thoughts to God:

Dear God,
When I think of Heaven, I feel _____

_____

_____

_____

Old Testament (39 Books)

Law (5 Books)
These books tell about the law that God gave to Moses. They tell how the Hebrew people became God's people. Moses wrote the five books of Law. Other names for the books of Law are Pentateuch, Torah, and Mosaic law.

Genesis
Exodus
Leviticus
Numbers
Deuteronomy

History (12 Books)
These books tell about three stages of Hebrew history during which God was preparing His people for the coming of Jesus: theocracy (the period of time when the people were ruled by God), monarchy (the period of time when God's people were ruled by a human king), and post exile (the period of time after God's people were freed from captivity).

Theocracy	Monarchy	Post Exile
Joshua	*1 & 2 Samuel*	*Ezra*
Judges	*1 & 2 Kings*	*Nehemiah*
Ruth	*1 & 2 Chronicles*	*Esther*

Poetry (5 Books)
These books are a collection of songs, stories, and wise sayings that express thoughts and feelings of the Hebrew people.

Job
Psalms
Proverbs
Ecclesiastes
Song of Solomon (Song of Songs)

Prophecy (17 Books)
These books contain God's messages, which the prophets spoke to the Hebrew people. Five of these books are called the major prophets because their books are long. Twelve are called minor prophets because their books are shorter. Each book of prophecy, except Lamentations, is named for the prophet who wrote it. Jeremiah wrote Lamentations.

Major Prophets	Minor Prophets	
Isaiah	*Hosea*	*Nahum*
Jeremiah	*Joel*	*Habakkuk*
Lamentations	*Amos*	*Zephaniah*
Ezekiel	*Obadiah*	*Haggai*
Daniel	*Jonah*	*Zechariah*
	Micah	*Malachi*

New Testament (27 Books)

Gospels (4 Books)
These books tell about the life and teachings of Jesus. Each writer wrote his book to help a different group of people understand why Jesus came to earth. Each Gospel is named after the man who wrote it.

Matthew
Mark
Luke
John

History (1 Book)
The book of Acts is the only New Testament book of history. It tells about the beginning of the church. Luke wrote Acts.

Acts

Letters (21 Books)
The letters were written to encourage and help Christians. Paul wrote thirteen of the letters to churches and individuals, and they are named for who received them. Eight letters were written by other people. These letters, except Hebrews, are named for the person who wrote them. Hebrews is named for who received it. This division is also called the "epistles," which means letters.

Letters from Paul	Letters from others
Romans	*Hebrews*
1 & 2 Corinthians	*James*
Galatians	*1 & 2 Peter*
Ephesians	*1, 2, & 3 John*
Philippians	*Jude*
Colossians	
1 & 2 Thessalonians	
1 & 2 Timothy	
Titus	
Philemon	

Prophecy (1 Book)
The apostle John wrote the book of Revelation when he was exiled on the island of Patmos. This book tells about events that will happen just before Jesus returns again.

Revelation

Genesis	2 Kings	Isaiah
Exodus	1 Chronicles	Jeremiah
Leviticus	2 Chronicles	Lamentations
Numbers	Ezra	Ezekiel
Deuteronomy	Nehemiah	Daniel
Joshua	Esther	Hosea
Judges	Job	Joel
Ruth	Psalms	Amos
1 Samuel	Proverbs	Obadiah
2 Samuel	Ecclesiastes	Jonah
1 Kings	Song of Solomon (Song of Songs)	Micah

Nahum	Romans	Titus
Habakkuk	1 Corinthians	Philemon
Zephaniah	2 Corinthians	Hebrews
Haggai	Galatians	James
Zechariah	Ephesians	1 Peter
Malachi	Philippians	2 Peter
Matthew	Colossians	1 John
Mark	1 Thessalonians	2 John
Luke	2 Thessalonians	3 John
John	1 Timothy	Jude
Acts	2 Timothy	Revelation

Things We Know

List student names in the first column. Use a check mark (or sticker) to record information that has been recited from memory.

Student	3 Stages*	8 Eras**	Time Line: Creation to Patriarchs	Time Line: Creation to Judges	Time Line: Creation to Prophets	Time Line: Creation to Return	Time Line: Creation to Jesus' Life	Entire Time Line in Order
1								
2								
3								
4								
5								
6								
7								
8								
9								
10								
11								
12								
13								
14								
15								
16								
17								
18								

*(Promised Salvation, Provided Salvation, Presented Salvation)
**(Creation and Fall; Patriarchs; Exodus & Conquest; Judges; Kings & Prophets; Exile & Return; Jesus' Life; Early Church)

For the Record

Fill in the dates across the top and place a check mark or a sticker in the box when you are able to demonstrate the skill listed. Continue to practice each skill, even after you mark it off, so that you can demon strate each of the skills whenever asked.

I can separate the Old Testament section from the New Testament.																					
I can find the book of Psalms.																					
I can locate a specific chapter and verse for each:																					
• book of the Law																					
• book of history (Old Testament)																					
• book of poetry																					
• a book of prophecy (Old Testament)																					
• book of the Gospels																					
• book of history (New Testament)																					
• book of letters (or epistles)																					
• book of prophecy (New Testament)																					
I can recite:																					
• Bible divisions																					
• all Old Testament books																					
• all New Testament books																					
• books of the Law																					
• books of history (Old Testament)																					
• books of poetry																					
• books of prophecy (Old Testament)																					
• the Gospels																					
• books of history (New Testament)																					
• the books of letters (or epistles)																					
• a book of prophecy (New Testament)																					

ALMIGHTY

Almighty: all-powerful; a name given to God.

altar (ALL-ter): a mound of earth or stones on which incense or animals are burned as an offering to God.

Amos: a shepherd from Judah who became a prophet to Israel. The general theme of his Old Testament book is God's judgment.

apostle (uh-POS-ul): one who is sent forth on a special mission. Jesus chose 12 of His disciples to be apostles (Luke 6:12-16). Judas betrayed Jesus. After the resurrection, Jesus gave the 11 remaining apostles the job of spreading the gospel (Matthew 28:19, 20). Later, Jesus chose Saul to be an apostle to the Gentiles (Acts 9:1-19).

Bethlehem: a village on a Judean hill, about five miles south of Jerusalem. Rachel was buried near Bethlehem (Genesis 35:19). As the birthplace and home of David, it was the "town of David" (Luke 2:4, 11). Jesus was born in Bethlehem (Matthew 2:1; Luke 2:1-18).

CITY OF DAVID

bread: 1. a food made from dough that is made with flour and water and sometimes yeast; 2. often used to mean food in general. In Jesus' day bread was the most important food in a person's diet. Jesus called himself the "bread of life" (John 6:35-51), because He is the source of spiritual life to everyone who believes in Him.

Caesar (SEE-zer): a title used for the emperor of Rome. Caesar Augustus ruled when Jesus was born (Luke 2:1); his successor, Tiberius Caesar, reigned A.D. 14–37 (Luke 3:1); Claudius Caesar reigned A.D. 41–54 (Acts 11:28; 18:2); and Nero reigned A.D. 54–68 (Acts 25:10-12; Philippians 4:22).

Caiaphas (KAY-uh-fuss): the high priest in Jerusalem at the time of Jesus, about A.D. 17–36.

City of David: another name for Jerusalem. When David conquered a fortressed area of the city and made his home there, he called that area the City of David (2 Samuel 5:9). Later the entire city was known by that name.

CORNELIUS

Cornelius (kor-NEEL-yus): a Roman centurion in Caesarea, a devout man and the first Gentile to become a Christian (Acts 10).

doctrine (DAHK-trin): teachings; something that is taught.

Euphrates (yoo-FRAY-teez): the largest of two great rivers in Mesopotamia. It flows for 1,750 miles from the Tarsus mountains to the Persian Gulf. Sometimes called the great river, its name means "that which makes fruitful." The Euphrates was one of the rivers of the Garden of Eden (Genesis 2:14).

faith: a firm belief or trust in a person or thing; belief in what God says, even though one cannot see or understand everything.

foreign altars: See idol.

Genesis: "origins" or "beginnings." The first book of the Old Testament. Moses is credited with writing Genesis.

Holy City: See Jerusalem.

Holy Spirit: a part of the Trinity—God the Father, Jesus, and the Holy Spirit. He is the comforter, sent by Jesus after He ascended back to God. The Holy Spirit directed the writing of the Bible. He lives in each Christian to help him live the Christian life.

JERUSALEM

idol: something worshiped as a god, often an image of a god or goddess made out of wood, stone, or metal. In the Old Testament, the Israelites often sinned by turning away from God to worship the idols of other groups of people.

interpret: to explain or to tell the meaning of something.

interpretation: the process by which the meaning of something is understood.

Israel (IZ-ray-el): 1. the name God gave to Jacob (Genesis 32:28); 2. Jacob's descendants, the 12 tribes of the Hebrews; 3. the 10 tribes that made up the northern kingdom of Israel.

James: a fisherman, son of Zebedee and brother of John (Mark 1:19). James became one of the three disciples who were closest to Jesus (Matthew 17:1; Mark 5:37; 14:33).

Jerusalem (jeh-ROO-suh-lem): the Holy City and well-known capital of the united kingdom. David conquered the city and made it his capital (2 Samuel 5:6-10). Solomon built the temple in Jerusalem (1 Kings 6). Jerusalem was a holy city to the Jews because they came to worship at the temple. In 586 B.C., the city was destroyed. Later, Persian rulers allowed Jewish exiles to return to their homeland and rebuild the Holy City and the temple (Ezra, Nehemiah). In Jesus' day, Palestine was under Roman rule, but Jerusalem remained the Jewish religious center. At

LAZARUS

Lazarus (LAZ-uh-rus): 1. brother of Mary and Martha whom Jesus raised from the dead (John 11); 2. the beggar in the parable of the rich man and Lazarus (Luke 16:19-31).

light: something that makes vision possible such as the sun or a lamp. Jesus called himself the "Light of the world" because He makes it possible for believers to see the difference between evil (darkness) and righteousness (light). Those who believe in Jesus have walked out of darkness into the light (1 Peter 2:9).

Mesopotamia (MESS-o-po-TAY-mee-uh): "the land between the rivers." It is the region between the Tigris and Euphrates rivers, extending from the Persian Gulf to the mountains of Armenia. Some famous Old Testament cities of Mesopotamia were Ur, Babylon, Haran, and Nineveh.

Messiah (meh-SYE-uh): "the Anointed One." The word was originally used for any person who had been anointed with holy oil (Leviticus 4:3, 5, 16; 2 Samuel 1:14, 16). The title later came to have a greater meaning referring to the coming promised Savior (Jeremiah 23:5, 6; Isaiah 9:6, 7; Micah 5:2-5).

Micah (MY-cah): a prophet to both Israel and Judah who wrote a book of the Old Testament. Micah warned of the defeat of nations and rulers who do not obey God.

PHILIP

Nazareth (NAZ-uh-reth): a town in a secluded valley in lower Galilee. It was the home of Mary and Joseph (Luke 1:26, 27). Jesus grew to manhood in Nazareth and lived there until He was about 30 years old (Luke 2:39-52; 3:23).

Patmos (PAT-mus): a small island in the Aegean Sea, off the cost of Asia Minor. When the apostle John was an old man, he was exiled there by the Roman government.

Paul: a Jew named Saul of the tribe of Benjamin; a Pharisee, yet a Roman citizen (Acts 21:39; Philippians 3:5). He was born in the city of Tarsus and learned the trade of tent-making. Saul became a Christian and a great apostle to the Gentiles after receiving a vision of the risen Christ (Acts 9:1-20). The apostle Paul made three missionary journeys, establishing churches in Asia Minor, Macedonia, and Greece. He suffered many hardships for his faith. The following books in the New Testament were written by Paul: Romans, 1 and 2 Corinthians, Galatians, Ephesians, Philippians, Colossians, 1 and 2 Thessalonians, 1 and 2 Timothy, Titus, Philemon, and possibly Hebrews.

Philip: 1. one of the 12 apostles; 2. one of the seven deacons chosen by the early church (Acts 6:5). Persecution scattered the Christians, and Philip became an evangelist.

PROPHECY

prophecy (PRAH-feh-see): 1. a statement of the will of God; 2. something told or written that will happen in the future.

prophet (PRAH-fet): 1. one who spoke God's message to the people; 2. one who told events that would happen in the future; 3. a man who spoke in another's place.

rabbi (RA-bye): a title meaning teacher or master.

repent: to change one's own heart, mind, and direction; to be sorry for sin and to decide to turn to God.

Rhoda (RO-dah): a servant girl of Mary, the mother of John Mark (Acts 12:12-17).

Sabbath (SA-beth): the seventh day of the week, as set apart by God as a day of rest and worship. It began at sundown on Friday evening and ended on Saturday evening.

shepherd: 1. one who cares for a flock of sheep, a common occupation of Bible times; 2. a name for God that describes His care for His people (Psalm 23); 3. a name for Jesus, who as the Good Shepherd gave His life for the sheep (John 10:1-18). Sheep were highly valued in Jesus' day and a good shepherd knew and named each sheep in his care. A shepherd often lived with his sheep so that he could protect them. A good shepherd was always ready to

ZION

protect his sheep and to give his life if necessary.

shield: 1. a piece of armor carried on the arm, used for protection; 2. a word to describe God and to show how He protects His people (Psalm 3:3).

Simon: 1. Simon Peter, see Peter; 2. Simon, a sorcerer at Samaria who was severely rebuked by Peter (Acts 8:9-24).

synagogue (SIN-uh-gog): 1. a meeting place for Jewish worshipers in New Testament times and later; 2. a congregation of Jewish worshipers.

Tigris (TYE-gris): the lesser of two great rivers of Mesopotamia. It rises in the mountains of Armenia and flows for 1,150 miles to join the river Euphrates before emptying into the Persian Gulf. *Tigris* means "arrow." It is one of the four rivers of the Garden of Eden (Genesis 2:14).

tunic (too-nic): a simple slip-on garment made with or without sleeves, worn as an under or outer garment by both men and women. It was usually knee-length or longer and was belted at the waist.

Zion (ZYE-on): a name for Jerusalem, especially the hill where the temple was located; also used to mean Heaven or the heavenly city, the new Jerusalem (Revelation 14:1).

APPENDIX

Sample Bible Concordance

AFRAID

Afraid (fear)
Ps	27:1	of whom shall I be *a*?
Lk	1:13	"Do not be *a*, Zechariah; your
	1:30	"Do not be *a*, Mary, you have
Heb	13:6	The Lord is my helper; I will not be *a*.

Beginning
| Ge | 1:1 | In the *b* God created the heavens |

Believe
Mk	16:16	but whoever does not *b* will be
Lk	1:20	because you did not *b* my words,
	24:11	But they did not *b* the women,
	24:25	to *b* all that the prophets have
	24:41	And while they still did not *b* it
Jn	1:7	that through him all men might *b*.
	11:42	that they may *b* that you sent me."
	20:31	written that you may *b* that Jesus is

Book
| Jos | 1:8 | Do not let this *B* of the Law depart |
| Jn | 20:30 | which are not recorded in this *b*. |

CREATED

Bread
Dt	8:3	teach you that man does not live on *b*
Mt	4:4	'Man does not live on *b* alone
Jn	6:35	Jesus declared, "I am the *b* of life.
	6:48	I am the *b* of life.
	6:51	I am the living *b* that came down from heaven.

Commands, Commandments
Dt	6:6	these *c* that I give you today
Ps	119:35	Direct me in the path of your *c*
Ecc	12:13	Fear God and keep his *c*,
1Jn	5:3	This is love for God: to obey his *c*.

Covenant
Dt	7:9	keeping his *c* of love
2Ch	15:12	They entered into a *c*
Mt	26:28	blood of the *c*, which is poured out

Created
| Ge | 1:1 | In the beginning God *c* the heavens |

CROSS

Cross
Jn	19:17	Carrying his own *c*, he went out
	19:19	prepared and fastened to the *c*
	19:25	Near the *c* of Jesus stood his

Crucified
Lk	24:7	be *c* and on the third day be raised
Jn	19:16	him over to them to be *c*.
	19:18	Here they *c* him, and with him two
	19:32	of the first man who had been *c*
Ac	2:36	whom you *c*, both Lord and Christ

Disciples
Mt	5:1	His *d* came to him,
	26:17	the *d* came to Jesus and asked,
	26:19	*d* did as Jesus had directed them
	26:26	and gave it to his *d*, saying,
	28:19	Therefore go and make *d*
Lk	8:22	One day Jesus said to his *d*,
	8:24	The *d* went and woke him, saying,
	8:25	is your faith?" he asked his *d*.
Jn	1:35	was there again with two of his *d*.
	6:3	mountainside and sat down with his *d*.
	6:8	Another of his *d*, Andrew,
	6:12	to his *d*, "Gather the pieces that
Ac	9:38	so when the *d* heard that Peter was

INSTRUCTION

Doctrine
| 1Ti | 4:16 | Watch your life and *d* closely. |

Dream
Mt	2:13	the Lord appeared to Joseph in a *d*.
	2:19	appeared in a *d* to Joseph in Egypt
	2:22	Having been warned in a *d*,

Earth
| Mt | 5:13 | "You are the salt of the *e*. |
| | 28:18 | and on *e* has been given to me. |

Faith
| Heb | 11:6 | without *f* it is impossible to please God, |

Forever
| Heb | 13:8 | same yesterday and today and *f*. |

God
| Ro | 3:23 | sinned and fall short of the glory of *G*, |
| Heb | 11:6 | without faith it is impossible to please *G*, |

Heart
Mt	22:37	with all your *h* and with all your soul
Mk	12:30	with all your *h* and with all your soul
Lk	10:27	with all your *h* and with all your soul

Instruction
| Pr | 13:1 | A wise son heeds his father's *i*, |

Jesus

Heb	13:8	*J* Christ is the same yesterday and

Law

Dt	17:18	on a scroll a copy of this *l*,
	17:19	follow carefully all the words of this *l*,
	17:20	turn from the *l* to the right
Jos	1:7	obey all the *l* my servant Moses
	1:8	Do not let this Book of the *L* depart
Ps	119:1	according to the *l* of the Lord.
	119:18	wonderful things in your *l*.

Light

Ps	27:1	The Lord is my *l* and my salvation—
Jn	8:12	"I am the *l* of the world.
	9:5	world. I am the *l* of the world."
	12:46	I have come into the world as a *l*,
1Jn	1:5	God is *l*; in him there is no darkness

Love

Mt	22:37	"'*L* the Lord your God with all your
Mk	12:30	*L* the Lord your God with all your
Lk	10:27	"'*L* the Lord your God with all your

Medicine

Pr	17:22	A cheerful heart is good *m*,

Mercy

Mt	5:7	for they will be shown *m*.
	18:33	Shouldn't you have had *m*
Lk	1:58	the Lord had shown her great *m*,
	1:78	because of the tender *m* of our God,
	10:37	"The one who had *m* on him."
	18:13	'God, have *m* on me, a sinner.'
Php	2:27	But God had *m* on him,

Messiah

Jn	1:41	"We have found the *M*" (that is, the Christ).
	4:25	"I know that *M*" (called Christ)

Mind

Mt	22:37	with all your soul and with all your *m*.'
Mk	12:30	with all your soul and with all your *m*
Lk	10:27	with all your strength and with all your *m*';

Miraculous

Jn	6:2	they saw the *m* signs he had
Ac	2:43	*m* signs were done by the apostles.

Money

Mt	21:12	the tables of the *m* changers
Mk	11:15	the tables of the *m* changers

Receive

Ac	20:35	'It is more blessed to give than to *r*.'"

Shepherd

Ps	23:1	The Lord is my *s*, I shall not be in want.
Isa	40:11	He tends his flock like a *s*:
Jn	10:11	"I am the good *s*.
	10:11	The good *s* lays down his life for
	10:14	"I am the good *s*; I know my sheep

Sinned

Ro	3:23	for all have *s* and fall short of the glory

Soul

Mt	22:37	with all your *s* and with all your mind.'
Mk	12:30	with all your *s* and with all your mind and
Lk	10:27	with all your *s* and with all your strength

Strength

Mk	12:30	with all your mind and with all your *s*.'
Lk	10:27	with all your *s* and with all your mind';

Today

Heb	13:8	Jesus Christ is the same yesterday and *t*

Word

Ps	119:9	By living according to your *w*.
	119:11	I have hidden your *w* in my heart
	119:37	preserve my life according to your *w*.
	119:89	Your *w*, O Lord, is eternal;
	119:105	Your *w* is a lamp to my feet
2Ti	2:15	who correctly handles the *w*
1Jn	2:5	if anyone obeys his *w*,

Words

2Ch	15:8	When Asa heard these *w*
Ps	119:130	The unfolding of your *w* gives light;
	119:160	All your *w* are true;
Mt	7:24	everyone who hears these *w*
Lk	1:20	because you did not believe my *w*,
Ac	2:40	With many other *w* he warned them;
Rev	21:5	for these *w* are trustworthy
	22:7	Blessed is he who keeps the *w*

World

Jn	8:12	he said, "I am the light of the *w*.

Worship, Worshiped

Ex	23:24	or *w* them or follow their practices.
	23:25	*W* the Lord your God,
	34:14	Do not *w* any other god,
Ps	29:2	*w* the Lord in the splendor
	86:9	will come and *w* before you,
	95:6	Come, let us bow down in *w*,
Mt	2:2	and have come to *w* him."
	4:9	"if you will bow down and *w* me.
	4:10	For it is written: '*W* the Lord your God,
Jn	4:24	and his worshipers must *w* in spirit
Rev	11:16	fell o their faces and *w* God,
	14:7	*W* him who made the heavens,

Yesterday

Heb	13:8	Jesus Christ is the same *y* and today

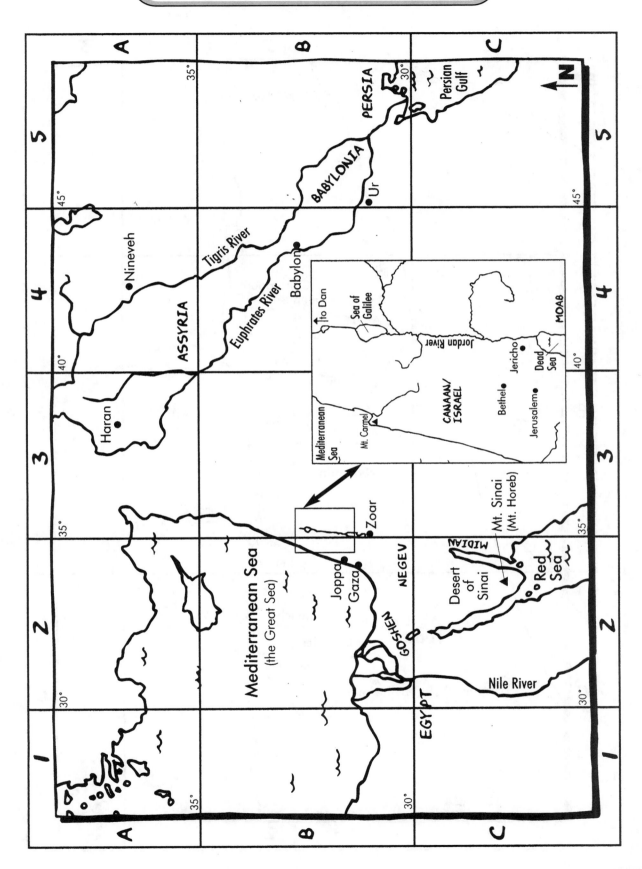

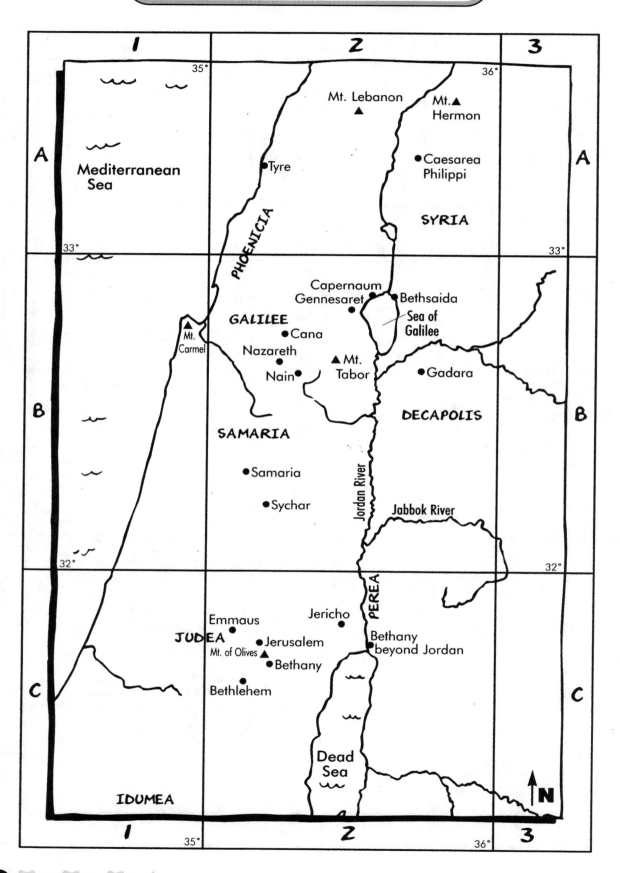

APPENDIX

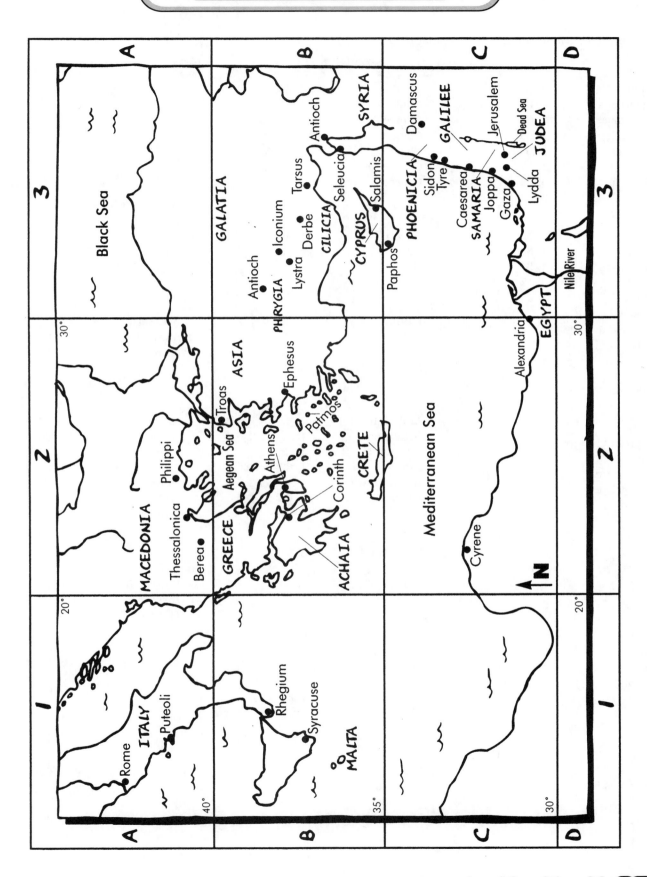

Black Sea

GALATIA

SYRIA

Damascus

GALILEE

Jerusalem

Dead Sea

JUDEA

Antioch

Tarsus

Seleucia

PHOENICIA

Sidon

Tyre

Caesarea

SAMARIA

Joppa

Gaza

Lydda

Iconium

Derbe

CILICIA

CYPRUS

Salamis

Antioch

Lystra

PHRYGIA

Paphos

30°

ASIA

Ephesus

Alexandria

EGYPT

Nile River

Troas

Patmos

CRETE

Athens

Mediterranean Sea

Philippi

MACEDONIA

Corinth

ACHAIA

Thessalonica

Berea

GREECE

N

Cyrene

20°

Rhegium

Syracuse

MALTA

ITALY

Puteoli

Rome

40°

35°

30°

APPENDIX

Index to Maps

(map number, grid location; * = inset map)

Creation

Adam & Eve

Garden of Eden

Noah

Tower of Babel

HOPE

2100 B.C.

Abraham

Isaac

Jacob

Joseph

Slavery in Egypt
400 years

NATION

| Moses | Passover | Exodus | 12 spies | Israel wanders 40 years | Joshua | Jericho |

LAND

| Promised Land: 12 tribes | Deborah | Gideon | Samson | Ruth | Samuel |

DELIVERANCE

930 B.C.

Saul	David	Solomon	Divided kingdom	Ahab & Jezebel	Elijah & Elisha
40 years	40 years	40 years	400 years	in Israel	in Israel

722 B.C.

605 B.C.

Daniel taken captive

Isaiah	Assyria	Manasseh	Josiah	Babylon seizes	Jeremiah
in Judah	scatters Israel	in Judah	in Judah	Jerusalem	in Judah

FAMILY

586 B.C.

| Many from Judah taken to Babylon | Ezekiel in Babylon | Babylon destroys Jerusalem | Fiery furnace | Cyrus lets Judah go home |

457 B.C.

538 B.C.

444 B.C.

GOD'S LAW RENEWED

| Zerubbabel rebuilds temple | Daniel | Esther | Ezra rebuilds people | Nehemiah rebuilds wall | Silence 400 years |

RESTORATION

Jesus, Mary, & Joseph

Jesus' baptism

Calls the Twelve

Feeds 5,000

Walks on the water

Peter's confession

Transfiguration

Triumphal entry

Last Supper

Crucifixion & burial

Resurrection

Great Commission

SALVATION

A.D. 30

Pentecost

Peter & John
heal a lame man

Stephen
stoned

Philip & the
Ethiopian

Saul's
conversion

Peter &
Cornelius

Paul &
Barnabas

Paul, Silas,
Timothy

Paul

Paul's
journey

John

ETERNAL LIFE

Time Line Pieces

 Creation	 Adam & Eve	 Garden of Eden	 Noah	 Tower of Babel
2100 B.C.  Abraham 2100 B.C.	 Isaac	 Jacob	 Joseph	 Slavery in Egypt 400 years
 Moses	 Passover	 Exodus	 12 spies	 Israel wanders 40 years
 Joshua	 Jericho	 Promised Land: 12 tribes	 Deborah	 Gideon

Samson

Ruth

Samuel

Saul
40 years

David
40 years

930 B.C.

Solomon
40 years

Divided kingdom
400 years

Ahab & Jezebel
in Israel

Elijah & Elisha
in Israel

Isaiah
in Judah

722 B.C.

Assyria
scatters Israel

Manasseh
in Judah

Josiah
in Judah

605 B.C.

Daniel taken captive

Babylon seizes
Jerusalem

Jeremiah
in Judah

586 B.C.

Many from Judah
taken to Babylon

Ezekiel
in Babylon

Babylon destroys
Jerusalem

Fiery furnace

DECREE OF CYRUS

Cyrus lets Judah
go home

 Zerubbabel rebuilds temple	 Daniel	 Esther	 Ezra rebuilds people	 Nehemiah rebuilds wall
 Jesus, Mary, and Joseph	 Jesus' baptism	 Calls the Twelve	 Feeds 5,000	 Walks on the water
 Peter's confession	 Transfiguration	 Triumphal entry	 Last Supper	 Crucifixion & burial
 Resurrection	 Great Commission	 Pentecost	 Peter & John heal a lame man	 Stephen stoned

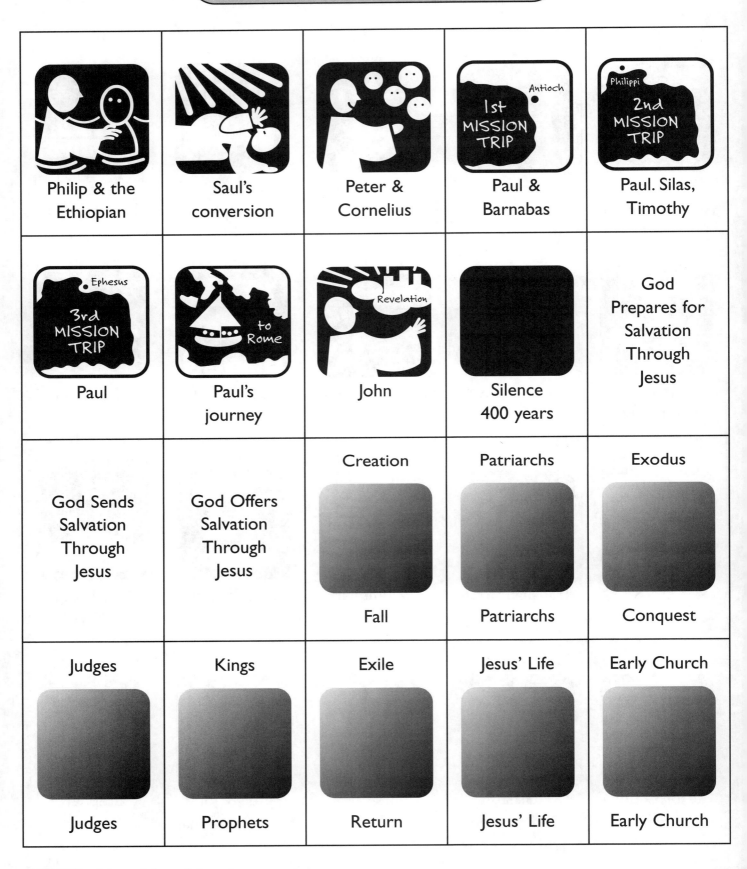

Philip & the Ethiopian	Saul's conversion	Peter & Cornelius	Paul & Barnabas	Paul. Silas, Timothy
Paul	Paul's journey	John	Silence 400 years	God Prepares for Salvation Through Jesus
God Sends Salvation Through Jesus	God Offers Salvation Through Jesus	Creation / Fall	Patriarchs / Patriarchs	Exodus / Conquest
Judges / Judges	Kings / Prophets	Exile / Return	Jesus' Life / Jesus' Life	Early Church / Early Church

Route 52 Road Map

Year 1

Year 2

Ages 3, 4

DISCOVER GOD'S LOVE (42071)

- God Is Great
- God Is Love
- God Is Good
- God Sends His Son, Jesus
- God's Son, Jesus, Grows Up
- God's Son, Jesus
- We Can Know Jesus Is Our Friend
- We Can Know Jesus Is Close to Us
- We Can Be Jesus' Helpers
- We Can Learn to Help
- We Can Learn to Share
- We Can Learn to Love God

DISCOVER GOD'S WORD (42075)

- God Made the World
- God Made People
- God Cares for Me
- Jesus Is Born
- Jesus Is God's Son
- Jesus Loves Us
- Be Thankful
- Help Jesus
- Discover About Myself
- Learn from the Bible
- Talk to God
- Help Others

Ages 4-6

EXPLORE BIBLE PEOPLE (42072)

- Learning That I Am Special (Joseph)
- Learning to Trust God (Gideon)
- Learning to Do What Is Right (Nehemiah)
- Learning to Be Brave (Esther)
- Learning to Pray Always (Daniel)
- Learning to Obey God (Jonah)
- Learning to Love People
- Learning to Be Happy
- Learning to Be Thankful
- Learning to Share
- Learning to Help Others
- Learning to Follow Jesus

EXPLORE BIBLE STORIES (42076)

- Learning About God's Creation
- Learning That God Keeps His Promises
- Learning About God's Care
- Learning About Baby Jesus
- Learning to Be a Friend Like Jesus
- Learning to Follow Jesus
- Learning About Jesus' Power
- Learning That Jesus Is the Son of God
- Learning About the Church
- Learning to Do Right
- Learning That God Is Powerful
- Learning That God Hears My Prayers

Ages 6-8

FOLLOW THE BIBLE (42073)

- The Bible Helps Me Worship God
- The Bible Teaches That God Helps People
- The Bible Helps Me Obey God
- The Bible Teaches That God Answers Prayer
- The Bible Teaches That Jesus Is the Son of God
- The Bible Teaches That Jesus Does Great Things
- The Bible Helps Me Obey Jesus
- The Bible Tells How Jesus Helped People
- The Bible Teaches Me to Tell About Jesus
- The Bible Tells How Jesus' Church Helps People

FOLLOW JESUS (42077)

- Jesus' Birth Helps Me Worship
- Jesus Was a Child Just Like Me
- Jesus Wants Me to Follow Him
- Jesus Teaches Me to Have His Attitude
- Jesus' Stories Help Me Follow Him
- Jesus Helps Me Worship
- Jesus Helps Me Be a Friend
- Jesus Helps Me Bring Friends to Him
- Jesus Helps Me Love My Family
- Jesus' Power Helps Me Worship Him
- Jesus' Miracles Help Me Tell About Him
- Jesus' Resurrection Is Good News for Me to Tell

Ages 8-12

GROW THROUGH THE BIBLE (42074)

- God's Word
- God's World
- God's Chosen People
- God's Great Nation
- The Promised Land
- The Kings of Israel
- The Kingdom Divided, Conquered
- From Jesus' Birth to His Baptism
- Jesus, the Lord
- Jesus, the Savior
- The Church Begins
- The Church Grows
- Reviewing God's Plan for His People

STUDY GOD'S PLAN (42078)

- The Bible Teaches Us How to Please God
- Books of Law Tell Us How God's People Were Led
- History and Poetry Tell About Choices God's People Made
- Prophets Reveal That God Does What He Says
- God Planned, Promised, and Provided Salvation
- Gospels Teach Us What Jesus Did
- Gospels Teach Us What Jesus Said
- Gospels Teach Us That Jesus Is Our Savior
- Acts Records How the Church Began and Grew
- Letters Instruct the Church in Right Living
- OT People and Events Prepare for God's Plan
- NT People and Events Spread God's Plan

Ages 8-12

GROW UP IN CHRIST (42080)

- Growing in Faith
- Growing in Obedience
- Growing in Attitude
- Growing in Worship
- Growing in Discipleship
- Growing in Prayer
- Growing in Goodness
- Growing in Love for Christ
- Growing in Devotion to the Church
- Growing in Grace
- Growing in Confidence
- Growing in Hope

STUDY JESUS' TEACHINGS (42079)

- Jesus Teaches Us About Who God Is
- Jesus Teaches Us That God Loves Us
- Jesus Teaches Us How to Love God
- Jesus Teaches Us About Himself
- Jesus Teaches Us to Do God's Will
- Jesus Teaches Us to Love Others
- Jesus Teaches Us About God's Kingdom
- Jesus Teaches Us How to Live Right
- Jesus Teaches Us the Truth
- Jesus Teaches Us About Forgiveness
- Jesus Teaches Us About God's Power
- Jesus Teaches Us About God's Word

A 52-Week Bible Journey . . . Just for Kids!

Ages 3 to 4

Discover God's Love

Help young children discover what God has done, thank Him for what He made, celebrate Jesus, begin to follow Jesus, and practice doing what God's Word says.

Product code: 42071

Discover God's Word

Help young children discover what God's Word says about the world, who God is, what He wants them to do, and Bible people who loved God.

Product code: 42075

Ages 4 to 6

Explore Bible People

Stories of Bible people will help children learn that they are special, how to trust God and choose to do right, how to love and obey Jesus, and how to help and share with others.

Product code: 42072

Explore Bible Stories

Bible stories will help children learn about creation, God's promises, power and care, who Jesus is and what He did, and how to follow Jesus' example and teaching.

Product code: 42076

Ages 6 to 8

Follow the Bible

Young readers will learn to follow Bible teachings as they look up Bible verses, experience basic Bible stories, and practice beginning Bible study skills.

Product code: 42073

Follow Jesus

Young learners will learn to follow Jesus as they experience stories from the Gospels. Through a variety of activities, children will worship, follow, and tell about Jesus.

Product code: 42077

Ages 8 to 12

Grow Through the Bible

Kids will grow in their understanding of God's Word as they investigate the Bible from Genesis through Paul's journeys and letters.

Product code: 42074

Grow Up in Christ

Kids will grow up in Christ as they explore New Testament truths about growing in faith, obedience, worship, goodness, prayer, love, devotion, grace, confidence, and hope.

Product code: 42080

Study God's Plan

Kids will study God's plan for salvation by exploring Bible people and events, Bible divisions and eras, and Bible themes and content, all while practicing Bible study skills.

Product code: 42078

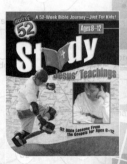

Study Jesus' Teachings

Kids will study what Jesus teaches about who God is, His love, how to love God and others, about God's kingdom, truth, forgiveness, power, God's Word, and doing His will.

Product code: 42079